W9-BJE-506

EMOTIONAL RESILIENCE

Also by David Viscott

Finding Your Strength in Difficult Times
Emotionally Free
I Love You—Let's Work It Out
Winning
Taking Care of Business
The Viscott Method
Risking
The Language of Feelings
How to Live with Another Person
The Making of a Psychiatrist
Feel Free

EMOTIONAL RESILIENCE

Simple Truths for Dealing with the
Unfinished Business of Your Past

DAVID VISCOTT, M.D.

HARMONY BOOKS   NEW YORK

Published by Harmony Books,
a division of Crown Publishers, Inc.,
201 East 50th Street, New York, New York 10022.
Member of the Crown Publishing Group.

Random House, Inc.   New York, Toronto, London, Sydney, Auckland

Harmony and colophon are trademarks of Crown Publishers, Inc.
http://www.randomhouse.com/
Printed in the United States of America
Designed by Barbara Balch

Library of Congress Cataloging-in-Publication Data

Viscott, David S., 1938–
    Emotional resilience : simple truths for dealing with the
unfinished business of your past / by David Viscott. — 1st ed.
        p.   cm.
    Includes index.
    1. Attitude (Psychology) 2. Attitude change. 3. Self-defeating
behavior.   I. Title.
BF327.V57   1996   96-407
158′.1—dc20   CIP

ISBN: 0-517-70240-1

10 9 8 7 6 5 4 3 2 1

First Edition

For Alan and Allene Fisch

Astringent truth
Liberate me
From the nostalgia
That taints
My spiritual pedigree

Contents

ACKNOWLEDGMENTS

Editing a book of this complexity is a daunting task. So much meaning has to be condensed and still remain accessible and readable. So many ideas need to be organized and presented. The reader and his or her needs must continually be kept in mind as well as fidelity to the author's style and principles.

In a writing career spanning several decades I have worked with many editors, most of them excellent, but none of them had the compelling love of a work that Shaye Areheart has so generously displayed and so thoughtfully put into practice. Often, after a long period in which she worked on the manuscript and returned it to me for my feedback, I found myself unable to find signs of her work and in reading through was unable to tell what she had deleted. The invisible mending of the best editor is a sign of love and devotion.

I have been fortunate indeed, and in this work I have felt loved and my work cherished. Thank you, Shaye.

I would like everyone to know that I love my agent Muriel Nellis, and I am saying so out loud. She is an agent in the very best sense of the word, agent meaning tireless champion of what is right and best. She believed in me, and that belief has made all the difference.

I would like to thank you, the reader, for being so giving of your affection and attention over the years. In this work I want to take you closer to yourself and reward you for your loyalty. In the truest sense you are always in my mind and heart, and I do this work for you. Without you all this is for nothing.

I want to thank my wife, Katharine, for her enduring patience, listening to me talk endlessly about all my ideas and responding as if she was listening to them for the first time.

I want to thank my mother for loving me so much, for reminding me I was one of the fortunate, for teaching me to be open to the gifts that all those who have come before have given to me and making me feel privileged for being able to give to others.

EMOTIONAL RESILIENCE

INTRODUCTION

HOW THE TRUTH HEALS

If you lived honestly, your life would heal itself.

As I look back on three decades of helping patients to cope with stress and understand their disappointments, this statement stands out as a singular truth. In nearly all the therapeutic breakthroughs I have seen, it was the acceptance of some previously concealed truth that allowed healing to begin.

The principal directive of psychotherapy was to help the patient become more truthful about his feelings. Being a therapist was a lot like being a choreographer of emotions. Relating a vague or troublesome feeling to the event that caused it placed the emotion in perspective and made sense of it. No matter how complicated the emotion or how confusing the situation, the simplest truth usually made the biggest difference.

When a person lost someone close to them, it was the truthful acceptance of that painful loss that initiated the mourning process and led to relief.

The essence of family therapy came down to helping to raise the level of truth in communication between family members. That higher standard of truth healed the fractured love when it could be healed or, when it could not, gave family members the courage to believe in themselves, take responsibility, and survive independently.

Similarly, the goal of couples therapy was to get the partners to reveal how they really felt about each other. No meaningful gains could be made until both partners arrived at the same level of understanding. More than anything else, whether a marriage failed or succeeded depended on how much truth the partners could tell or hear. On the other hand, the smallest lie could defeat trust, create suspicion, and block the expression of love. Only when the partners expressed their true feelings, no matter how unpleasant, could the relationship begin to right itself.

Resolving anxiety required that patients examine some painful truth that they had pushed aside. Dealing directly with the old problem allowed them to live in the moment again with confidence, rather than dreading that a nameless terror might at any moment be mysteriously reactivated and paralyze them.

Healing depression also required that patients candidly admit some old hurt. This allowed them to understand that the anger they were trying to conceal came from their being injured, not because they were bad. Truthfully accepting hurt and anger resolved guilt and allowed patients to forgive themselves and others. Only then did depression begin to lift.

Overcoming addictions, whether drug, alcohol, gambling, or overeating, always required accepting and living in a greater truthfulness. At the heart of every addiction was an anesthetized old hurt, seeking to be released. Some chemical or self-destructive behavior reinforced the lie and made it more difficult to correct. Accepting the painful truth, rather than running from it, was the beginning of sobriety. Nothing less succeeded.

It became clear that *resolving most of life's difficulties required telling or hearing the truth.* When a friendship went sour, it was usually because of a misunderstanding, a distortion of the facts. What friends yearned for was to have a chance to air the truth and set the matter straight.

When people struggled with their parents or children, it was largely because of the distortions that had been allowed to establish themselves between them. What family members sought was to be clearly understood.

People's greatest regrets involved wishing they'd had the chance to tell the truth so someone could have known how they really felt. When people said it was too late, what they really meant was, it was *too late to tell the truth.*

The truth had power to heal, to protect, to guide.

Living in the truth was living free and at one's best.

On the other hand, living in a lie eclipsed the joy of the world and lowered people's self-esteem. Concealing lies drained people's energy so they didn't have enough strength to do their best. It was harder to look out for themselves. When people lived in a lie, they seemed to invite trouble into their life rather than make it better.

Lies complicated.

The truth simplified.

An obvious question presented itself: why was telling the truth so powerful? Philosophers, poets, healers, and religious leaders have always urged people to be honest. It has long been known that confessing the truth relieves guilt. Telling the truth makes you feel better, but why? What is the power that the truth contains?

In my practice I pondered this question and sought to take advantage of the truth's healing power. I realized my patients forgot most of what took place during therapy sessions, and I began to tape them so they could replay them in private. I expected they would benefit from hearing my advice and comments again since I could seldom remember exactly what I had said when asked to repeat it, and felt my original wording was usually the most effective. This led to an unexpected discovery.

Many patients soon began telling me that they were troubled by what they heard on their tapes. Some said they disliked the sound of their voice. Others said the session became too painful to listen to. Eventually the real reason for their aversion became clear. Patients could not stand listening to themselves distort the truth or misrepresent themselves. They cringed at hearing the way they sounded when they lied. They seemed like less of a person, a child, like someone living in a dreamworld, and it bothered them. What stressed them the most, however, was the truth they sensed hidden just below their lies, struggling to be released.

Approaching this concealed truth made my patients increasingly uncomfortable. They yearned to know it but were afraid of what they would discover. It was a turning point for many of them. Some were strongly motivated by their discomfort and eagerly embraced the fearful truth. They had to know. It was as if hearing themselves lie activated the displeasure of a higher, more spiritual self within that could no longer tolerate deception. They seemed to have found their healing self, and when they did, a natural process of recovery began.

I tried to reinforce this natural process. I designed an exercise asking patients to replay the tape of their session and write down every lie they heard themselves tell. Then I asked them to correct the false statement. Finally, I asked them to explain the difference between the two statements. Did they wish to avoid something painful? Had they been pretending life was better? Were they hoping for the impossible? In a sense the exercise was a method for helping patients tell the truth about their lies, and it worked.

Making these corrections made it possible for patients to listen to their tape again and progress rapidly. Patients began to recognize not only the lies they told but also their style of distorting. They began to put aside their denial and pretense and look at their hidden feelings, needs, and desires. They were able to stop making excuses and admit that their life had not turned out the way they wanted. Most importantly they were willing to take responsibility for their role in their problems instead of blaming others.

Reaching this new level of honesty released a surge of positive feelings and motivated patients to work harder. Facing and accepting the truth created a momentum of healing. It was as if the more truth they told, the more powerfully their healing self manifested in their lives.

When I reviewed my patients' workbooks and saw the large number of lies they'd uncovered, I realized I had largely been unaware of when a patient was distorting the truth. For the most part, only the patient had the ability to discover his underlying deceptions. In a sense that meant the patient had to heal himself. Fortunately, the exercise for telling the truth undermined the defenses that held in old feelings and made patients eager to unpack their hearts and grow.

I was witnessing the wholesale release of a powerful healing process that I had only speculated on before when I was a resident in training. I remembered some of the questions I'd wondered about then: when, why, and how do people get better? I felt those questions were beginning to be answered.

The healing process seemed so spontaneous that I called it Natural Therapy. I sought to define this process through a series of therapeutic workbooks that I had my patients use to facilitate their healing. I began to ask how this process worked, what got in its way, what happened when it was blocked, and what could be done to release it?

This led me to study human emotions and to define the Feeling Cycle. I realized that the name given a painful feeling depended on when the pain occurred. *Pain in the future was called anxiety. Pain in the present was called hurt and experienced as sadness or disappointment. Finally, pain in the past was called anger. When a person held in his anger, it turned on him and was experienced as guilt. Depression was the depletion of energy from holding anger inside.*

When I analyzed the forces that kept these feelings hidden, I discovered that the same defenses that blocked feelings also blocked people from knowing or telling the truth. I found that all defense mechanisms belonged to three major defense types: denial, blaming or excuses, and pretenses. I also realized that everyone used all these defenses, depending on the kind of pain they were defending and their personality type.

This led me to define personality types by the way each avoided pain during different stages of childhood. Thus the dependent character was sensitive to the loss of love and used denial to protect himself. The controlling character blamed or made excuses when his power was threatened. Finally, the competitive person pretended not to care when he failed. Most people seemed a mixture of all three personality types and defenses.

My investigation into the healing process focused on the positive aspects of life. I tried to understand the forces involved in risk taking and to define how the different character types approached risks. I also began to explore the creative process.

I began to define the dynamics of the natural therapeutic process. When a feeling was not expressed, it created a condition of tension. Emotional stress was simply the pressure of an unexpressed feeling. I called the condition of withholding feelings Emotional Debt. Put simply, you owe the expression of a hidden feeling.

When you are in Emotional Debt, you suffer because you are afraid to tell the truth about your feelings. After a while your defenses become more rigid, and it is increasingly difficult to recall the truth. Your withheld feelings distort your life and consume your energy.

There was no such thing as emotional credit, although the more honest a person was, the more resilient he became, and the easier it was for him to endure stress.

Two points became clear.

Emotional illness was a storage disease.

The secret of mental health was to tell the person who hurt you that they hurt you, when they hurt you.

TOXIC NOSTALGIA

I then turned my attention to the study of the positive side of the Feeling Cycle, seeking to define how the various character types and defenses interfered with the experience of pleasure. I became aware of an intrusive phenomenon I had always been familiar with but never really recognized as a distinct mental process.

Like all psychiatrists, I often heard patients report how some trigger mysteriously caused old feelings to reappear as if out of nowhere, ruining their good times by paralyzing them with fear or filling them with anger or unresolved hurt. I reasoned that the source of these intrusive emotions had to be feelings that were stored in Emotional Debt. When these old feelings and attitudes were suddenly precipitated, it was as if a prefabricated mental state had suddenly been superimposed on the present. I called this intrusion Toxic Nostalgia and sought to understand and define its dynamics.

Although they created a lot of problems when they escaped, the *old emotions* released as *Toxic Nostalgia were just attempting to be resolved.* It became clear that the amount of stored feelings in Emotional Debt determined the potential for Toxic Nostalgia. It followed from this that any effective therapy had to decrease the volume of old stored emotions and also prevent newer feelings from being withheld. Storing feelings by not expressing them in a timely fashion is the mechanism by which you become emotionally damaged.

Toxic Nostalgia represented the way these repressed feelings resurfaced in order to be addressed and finally put to rest. It was clear that Toxic Nostalgia was the most important element in the natural healing process, and studying it became the focus of my work.

THE NATURAL HEALING PROCESS

The natural healing process is always working within you. It helps you resolve your emotional as well as physical pain. Every wise physician knows that the best he can do for a patient is to assist nature in healing. The heart of this process involved dealing honestly with life's problems by taking feelings and events at face value as they occurred. Facing life directly leads to resolution of the problems that can be solved and acceptance of those that can not.

If you acted with total honesty, expressing your true feelings to the person who most needed to hear them, you would be doing your part. The benefits you would receive would be peace of mind, enduring health, and comfort with yourself just as you are. You would also age slowly because the energy used to confine emotions would be free to heal you and keep you young instead.

The natural therapeutic process serves to keep you open and emotionally free. Because this healing process is blocked by self-deception and avoiding the truth, you are the main reason the process fails. When you refuse to look at what hurts you, you get in its way, and you live with anxiety, stress, and depression. Self-doubt and worry become your companions. You already possess this natural healing power. In a sense, it is yours to lose.

This book is designed to awaken you to the ancient knowledge that is within you. It will show you how to get out of your own way and allow this powerful healing process to function. It will teach you how to make Toxic Nostalgia work for you.

You are the real guru in your life. All you need to do is surrender to the truth. Telling the truth, especially in difficult circumstances, is the key: it's the easiest instruction to understand, the most difficult hurdle to leap, and results in the greatest relief you can know.

TEST YOURSELF

From time to time everyone is troubled by their unresolved past feelings intruding into the present. When you have settled your problems, forgiven those who have hurt you, and accepted yourself as you are, these intrusions are minimal. However, when old hurts still trouble you and you have not come to peace with your family or yourself, your life feels repetitive and you easily succumb to bad moods. This intrusion of the past into the present is called Toxic Nostalgia. It limits your freedom to act and diminishes your emotional resilience, for when old feelings are triggered they confuse you and hold you in their grip. Your confidence falls and it is difficult to act in your own best interests or even to see your options clearly.

The following quiz will help you see how vulnerable you are to toxic nostalgic intrusions. Be as honest as you can in responding to the following questions.

Indicates how much of the time the following statements are true	Rarely	Occa-sionally	Often	Most of the time	Almost always
Percent of the time the following is true	less than 10%	10–40%	40–60%	60–85%	85% plus
1. I worry					
2. I feel guilty					
3. I regret my actions or comments					
4. I have difficulty making decisions					
5. I feel resentment or hold grudges					
6. I feel uncomfortable with myself					
7. I fear admitting or making mistakes and accepting criticism					
8. I worry what other people think of me					
9. My problems feel repetitive					
10. I hold feelings inside					
TOTAL					

SCORING

Rarely 1; occasionally 2; often 3; usually 4; almost always 5

UNDERSTANDING YOUR SCORE

If you are under twenty years old subtract 3 points.
If you have just suffered a major loss, illness, or setback, or are in recovery your score will
be lower as a reaction to this loss.

11 OR LESS. You live in the present with occasional intrusion of the past. You
are either extremely well adjusted or you may not be completely truthful, shad-
ing your answers to appear stronger than you are.

Your growth depends on being as honest as you can. Pay attention to
the feelings you would like to brush away, for they reveal your tendency
to hide. Remember that attaining perfection is impossible. Your goal is true self-
acceptance, accepting yourself as you are.

12–16. You are generally open and working to be better. Your life is not
problem-free and you are not on top of every situation, but you are willing to
look at life honestly, take responsibility and grow. Past feelings sometimes persist but are mostly on the way to being resolved rather than becoming obsessions.

You will achieve the greatest momentum toward personal growth by being
more open about admitting your weaknesses. Accepting your limitations is the
first step in working on them. Trust yourself in spite of mistakes you have made.
Believe in yourself in spite of your failures.

17–21. Your have difficulty in letting go of the past. You frequently feel burdened by old feelings and tend to be defensive in accepting responsibility for
your actions. You tend to be closed under stress and make matters worse by
holding feelings in, wasting a lot of energy. Stress is mild but common in your
life.

You need to be more honest about forgiving, not just forgiving people to
avoid dealing with the problem, but also by being willing to talk about your
feelings with the people who have hurt you. Face all your feelings. You are
stronger than you know. Pride and appearances are not as important as you
think.

22–30. You did not need this quiz to tell you that life is not going well. You
are continually being distracted by old emotions. Your self-confidence is frequently shaken. You are not a stranger to moodiness and depression. Anxiety
is a large component of your life. Much of your energy is lost by holding feelings in Emotional Debt. Old feelings are easily triggered. You tend to be defensive rather than open. It is difficult to give freely and to enjoy life without

thinking of the negative possibilities. Forgiving others is a problem. Stress is moderate.

You are far too tough on yourself. This comes mainly from internalizing your anger when you are hurt rather than being forthright in expressing it. You need to trust yourself and your goodness. Your fear of rejection has too much power over you. Risk expressing your feelings even though you fear the consequences. Holding feelings in is defeating you.

31–36. Your life is wrapped up in unresolved feelings. Old problems compound new ones. Stress is high. Your ability to concentrate is diminished. Listening to other people is difficult. You are in a rut, commonly feel trapped, in over your head, and hopeless. You often feel on the edge and too overwhelmed to take responsibility for yourself. The past seems to cling to you in the form of grudges and resentment.

You need to place far less emphasis on what other people think and want. Concentrate on your own needs. Be more direct and timely in making emotional statements to people who hurt you. Too much of your life is spent catching up with the past rather than living spontaneously in the present. Try letting go instead of holding on.

37–42. You have significant difficulty being truthful. Anything that can inhibit you does. At the same time anything that can trigger your past feelings disturbs you. Therefore, everything feels like a problem to you. You are living in the past and probably don't even realize it. Your feelings stored in Emotional Debt frequently break loose as toxic nostalgic displays, leading you to overreact and seem unstable or hypersensitive to others. Your life is out of balance and it is difficult to tell what is real at times.

While this may be a little hard to hear, most of your problems are not the result of the way others have treated you, but rather from the way you have chosen to respond to them. You need not only to forgive others, but also yourself for allowing your life to drift so far away from truthfulness. You can always turn it around if you decide to take the risk of other people not liking you. Take responsibility for everything in your life instead of blaming others. If you can do that you'll find the power to change.

OVER 43. You are probably depressed and therefore this score comes from exaggerating the negative aspects of your life. You feel hopeless and powerless much of the time. The previous description also applies to you.

Your life is seized in the grip of the past. It is hard to find the energy to become involved in the present let alone deal with the overwhelming issues of the past. There is a way to take control of this seemingly insoluble situation and make it better. It begins with being more truthful and expressing what you feel, as hard as that may seem right now.

It should be clear from these responses that everyone suffers from Toxic Nostalgia to one degree or another. At those times you are robbed of spontaneity and the ability to respond to situations easily and naturally.

This book is designed to help you achieve and preserve your emotional resilience, so you can face the difficult threats of the present and manage them effectively without being drained, feeling bad about yourself, or second-guessing your actions. As you come to understand how feelings work and what blocks their expression, how the mourning process is undermined, and how stored feelings subvert your best intentions, you will begin to see the inner workings of your own mind and heart. Therein lies the key to releasing the past and getting on with your life.

The methods described in this book suggest taking emotional risks. The reward is great. Mastering these techniques offers the promise of a new personal freedom based on an increased flexibility in dealing with the world. This new openness will help you overcome self-consciousness and give you increased confidence based on trusting and accepting yourself.

You deserve no less.

WHEN OLD FEELINGS DISCHARGE

WHILE COMPLEX EMOTIONS can be reduced to a simple formula, simple emotions can seem incomprehensible when you are embroiled in your own difficulties.

When you hold on to a painful feeling, rather than express it spontaneously, you begin to distort it. The longer the feeling is stored, the more distorted it tends to become. While the event that caused the original injury is probably a discrete incident, storing the feeling is likely to make your recollection blurry.

For example, even though a person might have been terrified when he was lost in an amusement park when he was five years old, he would find it difficult today to recall the exact emotions he felt then. He might be able to remember some facts, but the memory of his old feelings would be altered both by recent history and the opinions he later formed about the event. He may have found being lost so uncomfortable that he would now find it difficult to remember any feelings and would hardly remember the incident. Most likely, being lost was a hurt that was allowed to heal. He learned to trust his parents again and realized that being lost was just a mistake. He was not being abandoned.

On the other hand, imagine that the person who was lost in the amusement park came from a home where he suffered serious neglect. His retelling of being lost in the amusement park would likely include some other unexpressed old hurts too vague to be remembered. The incident of being lost would become a symbol for being neglected, and the emotion he felt would be exaggerated in support of his belief.

In this way the memory of a painful event can stand for many stored emotions.

HIDDEN FEELINGS

Hidden feelings are always trying to make a case in exactly this way. When you are hurt and retain the feeling, the hurt is converted into anger, and the anger grows. Your mind continually collects other examples of your being hurt to justify your feeling angry. To feel angry without knowing why is extremely disruptive. Eventually, you turn the anger against yourself and begin to doubt your goodness. After all, if you can be this angry for no reason, you may well begin to wonder if you might be a bad person. This is the dilemma that causes suffering in depressed people. Without a good reason for being angry, people beat themselves up emotionally.

When your mind searches forward and backward trying to justify your anger, it is not especially accurate, only approximate. The hurtful memory you locate is likely to be distorted, contaminated by many feelings. Should you decide to express yourself, your story may make sense to you but will be highly slanted and may bear little relationship to what others remember. Both your and others' recollections will be self-serving. You will be trying to prove you were injured, and they will be trying to show that they were innocent and you are mistaken.

When you are in Emotional Debt, you always suffer. Because unresolved feelings live inside you, you feel as if you are trying to contain a powerful negative energy that is continually seeking to be discharged. As a result you feel unsettled, jittery, off balance, or fearful of losing control. You look for a safe release valve, but when you find a way to express your feelings, you often tend to overdo it and hurt others.

When you are in Emotional Debt, you may not even be aware of the specific hurt that is troubling you, although it is common for people to target an obviously neglectful or wanting parent, spouse, or boss as the source of all their problems. There is much more to your hurts than what you choose to remember or whom you blame. You are always responsible for some part of your problem. The reason you suffer is not because you have been hurt, but because the way you choose to deal with the hurt has kept it from resolving naturally. You need to take responsibility for the part you played.

The essence of Emotional Debt is that hurt is stored as an amorphous merge of anger and guilt. The feelings in Emotional Debt are usually expressed as Toxic Nostalgia after being triggered, and so they are displayed suddenly and often seem overstated. Therefore, when people in Emotional Debt do blow up, instead of relieving their pain, they frequently make it worse by hurting others.

This only undermines their self-esteem. Fearing that there is something wrong with them for being so angry, they repress even more feelings. Typically, the person in Emotional Debt begins to doubt himself and his stability.

This is understandable, because while anxiety, hurt, and anger are all accompanied by physical sensations, guilt—which is anger turned inward—is dealt with primarily by the mind. The mind reasons and makes arguments for and against the self, depending on how much stored anger or guilt there is to rationalize.

When the anger is slight, it is easy to blame others for hurting you. However, when withheld anger grows, you begin to accuse yourself for having such dark visions of revenge. From time to time everyone has retaliation fantasies. They are generally excused as being justified by the present situation, but to a person in deep Emotional Debt, these sinister internal dramas can be disturbing, seen as proof that the sufferer is evil, which only produces more guilt.

It is in this caldron of self-justification and self-vilification that feelings stored in Emotional Debt churn. Additionally, because strong defenses are already in place to contain feelings, a person in Emotional Debt immediately seeks to conceal new hurt when it occurs, thus adding to the volume of unexpressed feelings. The discomfort of being in Emotional Debt is aggravated both by the added weight of each newly concealed hurt and by the sufferer's growing fears of losing control.

It is common when you are in Emotional Debt for old hidden emotions to seek opportunistic expression by joining in with the expression of a current hurt. This leads you to overstate your case and become sarcastic or hypercritical. You may even seem petty or mean-spirited, and should you hurt others, you now become the villain. This is why people in Emotional Debt tend to shy away from being open and instead pull further into their shell and obsessions, endlessly vacillating between self-condemnation and justification.

DISTORTION

A story that made headlines a few years ago illustrates the extent to which reasoning can be distorted by stored pain. An old widower, reclusive after the death of his wife, was annoyed by some boys who stole apples from his orchard. When the boys ignored his warning, the old man shot into the trees and killed two of them. As he was taken away, he explained pitifully, "But I warned them," as if that were enough to justify his actions. Obviously, he had so rationalized his actions in his own mind that he lost touch with reality.

Although this example is extreme, it reflects how all feelings stored in Emotional Debt undergo distortion. As new hurts are held in, they are combined with the old, adding to the pressure and the potential for discharge as Toxic Nostalgia. If the feelings are allowed to build to intolerable levels, they can be triggered by a symbolic emotional event and be released without sufficient consideration of the consequences, as in this tragic case. The old man felt robbed because fate stole his wife from him—his inner struggle. When the boys stole his apples, they reawakened the feelings of outrage and powerlessness that he felt when his wife died. He was highly charged to protect himself from the next robbery and to avenge the old one by proxy.

Even when you are in Emotional Debt, most people remain in far better contact with reality than that unfortunate old man. Although you may distort the truth, you generally reconsider putting your angry feelings into action. You question yourself and wonder if you played a role in your misfortune. So although your old hurts and frustrations prime you to express yourself, your self-doubt and discretion keep you from acting.

TOXIC NOSTALGIA

Have you ever found yourself in an emotionally confining situation, feeling as if you would burst? Many people have experienced the pain of being trapped in an unhappy relationship, pursuing the wrong educational path, tyrannized by controlling parents, or locked in an impossible financial situation. You may feel like a prisoner in a thankless job, a marriage of diminishing convenience, or enrolled against your will in a cause you do not support. In such confinements, you suffer the most when you discover you can make a good case for hating yourself. You despise your powerlessness and negativity.

Although initially your doubts hold you back, the longer you conceal your true feelings, the stronger the case you make for taking action and the more likely you are to do something you'll regret. You want to do something about your situation. You want to act but fear the consequences. At some point your self-justifying logic becomes inflexible and unable to contain your discontent. It is then that you are most likely to be pushed into trouble by some seemingly trivial event and say things you wish you could take back or jeopardize your position by acting impulsively.

Your precipitous actions are usually awkward, embarrassing, and self-defeating. You hurt others most when you find yourself propelled into action. The words are out of your mouth before you have a chance to think about what you are going to say. You struggle to hold yourself in check as an overwhelming fear of losing control sweeps over you and clouds your reasoning. You find yourself defending an indefensible position or rash action. You can barely remember what started it all. You just try to hold on.

Toxic Nostalgia describes the symptoms produced when concealed emotions are triggered. Typically something in the present so strongly reminds you of some unfinished emotional business that it reawakens those old feelings and brings them to life again. Those feelings can lead you to take action before you are even aware of them. At other times you can be plagued with a sudden painful feeling that holds you captive. Even if your recollection of the event that caused the feeling is lost, the persistent emotional echoes make it feel like the past is happening all over again.

Toxic Nostalgia often feels like a mystery. You ask, Why am I feeling this way? What does this disturbing occurrence mean? Am I crazy? There are many pieces missing from the puzzle you are trying to solve. Many facts are hidden or distorted. The explanations you give for your symptoms are highly personal and usually reflect your defensive style, your blind spot.

WHERE ANGER GOES

When you direct your anger outside, you act self-righteous. You review the evidence, uncover more hurt, and add it to your slanted argument. It makes no difference what the truth is. How you feel makes you believe you are right. You're out to prove others are bad and that you have been hurt by them.

When you turn your anger inward, you wonder, What is wrong with me? Why am I this vengeful? As your self-esteem falters, your doubt grows. The people who hurt you don't seem so bad. You feel guilty and fear you may have been wrong to accuse them. You wonder if you even provoked them to hurt you. Even worse, because you feel so guilty, you begin to feel you deserve to suffer.

When you hold anger inside, you try to reason your pain away—not a good plan, for the mind is not designed to feel. You need to feel pain before you can accept it. Accepting pain means putting what you have felt into perspective, a function of reason. However, if you place your pain in perspective too quickly, saying, "Everything works out for the best," when it clearly has not, some pain is excluded from being felt and still needs to be mourned. So the mind has the power both to heal you and prolong your suffering. Until you feel your pain, the mind can grant only limited relief.

LIFE'S IMPORTANT QUESTIONS

When the mind manages pain, instead of feeling angry, you obsess, analyze, blame others, and try to absolve yourself. What is curious is that no matter what form your obsessions take, they are all derived from the following questions:

Am I lovable or unlovable?
Am I good or bad?
Am I smart or stupid?
Am I right or wrong?
Am I worthy or unworthy?
Am I attractive or unattractive?
Am I a success or failure?

Even when you wallow in negative feelings, your mind still struggles to affirm the positive response to these questions. However, as you slip into deeper Emotional Debt and become more guilt-ridden, your conviction falters. As it does, even an innocent comment that suggests one of these negative descriptions might be true can cause your self-esteem to drop. Now, instead of protesting these negative accusations, you embrace them. You are the first to claim you are unlovable, stupid, not good, or a failure. It is as if your mind has stopped reasoning on your behalf and now works against you.

The same withheld feelings that lead you to search for negative answers to these questions are also the driving force behind Toxic Nostalgia, causing these feelings to spill over into the present. It's important to remember that these old feelings resurface in order to be resolved, not to punish you.

If there is a power shaping your life, it is within you and yours to master by being more honest.

Because the old feelings of Toxic Nostalgia have been concealed, their sudden intrusion usually comes as a shocking surprise. When anxiety breaks loose from its ancient moorings, you feel adrift in a sea of unexplainable turmoil. When anger breaks free of defenses, you feel out of control and often suffer a severe blow to your self-esteem. You recoil as your negative outburst seems to reinforce your worst doubts about yourself. It is no wonder you often withdraw following a display of Toxic Nostalgia, convinced you are crazy or bad. This fearful withdrawal leads you to withhold more feelings and raises the likelihood of future displays of Toxic Nostalgia.

Toxic Nostalgia can take many forms, including anxiety attacks, sudden mood swings, inhibited grief, inappropriate emotional responses, prejudices, playing the victim, being rigid, overreacting, hypersensitivity, misperceiving, finding the negative in positive situations, acting self-destructive either in repetitive behavior or thinking, plus many more. All of these manifestations are driven by Emotional Debt.

THE SEARCH FOR UNDERSTANDING

In order to unlock the mystery of Toxic Nostalgia, the most effective psychotherapists guide patients to understand the meaning of their hidden feelings. The realization they seek to liberate in their patients is "Aha! Now I know what happened to me." Of course even the clearest insight is framed by distortions that must still be sorted out before you act on them. Having just uncovered and understood one old hurt, a person may now mistakenly conclude that because he believes he has proof that others injured him, he is justified in responding to all the wrongs he suffered, even those he exaggerated, combined, or made up.

For example, imagine that someone who suffered from frequent rejections suddenly remembers being lost at an amusement park as a child and recalls all the feelings of panic he had then. Combining those feelings with his long-standing feeling of betrayal and disappointment from his parents' negligence, he now believes he was not lost but purposely abandoned. In the expressive flush of his recaptured memory, many other emotions and partial memories are also awakened. As he "remembers" these additional hurts, he weaves a story from fragments to fit his accusatory logic.

Having identified "the source" of all his pain, he decides to confront his parents. In his own mind his report feels accurate and long overdue but seems fabricated and repetitious to them. Since they do not relate to the scenario he portrays, his presentation only makes things worse. He feels rejected again. Now his old feeling of abandonment is reinforced by the fresh insult. He takes the ill-fated confrontation with his parents as proof that he was and continues to be intentionally victimized.

Where is reality in all this?

How do you express an old injury so that it is relieved?

How do you get others to hear your pain?

What should you do when others come forward with a story you know is either false or so exaggerated you cannot relate to it?

PROBLEMS IN RECALLING

Even if there is a basis in fact for the original injury, almost all stored emotions downloaded during Toxic Nostalgia are distorted, especially those involving childhood injuries. This is understandable. A young child has a limited ability to deal with overwhelming emotional events. Gripped with fear, the child seeks to deny what he cannot manage. Later on, when he attempts to recall the injury, his mind weaves a story, making up the part he denied in much the same way the mind assembles incoherent mental fragments on awakening to create a dream. Often the child cannot remember the actual event but only his cover story, his fantasy.

Probably all memories of both painful and pleasurable events are distorted. When an old feeling surfaces unconnected to the original events that caused it, it searches to attach itself to events in the present to make sense of itself. Connecting emotions with events seems the natural imperative of the mind and satisfies its innate sense of order and need for an explanation.

That search also causes you to believe in your distortions. You exaggerate or diminish the truth to placate your hidden feelings. What you cannot face, you tend to deny. What you dislike in yourself, you blame on others. What you cannot accept, you pretend you do not care about.

You are not evil, stupid, or crazy. Neither are most of the people who have hurt you. Unpredictable accidents happen to everyone. Illness claims loved ones. People become distracted by the stress of life. Sometimes they get careless and say things they don't mean. Sometimes they are neglectful or unsupportive. Sometimes there are real villains, and innocent people are abused. Other times, innocent people are hurt unintentionally and no one is at fault. Even then you still want to make sense of what you feel. You want a target for your anger.

In some way you distort everything you experience.

LOOKING BACK

The concept of Toxic Nostalgia also applies to positive feelings. An idealized recollection of a perfect past can intrude to sully today's joy by invidious comparison. Since idealized recollections are perfect and reality is not, such intrusions can act as spoilers to an otherwise pleasant experience. When your grandparents unfavorably compared the present to the way it was in their day, they were demonstrating Toxic Nostalgia and revealing how the mind alters memory with time.

You yearn for the innocence and freedom of childhood. You seek to recapture the happy times you believe you lost. You idealize your childhood experience most when you find the present disappointing, and you flirt with disaster when you try to re-create old feelings in the present. Sometimes you mistakenly seek the comfort of your mother's love in your present lover or tragically set yourself up by placing trust in an unsuitable employer, expecting him to protect you the way you imagine your father did.

When you cling to these past idealizations, the present always seems to fall short, unable to meet your unrealistic expectations. You can only lament what has been, what has passed, your absent loved ones, and days gone by. In some way these toxic nostalgic intrusions result from your inability to let go of the past, mourn the loss of those who are no longer with you, and move on with your life.

Idealizing the past is another form of Toxic Nostalgia in which the hurtful loss has been coated with unresolved yearning. Some people can only deal with their unhappy past by pretending they were always happy then. It is hard to abandon an idealized past, especially when your perception serves to cover a hurt you don't want to admit.

Everyone distorts the past. Who has returned to his childhood home and walked down the old familiar streets and not found his memory at variance with reality? In the middle of the most familiar of all settings, you are likely to find something strangely absent. Missing perhaps are the distortions you cradled to make your life tolerable or the lies you told yourself that made the place seem even lovely. Instead the place seems stark, empty, or emasculated when you return. You marvel at how small everything is, how much your fear and innocence exaggerated the size of it. You try to relate to your old home but find it is not the same. The old feelings you thought lived here seem to have come unattached. In the end you prefer your memories of the way home was to what you see when you revisit it.

You wonder how much of your past was real, or if you imagined it all.

VISITATIONS FROM THE PAST

Toxic nostalgic intrusions, whether positive or negative, are always disquieting because they occur beyond your control and expose your unresolved feelings and persistent vulnerability. They reveal you to be needy, irrational, or vindictive, and their inclemency makes others want to avoid you. These intrusions can be sudden or the sum total of the way you are.

The weight of your emotional baggage burdens the present moment. You find it difficult simply to be yourself. Too much history has to be explained to understand you. Much of the evidence you cite does not stand up to close scrutiny. You discover that the facts you earnestly believed in were somehow embellished. Much of what you recollect to justify your thinking feels like a realistic dream or a dreamy reality. You begin to wonder, Am I real or a phony?

The main task of the natural therapeutic process is to sort out your cherished distortions and emotional anachronisms to determine and accept the painful truth that lies beneath them, a process called working through. However, it is impossible to discover the truth as it actually happened. Some people find it exceptionally difficult to relinquish their unique view of history because that view exonerates them from responsibility. Time, it seems, makes liars of us all.

It is much more practical to treat all feelings as if they were composites and reflect not so much a single truthful event but your total life experience. Even so, old pain is best resolved by admitting as much truth as possible, taking as much responsibility as you can, and forgiving others. This is the heart of the therapeutic process.

The natural therapeutic process obliges you to face your feelings and learn what they mean. As you grow, you learn how you distort the truth. You become wiser and more understanding. In the end you come to accept both the fact that you were injured and how your silence has added to your suffering. You learn these lessons at a very high price, paying for them in misery, time, and lost opportunity. You could have been better sooner if only you had been more honest.

THE MANIFESTATION OF TOXIC NOSTALGIA

The following case illustrates many of the typical features of Toxic Nostalgia and Emotional Debt.

Suzanne was a schoolteacher in her late thirties who sought help for debilitating anxiety attacks that had plagued her for almost twenty years. Her problem first manifested as a fear of riding in elevators and then expanded to a fear of going into any enclosed space. Therapy and medication directed at helping her cope with her symptoms were only marginally helpful.

When asked to recall her first episode of panic, Suzanne immediately protested that she couldn't remember. After persistent questioning she finally blurted, "It was in Chicago, at the Empire State Building."

Hearing herself speak, Suzanne realized she'd made a mistake and corrected it, saying it must have been at the Sears Tower in Chicago. On reflection, she remembered that her only visit to Chicago took place many years after her symptoms started. In a sense Suzanne felt that to cause such severe symptoms the elevator in question would have had to be in one of the tallest buildings in the world, an example of how stored feelings shape your recollection of events.

Suzanne finally remembered that the elevator in which she had had her first anxiety attack was a short one indeed, traveling over only three stories. It was located in a restaurant where she was going to lunch with her sister and parents. It was pointed out that the elevator ride must have seemed to her as if it were taking forever, making the building seem taller. On hearing this explanation, Suzanne recalled the feeling of being trapped and with it some additional memories.

Suzanne remembered that at the time of the first attack she was nineteen and had just finished her first year in college, which she considered the worst time in her life. She had desperately wanted to pursue a dancing career, but her mother insisted she qualify as a teacher to protect her options. The implication was clear. Her mother did not believe Suzanne possessed enough talent to enjoy a successful dance career. Suzanne was hurt but meekly acquiesced.

She was deeply disappointed in school and barely managed to make passing grades. Because she spent so little time dancing, her performance began to slip, and she began to doubt her talent. It also made her mother's opinion seem like prophesy and her advice to pursue an alternate career a wise assessment.

Suzanne's parents were both artists and familiar with the world of performance. They had for a long time been determined to persuade Suzanne's younger sister, Kim, to become a cello soloist. Ironically Kim did not want to be a soloist because the pressure was so intense. So while her parents did not believe in Suzanne at all, they believed in her sister to an excessive degree. This only added to Suzanne's frustration and hurt.

When her mother and father made plans for the lunch it was clear that they had two main items on their agenda. They wanted to convince Suzanne to complete her teaching accreditation and give up her dancing career and to coax Kim to become a soloist.

As they all drove to the restaurant Suzanne mentally rehearsed her plea to study dance, but when she searched for evidence to prove that she had talent, she had only the past miserable year to fall back on. Her former achievements now seemed distant and unconvincing, and her low self-esteem made it easy for her to discount them. Kim, however, was already arguing with her mother. Suzanne became increasingly uncomfortable listening to Kim express herself. She wished she could express her feelings as directly but feared she would lose control.

Walking to the restaurant, Kim became sarcastic and bitter. Her mother gave her an inhibiting glare, but Kim bravely persisted. Suzanne remembered how her mother's look had always silenced her when she was a child. She'd always given in and never protested. Suddenly Suzanne hated herself for being so weak. She wanted to express herself as well.

Suzanne's resentment increased as they waited for the elevator. She was about to tell her mother how she really felt when the elevator door opened. She decided to say nothing and stepped inside, holding back the long-repressed words of defiance just as they finally approached her lips. As she did, the elevator door closed with a thud. Suddenly, Suzanne felt trapped within the elevator, and within herself. Fear came over her and grew into a suffocating dread. She became dizzy and frightened as her heart started to pound. She felt she would burst. She ached desperately to be free of her confinement in the elevator and from confining her explosive anger.

By the time the elevator reached the restaurant, Suzanne was in an uncontrollable panic, convinced that her surfacing feelings were caused by riding in the elevator, a much more acceptable belief than admitting she was angry at her parents and feared losing their approval and love if they found out.

Because Suzanne's anger had never come so close to the surface, she never before knew just how angry she'd been, and this realization undermined her self-esteem. She felt as if for a dark moment her secret had made itself visible, and this convinced her she was bad.

It is when an unacceptable feeling is repressed that the symbolic emotional trigger is selected and invested with its disruptive power. Suzanne was never particularly fearful about elevators until she associated her fear of losing control with them. Had she been sitting at the table in the restaurant, holding a knife at the time she repressed those very same emotions, she could equally have developed a terror of sharp objects, fearing she would take a knife and hurt someone. When the trigger is separated from the inhibited emotions that it comes to symbolize, it becomes a mystery of its own.

Over the years, Suzanne lost her courage to dance, but her anger persisted. As her need to repress her anger grew, Suzanne's fear became more generalized, and she came to fear any enclosed place. If she could avoid a confining place she could avoid her confined anger.

THE LEGACY OF TOXIC NOSTALGIA

No one expresses his feelings completely the moment they occur. Therefore, everyone stores some emotions. Your capacity for Toxic Nostalgia depends on many factors: how many feelings you have concealed, how much you fear expressing them, your openness, your fatigue, and your honesty, to mention a few.

From time to time everyone suffers from occasional bouts of unexplained sadness, anxiety, irritability, and unreasonableness. All these symptoms are manifestations of Toxic Nostalgia. Rather than seeing these symptoms as a weakness, you should take them as an opportunity to learn to deal with your feelings more openly.

What follows is an explanation of the natural therapeutic process and a plan to use the special opening created by Toxic Nostalgia to your advantage. The purpose of Toxic Nostalgia is always to initiate the healing process and clear up the emotional debts you have not expressed.

. . . AND THE PROMISE

The natural healing process keeps you well and heals you when you are troubled. There is a simple optimism inherent in this process, an affirmation of the purpose and worth of life. The process can help you resolve your pain so you can be free to make your special contribution. Ultimately, it seeks to make us all emotionally free so that we can solve the problems of the planet, insure safety and justice, and reach for the stars.

In our feelings we are all one.

HOW NATURAL THERAPY WORKS

THE ANATOMY OF AN EPIPHANY

*T*HE TRUTH YOU RESIST is the battle you fight.

The natural therapeutic process directs you to recognize and accept your losses and disappointments so that you can put them in perspective. It does this by continually presenting your pain and dissatisfactions to you, bringing them to mind, disturbing you and reminding you to deal with them. To heal and grow you must admit that you are not happy and then understand why.

The pain you resist pools within you and incites you to engage in empty symbolic struggles over and over, whereas the pain you mourn frees you to move on and live your life spontaneously. This natural process is also concerned with helping you find yourself. It forces you to examine your discontent, to ponder your purpose, and so it directs you to seek self-fulfillment. Thus, this process has two distinct goals: motivating you to become emotionally free, and encouraging you to discover and develop your true talent. What's the point of becoming emotionally free if you aren't going to do something meaningful with your life, something that matters to you?

Just as gravity pulls water, there is a natural direction to this process, a momentum that inclines you toward emotional health and spiritual growth. The process can lead you to see and confront your self-deceptions and acknowledge your unhappiness. Only then can you deal with them and move on.

If you fear accepting your feelings or deny what happened to you, you are forced to bear the burden of holding back the inevitable. When dammed-up old emotions eventually flood into the present, they sometimes wash away your emotional fortifications, causing great upheaval. At the same time it is only when your defensive barriers are lifted that the healing process is free to do its work. Facing your discontent heals you.

The natural process always tends toward openness and release. You oppose it at great cost and suffering.

THE IMPERATIVE OF NATURAL THERAPY

The natural therapeutic process directs you

> *To express your feelings.*
> *To mourn, forgive, and heal.*
> *To admit the lies you tell.*
> *To understand why you tell them.*
> *To understand your true needs.*
> *To give up false expectations.*
> *To accept yourself as you are.*
> *To create your own life, free, productive, and happy.*

YOU

You can only be happy as yourself.

What you were meant to be is the person you already are.

It has taken everything that has ever happened to you for you to have turned out the way you are today. If you become the success you dream of and look back on your most troubled times, you will see the contribution that adversity played in making you more honest and more real, and how it motivated you to change.

Do not lament any part of your life. Every hardship can teach you a valuable lesson. Every problem you encounter is partly the result of something in the past you did not understand, did not take responsibility for, or wished to ignore.

Of course, terrible misfortunes still happen to innocent people, totally out of their control. Some people through no fault of their own are abused, damaged, victimized, and treated unfairly. Even so, the way a person has been treated does not irrevocably shape the way he turns out. There are people who have every advantage whose lives are ruined because they see themselves as victims of trivial injuries and blame others for their failures. On the other hand, there are those who suffer unspeakable abuse and deprivation but overcome their past to make contributions that elevate the spirit of mankind. It is not what happens to you that shapes you, but how you choose to react to it.

The natural therapeutic process is the healing force that makes the difference, levels the playing field, and gives people a chance to succeed beyond the
circumstances of their birth and education, their mistreatment and misfortune.
Being conversant with the truth and learning to express your feelings honestly
is the method that it employs. Only those who face their pain truthfully can let
go of it and move forward with their creative energy and self-esteem intact.

The goal of the natural therapeutic process is not merely to tell the truth, but
to understand how your needs and self-doubts lead you to distort that truth or
postpone acting on it.

THE AWAKENING

You must sometimes endure a life of pain before you are ready to admit what
everyone else can plainly see. Only then can you begin to live openly. The forces
that finally drag you to the bottom are usually of your own creation. The very
barriers you erect to protect yourself become too costly and too emotionally
exhausting to maintain. Your life becomes consumed by the empty activities and
meaningless rituals and symbols you invent to hide from disappointment. Your
attempt to protect yourself becomes your undoing.

Eventually there comes a day of awakening and reckoning. Your epiphany is
both inevitable and totally unexpected. It is often triggered by a trivial detail
that somehow slips past your defenses. In the moment of your illumination, you
finally see yourself as you are and are forced to surrender to the truth lest your
false illusions forever obscure your best self. It is characteristic of these sudden
awakenings that they not only permit you to see your weaknesses but also allow
you to see your strengths. You realize you can face what you've so long avoided.
This gives you the courage to let go of what does not work and, even though you
are flawed, to believe in yourself.

Until you reach such a day, you often live a self-deceptive way of life. You try
to convince yourself that what you have chosen is what you really want. You
channel your unfulfilled emotional needs toward some materialistic or compulsive goal and pronounce yourself happy. It's characteristic of such false goals that
their ability to satisfy quickly wears thin. You always need to achieve more to
slake your unmet discontent.

Stanford, a prominent physician who always bragged about his loving marriage, began to have compulsive affairs that left him confused and torn with guilt.
He protested that he really wanted to be faithful to his wife and was certain they

loved each other. Although his cheating was out of control, he could not explain why he was unfaithful and refused to admit that his marriage was in any trouble.

Stanford built an extravagant beach home that was beyond his means and held it up to the world as proof of his marriage's stability. When Stanford's wife discovered his affairs, she shocked him by refusing to discuss reconciliation and taking immediate steps to get a divorce. Deeply wounded and yet unable to grasp her rejection, Stanford insisted on keeping the beach house as part of the settlement. Even though it was an unaffordable excess, he couldn't let it go. Because it was an extension of his denial, keeping the house allowed him to hold on to his belief that his wife had loved him.

One weekend after his painful divorce, Stanford went down to the shore to enjoy his retreat, his symbol of happiness. As he paced on the spacious verandah surveying Nantucket Sound in the nippy spring air, the place seemed anything but a consolation. He began to think of his marriage and why he'd built the home in the first place. He remembered how he'd driven the architect crazy with all his changes, insisting that everything be just right.

His old critical attitude reawakened by that memory, he began to scrutinize the porch. He noticed that one of the shutters was crooked and had been improperly mounted. He became irritated. When he began to adjust it he found that it had been painted on only one side. Suddenly he felt cheated. A swell of anger built up in him and he began to curse the contractor when, just as abruptly, he became weak and dizzy. He slumped back into a wooden deck chair and began to weep as the feelings he had refused to recognize flooded over him.

Discovering that the shutter only appeared perfect on the surface but was flawed when he examined it closely pierced his pretense. He realized for the first time that he had created the perfect place to conceal the fact that his marriage was lacking love. The awareness came unexpectedly, precipitated by a tiny detail that suggested to him that he had also been maintaining a false facade.

It was the first time Stanford allowed himself to feel sad about being deprived of affection. Acknowledging that his wife did not love him justified his hidden resentment and made perfect sense of his affairs. He was lonely and desperate for love. He wasn't proud of cheating, but at least now he understood why he had done it. It helped him believe in his goodness again.

When, instead of mourning your losses, you attempt to replace what has been taken away, the natural healing process becomes sidetracked. However, the process still lives within you. It will seize any symbolic opportunity to open your eyes and initiate its therapeutic course.

* * *

Chelsea was shattered by the sudden death of the only man she ever loved, a passionate, caring, sensitive man for whom she had left her husband. Her grief was inconsolable, and she did everything she could to get over it except to mourn. She changed jobs and became socially involved, but her grief lingered and oppressed her. She tried to escape by becoming involved in one tumultuous and disappointing love affair after another. Finally, she gave up all hope and sank into despair. However, just when it appeared she would begin to face her blocked mourning, she miraculously met the perfect man—well, almost perfect.

Although he had everything—status, money, family, palatial homes—he lacked passion. He was emotionally distant, passive and cool, something Chelsea had long claimed she would never settle for. Nevertheless, she abandoned her promising career and threw herself into the new relationship which was stable and financially comfortable.

To make up for what was missing emotionally, Chelsea became obsessed with redecorating three homes. For the first time in her life she could have any accessory she wanted, any fabric or painting. Her life became a circle of decorators, architects, builders, landscape gardeners, and color consultants. She even hired artists to paint pictures of her homes. All she could talk about was her passion for materialistic interests. Finally, Chelsea alienated her friends.

To quash the unmourned pain that lived within her, Chelsea took on even more projects, until one day she found herself on a shipping dock, supervising the unloading of a crate of Italian marble, trying unsuccessfully to exactly match the pink drapes in her new kitchen. Sitting on the dock for the entire day with hundreds of pieces of marble spread around her as workmen dutifully loaded and unloaded boxes, Chelsea became frustrated and then mysteriously sad. Suddenly she realized that all this time she'd been trying to match the man she'd lost. As she admitted the futility of her obsession, she dissolved into deep sobs and for the first time surrendered to her sorrow.

Chelsea could no longer fight the destiny of her feelings or the momentum of the healing process. In her new relationship she found herself living with an aloof stranger who did not speak her emotional language. Something had to give. Her defensive maneuvers had finally carried her so far away from herself that she could no longer deny that she had drifted off course.

In the moment of your painful realization, you are forced to admit how foolish you were to pretend or deny what you now realize is true. Like Chelsea and Stanford, you have to give up your false passions and focus on what you have really loved and lost. As you allow yourself to mourn, your old diversions seem farfetched, almost childish ways of avoiding pain. You can suddenly see how desperate you must have been to be led so far astray. Now you can begin to pick up the pieces of your life.

There is a great natural wisdom reflected in the momentum of this healing process. It directs you to express your feelings, to accept your true desires, to claim your place in the world and take risks to fulfill yourself.

FEAR KEEPS YOU FROM YOUR TRUE PASSION

Real passions stem from your talent or true love and energize you. It is difficult enough to follow what you love when you are aware of it, but when you're living falsely, you have limited knowledge of your true passions, and risking anything for them seems difficult indeed. Further, when your energy is drained by a job you hate or meaningless routines, you find it hard to believe in yourself. While you may claim that your fear of being alone prevents you from letting go of a situation that no longer seems to satisfy you, it is really not your loneliness you fear, but the painful realizations that may come to you when you are by yourself and have nothing to divert your attention.

What is it you fear?

> *You fear that you have squandered your chances.*
> *You fear you have no talent.*
> *You fear starting over again.*
> *You fear admitting you were wrong, foolish, or prideful.*
> *You fear being embarrassed.*
> *You fear admitting you made mistakes.*

Mostly you fear admitting that you were hurt, that you were not loved or that someone used you.

CORRECTING FALSE CHOICES

Your particular pattern of making the wrong choices began in childhood. Perhaps you were motivated to please people or to prove you were worthy by becoming the biggest, the best, the richest, or the smartest. While these seemed like good reasons years ago, they may have led you to make choices that didn't turn out to be in your best interests. Like everyone else, your life today is littered by the detritus of your bad choices.

The resentment that comes from career frustration is managed by the natural therapeutic process as just another in a series of buried hurts. Your suppressed displeasure over your work is stored in Emotional Debt, where it merges with other stored anger. When you feel others don't appreciate you, this anger is likely to be suddenly downloaded, especially toward spouses and children—another intrusion of Toxic Nostalgia.

Just as other hidden angers need to be attached to their related hurts, the cause of your career dissatisfaction needs to be understood. When you find the source of your disappointment, it becomes a driving force for making changes, just as uncovering an old hurt does. You correct mistaken career decisions by admitting you're dissatisfied and understanding what led you to make the choices you did.

Of course your biggest difficulty in solving your career problem is admitting that the person most responsible for your unhappiness is probably yourself. You are the one who took the wrong risk or failed to risk at all. You are the one who was afraid to declare yourself and pursue your dream. You are the one who was afraid of hard work or confronting your limitations. You're the one who took the easy path.

After you spend too much time in a job that is wrong for you, you develop a bad attitude and have trouble listening to criticism, insisting you are right. You stop believing in yourself. You become lazy, sloppy, and try to get away with as much as you can. On the other hand, you might struggle to do perfect work just to please others or win their appreciation but not derive any personal satisfaction or feeling of accomplishment from your efforts. Had you been doing what you loved, you would have none of these problems. You'd love your work, give your best, and succeed on your own terms. The truth is that you injure yourself the most by not going after what you really want.

To make a career change you must first take responsibility for the damage you have caused yourself. Once you do, you empower yourself to act. Directing your anger at your bosses, the company, or the political system only dissipates your energy. Since the real fault is yours, getting angry at others increases your feelings of frustration and helplessness. Taking your bitterness out on the family you care about for not appreciating you only lowers your self-esteem. Accepting the blame for your own disappointments also hurts, but only once. Acting positively to correct that hurt is the beginning of healing.

When you make the wrong career choice there are warning signs everywhere. You probably disregarded them because the pay was good, the job prestigious, or you were living out someone else's dream. Somehow it all catches up with you. When you set your passion aside and choose a career just to please your parents, you somehow always manage to fall short of their expectations. Often they respond with resentment and criticism. Should you succeed strongly, you're more likely to inspire envy than praise.

You can never please a person who is not happy with himself.

You probably chose the wrong career because you were afraid to risk failure in a pursuit that really meant something to you. It's always easier to risk something you don't really care about. If you fail at what you love, you have no place to hide. This explains why there are so many professionals who should have been artists. Professions are safe.

In time the hurt from your mistaken choices builds into a nagging doubt: something is wrong; you are not living the life you were supposed to live. It is that unrelenting disquiet that builds in Emotional Debt. When you can finally be honest and admit it, this pain creates the momentum of change.

The fact that your bad choices make you unhappy is a reflection of the dynamics of the natural therapeutic process, just the way your hurts build into anger, disquieting and propelling you to resolve them.

Like your failure to speak your feelings, your bad choices were also inspired by desperation, loneliness, and the fear of rejection. You still cling to these choices for the same reasons. At first you ignore your misgivings about your mistaken choices and may struggle even harder to become a success. It is often only when you achieve success, or finally do acquire what you struggle for only to discover that it doesn't make you happy, that you become willing to admit your unhappiness and seek your true destiny. It may take a long time to reach this point, but finally your pain makes you wiser.

You are never too late to take risks to find yourself. If you are not willing to take the necessary risks when you see the falseness of your life, your accumulated discouragement drowns your spirit. You become rigid, set in your ways, determined to show that you were right and made the right decisions. In your pretended contentment and "success," you become as autocratic and mean, as controlling and difficult as the worst boss you ever hated. At some point you may even come to realize that what was wrong with him is what is wrong with you.

There are reasons for feeling the way you do.

There are reasons why you are where you are right now.

Seek to understand them.

It is never too late to admit the truth of your feelings or to look for your true passion. You have everything to gain.

ADJUNCTS TO NATURAL THERAPY

MANY ACTIVITIES SUPPORT the natural healing process, including emotional expression, work, play, and love. Because healing is natural and has been described since earliest times, it is well represented in literature, poetry, folklore, and the lyrics of popular songs, as well as in scientific journals. It seems everyone is in the business of getting over what hurts and learning to lead productive, happy lives.

Probably no observer of the human condition ever described the process more eloquently than Shakespeare.

> *Give sorrow words, the grief that does not speak*
> *Whispers the oe'r-frought heart and bids it break.*

THE CARDINAL PRINCIPLES OF NATURAL THERAPY

> *Respect yourself.*
> *Face the truth, even if it hurts.*
> *Identify your feelings.*
> *Express them to the person who inspired them.*
> *Be prompt. Don't wait for ideal conditions.*
> *Be simple. Long explanations are unnecessary.*
> *If the other person hears you, you have succeeded.*
> *If he refuses to hear, understand whom you're dealing with.*
> *Be willing to accept the situation as it is.*
> *Let go of your hurt and forgive.*
> *Move on.*

TELLING THE TRUTH

Most of the time you already know the truth, but you want to look the other way in the hope that what is disturbing you will go away or get better on its own, or that you will find you were mistaken and that nothing is really wrong.

Sometimes problems do seem to get better on their own. However, the fact that something disturbs you is a private signal, your cue to take notice and sometimes action. When you turn away from a hurtful situation because it hasn't turned out the way you wanted or because you fear that acknowledging your disappointment might dispel your illusions of happiness, your problems almost always get worse because they are allowed to become entrenched and grow without opposition.

Like everyone else, you're probably afraid of speaking candidly because you do not want to be rejected. You want to be loved. At least you want other people to like you. Yet when you present a false picture of yourself, concealing what you really feel or believe, how can others be expected to know you, let alone like you?

Hiding your true feelings is the source of most of your loneliness and suffering. When you hide your feelings, you become lonely for the part of yourself you've excluded from your life. If you think about it, the reason you avoid people is that you cannot be yourself in their presence. Having to be false and withhold your true feelings is stressful because your hidden feelings are always trying to surface.

By withholding feelings you begin to lose touch with the truth and doubt yourself.

When hiding emotions becomes a pattern, a backlog of unspoken hurt wells up inside and your anger makes you feel brittle and question your goodness. You fear rejection if you finally do express yourself.

When you hide from the truth, your procrastination and silence always make you suffer.

ADMITTING THE HURT

Admitting that you are in pain or unhappy is a crucial step in the healing process. Saying you are unhappy means you do not like the way you feel.

Many people have pushed their feelings so far away that they don't recognize or admit they're in pain until they find themselves overwhelmed by trying to control what cannot be controlled or to manage what has become totally unmanageable.

Hiding from pain is always destined to fail.

Blaming others for your misfortune only creates more problems.

Trying to fix or change people is a futile task that usually backfires.

It is a peculiarity of human nature that no matter how often people hear these truths, they still have to suffer their own mistakes before they understand and accept them. Often people have to hit bottom in order to concede that there must be a better way than the one they have been following. When a person is in denial, his loved ones and friends can often see his pain and the hopelessness of his struggle long before he can. After trying to help and being pushed away, others usually withdraw. Now the sufferer, ever the victim of circumstance, complains he's been abandoned and betrayed.

By contrast, people who are emotionally open are not ashamed to be having problems and easily admit their pain. They are willing to speak out and deal with their disappointments. When a situation cannot get better or is abusive, they let go. Their willingness to be honest keeps their self-esteem high. They are prepared to do what is right, and so they suffer the least.

The more pain you tolerate, the less alive you feel. In time you become numb, and the level of pain necessary to get you to change can be life threatening. We all know people who practically have to die from stress before they can admit that their lifestyle, habits, or relationship is killing them.

While the triggers that lead to life-changing realizations may seem trivial, like Stanford's unpainted shutter, they allow us to see formerly concealed truths. To initiate the healing process, a painful realization must exceed your threshold of denial and be felt.

IDENTIFYING THE SOURCE OF THE INJURY

If you are afraid of rejection, naming the person you are angry with can be a fearful task. Suzanne developed anxiety in the elevator because she found it difficult to admit she was angry at her mother. Only after she admitted that her mother had hurt her could Suzanne allow herself to express her anger. When she did, her symptoms cleared.

Identifying the source of your hurt is a critical point in the healing process. Your hurt justifies your anger.

Admitting your hurt allows you to direct the anger at its correct source without feeling guilty.

Not identifying the hurt makes you feel bad, like a person who is angry for no good reason.

TAKING RESPONSIBILITY

Taking responsibility for your feelings and where you are in your life is a vital part of the natural healing process.

No matter how much Suzanne might feel her mother had hurt her, it was her job to speak up. To do this she needed to believe in herself and risk losing her mother's love by expressing her feelings. Sometimes it takes a lot of pain for a person to get to that place.

No matter how badly someone hurts you, it's always your responsibility to stand up and defend yourself. If you were a helpless child and felt threatened, it is understandable that you would be silent rather than risk anything that might jeopardize your safety or make matters worse. However, when you are an adult it is hard not to feel like a coward or that you are betraying yourself when you acquiesce.

Even if you were a helpless victim, you may still regret that you didn't do or say something. You wish you had put up a fight, screamed, run away, or told someone. It may not have worked, but at least you would have protested, asserted some power. When memories of the painful event surface years later, you are likely to obsess over your inaction and passivity. Old hurts haunt you until you decide to take responsibility for acting on them.

Even if you were totally innocent, it's wise to take responsibility for some part of the damage that was done to you, not to excuse the other person but to reclaim your power. If you can accept that there was something you could have done to protect yourself, you can believe that you still have the power now to defend yourself. Taking back power allows you to give up your investment in being a victim and to heal.

One of the difficulties in treating a victim of incest is that the abuser was often a trusted person and the sexual violation may have afforded the victim some yearned-for emotional intimacy. Further, because genitalia are designed to produce pleasurable sensations, some abuse victims experience erotic awakening and orgasm. This sexual pleasure, as well as the emotional gratification and attention they receive, often seals the lips of these victims, who mistakenly come to believe that because in some way the abuse fulfilled their needs, they were responsible for causing it.

It is in the nature of children's self-perception that they believe that if they did something bad, they *were* bad. Therefore if they experienced something pleasurable in a bad act, they reason that they must have wanted it and were bad for feeling that way. This reasoning is the compromising force in all abuse.

Until you make it a habit to take responsibility for everything in your life, doing so can be a great hurdle.

You must take responsibility

> *For tolerating being treated the way you are.*
> *For accepting a life that doesn't make you happy.*
> *For living with an addict or alcoholic.*
> *For failing in your career or relationship.*
> *For your mistakes, especially the ones that you repeat.*
> *For remaining silent in the face of injustice.*
> *For not speaking out.*
> *For holding on to your pain.*
> *For not forgiving and choosing to suffer.*
> *For being the way you are, where you are.*

It may seem difficult and unfair, but if you take responsibility for everything in your life, you claim the power to change it.

Taking responsibility for nothing insures that you will stay a victim.

EXPRESSING YOUR HURT

The healing process begins when you express your pain.

How should you express your pain?

Simply: Say you have been hurt in a way that makes your pain known.

Directly: Tell the person who caused it.

Openly: Don't conceal it, deny it, or pretend it did not matter.

Vulnerably: Don't punish others or start a fight just to show you're tough. You were hurt. Say so. It's more effective.

Without fear: Whatever the other person will do when you tell him or her you are hurt cannot be your concern. Expressing your hurt is your only business. Don't let your fear of rejection silence you.

Honestly: Separate the pain of the present from the pain of the past.

Stay in the present moment, the present hurt, the present situation. Do not go into the negative history between you and the other person, citing prior damage and insensitivity. It will be seen as hurtful, paint you as someone bearing a grudge, and weaken your case.

Finish your complaint and let go. Don't nag. Remember that the person you are expressing feelings to is someone close to you and you want them to have an opportunity to recover from the confrontation. So avoid overkill. You made your point. Don't forget to take a breath. The reason you may feel incomplete is that there is old anger still inside you. This is your responsibility, and the present situation may not be a good time to let it out. You have to pick your time and place to let out old feelings.

WHEN TO RESTRICT EXPRESSIONS OF HURT

You may feel tempted to express hurt outside your intimate circle, but doing so usually complicates situations, provokes people who have no interest in trying to understand you or in being patient or kind, and can be entirely inappropriate, especially in business situations. If the people who love you have difficulty dealing with you when you express your feelings, you can expect acquaintances to be far less tolerant.

When you go out into the indifferent world, don't allow anything anyone says or does to get to you. If someone cuts you off in traffic, let it go. Ask yourself, What difference does it make? Then if you pull up behind the car that cut you off at the very next light and observe the driver quietly, you'll realize the poor fellow is a troubled soul. You'll be home soon enough. Your job is not to allow yourself to be hurt by the circus out there. Just be an observer. Enjoy the parade.

The horrors of the day are what stick to you. Another person walking your exact path might not even notice the innocent hurts you take to heart. If you are emotionally troubled by the insensitivity you encounter, it only means that your shield isn't big enough or thick enough. If that's so it's likely that your defenses have been worn thin by personal troubles. Settle your problems with the people you care about and you'll be less likely to get upset by the miscellaneous and bumbling galoots you meet.

Don't express hurtful feelings at work. This is the last place you should allow yourself to be vulnerable. Expressing hurtful feelings at work will always backfire. You'll appear unprofessional or unbusinesslike.

Expressing your displeasure in a firm but pleasant manner is the best way to voice your unhappiness as a customer, in a restaurant, or with a professional. If you remain businesslike, people will want to help you and you'll get satisfaction. You only create additional problems when you make a scene. If you do, you'll find that other negative feelings will surface and cause you to overstate your case. Then you'll seem difficult, even menacing, to others. They'll feel threatened and less likely to be supportive or helpful. Remember people are afraid of losing their jobs and will have a need to paint you as unreasonable or crazy to save themselves.

When strangers do treat you badly, don't take it personally. Don't allow yourself to be provoked, and don't respond. Just get out of their way. Even if the bad behavior is directed at you or your specific actions or comments, assume it has nothing to do with you. The other person is difficult, or is emotionally over-whelmed. Who else would make an issue out of a minor incident?

Move on. You have nothing to prove.

If this is a person you have to deal with, do so at another time. When the person has cooled down, he'll be anxious to make good if he was out of line. If you argue when the other person is irrational, you'll only make an enemy and be-come the target for all his repressed feelings.

If you find you are often treated rudely by strangers, you should question if you are acting in an insensitive manner and hurting others. Acting entitled, haughty, ill-mannered, arrogant, and demanding is not pleasant, even if you are the customer. So if this is a common experience for you, you ought to think about what you're really angry at.

Again, admit your hurt to yourself and express it to your loved ones and your friends. The moment you present an emotional grievance elsewhere, you're on shaky ground. With the exception of displaying grief over a well-identified loss or accident, no one really takes people seriously when they let their emotions out in public. This is why people in mourning wear black armbands, to let others know of their special sensitivity. Generally, people regard public emotional displays as an embarrassing waste of time. Don't set yourself up to be hurt by expecting the world to be sensitive to your needs or care about your pain.

FORGIVING

Forgiving means letting go of your hurt. Without forgiving you cannot grow.

People often keep their pain alive to show the world how badly treated they were. They damage themselves the most by doing this. The world does not care about your past. The world only wants to know what you have to give today. When you hold on to old pain, self-pity taints your gift to others and you seem like a martyr.

Letting go of your hurt opens the gateway to acceptance, the object of the mourning process. You release your hurts to diminish your burden so you can live freely in the present. That's why every society ritualizes funerals and losses in order to facilitate this outward expression of grief.

You cannot correct or alter what has been done to you. You need to forgive the people who hurt you.

Forgiving does not mean that you have to be friends with the people who hurt you. It only means that you no longer allow your old hurt to cause you to suffer. You need to let go of your hurt. Even if your happiness and success relieves the guilt of the people who hurt you or even brings them pleasure by allowing them to point to your situation as proof that they treated you well, you are still the beneficiary of letting go.

If you are holding on to your hurt to show others that they injured you, you are wasting your life. If you expect others to apologize for hurting you and wait until they do, you will suffer for a long time. You cannot delay your well-being by waiting for someone to make good. If the other person was going to apologize, he would have done so by now.

Let go.

It's time to forgive and move on.

ACCEPTING

Accepting a loss is the most difficult part of the therapeutic process. Before you accept a loss you struggle with reality. You deny the obvious and refuse to admit what is so. You battle within yourself. Long after it is clear that others have stopped caring, you debate the possibility of recapturing their affection. You brush painful facts away to keep hope alive. Until you accept your losses, you are not living in the real world.

Acceptance is learning to live with a new reality. Acceptance is never complete. No loss is ever totally mourned. Even years after losing a love, an unmourned fragment of the loss can pierce you when you least expect it. It takes your breath away in a shuddering moment and leads you to mourn anew.

Toxic Nostalgia, the unexpected recapitulation of grief, is the most characteristic part of the natural healing process. Some trigger awakens the old hurt, and you are presented with another opportunity to feel your loss, examine your heart, and come to peace, hopefully in a more serene place.

Accepting that the process works in this way can be reassuring to you when these old feelings return. You are at the center of an emotional mill grinding exceedingly fine. Do not push the old pain away. Be patient. Observe. Remind yourself that these returning emotions are just another step on the way to acceptance. On the way to a more open and free self.

NATURAL THERAPY—THE TOOLS

The object of the natural therapeutic process is to place the losses you suffer in a healing perspective.

The most important rule is to express your pain the moment it occurs. The following well-known emotional outlets help express and resolve emotions. Understanding how they work will increase your awareness of the healing process and allow you to take greater advantage of them.

TEARS

The great physician Sir William Osler once said that the hurt that does not find its expression in tears may cause other organs to weep. The wisdom of this observation holds true everywhere in life. It is typical for asthma sufferers to report that they do not often cry and that after they learn to shed tears their asthma frequently improves.

Having a good cry is a cathartic experience, while inhibiting tears creates stress. To prove this, you need only go to a sad movie and swallow the lumps in your throat instead of giving in to your tears. Holding back tears is painful, causing muscle tension and chest discomfort. In a word, inhibiting tears makes you sick. The muscle tension required to put on a "game" face and deny your tears is responsible for much of our high blood pressure and coronary artery disease.

The tears you shed as a member of the audience are a form of Toxic Nostalgia, in which some telling detail serves to unlock your hidden emotions. Being moved by events in a public movie theater gives you both permission and the disguise to mourn by proxy.

Teaching boys that men do not cry is lying to them about the importance of tears. Women today assuming masculine roles in the workplace have also acquired a masculine style of inhibiting tears. As a result they are now developing disease patterns similar to men's.

Don't be afraid to cry. Expressing your tears is vital to mental and physical health. If something is worth your love, it is worth your tears. The emperor Nero so valued his tears that he had them sealed in glass containers "so people might see for whom Nero wept."

Crying over a loss commemorates the loss, punctuates the emotion, and makes it more real. Crying documents the pain, lets others know how much something meant to you. The whole concept of keeping a stiff upper lip is a cultural aberration against the forces of nature. Tears lubricate the pathway of emotional expression and facilitate release, allowing the process of healing to begin. Tears can bring emotional absolution and relief, making you human and whole again.

Tears at the right time and in the right place have such healing power as to make them seem almost holy.

PROTESTATION

Protestation plays an important role in the natural therapeutic process. Protesting is standing up for yourself.

Protesting is defending your beliefs, your boundaries. It is a declaration that you will not permit trespass. The purpose of displaying anger when you are hurt is to define the limits of your toleration and make your point with force so that no one will mistake your intentions. It is an affirmation of strength and survival.

All creatures give warnings when they are injured or threatened. Your capacity to protest may have been inhibited by your fear of rejection or the politics of your family structure that convinced you that protesting was impolite, ungentlemanly, or unladylike. Raising your voice may have been regarded as uncouth or disrespectful.

In spite of what you have been taught, there is great therapeutic value in protesting when someone you love has hurt you. The value of remaining silent in the face of injury from a loved one is hard to defend. If you say nothing when you are hurt, you only allow the protest to be muffled and turned against you. The consequences of this are horrendous, for nothing destroys your love for another person like harboring resentment.

People pretend that they love other people but do not like them. The truth is that you cannot feel love for someone you do not like. The reason you do not like another person is that they have hurt, insulted, offended, or disappointed you. In the face of these negative feelings, it is pure self-deception to claim that you actively feel love for them. What you are really saying is that you remember feeling love for them and that you probably will love them when the hostility between you decreases, but right now you do not.

Many parents struggle with difficult children during periods of adolescent rebellion, also claiming that they love, but don't like, them. Their children know that their parents are just hiding their anger. Being difficult, the kids now test their parents to get them to show their true feelings.

Adolescence is troublesome because it is a time of protest, when adolescents who do not know who they are and are afraid of expressing their feelings act them out instead. They aggravate their parents by reminding them of unresolved problems from their own childhoods. Parents don't want to remember the past, which is why they try so hard to control their children. Often the adolescent is making the very same protest that his parents lacked the courage to mount.

Protesting is a powerful and emotionally redemptive act, if you make your protests at the right time and to the right person. You must rise to the disputes of your heart. You must make your emotional case. You must go into battle with the foe who torments you.

What do you risk when you protest?

You risk discovering that the other person does not love you or care about your feelings.

You risk discovering that you were mistaken.

You risk hurting other people's feelings.

You risk proving to others that you don't care, that you're disobedient or disrespectful.

You risk retaliation, being humiliated or ignored.

But if you do not protest:

Others will not know what you feel or what matters to you.

Others will not know they have trespassed and will more than likely do so again.

You will not clear the air.

You will not resolve your injury when it occurs, which is the best time to make your case, to be heard, believed, and taken seriously.

If you don't protest, how will others know they've hurt you? They will have had no warning to keep them from hurting you again. If they do hurt you again, even if it is also unintentional, you will be convinced they meant to hurt you and you'll be more likely to overreact. Filled with mistaken resolve, you'll end up doing the most damage.

Go on, protest! Tell the other person how you feel.

Dispute your injury. Speak up when you are hurt.

You may be surprised to find that the injury was just a mistake.

Be willing to accept apologies and let go.

Just be aware that if you are new to speaking up, you run the risk of unleashing old anger when you do. So try not to overreact.

DREAMS

Dreams have been an object of fascination since the beginning of recorded history. People have always speculated on the meaning of dreams, hoping to divine the future and understand themselves. The Chinese philosopher Chuang-tzu placed the problem in perfect perspective when he asked, "Yesterday I dreamt I was a butterfly. How do I know that today I am not a butterfly dreaming I am a man?" A Roman emperor had one of his soldiers put to death when he learned that the soldier had dreamed he killed the emperor.

The reason dreams have been taken so seriously is that there is truth imbedded in them. The way this truth appears can be frightening and confusing. In those moments when you view your dreams with lifelike clarity, you may think you are on the brink of profound understanding, but you are merely witnessing changes in your state of consciousness, the so-called hypnopompic and hypnagogic phenomena.

Freudian analysis focuses greatly on dream content and dream work as a mirror of the unconscious mind and a guide to decoding the hidden. The Jungian view sees dreams as a window to a collective unconscious that symbolically links us all.

For the purpose of this book, these philosophical considerations are set aside to consider the practical question: What is the role of dreaming in the natural therapeutic process? How do dreams process feelings and expedite the resolution of Emotional Debt?

Dreaming is critical to your emotional well-being, but not just because dreams help you stay asleep and get adequate rest. Dreams help you process those daily emotions that you did not completely settle. Children, especially newborns, dream extensively, as if their dreams compensate for their lack of verbal ability to express themselves. You process a considerable bulk of your daily emotional responses in your dreams, greatly reducing the amount of emotions that you would otherwise store in Emotional Debt.

Obviously merely dreaming about a painful event isn't all that is needed to resolve it. The most important function of dreaming is to bring emotions that you have set aside to your attention again. To make the best use of your dreams, use them to recognize emotions you may have avoided. In order to understand the feelings you encounter in your dreams, try to relate them to real events in your life.

In deciphering your dreams, keep in mind that dreams employ a symbolic language that is both literal and childlike. If you felt as if you "got killed" in the stock market today, you may dream tonight that you have murdered a relative in a supermarket. Instead of being killed, you become the killer. The relative may be the person who would have been damaged, that is "killed," by your financial loss in the market.

Your hidden feelings also shape your dreams. The events of the present cause your older feelings to resonate, activating them and pulling them away from their ancient defensive moorings and floating them to awareness in the dream state. Freed up, these older feelings combine with more recently stored emotions and, disguised together, present themselves in the dream, seeking to be expressed and resolved. Indeed, some people will first begin to recall a painful childhood event through nightmares. In a sense dreams are another form of Toxic Nostalgia, a triggered remembrance of pain.

In complicated dreams, identify the predominant feeling rather than trying to understand the meaning of the symbolic camouflage. Most dreams are easily understood if you keep them simple. Identify feelings such as anxiety, hurt, anger, and guilt. Don't attach too much meaning to the intensity of the feeling. Don't worry about what you perceive. It's just a representation of what you've already experienced.

Sexualizing a relationship is common in dreams, but it implies closeness as much as sexual attraction. Dreams usually contain elements of the previous day's events in which scenes are revisited and replayed in altered form. In your dreams you may see yourself trouncing your enemies as you compensate for your earlier ineffectiveness. Then again, even though you performed successfully that day, you may see yourself being beaten by your opponents as the dream gives expression to the self-doubts you concealed earlier in order to find your courage.

Think about your dreams and try to understand what they mean. Your first guess is often the correct interpretation. If you can't guess, just make something up. The first idea that comes to your mind will often be full of meaning. Bear in mind that there is almost nothing you will discover in your dreams that you did not already know.

On the first anniversary of her divorce from her abusive husband, Jeannie began to have troublesome dreams. Some were reenactments of the violence she suffered. In others she was the oppressor. Still other dreams were highly erotic and charged with emotional closeness. Jeannie was worried that the dreams meant she was the bad one or that she really wanted to be with her husband in a loving way and had been mistaken in leaving him.

Jeannie's dreams reflected her neglected emotional concerns. She'd been so determined to put her failed marriage behind her that she decided to banish all her feelings. When it was pointed out that her dreams reflected her anger at her husband she easily accepted that but had difficulty admitting she secretly yearned to be back with him. To find the courage to separate, she had decided to paint her husband as totally bad and deny their positive experiences.

Shutting out a loss is not mourning or letting go.

Jeannie's fear that in spite of feeling hatred for her husband she also longed to be with him tormented her. Her dreams made her examine precisely the feelings she could not face. When she finally was able to state that although she partly wanted to go back to her husband, she much preferred being alone, her dreams began to fade. This shift in admitting her true feelings hardly seems earth-shattering, but integrating these two opposite feelings of love and hate into a conscious awareness was the work that the dream accomplished and exactly the realization that allowed Jeannie to move on.

When a hidden emotion is stirred, it is typical to begin dreaming about it. In fact, your very first awareness of an old pain may come in your dreams.

Emotions contained in dreams follow the same dynamics as emotions in the waking state, although they are not subject to the same rules of reality testing. There is little reality in dreams, just enough to anchor our fascination. While the anger in a dream always comes from some hurt, it may not be possible to identify that hurt accurately within the context of the dream.

Painful feelings are often disguised in the intricate dreamscapes they inspire. Events and people as well as time and place are frequently distorted. Rather than trying to understand every detail of a dream, it is far more useful to identify the feelings of the dream in general terms and accept them as representations of feelings that may be hidden within you. Just accepting the possibility that such feelings exist can provide a therapeutic opening, just as it did for Jeannie.

There is more evidence of the healing power of dreams. It has been noted that some antianxiety agents increase the anxiety people experience in dreams. It is likely that releasing anxiety in dreams lowers the reservoir of anxiety seeking expression from Emotional Debt. Facilitating the expression of a hidden feeling in dreams may be the therapeutic mechanism of psychoactive drugs. People taking antidepressants often report an increase in the amount of anger in their dreams. The dynamic is simple to understand. Keeping anger from expression depletes energy. It is this depletion of energy that causes depression. Therefore releasing anger in dreams would free psychic energy from the task of binding feelings and allow the depression to lift.

GETTING DISTANCE

Time is the distance between two events.

It is often said that time heals all wounds. Time helps by putting distance between you and a terrible experience, making the danger seem farther away, giving you room to gather your senses so you can place the loss in perspective. Over time you find the courage to review what happened to you, take stock of the damages you suffered and make adjustments. Although many wounds never heal fully, they still need to be placed in perspective.

On the other hand, if you don't deal with your painful experiences, time only makes matters worse. Hiding from old feelings can ruin your life.

It can be helpful to make some distance in the middle of a tumultuous situation and observe yourself without emotions. Because you have deep feelings about the very thing you are trying to be dispassionate about, this is not easy. You have to avoid arguing, responding, defending, or justifying yourself.

The object is to keep from being emotionally involved. Try to play the role of a noncombatant gathering information. You ask, "Please explain," and comment, "Is that so?" and you permit others to display their feelings and beliefs without opposing or correcting them. You just want to see the situation and others as they are, warts and all, without getting drawn into the madness.

Be sure that you don't act haughty, superior, or pretend to be indifferent. This will only make the situation worse. Simply saying you are hurt or angry is enough to allow you to show that you have feelings and still keep your distance so you can observe the situation.

GAINING PERSPECTIVE

It is also helpful to observe yourself from a distance to get a more truthful perspective on your disappointments.

Think of a hurt that you suffered when you were in grade school, a teacher's unfairness, a bully's intimidation, a friend's rebuff. See your past from the perspective of this moment, and note how your pain has faded and is no longer alive in you. In order to feel it you have to put yourself in that older space and reenact the hurt.

The healing process has placed your pain in perspective. To see today's events in perspective, imagine you are twenty or thirty years older, looking back on this moment. Answer the following questions about your present disappointment from that point of view:

> *Why did you think what you lost was so important to you?*
> *How much did you exaggerate its worth?*
> *Did you need a consuming love to believe you were lovable?*
> *Did you need power to make you feel strong?*
> *Did you need the applause of others to prove your worth?*
> *What were you dependent upon? And why?*
> *What were you trying to control? And how?*
> *What were you pretending to be? Why didn't you accept yourself?*
> *How did you survive this loss?*

How much did you want or love what you lost?

Why weren't you more careful, caring, or hardworking?

Did you really do your best?

What did you hold back and why?

What did you believe that was untrue?

Why did you believe it?

What did you really want?

Did you have an inflated view of your worth?

Were you sincere?

Try to see the influence of your past on your present attitude and to recognize when your responses are exaggerated or the result of unrealistic expectations, unresolved feelings, and false hopes.

When you practice detachment you start to think thoughts you may not have had the courage to address before. You may find that what you think you need is an illusion. You are able to admit your shortcomings and weaknesses.

You need to see yourself as honestly as possible and measure yourself by your own standards. You need to be free to ask yourself what you want, why you are where you are, what you are getting out of your relationship or job, and to hear your truthful answers to those questions.

LAUGHTER

Laughter is an important adjunct to the natural therapeutic process. Where a dream may buoy an old painful feeling to the surface so that it becomes accessible to healing, laughter inserts the healing perspective into the middle of pain and allows you to see yourself from a new point of view.

Laughter can act as a positive force, releasing you from denial and allowing you to take yourself less seriously. When you laugh, you trigger relief. Some people who are trying their best to stay sad seem resentful when someone makes them laugh. It is as if the ability to laugh, by involuntarily accessing the perspective of healing, confers the belief that things are not so bad and undermines self-pity and self-destructiveness.

Laughter heals.

RELIEF

Relief is a central part of the healing process. Feeling relief does not necessarily mean all negative feelings have been resolved. Feeling relief only indicates that the pain has for the moment subsided and that you have come to more acceptable terms with it and yourself. Relief grants you a more truthful perspective.

Often you don't know how much something means to you until you lose it. If somehow you are granted a second chance and what you thought you lost is returned to you, the relief you feel measures its worth to you. When the danger is past, it is safe to admit your fear. It is for this reason that people who act tough in the face of peril find it easier to show their fears at happy occasions. Think of soldiers and their families reuniting after a war.

In some way relief is the truest of feelings. In terms of the natural therapeutic process, the best use of relief is to allow it to help you define what really matters to you. Then you are better able to protect and value what you love.

Relief allows you to ponder the fragility of life and to realize how close to the edge we all live. Let relief direct you to find and commit to your life purpose.

OTHER NATURAL HELPERS

Even though the following aids may sound obvious, they serve an important role in the natural healing process, promoting well-being and inducing calmness. Don't underestimate the therapeutic value of any of these ideas. Much of what is wrong in your life could be greatly improved by following this simple advice.

SLEEP

If you think of what the words "a good night's sleep" mean to you, you cannot take sleep for granted. A good night's sleep is a mercy and always makes you feel better, whereas if you go without sleep, you become irritable, depressed, and your thinking becomes confused. When you are deprived of sleep for days at a time, you can develop tremors and hallucinations. Depriving people of sleep is a form of torture in which defenses crumble, the will is weakened, and perspective is lost. Getting regular sleep has the exact opposite effect.

Regular sleep protects your body's natural circadian rhythm and stabilizes your endocrine and immune systems. Regular sleep provides the necessary opportunity to dream so you can process the emotional residue of the day.

There is much healing in sleep. Everyone has had the experience of emotional stress improving after a good night's sleep. Several good nights of sleep in a row give your mental mechanisms a chance to restore themselves. Your brain needs time to recuperate, preferably time free of additional challenges. Often newly arrived patients in mental hospitals get better just by being separated from stress and allowed to get some rest. If you give yourself this same opportunity, you do yourself untold good.

Sleep makes you feel normal. Regular hours and ample sleep will improve your memory and concentration. A person with a good night's sleep is the best prepared to succeed. Sleep should be an indispensable part of your schedule.

RELAXATION

Our age assaults us: congested traffic, sensationalist media, a huge, aloof government, a justice system that is slow and costly, crime in the streets, graffiti, and pollution. You need time each day to relax, to let go and simply be at peace, time without a plan or schedule.

Sitting in front of the television, clicking away at a remote control, is not the kind of relaxation that will work. Neither is pouring a stiff drink.

You need to be able to sit down alone and allow yourself to become quiet and still. Simple reflection is best: a walk in the woods, by the shore of a lake, or time spent in a garden. Find your own retreat and use it.

VACATIONS

You need a vacation. Everyone does. You make excuses why you can't: time, pressure, money. Nevertheless, you must figure out a way to take a vacation. It doesn't have to be long, and it doesn't have to be expensive. Every now and then you *need* to get away for a while.

MEDITATION

Although meditation is not strictly speaking a natural process, it creates "down time" in which the mind can restore itself. Much has been written about this, but if you want to meditate and achieve its benefits, the following basic steps will guide you.

Select a quiet place where you can comfortably sit, undisturbed, for fifteen to twenty minutes.

Pick a mantra, a nonsense word. Choose any two- or three-syllable word. Here are two famous mantras from Hindu meditative practice: *Om! Mane padme Om!* and *Om nemah shevaya.* Or just make up a word or phrase like *My Iowa,* which is easier to remember and will work as well. A mantra should become unobtrusive. Its purpose is just to numb your mind while you meditate. There's no mystery to this.

Close your eyes and breathe evenly and deeply.

Repeat your mantra silently to yourself throughout the meditation. Repeating the mantra blocks the brain from thinking and induces relaxation.

With your eyes closed look for a blue area appearing out of the darkness and try to float through it. This is not easy to do, but it focuses your mind to the right place, a metaphor to induce deep relaxation.

Advanced technique: in the middle of the blue spot, discern a rotating star and try to stop it from rotating.

That's all there is to meditation. It is very relaxing, it lowers your blood pressure, and it's refreshing. Meditate daily or once a week. Experiment to find what is right for you.

DIET

Millions of words have been written on this subject. Here are the most important ones.

> *Moderation.*
> *Low fat.*
> *Fruit in the morning.*
> *Complex carbohydrates for lunch.*
> *Moderate protein for dinner, six to eight ounces of fish or*
>   *poultry. Little red meat.*
> *Fruit between meals for snacking.*
> *Avoid eating after nine in the evening.*
> *A glass of wine is fine. Two per day is the limit.*
> *Six to eight glasses of water a day.*

Eat slowly, allow your natural appetite suppressor, the appestat, to tell your brain that you are sufficiently fed. That takes fifteen minutes. Obese people eat too fast.

Sumo wrestlers work out on an empty stomach. Then they eat and immediately take a nap. To lose weight, do the opposite. Exercise after eating complex carbohydrates, and go to bed a little hungry.

Chew your food and savor it. Don't eat when you are angry. Calm down first. There is no law that says you have to have a big meal if you're not hungry. Try a peach instead.

If you overindulge, just eat normally at the next meal. Don't try to compensate by starving yourself.

Light fasting, such as clear liquids, one day a week is also beneficial.

Celebrate! Food is not just fuel. At least once a week share a meal with some friends. Create occasions that celebrate life and friendship. Start using your best china and silver for yourself. Put candles and flowers on the table. You deserve it.

ENTERTAINMENT

The purpose of the arts is to touch your heart and remind you of your spiritual nobility. What do we really know of the earliest people besides the art they left behind? As the most enduring human testament, our art is our history.

This world resounds with our artistic and creative legacy. Consider architecture, fabrics, design, graphics, music, textiles, literature, drama, dance, oratory, cuisine, furnishings, vehicles, and dreams of visiting distant planets. They all testify to the fact that we are a race of artists, seeing what is, thinking what could be, and creating it.

The purpose of the natural therapeutic process is to make you happy and productive. You should either create art or enjoy and support it. The business of the world serves to feed and clothe you and make the creation and enjoyment of art possible.

At least once a month you should attend a concert, visit a museum, walk through an art gallery, read some poetry aloud, sing a song from beginning to end with all the right words and in tune.

If you ever played a musical instrument as a kid, consider taking a few lessons. You'll be amazed at how much pleasure you'll get. Join a choir. Look in the entertainment section of your newspaper and pick out one cultural event to attend each weekend. Tune in to a classical music station for at least an hour a day. It will connect you to a deeper sense of peace. Go to the theater. See a good movie. Read a book just for fun.

The arts define the purpose of civilization. You enrich your life by participating in them.

HOBBIES

If you are trapped in an unrewarding job or haven't found or pursued your true passion, you really need a hobby. Your hobby should be something you love and take seriously. The most successful people have turned their hobby into their life's work. Fish, paint, garden, travel, go to flea markets and shows. Do whatever you love to do, but begin to do it. You need to find and make time for your passion. A hobby is a good place to start.

SEX

Sexual release is a wonderful thing, but it easily gets overrated. The younger you are, the more overrated it tends to get. When your hormones rule, your life suffers. Sexual energy infatuates your mind and stimulates your body. All well and good. When it is out of control it can preoccupy you and draw you into incongruent misalliances, situations of enormous stupidity, embarrassing silliness, and often deep regret.

When sex is not good in a relationship, it becomes a big part of the relationship. When sex is good, it remains a small part of the relationship.

Still, sexual release fulfills deep needs, and its benefits cannot be denied.

However, when sex becomes obsessional or addictive, it causes more problems than it solves. Such sex leaves you hyperirritable and always wanting more. You act as if you are caught in a neurological short circuit. You can't tell whether you are overstimulated or really need a lot of sex to satisfy you.

Sex with romance is exciting. But romance is hard to trust because it is the stuff of pretense and leads partners to use each other in order to fulfill their fantasies. This is fun as long as no one gets hurt and providing the absence of enduring affections doesn't matter to you. Sometimes romance is used as a way to justify recreational sex. Recreational sex requires an explanation, a justifying logic. You do it to prove something to yourself, that you are lovable, potent, attractive, not alone.

Sex with strangers is an act of desperation.

Sex to prove love is draining. So is obligatory sex, mercy sex, controlling sex, and dependent sex.

Sex with love is the only satisfying sex and the only sex that lasts.

Sex should be natural and fun. The best sex involves laughter and talking. Sex should be freely and mutually given, without any strings; otherwise it is a form of commerce no matter how it is disguised.

Try to avoid using sex as a sleeping pill. It takes too much of the edge off the excitement and makes sex boring. Have sex when you are rested, during the day, in the light. Be experimental, adventuresome, naughty if you must, but try to make a little production out of it. Teasing is permitted, but only if it's in fun and designed to increase pleasure by making sex more exciting.

Sex in the context of a loving, mutually committed, monogamous relationship feels best, lasts longest, and ultimately has the most beneficial and healing effect.

EXERCISE

Exercise is a good coping mechanism, especially if you exercise regularly, as long as the form of exercise you choose is comfortable to you and will produce emotional release. Aerobic exercise releases endorphins, enkephalins, and raises brain serotonin for hours. These in turn increase feelings of well-being, lift depression, and restore normal brain functioning.

Twenty to thirty minutes a day of aerobic exercise has been shown to have significant positive benefits for people recovering from addiction and greatly reduces the chances of relapse.

Perhaps the greatest benefit of regular exercise is that it provides a time in the day you can look forward to when you can shed stress and tension.

SHARING

In the battle against loneliness, sharing is the weapon of choice. You share your pain, and it diminishes. Sharing your pain with the person who caused it resolves it. Even telling someone who is sympathetic makes you feel better.

Why?

Sharing allows you to take the pain from inside you and bring it out into the world. Once pain is separated from the reinforcement of other stored anger, it resumes more normal proportions, seems less awful, and can be put aside.

When you share and another person supports your point of view, your fear that you are imagining your hurt or being overly reactive diminishes. In a real sense, sharing makes you sane again.

Sharing the good reinforces the good. Think about the times you've seen a rainbow. The first thing you do is urgently cry, "Hurry, look!" as you seek to share the experience.

Rainbows quickly fade, so sharing a rainbow is being present together in a fleeting moment. A rainbow by its very nature is a thing of momentary conditions and unique perspective.

In some way sharing a rainbow is like validating the good times in life. In fact, sometimes it is the sharing that makes the good times what they are. Seeing a loved one's joy, a friend's predictable reaction, or a child's fascination reminds you of your emotional connection to others and makes the world seem smaller.

An unshared rainbow is no less beautiful, but sharing allows you to lock the singular experience in two memories.

FRIENDS

All you need is one friend, but still you need that friend, someone you can talk to who listens, cares, and understands.

Think about that last phrase: *listens, cares, and understands.*

If you want to have a friend, you have to be a friend. If you do all the talking, always ask to be cared for and understood, and give nothing back, what is the point of the friendship to the other person?

A friend is not someone to borrow money from, nag, criticize, use, or abuse.

A friend is not there to do things for you that would compromise himself. A real friend would not ask that of another.

The best friends share the same vulnerability and therefore understand from firsthand experience the peril each faces. When two people come through for each other under adversity, their friendship has already started.

As far as the natural process goes, your friends share the secrets that you reveal to yourself when you relinquish your lies and distortions. Friends are natural confessors. It's good to be able to tell someone how badly you screwed up and have them tell you that they once did even worse. The truthfulness that friends share reinforces the truthfulness of the natural process. Friends tell the truth and demand to hear the truth.

People who lie to their friends have no friends.

LOVE

There's no way around this. You need to love and be loved.

Love is caring about another person's feelings as if they were your own.

You cannot be loved by someone who does not love himself, who is dishonest, who is filled with anger, or who has low self-esteem.

Of course people make excuses for other people not loving them all the time. They are only fooling themselves. Someone either loves you or doesn't.

If you have difficulty accepting and loving yourself, it probably has more to do with holding in anger than anything else, because your internalized anger constantly tells you that you are unlovable. It follows that no amount of love can make a person who doesn't feel lovable love himself.

Love is a powerful healing force, but you have to love yourself to love in return.

Being loved does not make you believe in your lovability. Self-acceptance and peace of mind are your business alone.

Self-love is the only true antidote to loneliness.

When you think about it, you're really no less alone when you have someone to love than when you don't. While your emptiness can sometimes be filled by another person, it is only a momentary respite. When that person's love is removed you still have to deal with your emptiness. While another person's love can reassure you, only you can find contentment with yourself.

Finding your beloved may consume, divert, and amuse you, but it will not placate a heart that longs for itself. While love may have great appeal, it is a brief balm for a person who senses he has no purpose.

Finding another does not mean you can abandon the search for yourself. It is typical when you fall "in love" that you pull away from your friends and work and surrender to the forces of discovery and confession in which you now find yourself enveloped. You plumb the depths of your mutual understanding and marvel at the similarities you share. When this recess from reality is over and you begin to return to your usual life, you must find yourself again in order to keep your love alive.

If you sacrifice a part of yourself to keep a relationship alive, you will eventually leave the relationship to regain the part you gave up.

Before you can love another you need to believe you are worthy of love. Otherwise the other, no matter how generous and understanding, becomes a substitute for your own self-esteem. If you haven't found yourself, you end up needing the other too much. Then the other person's love becomes your reason for living, and your love a dangerous and destabilizing attachment.

The relationship can become an addiction. Then you believe you need the other person to be with you all the time. You suffer without him. The relationship eventually is burdened by unrealistic expectations and bitter accusations. If the other person has to be everything to you in order to make you feel complete, he soon loses himself and has to leave you to be himself again.

You can live your life without the love of another person, but you cannot survive joyously unless you love yourself. That lonely place within you is not filled by receiving love, but by giving.

WORK

You need to be doing your life's work. The purpose of the natural therapeutic process is to free you to do your life's work effectively.

Conversely, finding your life's work heals you by building self-esteem and allowing you to be more self-accepting and more honest.

If you don't know what your life's work is, you need to find out.

If you are pursuing your own destiny, it matters very little how hard you're working. Hard work on the way to fulfilling a dream or defining yourself is a great privilege. You think, "At last I'm doing what I'm supposed to do." Digging a drainage ditch for your own garden feels like an accomplishment. Digging someone else's ditch never feels as good.

Most of the stress you suffer at work comes from hating your employer and the way you are treated, not from the workload. When you feel appreciated and applauded for your efforts, you can handle a large workload. Resentment destroys your capacity to work and builds stress.

Your work should inspire you and energize you.

Your work should allow you to define and fulfill your life's purpose. You should feel that your work takes you further along the road to self-discovery, at a pace where you continually develop new skills and confidence, where the more you give, the more you get.

Your work should be where you discover and practice your talent. However, the place you discover your talent may not offer you the best opportunity to perfect or display it. You have to create your own life plan. In order to perfect your skills and keep growing, you continually need to gather your resolve, readjust your direction, and sometimes start all over again.

There are no rules.

MENTORS AND MASTERS, GURUS AND TEACHERS

You need to let the dissatisfaction you feel with your work lead you to a teacher who can help you find the best within yourself and draw it out.

Clark, an accountant, moved to Vermont to join a pottery studio and fulfill his lifelong dream of becoming a potter. After a few years of success, he found his work repetitive and became discouraged. He felt there was more beauty trapped inside him that he did not know how to release.

At great personal sacrifice he moved to Japan to apprentice to a master potter. Slowly he progressed from chopping wood for the kiln and preparing clay to making pieces of his own. Along the way he relearned all his technique and refined his aesthetics. After seven years, Clark returned to Vermont and established his own business. His work as a master was much simpler than it had been as a novice, but now each piece contained part of his soul and imitated perfection.

You need to be apprenticed to your life's dream as well.

Find a teacher.

Where?

Whoever can teach you is a good first place to start.

Keep looking.

TALENT

Do you have any talent? Stop doubting yourself and take a risk to find out. You have to believe talent is there to see it. It is common to doubt yourself, and it takes very little doubt to give up.

Clue: your talent is always related to what you love most.

Your ability to love something comes from being able to perceive and appreciate its details; in other words, you love what you love because you have a special sensitivity. A musician's love for music depends on his sensitive hearing. His gift still has to be developed.

Unfortunately, when you are a child and see another child with talent, you disregard how hard he worked to perfect his gift and mistakenly believe that because you cannot do as well the very first time, you must lack talent. This attitude tends to persist.

Your fascination for anything reveals a special appreciation. That in turn reflects your talent.

Don't judge your talent.

Don't measure it.

Just follow it.

Your work should provide an opportunity for you to give not merely your best effort but also your best self. It should provide a platform on which you can stand to declare your philosophy, express your caring, and affirm your alliance with the world. When your work connects you to others, it gives you a sense of purpose that is greater than yourself. When you give your unique gift, you develop a profound belief in the worth of the world.

Knowing that you are making a difference goes a long way toward getting you through difficult times. It is a wonderful thing to know that you participated in a greater cause, that you made the lives of others better, that without your being here the world would be diminished.

Your work should help you define the difference you were intended to make.

When it comes down to the ultimate truth, believing in the difference you made is all you've got.

When you give your deepest, truest gift away, you are never lonely again.

BELIEVING IN YOURSELF

Believing in yourself is your first job. If you don't believe in yourself, who should? Believing in yourself is a leap of faith. Some people act as if they always believe in themselves. They display bravado and ego. That's not believing in yourself, that's merely pretending. Still, pretending is often the first step toward believing in yourself.

You need to believe in yourself in spite of your weaknesses and failures. Do not disregard your shortcomings, admit them and learn from them. No one is perfect. No one expects you to be, but you still need to be perfectly honest about your failures. That honesty is the source of your strength.

Believe in yourself, even when you are wrong and have hurt another. Remember, only good people feel bad about hurting others, and only people who feel humility about their shortcomings find the courage to correct them.

You may think it would be easier to believe in yourself if you had accomplished everything you wanted in life or were rich and famous. Not true. Belief in yourself comes before accomplishment, not afterward. A person who does not believe in himself is not persuaded otherwise by his accomplishments.

Believing in yourself is a state of mind. It comes from your commitment to yourself as a good person, a person who is willing to admit hurt and express it. There is no greater destroyer of self-belief than holding hurt inside and polluting your self-image with negative messages of guilt.

While all these elements play their part in the natural therapeutic process to heal and free you, believing in yourself, your goodness and worth, is the best place to begin.

THE FORCES THAT WORK AGAINST YOU

MOST OF YOUR PROBLEMS come from not wanting to see things as they are. When you resist being honest, you defeat the natural healing process. The defensive attitude you adopt to protect yourself gives you no peace. You are always expecting some undeniable truth to cut through your facade and remind you of how you truly feel. Your fear of approaching stressful situations triggers the release of Toxic Nostalgia.

DISHONESTY

Dishonesty—which can take different forms—works against the natural therapeutic process, creating additional suffering, and prolonging mourning.

Not wanting to know is a form of denial, a wish to keep pain away by denying its existence. When you don't want to know, you assume that the situation will get better by itself or that someone else will take care of it. When you deny a problem, you still have some awareness that it exists but cannot exactly identify or prevent it. For this reason denial often thinly conceals a feeling of helplessness or impending doom. You feel like a besieged child, powerless and trapped.

Refusing to accept blame for your actions is an indication that you're afraid to appear weak or flawed. If you can't take criticism, you become difficult to approach and teach. Since you need to be right, you try to prove you are strong and smart, that you already know what others are trying to tell you. You make excuses for everything. In your heart you feel guilty and secretly fear any confrontation that may prove you're bad.

Pretending you planned it that way is another way to dodge taking responsibility for or admitting failure. It is easy to see how this subverts the healing process. If you insist you did nothing wrong and pretend to be happy with what you got, where is the momentum for change? When you avoid the truth by pretending everything is the way you intended it to be, you are forced to repeat your mistakes until something so bad happens that you can no longer pretend it doesn't matter.

Whatever lie you tell, it reveals both your needs and the way you truly feel about yourself.

If you hide from the truth, you reveal that you feel you are too weak to care for yourself.

If you blame others, you fear being imperfect.

If you exaggerate and brag, you're not sure of yourself.

Your dishonesty keeps you prisoner and primes you to explode when you can no longer hide.

SECONDARY GAIN

What is commonly called secondary gain is an exaggeration of hurt in order to achieve pity, favor, or any consideration you wouldn't have received if you were well. A comment as innocent as "Please speak a little softer, I have a terrible headache" is a form of secondary gain. It's common in childhood to act sick in order to avoid taking a test or to get attention from your mother. However, using illness to avoid responsibility as an adult can easily become a habit.

Exaggerating hurt is always destructive to your well-being. You engage in it not out of trickery but out of low self-esteem or when you are afraid of standing up and being evaluated on your own merits.

Consider beggars, who are professionals in the business of using their pain to control others. They manipulate you by making you feel sorry for them. While you may be swayed to give you have trouble taking them seriously. At best you pity them. At worst you resent them for the bad feelings they arouse within you and for their coercion.

Any manipulative pretense alienates others, who feel put off by your actions even if they don't say anything. Any reluctance to accept your story, any sign of disbelief, insults you and obligates you to parade your "disability" and shame the other person for even suggesting you are pretending. How dare someone question your sincerity when you feel this bad?

Acting weak or disabled interferes with the natural healing process by diverting you from the very truth you most need to confront. You need to admit that in the very weakness you are pretending to display there is also some truth.

BAD ATTITUDES

Bad attitudes have the power to defeat you. They create an air of dishonesty about you and alienate others who then resent you.

FALSE PRIDE

Because it involves positioning yourself as having been shamefully insulted or betrayed beyond forgiveness, false pride leads you to suffer your hurts deeply. When you indulge in false pride, you oblige yourself to live in the past. False pride leads you to make much of an affront and suggests that you are morally superior to others who, in your view, must be seen as villains.

False pride is closely related to the exaggeration seen in secondary gain. You feel committed to acting offended. You're trapped because you cannot get over your hurt without undermining your position of superiority. As a result you can't accept the world as it is and are robbed of peace of mind.

When you act prideful you claim others are inconsiderate or unappreciative. You're always searching for someone to agree with you. You're irritable and difficult to please and hard to be around. Others feel uncomfortable and pull away. As a result you become susceptible to even more betrayal, abandonment, and insult.

You also exhibit false pride when you act as if someone didn't hurt you when they actually hurt you deeply. Pretending not to be hurt while exaggerating other injuries can confuse you and isolate you from your true feelings. After a while you don't know what really caused your pain, whether you were actually hurt or just pretending.

To overcome false pride, admit your imperfections and be willing to forgive yourself for pretending. Only when you can accept yourself, even though you are flawed, can you forgive others as well.

RIGHTEOUS INDIGNATION

Righteous indignation takes false pride one step further, to retaliation. Your overstated pain leads you to believe you have the right to humiliate and punish others. You appear eager to get even. "Now I've got the goods on you!" are the words written on your lips.

When you feel righteously indignant, you're just afraid of being open about your hurt. Although you don't want others to see it, you have a large store of anger from many sources in Emotional Debt and are searching for an opportunity to let it out. So in a sense righteous indignation is like purposeful Toxic Nostalgia, where you lie in wait for others to make mistakes or say the wrong thing to allow you to download your feelings and blame others for making you do so.

Righteous indignation blocks the healing process by keeping you from taking responsibility for your actions. Blaming others diminishes your power to heal yourself, while overreacting causes you to hurt others and makes you feel even more guilty.

PRETENTIOUSNESS

Pretentiousness leads you to devalue the importance of other people. If you pretend that you are superior in order to avoid admitting you are hurt, you are perceived as putting other people down. People see you as cold and aloof, which is unfortunate, because you are really just too frightened to admit you care. Down deep you don't believe you can survive the embarrassment of hurt, rejection, or failure.

When you pretend, you block the natural therapeutic process from getting to work. How can you begin to mourn something you claim you don't care about? Pretentiousness causes you to form a callus of indifference around you, which alienates others and deprives you of the very contact you need to feel accepted.

Until you drop your pretenses, the healing process is suspended by false posturing. You cannot resolve a pretended emotion.

LOYALTY

Loyalty is a subtle enemy that does you a great disservice when it allows you to alter your view of the truth. Loyalty leads you to believe in others when you should not. Like everyone else, you compromise out of friendship when you know your friends are in trouble. You blindly run to their support, tell them they really didn't do so badly or that others were at fault, that they were cheated when they were really foolish or neglectful. You only do more damage because your friends need to learn their own lessons. They need you to tell the truth even though they may ask you to lie.

If you protect someone from his pain, you also rob him of his life.

Your allegiance to failing causes blinds you. You want something to work so badly that in spite of the evidence, you continue to assert what you want to believe, not what you know in your heart is true.

When your loyalty leads you astray, it often takes a calamity to set things straight. Then the realization—"I knew it all the time"—occurs to you, a realization that should have been there long before.

In fact, it was.

Your loyalty to these realizations should always come first and not compete with friendship, principle, pride, or dogma.

Loyalty is the enemy of common sense. You want to believe in what you think insures your survival. The reason government is so slow in recognizing the needs of people or instituting reforms has to do with misplaced loyalty. Loyalty to the system allows unspeakable injustices to be perpetuated in the name of standard operating procedure and politics.

Loyalty does not require bravery or original thinking. On the contrary loyalty is the social equivalent of secondary gain. To be accepted you have taken the lesser cause and have subverted honesty.

But no one can accuse you of being disloyal!

HOPE

Hope interferes with the natural healing process by leading you to expect to be saved and thus to postpone saving yourself.

When you have hope, you're really in denial. You are insisting: things aren't as bad as they seem; things will get better, the other person will change or will love you again someday. You should accept the truth as soon as possible and make adjustments.

Typically you count on hope when you're most afraid. You are going to have to face the loss or danger by yourself anyway—why lose time hoping for things to get better while they only get worse?

Hope is a reflection of powerlessness, a child's cry for its mother to deliver him in the face of the fearful unknown.

Hope has destroyed more lives than any other emotion, by thwarting the normal instinct to save yourself.

Hope keeps you from growing.

Give up hope.

The way things are is the way things are.

Unless you do something, nothing is going to change.

Instead of hoping, believe in yourself and act.

FALSE EXPECTATIONS

False expectations are unreasonable hopes that come from not taking responsibility for yourself or your present situation. They represent your wish to be compensated for past suffering. False expectations ruin the good times more than actual misfortune because they are always with you, while misfortune only sometimes happens.

If you expect people to be a certain way, they will disappoint you by just being themselves. If you expect something to be wonderful, you will probably be disappointed when it is just the way it is.

When you have false expectations, what you want is never here, never enough. You're always waiting for something better, which makes you overcritical and rejecting. Your standards are based on fantasy and hope. You find reality depressing because it doesn't reward you for what you've sacrificed. You always feel entitled to more and better to make up for what you gave or didn't get.

When you have false expectations you are never fully happy. No matter how good you feel, you compare your situation to something better. Nothing ever seems worth the effort.

You destroy your children when you have unreasonably high expectations for them. Those expectations usually come from failed false hopes for yourself.

Living in false expectations leads you to find hurt and disappointment everywhere and live in mourning over what you think should have been. You continually suffer private little hurts that make sense only to you. You silently pack these ineffable losses into Emotional Debt. As a result the mourning process is always with you. You experience a kind of mourning overload. Because you grieve over these false disappointments, you find it difficult to mourn the real losses you suffer. It is as if you so often sound false alarms to the healing process that it loses its effectiveness.

Since your disappointments only make sense to you, others see you as oversensitive and morose. You appear so difficult to please that others become frustrated and stop giving to you. As a result you feel isolated, the lonely keeper of impossible standards that the world cannot meet. You may become unforgiving and cynical as your world turns in on itself in a spiral of self-pity. Only you know how much others have let you down. Only you know how much you have tried and given. Only you know how much you suffer.

In order to live fully, you have to give up your false expectations and accept yourself and the world just as it is. You have to let go of your suffering to see the world clearly. The world makes perfect sense exactly the way it is. When the truth can be told, everything can be understood. What might have been is not of concern to you, it is merely an energy-draining diversion that weakens your will.

If you must focus on what might have been, learn the lesson that your experience teaches you. What should you have done differently, and why didn't you do it?

Apply that lesson to your life.

The present is the truth. Don't lament it, just try to understand it. Make your expectations into goals for yourself, not criticism of others.

Pursue those goals.

SHAME

Shame and guilt both originate from anger being turned against the self. Shame is an older feeling, with its roots in childhood when you were unsure of yourself and too frightened to express your feelings openly. As a child you hadn't completed your emotional development, and so your defenses tended to be primitive and more rigid. While as an adult you feel remorseful for being angry or doing something bad, when you were a child you believed you were bad when you were angry or that something was wrong with you. As a result you shied away from revealing anything about yourself that could prove your fears true.

The hallmark of shame is that because you feel you are a bad person, you believe you deserve to be punished.

When you suffer from abuse in childhood you are likely to become a victim of shame. When addiction or severe emotional preoccupation is present in your parents, you get the feeling that there is no one who wants to hear your troubles. You internalize the hurt you feel and bury your resentment. You try to be perfect and win your parents' love. You may become a model child and adopt adult attitudes in order to cope and cover for their shortcomings. All this time you suffer more hurt and have more anger to conceal as you try to "fix" your home situation for which, thanks to your shame, you somehow feel responsible.

In fact, shame makes you feel responsible for everything that goes wrong. Like guilt, shame activates your mind to obsess over questions such as, Am I good, smart, attractive, or worthy? Sadly, when shame has been allowed to erode self-confidence, it is easy to convince yourself that these questions always have negative answers. Thus shame inclines you to manifest Toxic Nostalgia by believing anything that suggests you are bad, undeserving, or stupid, which in turn triggers feelings of worthlessness.

If you suffer from shame, you struggle through life. The fear of rejection paralyzes you and makes expressing your feelings a terrible risk. This leads you to accumulate an Emotional Debt made up of so many seemingly insignificant injuries that it is hard to know where to begin to let go or whom to forgive. Since these feelings all seem overblown because they have been incubating in silent resentment, harboring them makes you even more insecure about your worth. As a result you are often too quick to forgive and do so only superficially, without really letting go of your hurt.

If you were victimized or abused to the point where you no longer felt comfortable expressing feelings, most of the real damage done to you was the result of your being unwilling to vent your negative emotions. This is what created your unmanageable Emotional Debt, added to your guilt and shame, and lowered your self-esteem. You are set up to have intense Toxic Nostalgia when you risk expressing yourself, for older feelings are sure to burst forward at the same time that you express current hurt. This overreaction hurts others and convinces you that you're bad.

Everyone suffers from some degree of shame. Who does not believe he has a dark secret that would cause others to reject him if they only knew? Who is not afraid of admitting he is angry at someone he is supposed to love, someone who has fed and clothed him?

To overcome shame requires a leap of faith. In spite of all the negative evidence you can provide to support the opposite conclusion, you need to declare your worth and goodness. You need to remember that only sincere, good people feel bad about hurting others. Bad people never care whom they hurt.

If you suffer from shame, it should be obvious to you that the only person you don't feel guilty about hurting is yourself. Isn't it time you changed your opinion, declared yourself worthy of love and respect, and treated yourself better? Your shame will fade when you begin to take yourself and your value seriously. You deserve to love yourself, and give yourself the benefit of the doubt.

DRUGS AND ALCOHOL

The natural therapeutic process seeks to integrate your life experience by allowing you to understand and take responsibility for your strengths and weaknesses. To evolve into your highest self requires total honesty.

All chemical substances impede the natural therapeutic process's management of feelings. When pain is modified by chemicals it is stored unprocessed in Emotional Debt where it becomes excessive. This explains why people who use substances often seem crazy and volatile—drowning in sentimentality, rage, and blaming.

Ironically, addiction usually results from using a substance to dull the pain of the Toxic Nostalgia that the substance itself created.

People become addicted to chemical substances precisely because they numb emotional pain. In dynamic terms this means that these substances in-hibit, prolong, or with constant use completely arrest the mourning process by blocking the hurt. In a sense these substances mimic denial, making difficult problems feel less reachable and old feelings seem even more remote.

To heal you must acquire a point of view that allows you to take responsibil-ity for your suffering and accept what can't be altered. This perspective is a function of the higher brain, the very part of the mind that is most sensitive to emotional pain *and* the deadening effects of alcohol and addictive substances.

Although the likelihood of Toxic Nostalgia increases under the influence, the intoxicated mind does not process emotions but merely verbalizes them, and these triggered emotions only become a source of additional suffering. Every expressed emotion triggers another emotion, escalating the situation into drama and abusiveness. This explains the futility of trying to reason with an in-toxicated person even though it may be the only time he is talking about his feel-ings.

Typically, Toxic Nostalgia in the intoxicated state is characterized by im-mense anxiety, hurt, and anger. Even though there may be little relationship to a precise causative event, the intoxicated mind obsessively blames the usual vil-lains from the past who are seen as responsible for everything that ever went wrong. These tirades produce no relief and only lower self-esteem, motivating the abuser to seek oblivion.

The self-deception maintained by hallucinogenic drug users, that they can expand their mind or understand themselves better on drugs, is completely neutralized by their inability to integrate their intoxicated perceptions in a ben-eficial or lasting manner when they are sober. Such insight is like taking pictures of an unfamiliar landscape with your eyes closed and trying to make sense of them afterward. You are emotionally disconnected from your experience when you use drugs.

Alcohol, especially, has a depressive effect on the part of the brain responsi-ble for inhibiting the inappropriate expression of emotions. When this function is chemically impaired, any minor provocation that can trigger anger will do so. This explains why there are so many fights in bars and why alcohol plays such a powerful role in assaultive behavior. To the intoxicated person exploding with rage, the release of anger from Emotional Debt feels sincere. His chemically impaired mind obliges and comes up with a plausible rationalization for may-hem, and the anger is allowed to express itself, often tragically.

Intoxicating substances inhibit the natural processing of emotions and the at-tainment of a healing perspective. This explains why chronic alcoholics or drug users seem immature and stuck in the same emotional place. Their naiveté, which seemed sweet and charming when they were young, wears thin when they are expected to be adults. When they finally become sober they feel like children. Simple feelings terrify them. They think there is something wrong with them merely for feeling afraid, hurt, or angry.

When they begin to recover they still have to deal with volumes of unprocessed feelings. This makes them especially susceptible to bouts of Toxic Nostalgia. Even though these episodes of triggered feelings still present the opportunity for growth previously set aside by using the drug, they jeopardize the recovering addict's sobriety.

It takes a minimum of six months of sobriety for a chronic user to stabilize enough so that the natural therapeutic process can begin working again. Usually the first indication that the process has taken hold is the appearance of depression as the remorse and sadness that has so long been suppressed finally surfaces. This is also the most precarious time, when relapse is most likely.

LEGAL ENTANGLEMENT

It may sound peculiar to be discussing the law in relation to the natural healing process, but they are clearly antagonistic. While the law offers redress of grievances for being injured and there is enormous satisfaction in suing someone who injured you and recovering damages, the process involved in doing so exacts a dear emotional price and sometimes makes victory seem hollow.

The basic problem with appealing to the legal system to settle emotional difficulties is that the posture most likely to achieve success is one that requires you to engage in secondary gain, that is, to exaggerate the damage or display your injury to win sympathy. This prolongs the healing process.

Suing someone requires that you keep your anger alive as you seek to prove blame. Since ultimately your peace of mind depends on attaining forgiveness and letting go of your hurt, staying angry to fuel your vengeance diverts your energy from healing and commits you to living in the past.

At best legal encounters are awful. The frustration with procedural delays, postponements, and counterclaims only adds to your suffering. Worse, the torment that results from the disappointments of the legal process can be as great as that from the actual injury. When the case is over, you must still mourn the original loss. There is nothing left to do but mourn, which is why there is often such a letdown after a case is won.

By no means does this suggest that you should allow others to trample over your rights. Quite the contrary. It is intended as a warning. If you go to court, do so to seek monetary satisfaction, protection, or the delineation of privilege or custody. To survive the courts emotionally intact, you need to develop a lawyer's attitude, detached and indifferent. See it all as a kind of game.

Never enter the courts with the expectation of settling an emotional disagreement. Because attaching blame and excuses are at the heart of legal matters, becoming involved with the law almost always makes emotional situations worse. Healing depends on taking responsibility, being open and honest. The truth makes its own rules, and healing comes, not from proof of blame, but from acceptance of what cannot be resolved.

WARNING SIGNS OF EMOTIONAL DANGER

Inherent in the natural healing process are certain safeguards that alert you to danger. There is a bad feeling that you get when you misstate the truth. It can be a subtle uneasiness, a disquieting sense that something isn't right. It can be a wave of anxiety or sadness. Be still and ask yourself what just disturbed you. Correct what you just said so it is truthful.

Another sign that you may be in trouble is when you find yourself avoiding situations that are not especially dangerous. Ask yourself what feeling the situation brings to mind.

You may find yourself breaking into a sweat or developing signs of anxiety, shallow breathing, and rapid heart rate when a subject is mentioned or a certain person approaches you. Ask yourself how you have been hurt. You're probably afraid of losing control over your anger. When a sad memory returns, you are being reminded of some loss that is still being mourned.

Don't push it away. Identify and acknowledge the feeling. Put it into words by saying to yourself, I really miss her, I wish I had tried harder, it was a shame to give up when I was so close, or some other comment that states both your feeling of sadness and accepts some responsibility for the painful memory.

Your discomfort is a message telling you that something is wrong. Assume that you probably know what it is.

Use your feelings of discomfort to guide you to be more honest.

Examine your heart. All your answers lie there.

HOW FEELINGS WORK

*Y*OU *ARE* YOUR FEELINGS. While future generations may isolate your legacy from your emotions and evaluate you in terms of the gift you left behind, the way you feel about yourself right now, at this time and in this place, determines the quality of your life. You live in your feelings, and your happiness depends on whether you like the way you feel.

If you understand how your feelings work, you understand how your defenses operate, how your personality developed, and what motivates your behavior. Without understanding your feelings, you are a mystery to yourself.

HOW EMOTIONS EVOLVE AND ARE LINKED

Feelings do not just appear out of the blue. They are related to events, thoughts, dreams, and comments.

Your feelings are easy to understand once you have some perspective. However, there are few tasks more difficult than trying to understand a powerful emotion when it holds you in its grasp. The intensity of a feeling results not only from the events that caused it but also from any stored-up feelings that are reanimated. That is why strong emotions are so confusing.

THE BASIC FEELINGS

To begin with, there are two basic feelings: pleasure and pain.
The name given to these feelings depends on when the feeling occurs.

NEGATIVE FEELINGS

Pain in the future is anxiety. The pain hasn't happened yet. Thus anxiety is a warning of an injury or loss that could take place. Then again, it may be avoided or you could be entirely mistaken and there may be no danger. You may have merely misinterpreted what you perceived or it may have reminded you of something frightening, perhaps an old loss you haven't dealt with.

Pain in the present is hurt. Hurt is experienced as sadness and disappointment. Hurt is taking place right now. The evidence for the hurt is obvious, right in front of you. The damage speaks for itself. It requires little explanation for other people to understand your hurt. They are likely to be eyewitnesses. Hurt is the most real of all feelings, easiest to share with others and for them to comprehend.

Pain in the past is anger. Anger is resentment over being hurt. Therefore, anger always requires an explanation that relates it to the hurt that caused it.

When anger is not immediately expressed with the hurt that caused it, it is stored in Emotional Debt. There it is combined with other anger and to some extent made less real. Later, when you express the anger, you have to make a case for the hurt you suffered, because then it's more difficult for others to follow your reasoning. The longer you keep anger from expression, the more distorted it seems when you finally release it. When anger festers inside, it activates memories of other old hurts and takes on their anger. This is the main reason that anger confuses you. You don't understand the volume, intensity, or the seeming inappropriateness of old anger when it breaks through.

When anger is directed inward it is called guilt. It takes considerable psychic energy to withhold anger. The defenses that constrain anger are not specific but hinder the expression of *all* feelings, good and bad. This explains why people who repress anger don't seem loving. Your defenses not only direct your anger inward but also your attention, and thus preoccupy you.

The depletion of psychic energy to withhold anger is called depression. The energy that is required to keep anger from expression is part of the total energy available to solve problems, be creative, love, motivate yourself, and live your life. If energy is diverted from your life, the total amount of energy available to you is depressed. The more feelings you hold in, the more depressed you are.

Severely depressed people also experience a physical slowing down of body functions, sleep disturbances, and a depletion of vital brain chemicals that is more likely the result rather than the cause of the depression. Using drugs to reestablish the chemical balance is only a temporary solution and an inexact one.

The best way to heal and remain well is to learn how to express feelings in a more timely and appropriate way.

POSITIVE FEELINGS

Pleasure in the future is anticipation or excitement.

Pleasure in the present is joy.

Pleasure in the past is contentment.

These positive feelings will be discussed later. The focus here will be on the management of pain.

THE PURPOSE OF FEELINGS

Feelings in the animal kingdom are related to ensuring survival. While man has the capacity to evaluate a situation and place it in perspective, creatures with primitive frontal lobe development must rely on their instincts to insure their survival. For instance, painful feelings in animals are directly translated into physical response. However, in man they undergo subtle changes, the prejudice of memory and reason.

The glory of human intellectual abstraction, the capacity to create something from nothing, is also the seat of neurotic behavior. We believe in causes. We kill for revenge. We love and we hate.

Your capacity for abstract thinking also predisposes you to regard an old feeling that has been remembered as real and leads you to react to it as if it were actually happening. It is what your memory adds to your feelings that creates your difficulties. Thus when you say your problems repeat, you are really describing how your old feelings and memories from Emotional Debt persist into the present. Because he has a different past, another person facing the same stimulus as the one that triggered you would have an entirely different experience.

ANXIETY

THE PURPOSE OF FEAR

Fear is your protector. To put it bluntly, if you had no fear you would have been dead long ago.

When you are anxious, you feel something is wrong.

It is your job to understand why you feel that way.

The purpose of anxiety is to warn you of danger and to initiate those physiologic responses upon which a successful escape or defense depend. Anxiety increases your heart rate and breathing and causes blood to be shunted to the major extremities. Anxiety supports your survival.

In the animal kingdom there is little discrimination between different levels of anxiety—even a little fear will propel an animal to flee from danger. Because the human mind is capable of symbolic logic, it can imagine a situation as being the way it fears, needs, or wants it to be. Thus you can believe something is dangerous when it is benign or convince yourself that something is safe when it is clearly hazardous. Your reasoning can betray the original intention of your feelings.

Anxiety leads you to abandon your comfortable view of reality and look for possible threats. You become more sensitive, more focused on sound and movement. You go "on the alert" and begin to look for likely sources of danger. Your purpose is to define the threat and figure out how to meet it.

However, anxiety can also lead you to misinterpret what you perceive. Just as young campers listening to ghost stories become "spooked" and imagine they hear Big Foot bearing down on them, your anxiety can distort your perceptions, explaining why an overly vigilant soldier will shoot at a falling leaf, convinced he has seen the enemy.

Because anxiety begets anxiety, just talking about fear is threatening to some people. When you become afraid of being afraid, you tend to panic. When you do, your old fears are reactivated and seek expression. You feel disconnected from reality, as if you are living in a nightmare and can't wake up. You become suspicious and find danger wherever you look.

Your mind naturally seeks to understand the warning your anxiety is sounding. When you can't find an explanation, you search desperately to pin your fear on something, even if you have to make things up. You feel disoriented, awash in emotions. All you want is safety. Extreme fear can lead you to misinterpret reality and react to it with tragic results, for example, mistaking a member of your family for an intruder and shooting him.

Face your fears and understand them. Learn to see them as a message, not as a weakness.

Accept that it is okay to be afraid. However, it is not okay to pretend to be fearless.

Still, it's important to be brave in the face of fear and act in spite of it. Cowards use fear as an excuse. You have to do what you have to do in spite of your fear.

Confidence is your belief that you will survive being afraid.

If you let fear run your life, it will lead you to expect disaster. You'll constantly wonder what is going to happen next. You'll anticipate the worst and suffer needlessly. Most importantly, your concern for invented dangers will lead you to neglect your true concerns. When you live in fear, you bring upon yourself the very losses you most dread.

A child continually struggles to know the real meaning of his anxiety. When he is afraid he tries to decide whether something is dangerous and he should avoid it or if he's just afraid of failure and needs to be braver. He is reminded to avoid strangers. He is urged to overcome his shyness and play with new friends. It is confusing. Should he ignore his fear or respect it?

A child learns he must set some fears aside and oppose his natural instinct to run if he is to be successful, praised, or loved. He also needs to learn to avoid being a reckless showoff. He needs to learn that there are real dangers and evil forces in this world. It is also possible to be too cautious and withdraw from everything just to be on the safe side.

This struggle to interpret the paradox of anxiety continues throughout life.

THE UNKNOWN

No one can deal with the fear of the unknown, for it is fear without limitation. It contaminates your judgment and paralyzes you. The fear of the unknown is always with you. It lies there waiting to be called upon, the great spoiler. You reason that anything can happen. While there is some truth in that, there is also no truth in it. Fearing the unknown complicates your life and defeats the very purpose of fear.

The fear of the unknown always expands.

The purpose of fear is to define danger and limit your focus so you can save yourself.

Just because you know you are going to die someday, you don't stop living.

FEAR PREPARES YOU FOR DANGER

To deal with anxiety, ask the following questions:

> *Am I in danger?*
> *What loss am I facing: love, control, or esteem?*
> *Why is this risk important to me?*
> *What are the chances of this loss actually occurring?*
> *What can I do to prevent or limit this loss?*
> *Is the loss real, or am I imagining it?*

When was the last time I felt this way?
When was the first time I felt this way?
Did what I fear before ever come to happen?

Use your fear as a guide to help you understand and prepare for a challenge, not as an excuse for abandoning it. Every important risk involves fear. Don't run from your fear. Don't pretend to be fearless. You just want to recognize danger and learn to adapt to it.

PANIC—THE FEAR OF FEAR

The fear of fear is your enemy. It always escalates and causes you to lose perspective. Worse, because the fear of fear becomes isolated from reality, you don't know how real the danger is. You don't know how to act.

The first step in overcoming panic is to question if it is real. Just because you are panicked doesn't mean you're at all in danger. Panic is created when feelings of powerlessness are awakened and attach to whatever triggered them.

Because the panic response is so extreme, you naturally believe you are in grave danger. Your reaction releases the hormones of fear, which create additional disquiet, which in turn leads you to distort further. In a moment you are convinced the danger is real because it feels real.

Your fear of fear can become a burden to those who love you. If they are too understanding, they can become hostages to your fear. When you are preoccupied with your fears, you lose concern for other people. Others resent you for allowing your weakness to matter more than anything else in your life.

Jerry had suffered for years with his wife Nancy's chronic anxiety, calling her ten times a day to report on his activities. She was afraid Jerry was going to have an affair, the way her father had cheated on her mother.

One evening Jerry was in an accident on the way home and taken to the emergency room, where he required a dozen stitches. When he arrived home six hours late, Nancy greeted him in an angry panic, showering him with a tirade of accusations, totally ignoring his injuries.

For the first time in their marriage Jerry could see the problem clearly. He shouted for Nancy to pay attention, saying it was he who was injured, that reality mattered more than her fears and that her selfishness was making him want to leave her. By confronting Nancy with the worst of her fears and pointing out that she was causing the problem, he shocked her into a new awareness. For the first time Nancy was forced to reach beyond her fears and take action.

A little reality goes a long way to resolving irrational fears.

OVERCOMING YOUR FEAR OF BEING AFRAID

Your fear is mostly self-doubt. You build confidence by acting bravely. You destroy confidence by giving in to fear.

> *Admit and understand your self-doubts.*
> *Make a plan.*
> *Initiate that plan.*
> *Do the very thing you fear.*
> *Expect to be afraid as you do it.*
> *Do it anyway.*
> *Keep going.*

Today many people take antianxiety medication to cope with stress. Becoming dependent on such drugs interferes with your ability to develop confidence. If you do use a medication to help you manage frightening situations, try not always taking it automatically. For example, if you usually take medication before a fearful encounter, try postponing it as long as you can. Bring the medication with you, knowing you can take it if you feel you need it, but wait a bit. See how long you can postpone taking it. The longer you can wait, the more confident you will become.

If you feel better immediately after taking the medication, it isn't the medication that's making you feel better but the placebo effect. Put another way, your belief that you are safe lets you feel better.

That belief is always yours to tap if only you learn to trust yourself. Self-confidence is really nothing more than maintaining the belief that you are safe.

FACING YOUR FEARS

It's important to continue to take action in spite of your irrational fears while trying to understand them at the same time. The fear of fear can be an obstinate oppression, resisting all attempts to overcome it and demoralizing you by convincing you that you are weak.

If you don't trust yourself, you never feel completely safe. You worry about your hidden feelings bursting forward and betraying you or that you could be repaid by fate for your wrongdoing. You maintain a vigil, expecting the worst as a way of keeping yourself under control. Your avoiding behavior lowers your self-esteem and weakens your resolve to change.

You grow stronger when you face irrational fears. You discover that what you feared was not so fearful. Secret fears grow to unrealistic proportions. When you take action and face your fear, you develop a more realistic perspective.

As soon as you admit, "This isn't so scary," you are on your way. Facing fear is testing reality rather than relying on your preconceived belief. Facing fear is also growing up.

The question you must always answer is whether your anxiety or your self-doubt represents a real danger.

When you have low self-esteem you can come to fear everything.

Although most passengers assume that planes are safe, they still experience concern on takeoff and landings. Everyone gets at least a little frightened during severe turbulence. The more fearful passengers get even more afraid at such times. When the danger is past, most passengers experience relief. However, fearful passengers generally remain in dread, torturing themselves by staying in their terror, suffering until the plane lands and beyond. They can't get the incident out of their minds because their real fear has not subsided. *They doubt their ability to survive.*

The fear underlying the fear of dying in an accident has mostly to do with the fear that you have wasted your life. The people who fear death the most have lived the least.

If you are so afraid of something that you can't even look at it rationally, then you probably doubt your goodness, worthiness, or capacity to succeed. If you allow your anxiety to keep you from doing what you want, you don't learn to master the lessons you need to grow.

The bad news: The same lesson will repeat, and you can try to avoid the danger again.

The good news: The same lesson will repeat, and you can overcome your fear.

Since it is obvious that you are going to be faced with your critical lessons until you face them, here's an argument for dealing promptly with your anxiety.

You'll only be older and weaker next time.

Your self-esteem will be lower if you postpone.

You'll only waste more energy if you conceal your fear.

You'll miss that surge of belief in yourself that overcoming an obstacle gives you.

There are no insignificant gains in self-esteem. They all matter.

Granted, caution is important. However, never taking a risk is merely surrender.

You cannot really know the risk you avoid. The avoided risk is always a mystery and a source of perpetual intimidation. You only get to know a risk when you take it. Finally, the danger of a potential loss appears manageable to someone who is committed to taking a risk, while any obstacle is enough to block a person who is afraid.

The avoided risk remains the unknown forever.

HURT

THE PURPOSE OF HURT

The purpose of hurt is to limit the extent of the damage done to you.

If you didn't have the sensation of pain, you wouldn't know what danger to avoid. You'd be badly scarred and crippled.

The role of hurt is to tell you you've been damaged. You learn your life lessons in pain, so experiencing pain is necessary to grow. Feeling your emotional pain initiates the healing process. Pain in the present is as real a feeling as you can get. Expressing pain when it happens is vital to keeping yourself safe and your relationships honest.

Saying, "Ouch. That hurts," is the universal sentiment that causes others to hold back. It tells the dentist to ease up, the masseuse to be more gentle, and the ardent lover to change tactics. It lets others know that that they have gone too far. Telling someone they hurt you puts them on notice and tests their intentions. Knowing that you hurt and why helps them understand what is important to you.

Pain creates clear limits. It waves a red flag that says, "Go no further." It defines the edge of trespass. When you hurt another person, he says, "Ouch," and you stop what you were doing. You say you're sorry. You feel forgiven when he tells you his pain is gone.

Pain teaches children powerful lessons. However, when children experience too much pain, either by punishment or neglect, it damages their trust and lowers their self-confidence. When pain is accompanied by fear, the lesson it teaches may be exaggerated. Instead of learning to be appropriately cautious, the child may develop a dread of risking.

You're supposed to learn a lesson when someone hurts your feelings. Your hurt tells you that the person may not be trustworthy, that you need to protect yourself and be cautious about revealing your vulnerabilities and needs to him. Only you know how badly another person has hurt you, and therefore, only you have the final say as to how open you should be with him. Hurt is your private message. If it hurts you, it matters to you.

BOUNDARIES

Hurt teaches you when to establish limits with others. You have to declare how much you will tolerate. Limits are especially important with people you really care about. Because you allow only the people you truly love to see you with your guard down, the people you love have the power to hurt you the most.

Hurt forces you to declare yourself, to say you're hurt, to take a stand, to say "No!" *If you want to know how your life got off track, you need to look no further than the way you avoid speaking out when you are hurt.*

If you don't maintain boundaries, you'll find that other people will hurt you all the time, not because they're bad, but because they weren't told they were hurting you. It is not that people intend to ignore your rights, it's just that people naturally tend to be selfish. They just want what *they* want. If you don't object, other people will simply act in their best interests. For this reason, if you permit others to use you, you'll be used. If you allow others to hurt you, you'll be hurt. Try not to take it personally.

You are betrayed most by your hope that others will care enough to consider your feelings and not hurt you. Other people consider their feelings first. You can count on that. If you say nothing when they trespass, why should they hold back from hurting you?

It is difficult to assert yourself to someone who has become accustomed to violating your boundaries or using your property. They will even claim it is their right to do so. The practice of usage defines ownership and rights. If you allow people to use a shortcut across your property without posting a NO TRESPASSING sign, after a few years that shortcut becomes a public way and you lose all claim to it. Your rights are not guaranteed unless you are willing to defend them.

This holds true with feelings. If you don't express yourself when others hurt you, they believe that whatever they did was acceptable to you. If you do not protect your emotional boundaries, while you may not actually lose your right to object, you become so afraid of losing control of your stored anger that you feel too inhibited to object.

Most of the problems that you suffer would be solved if you could stand up for yourself at the time you are hurt, define your boundaries, and live in peace.

WHAT YOUR HURT TELLS YOU

Your hurt tells you what really matters to you. Your hurt tells you what is real.

It is an odd thing, but as much as you avoid pain, you need it to help you sort out your experience. "Pinch me so I know I'm not dreaming," reflects how people use pain. Slapping a person in hysterics can arrest the escalation of panic by focusing the person on his physical hurt. The power of pain is that it brings you into the present. The pain of the moment says, "You are here right now." Children who are head bangers often have a poor sense of reality. It is not that the head banging causes the problem, but that head banging is one of the ways such children use pain to ground themselves, to tell what is real. Hurt defines the boundaries of person and reality.

Hurt is a powerful motivator, but only if you do not deny it. If you accept that you are unhappy, your pain will lead you to make choices. Unfortunately, rather than do this, people often let their problems build to the point where they suffer and then feel too demoralized to act.

SUFFERING AND LOW SELF-ESTEEM

Abused women often deny that they've been battered because they don't want to take any action that might leave them all alone, their worst fear. They do not like or believe in themselves. If they had a better sense of self-worth, they wouldn't mind being alone with themselves. They sometimes minimize the abuse they suffer, commenting, "He never hits me with his fist," to rationalize their inaction. They deny their pain as long as they believe it could be worse.

People with low self-esteem avoid admitting their hurt. They do not want to discover that the other person hurt them on purpose or does not love them. They do not want to accept the hurt of rejection. They hope their pain will go away by itself, without them making a scene and risking abandonment.

WHY YOU DENY YOU'VE BEEN HURT

You don't want to take responsibility for or admit to your role in your own disappointment. You do not want to admit you can be hurt, or that you are vulnerable or powerless. You fear this would only show other people how you can be hurt again. You don't want to admit that you are unhappy. You want others to admire you as a success. You dismiss others' hurtful actions, pretending that they are just teasing or that you really aren't hurt.

Your hurt serves to protect you from further damage. Hurt is supposed to be painful in order to help you avoid it. When you deny your hurt, you're not being brave, merely reckless.

Admitting your hurt is the beginning of healing.

ANGER

THE PURPOSE OF ANGER

The purpose of anger is to reinforce the expression of hurt. Instead of holding in your hurt and allowing yourself to be damaged further, your anger urges you to exclaim, "Ouch! Hey, what are you doing? That hurt! Don't do that! Stop!"

To make it effective, the expression of hurt always requires revealing the edge of anger. You show a little anger to get others to stop hurting you. If you don't, you're depending on your display of hurt alone to protect you, which may not work. In the animal kingdom the conversion of hurt into anger is vital for survival since other animals only hold back when they are opposed.

Showing a little anger tells others you won't be trampled upon. Anger limits your injury by making you a little less safe to approach. The anger you show at the time you're hurt feels appropriate and in proportion. Because it is tinged with injury, its source is clear. The other person can readily understand it. If the injury was unintentional, the person who hurt you will be relieved that your pain has subsided and will hardly notice that you expressed anger with your hurt, unless that person is controlling and can't admit responsibility for his actions. Such people blame you for being in the way.

NEGATIVE EXPRESSIONS OF ANGER

People withhold anger for many of the same reasons they withhold hurt. They are afraid of being vulnerable, admitting the truth of the situation and their unhappiness with it.

Some dependent people, especially those who have been abused or trained by adversity to hide their feelings, are frightened by their anger. They fear that expressing anger will make them unlovable or a bad person. Typically they become so threatened by the prospect of losing control that they simply freeze. They tend to be irritable and easily brought to angry tears.

Other dependent people express anger by parading their hurt in a guilt-producing manner. This is a form of manipulation in which the victim tries to gain support against the person he claims hurt him. This also involves others in your private affairs. Such "victims" seldom admit that their manipulations hurt others.

Since they think revealing their hurt makes them seem weak, the only emotion controlling people feel comfortable expressing is anger. When they do express anger, they tend to be punitive, justifying their angry actions by recounting how their rules have been broken or how they have been disobeyed. They'd rather talk about their violated rules than their hurt feelings. If they could admit their hurt they could release it and forgive others, but then they would have no rationale for punishing others. Controlling people bear grudges and hold on to hurt for years, punishing, treating people unfairly by lording their power over those who hurt them.

Competitive people often express hurt in a demeaning way designed to hurt the other person's self-esteem by holding him up to the world for derision. Include here angry outbursts and embarrassing comeuppances. These displays seem unrealistic, as if the competitive person is living out a fantasy. Having planned his revenge, he is now guilty of overreacting. When his angry fantasies finally find expression, they tend to burst forth impulsively and recklessly and feel like vengeance. Even if you are not the target, this showy anger is humiliating to be around and explains how competitive people lose friends.

Anger is always more complicated to express than hurt. If you were more willing to express your hurt when it occurred, revealing anger would be a much more straightforward matter because it would occur simultaneously with the expression of the hurt that caused it. Unfortunately everyone tends to withhold hurt. After a while the hurtful event becomes distorted by time and is much more difficult to express. When you finally get around to expressing your hurt, it has largely evolved into anger, and your version of the original hurtful circumstances only makes sense to you.

If you wait too long to express your hurt and anger, you may discover that the incident is totally forgotten by the other person, who by now may doubt your story and even be offended by your accusation. Not only will he refuse to take responsibility for hurting you, he's likely to be surprised by your delayed complaint and regard it as a hurtful act against him. Delaying the expression of your hurt makes you seem like the villain.

The anger that develops in immediate response to a hurt is the only anger that is completely true. The longer you wait to express anger, the less real it becomes. If you wait years to express anger, it will seem ridiculously overblown, and you will seem a little crazy to be angry for so long.

Old anger often leads you to exaggerate the facts in order to rationalize and justify staying angry, so in a sense expressing old anger is telling a lie. This explains why expressing volumes of anger has limited therapeutic benefit. The natural therapeutic process does not move forward when a person lies. This is why people who are always angry can't seem to get better until they release their old hurt and forgive.

It is possible to realize benefits by encouraging a person to let out his old feelings by proxy at a safe target. This is a valid therapeutic technique, but it can get precarious. While ranting at artificial targets can easily produce a display of rageful emotion, doing so can be disorganizing to someone who is fragile and struggling to stay intact. For this reason so-called anger work, in which people are enthusiastically encouraged to scream, punch pillows, or use Styrofoam bats to strike out, can liberate more anger than the person feels comfortable managing, overwhelm his defenses, and precipitate a crisis of lowered self-esteem.

Ideally, expressing anger by proxy should employ as the target a tangible present injury that warrants the expression of anger. By encouraging the expression of that reasonable anger, the natural therapeutic process can be initiated and with it older feelings can also be resolved. The following illustrates how this is done.

When Miriam was widowed after fifty years of marriage, she developed an unrelenting burning sensation in her eyes but could not cry. In therapy it became clear that her symptoms reflected her withheld tears of rage. Her husband had always been affectionate and loving but had never been much of a wage earner. His insurance policy was meager, and his military benefits were used up at the funeral. Miriam found herself resentful over her severe financial restrictions.

Although it was the truth, encouraging Miriam to express her secret resentment toward her husband for failing to provide was seen as a dangerous tactic. To challenge her affection for him might mobilize more bitterness and run the risk of deepening her depression. Instead, she was encouraged to express her irritation at the Veterans' Administration and the Social Security Administration for their delays. The frustration she suffered by having to wait for checks was a natural topic of conversation. She was encouraged to complain about the rudeness of government personnel and the unfairness of the system. After a while she finally began to feel better and her depression lifted.

The anger that is triggered during Toxic Nostalgia cannot be resolved merely by expressing it. The original hurt that caused the anger must first be identified. The relationship between the hurt and the anger is the healing truth that needs to be retrieved.

Displaying old anger can hurt and infuriate the person you express it to, especially if he is in denial. This will cause him to reject you anew and confirm his view that you are irrational. To make matters worse he may expect you to apologize for hurting him. This can be very discouraging.

Additionally, expressing old anger just to get it off your chest always runs the risk of activating even more anger, leading to an irrational display of rage, florid Toxic Nostalgia. If you are depressed this can push you to the edge.

Old anger leads you to question your goodness and act self-punitively to relieve your guilt. This explains why it is common for recently hospitalized depressed patients to embrace menial behavior, such as scrubbing toilets and washing floors. They're doing penance, atoning for being bad. It makes them feel better.

POSITIVE EXPRESSIONS OF ANGER

Although you may experience some initial relief, expressing anger runs the risk of lowering your self-esteem by bringing you down to the level of your tormentor.

The best way to express old or recent anger is not to express it at all.

Instead, express the hurt that underlies your anger.

This accomplishes several important goals.

When you identify the hurt that's causing your anger, you no longer seem irrational. Suddenly there's a reason you feel the way you do. You have a case. Someone damaged you. You're not crazy.

The purpose of expressing hurt is to release it, to let go. This release of hurt forms the basis of forgiveness.

This may seem contradictory, but some people keep their hurt alive to justify feeling angry. Holding on to hurt is bearing a grudge. People who hold grudges think they know exactly how they have been hurt. They'll tell you what hurts, but they still won't let go. They won't forgive. Holding a grudge is a form of Toxic Nostalgia, except that the person holding the grudge forces the old feeling onto the present rather than it being triggered. The person who holds a grudge is probably hurting from many old injuries, nurturing his suffering as a way to avoid feeling guilty.

People who hold grudges find it difficult to release their hurt because to do so feels as if they're destroying the evidence that justifies their negative attitude. The fact that they are ruining their own lives by staying hurt and that others hardly notice their suffering is beside the point. Hurt has a way of rationalizing itself, even when most of the damage being done by holding on to it is done to you.

The greatest benefit of releasing anger by releasing hurt is that it keeps your feelings in the present. You address the person who hurt you and inform them that you were hurt, that you have been hurting, and that you still hurt. Thus the hurt that you are talking about is your present feeling. It is possible to mention that you feel resentment over the injury, but the greatest relief is felt by expressing the injury alone.

The following case illustrates the way in which old anger can influence a person's life as it continually seeks opportunities for expression in the form of grudges. It also shows how at heart people bearing grudges are suffering from guilt as well.

Patricia was a thirty-year-old woman, one hundred pounds overweight, who struggled all her life trying to contain her volatile temper. As she got older she increasingly found herself in angry situations, until in great frustration she sabotaged her job with a large company and moved to a small town where she hoped she could start over.

She rented a tiny cottage and began working in a video store, which she believed would not be stressful. However, after a few days she found herself becoming irritated over the smallest frustrations, such as a movie returned late or improperly rewound. Even though her boss reminded her that these extra charges added greatly to his profit, she treated customers rudely, often making nasty comments under her breath.

Patricia found herself returning home frustrated in the evenings and unable to get to sleep as she ruminated over the angry events of the day. One night she was jarred awake by the sound of a screen door slamming. Taking it personally, she jumped out of bed and caught a glimpse of a neighbor going back into her house. Patricia became furious, stormed across the street, slammed the lady's screen door, and quickly retreated. The following night she was awakened by rocks being thrown at her house and car. "For absolutely no good reason," Patricia puzzled.

Out of fear Patricia began to sleep in her car, but immediately another woman started to complain she was "bringing down the neighborhood." Patricia began to argue with customers at work, and after several warnings she was fired. Shaken by the recurrence of all her problems and wondering if she'd done anything to cause them, Patricia decided to seek help, complaining, "It's starting to happen all over again."

It was pointed out to Patricia that by overreacting to others' random anger she only reinforced it, drew their fire, and then used being attacked as an excuse for releasing her own stored anger. Patricia objected. When it was suggested that the problem would never have started if she had minded her own business, Patricia dismissed the idea. When asked if she thought others were out to get her, Patricia growled, "I'm not paranoid, just angry."

Patricia revealed that she had been angry for years, especially at her mother, whom she described as selfish, self-involved, and hurtful. The most painful part was that whenever Patricia protested against her mother's cruelty, her mother denied she'd ever hurt Patricia, ridiculed her, and called her "crazy."

Patricia struggled to stay in control, tolerating her mother's sarcastic assaults until, just after her sixteenth birthday, her father suddenly became ill. He'd been the only one in the family who cared for her or took her feelings seriously. When it was clear he was dying, Patricia's mother mounted a bizarre and mean-spirited campaign to blame him for everything that had gone wrong. Patricia was so shocked she couldn't believe her mother's abuse was actually taking place and remained silent. Patricia could no longer tolerate living in the house, and although her father badly needed her support, she moved out, wallowing in guilt as she left.

The loss of the only person who really loved her, her fury at her mother, and the anger she directed at herself for leaving her father overwhelmed Patricia. She tried to balance her anger by portraying herself as her mother's powerless victim. Although it was easier to feel that way than admit her guilt over betraying her father, her guilt still tormented her and led her to seek out self-destructive situations.

Although she was determined to make a life for herself, Patricia somehow found someone opposing her wherever she looked. She offended people in restaurants by being demanding and short-tempered. In traffic she would honk at the car in front of her so incessantly that daily she narrowly escaped being punched.

Patricia lived in a continual state of Toxic Nostalgia as her anger escaped from Emotional Debt, attaching itself to the slightest suggestion of insult. So much anger leaked out that she easily found reasons to be angry wherever she looked.

A plan was made to express her hurt to her mother, with whom she'd spoken every day all this time, playing the role of the nice daughter, never mentioning her real feelings. She was also encouraged to take responsibility for abandoning her father, but to see it as a reaction to her mother, not as an angry act for which she deserved punishment. Patricia had to admit that although she wasn't strong enough years ago to stand up for what she believed, in the present she could do so. Expressing her hurt at her mother became the cornerstone of her self-forgiveness, allowing her to feel good about herself.

Although Patricia's anger was a complex commingling of anger from many sources, it was still possible to resolve it through the expression of hurt. If Patricia had been encouraged to express her anger at her mother, the situation would have totally deteriorated. It was difficult enough for her mother to accept Patricia's hurt. When Patricia took responsibility for not being more honest, for stuffing her feelings down with food and for falsely accusing others, her mother finally conceded that she might have acted harshly and indicated that she'd been under a lot of pressure in those days. It was not much of an admission, but Patricia recognized that it meant her mother was sorry, and she was finally able to release her hurt, knowing that her mother would not change. She also stopped calling every day to make up for her guilt. Not long after this the world began to feel much more friendly to her.

GUILT

THE PURPOSE OF GUILT

Guilt has no purpose. Guilt does nothing to prepare you for danger or help you cope with pain. If anything, guilt makes matters worse by lowering your self-esteem and your sense of deservability. Animals do not feel guilty. They simply express their anger. If anything, guilt is a sign that the natural therapeutic process has gone awry. At fault of course is the human capacity for symbolic reasoning. We imagine that it is wrong to be hurt and angry, to be real and natural.

Conscience is not guilt. Your sense of conscience causes you to feel remorse after you have hurt someone or done something wrong. It is a function of your higher brain, the same part that is responsible for abstract thinking, creativity, and altruism. It allows you to rise above the self. Your conscience acts like a brake on your aggression, bidding you to hold back even before you have hurt others. Your conscience refers you to standards of behavior beyond that of the current swarm of feelings and helps you to overcome the tide of momentary emotions. Conscience allows you to persevere over your selfishness and your conformity to values of the pack. Your higher brain enables you to look beyond yourself and your present situation, to put yourself in the position of others and empathize with their pain.

If you find you have caused others pain, you feel remorse. When you have hurt others, you do not feel guilty—that is, you do not decide that you are bad—but rather that perhaps you were mistaken in your actions. To conclude that you are bad after hurting someone indicates that you are probably confirming some previously held belief. A healthy person believes in his goodness even when he does something wrong or hurts someone. A person in Emotional Debt uses any evidence of his wrongdoing to ratify his self-hatred. That feeling of self-hatred in turn is a manifestation of Toxic Nostalgia.

The higher brain that ennobles you is also the very part that enslaves you and is responsible for the self-destructive role guilt plays in your emotional life. The higher brain allows you to put the present into perspective and reconcile the past, to see events as cause and effect, even when they are sometimes totally unrelated. For this reason it is possible for you to feel guilty about what happened to another person merely because you once had an angry thought about that person or wished something bad would happen to him.

The higher part of your brain allows you to imagine what might or could happen. Thus, if you continually hold your hurt and anger inside, you can feel guilty for merely thinking of causing pain or displeasure. Believing in the destructive power of angry thoughts can be debilitating. It leads you to inhibit your normal feeling responses, fearing they could be dangerous. Having something happen to someone you have such angry thoughts about confirms such a belief, even when you know it doesn't make sense.

While guilt serves no obvious purpose, it remains the most complicated of all feelings. Your imagination can lead you far astray when it comes to feeling guilty. It is possible to assume responsibility for events over which you have absolutely no influence or control, to feel guilty about them and by so doing to punish yourself for years.

Insofar as the higher mind is concerned, there may not be all that much difference between sacrificing yourself for a greater good and sacrificing yourself for no good at all.

People are constantly trying to make sense of their guilt. When someone dies, people frequently say they feel guilty about what they did or what they said or what they could have done or should have said. It is also characteristic of manipulative people to use another's potential for feeling guilty to control them. The parent who reminds his child that one day, when the parent is dead, the child will regret not having been nicer is a prime example.

The best way to live is to be open with your feelings and keep them up-to-date, speaking the truth and allowing other people both the joy and the disappointment of dealing with you as you are.

When you try to please people by inhibiting your true feelings, you always end up feeling guilty and pleasing no one.

HOW DOES GUILT WORK?

Guilt is anger turned inward.

Another way of saying this is that guilt is anger that has not been identified as the result of some specific hurt. If the anger were associated with a particular injury, it would make sense and would have been expressed with the hurt. Guilt is anger that could not be justified and therefore was not expressed.

The greatest guilt is caused by condemning yourself for being angry and inhibiting the natural expression of your hurt and anger. Thus, if you comply with a parent who doesn't allow you to express your feelings, you become a candidate for more guilt than if you had spoken up. If you had, you might have hurt your parent's feelings. That is the price you pay for being real. You might have been rejected for telling the truth, but if you had, the situation would have been placed in the correct perspective. Then again, if you spoke up your parent might have come to understand that you have feelings, too. However, if you didn't ever speak up, such a parent would come to believe that your feelings simply do not matter—the boundaries question again.

When you stay silent after being hurt, out of fear of injuring such a parent, you only injure yourself instead. The anger that should have been expressed along with your hurt is now turned inward. The very anger you held in to keep from being bad now turns against you and convinces you that you *are* bad. You feel worse precisely because you didn't express your feelings. If suppressing your hurt and anger was being a good child, then being a good child should have made you feel good, but it never does. Suppressing hurt only makes you resentful and bitter.

A guilt-producing parent inhibits his child from honestly expressing hurt and anger.

Naturally this same mechanism holds true not only in your relationship with your parents but with everyone else. It is merely that your pattern of holding in feelings originated in your relationship with your parents and so the greatest amount of hidden resentment you have to get over usually starts with overcoming the guilt of childhood.

Unlike anxiety, hurt, and anger, guilt is not felt physically. The heaviness of guilt's burden does not prompt you to act to protect yourself, but to worry about your role in the past. Mostly guilt can be reduced to a series of mental messages that persuade you that you are unlovable, a bad person, wrong, stupid, weak, unattractive, or a failure.

It is easy to get lost in these messages, to test them and debate them internally. This inner debate over the messages of guilt is what obsessing is all about.

The event that leads you to obsess over any one of these messages is usually only a symbol. The real problem is that you have for a long time been withholding hurt and anger and paving the way for guilt. For that reason the guilt message you respond with has more to do with your character type and the way you defend against expressing your hurt and anger than the event that triggered it. This will be clearer following the discussion of defenses and personality types.

SUBTITLES OF GUILT

People who are guilt-ridden are simply obsessed with trying to understand the messages that their guilt is continually broadcasting to them. No matter how good their lives are, guilt-ridden people only seem to hear the negative subtitles their mind provides:

> *You're not deserving.*
> *You're terrible for even thinking such a thing.*
> *See, it is your fault.*
> *Now look at what you've done.*
> *Your parents were right. You're an idiot.*
> *No one in his right mind would want someone like you.*
> *You're never going to make it.*
> *You never should've done this.*
> *You never should've said that.*

It is important to point out that these mental comments are continually being superimposed on your mistakes and failures. While they are usually spoken in your own voice, it is often with the inflection of a parent or some person who did not believe in you. However, just because these thoughts recur doesn't mean you have to pay attention to them. As a matter of fact most of us brush such comments aside all the time. Just because an old condemnation breaks through into your awareness doesn't mean you have to take it seriously. It's just a form of mental background noise, an old forgotten emotional pathway echoing the way you used to feel. Let go of it.

The ease with which you can admit that you doubt yourself and feel this way is an indication of how healthy you are. If you were perfectly well-balanced and emotionally healthy, you would still hear these guilt messages when you were suppressing anger. Don't make too much of the messages; believe in yourself, correct your mistakes, express your feelings, and get back on track.

You tend to take these messages to heart when you have stored too much anger. That's understandable, because when you're in Emotional Debt these comments seem uncomfortably close to the way you secretly see yourself. As your stored anger increases, so does the pressure to express it. To maintain that delicate balance, your anger is directed inward and managed by your mind, in a sense by turning up the volume of these messages, balancing the anger, and also making the messages more difficult to ignore. Indeed, when you are in deep Emotional Debt, these obsessional messages become the only reality you can focus on, and they seem to drown out the outside world.

DEPRESSION

THE ONSET OF DEPRESSION

Guilt drives you further back into your mind, where you pay less attention to the world. The first purpose of this retreat is self-protective, to become non-combatant and spare other people the danger of your anger, your badness. Unfortunately, when you retreat from the pain of reality, you also pull away from the joys that validate life and make your struggle seem meaningful. As your energy is turned inward, you give up your exercise programs, your hobbies, and your external attachments. Work suffers, productivity drops, and with it self-esteem. Others pull away. The world becomes monochromatic. The intrusive subtitles begin to sound more and more like realities.

SUBTITLES OF DEPRESSION

You're better off dead.
You shouldn't have been born.
No one likes you.
No one cares . . . ever.
The world is against you.
You'll never make it.
You're a helpless baby.
You're trapped and powerless.
You're weird.
You're not a real man or woman.
You've been a fool to believe you could be happy.

At a glance it becomes clear that these messages are absurd, childish, the kind of statements children taunt each other with when they are angry. They would be almost comical were it not for the fact that when you are depressed you lack the energy to put these negative thoughts aside or refute them. You may actually believe them to be true, and tragically, you may even act on them.

Depression is a state of lowered energy. Your energy has been diverted to contain your anger. With the limited energy that remains it is hard to be productive, to do the work that supports your self-esteem, to love yourself or others.

Although depression, like guilt, does not serve a positive function, it is felt in the body. You become constipated and lose weight. You are unable to sleep. When you do, you have troublesome dreams that escaping anger leaves in its wake. When you're awake you're troubled by dark thoughts that can become so gruesome they challenge your belief in your goodness.

In this state you can make a more trenchant and comprehensive case for putting yourself down than anyone else. You've been a party to all your own negative behavior and thoughts. At the slightest question of your worth, your mind readily provides the proof that you are bad and deserve to suffer. You betray yourself. Depression is always your doing.

Richard was a seventy-year-old grandfather who had suffered from episodes of depression following his retirement. He had spent his life working for his family, never doing anything for himself. Although he complained about working so hard, his job was his identity and strength. When he retired he felt lost and without purpose.

Richard grew up in a poor family and decided when he was just a boy that he would redeem himself by making money. He thought he was vindicating himself by overcoming his poverty, but the sad truth was that his parents were not only poor but emotionally impoverished. His mother and father cited their poverty as the reason they did not give him what he needed, even when his need was just to be held, reassured, and told that he would amount to something.

Richard continually struggled to contain his feelings of resentment toward his parents. Although he became a success over the years, he found himself holding back emotionally from his children and began to wonder if he were no better than his own parents. Since he identified so much with his work, Richard's self-esteem began to slip shortly after his retirement, and he began to obsess about his childhood deprivation. Each time his anger surfaced, he pushed it down again. When his daughter invited him to his grandson's fourth birthday, he agreed to attend but with great reluctance.

When Richard saw his grandson receiving loving attention, he felt a pang of jealousy and then felt ashamed for feeling that way. When the blindfolded grandson smashed the piñata and presents showered down all around him, Richard was suddenly struck with a fearful urge to kill his grandson. The idea terrified him. Unsure about whether he would act on his feelings, Richard sought to gain safety for his grandson by putting distance between them and retreated.

Deeply troubled, Richard left the party early. On the turnpike Richard found himself behind an older couple driving a very expensive foreign car. Richard pretended that he was under their benevolent protection, a kind of compensation for not being cared for by his parents.

The fantasy calmed him down. Richard imagined what his life would have been like if this couple had been his parents. Feeling insulated by the good life he envisioned, Richard permitted himself to compare it to the deprivation of his own childhood and examine his parents' withholding without making excuses for them. He could see why he'd felt so jealous of his grandson. It all made sense now. He wasn't evil, he'd just been cheated by ungiving parents.

When, after an hour, the older couple exited the turnpike, Richard took the event personally and felt abandoned. A flood of old anger swarmed over him. Struggling to keep his anger in place, he became disoriented, took his foot off the accelerator, and coasted to the side of the road. State troopers took him to a hospital. Fortunately, the events of the day had brought the pain of the past to the surface and for the first time he was able to discuss it openly, forgive his parents, and resolve his lifelong depression.

Unlocking the Power of the Feeling Cycle

The events that trigger emotions always have deep connections to other hidden feelings. The triggering event is not the cause of the problem but a clue to what lies hidden. What gives a particular trigger its power to download past emotions is best understood in terms of the Feeling Cycle.

The Feeling Cycle defines the causal relationship of the emotions. Hurt that is not coped with the moment it occurs is transformed into resentment. If that anger is blocked from expression, it is stored in Emotional Debt, which has a limited, though inexact capacity. When this capacity is exceeded, your stored emotions become susceptible to being triggered.

When old feelings are triggered as Toxic Nostalgia they are usually combined with other emotions and feel exaggerated. In addition, as your feelings flood past your disabled defenses, you experience some anxiety over losing control.

Your feelings always make sense when viewed in the context of the Feeling Cycle. They have a purpose and a cause. For this reason when trying to analyze your emotions, try to avoid phrases such as "for some unknown reason," or "a feeling out of nowhere." You may not always like what you discover when you begin to understand them, but they are your feelings and they reflect the way you live your life. If you understand your feelings, your life is easier to manage.

KNOW WHAT YOU FEEL

Name your feeling: anxiety, hurt, anger, guilt, or depression. Speculate on what loss could cause such a feeling and when it might have occurred. You don't need to be sure, just having a suspicion is a clue.

Do not despair because you think your feelings appear to reflect a person you can't relate to or aren't proud of. It is precisely because you are reluctant to accept such feelings that they become a problem.

If you don't acknowledge your hurt and anger, you can't understand yourself. Understanding why you hurt lies at the heart of self-knowledge.

If you don't know what hurts you, you don't know what matters to you.

If you do not understand your hurt, your passion is also a mystery.

Your feelings are messengers. They are not final verdicts. Your feelings may be exaggerated, distorted, displaced, confused, and overstated, but they are *your* feelings. Accept your feelings as a part of yourself. You don't need to like them. You just need to be on speaking terms with them.

Understanding your feelings is the beginning of enlightenment. Without being conversant with your emotions, you cannot know if others are treating you unfairly or if you are just projecting your bitterness onto them. You cannot tell if you are being truly generous or are merely overcompensating for your repressed anger by being too kind. If you conceal your hurt by being too giving or trying to please others, you set yourself up for further disappointment.

UNDERSTANDING OLD FEELINGS

Understanding old feelings is more difficult because you need to unravel your self-serving distortions before you can see them clearly.

To see old feelings clearly you must first be aware of your imperfections and shortcomings. It is in trying to conceal these flaws that you are most likely to be defensive. You distort the past when you try to avoid responsibility for the negative part you played.

To see the past clearly you have to be willing to accept everything that ever happened to you as a fact. You also need to take responsibility for how you responded. Sometimes you were brave and stood up for yourself. Other times you ran, acted petty, lied, or cheated. If you are the sort of person who seeks to be perfect, seeing the past clearly is especially difficult. You feel compelled to blame others and rationalize unflattering information that comes to light.

Before you look at your past it is helpful to affirm your goodness to yourself. If you discover negative feelings and vengeful desires, you need to assume that you probably had good reasons for feeling that way. Don't insist you were always innocent or that others were always wrong. If you are going to come to terms with your past, you have to take responsibility. Keep in mind that anyone's recollection of the past will be full of distortions. Try to examine your past as a good person seeking the truth, knowing that there is nothing you can discover that will alter the fact that you are good.

DEALING WITH PAST HURT

For each painful event you recall ask yourself:

> *How were you hurt?*
> *Why did it hurt so much?*
> *How did you react?*
> *Why did you react the way you did?*
> *How could you have acted differently?*
> *What prevented you?*
> *What part of the hurt were you responsible for?*
> *What lesson were you supposed to learn?*
> *Have you learned it?*
> *What responsibility did you avoid?*
> *Are you still avoiding it?*
> *Whom do you need to forgive?*

ACCEPTANCE

Your life becomes understandable when you accept what happened to you and take responsibility for how you responded. If you search your past looking only for villains, be assured that you will find them, but you will not find peace.

If you are looking for your worst enemy, here are some clues.

That person is with you all the time, can read your mind, knows your innermost secrets, how you feel about everything, and has absolute control of your life. You are your proper study, not the external world. No one else has the power to do to you what you have done to yourself. Your troubles are an inside job.

When you heal and are your best, you will find that absolutely everything feels better, wonderful in fact, but nothing has changed but you.

Accept yourself, your mistakes, your selfishness and greediness just as they are, without explanations. You need to acknowledge your penchant for cruelty, even if it is only toward yourself. You need to recognize your dishonesty and your wish to avoid taking responsibility for hurting others, even if you did so in righteous retaliation for being hurt—or more appropriately, *especially* if it was in righteous retaliation for being hurt. The damage you do when you feel entitled to retaliate far exceeds any you cause through negligence. Accept that you are only human.

It is fairly easy to become sidetracked with elegant reasoning and elaborate rationalizations, which of course have the simple goal of blaming everyone else and exonerating yourself. The Feeling Cycle is a guide to the interior workings of your heart and mind. Understanding it will show you the reason for your suffering, help you combat the tendency to make excuses, and give you the courage to let go of the past.

Toxic Nostalgia derives its power from your dishonesty. If you dealt honestly with the pain of the moment, you'd undermine the influence of the past.

Accept your role in your own misfortunes. The more you accept, the more you can change.

You can't fix others. Even if you could, it would change absolutely nothing. You may dispute that if you wish, but it is true.

You are your own piece of work, and that should be enough to occupy you fully in this lifetime.

THE ARCHITECTURE OF LOSS

*E*VERYONE STRUGGLES TO LEARN his life lessons. You learn from your mistakes if you look at them honestly. You learn practically nothing from your successes.

Just because your life lessons are learned from pain does not mean that you need to suffer. Suffering is what happens when the natural therapeutic process fails. The purpose of this process is to allow you to get through your pain with as little damage to your self-esteem and energy resources as possible. People who suffer have postponed accepting the truth. They always want life to be different from what it is. In their desire to shield themselves from pain they compound their difficulties and prolong their distress. Suffering is the result of the mourning process gone awry.

The mourning process defines the steps from denial to acceptance in coping with a loss. Anyone who has lived through painful times knows that these steps are not predictable. While they can be described, they do not repeat exactly, and so each person's journey through mourning varies. Indeed, a person may mourn one loss with ease and inexplicably be plagued by another that just doesn't relent.

To understand a loss, you must know what you have lost, what it meant to you and why. The dynamics involved in some important losses, and the issues that must be dealt with, are as follows.

THE THREE TYPES OF LOSSES

The loss of love: this includes the loss of a loved one or the protection he afforded you, or the loss of yourself by physical injury, disfigurement, or death. Any event that can symbolically indicate you are not lovable, such as rejection or abandonment, is also treated as a loss of love.

The loss of control: this includes the loss of financial or political power or position, or anything that gives you influence over others. Underlying this loss is the fear of rejection. Losses of control make you more vulnerable to losses of love.

The loss of esteem: this includes failure, being embarrassed, losing face, and being seen as flawed. Also in this category is the loss of youth and beauty and with it your sexual allure. Anything that exposes your declining talents, or any slip in prowess that might cause others to see you as a has-been, can lead to loss of self-esteem.

The loss of physical and mental strength from aging or illness can be seen as either a loss of self, a loss of control, or a loss of esteem, depending on the person.

THE NATURE OF LOSS

Losses are measured by what they mean to you, that is, by the pain they cause you. So in a sense, no one can ever really know your grief. Even when shared, your loss must be endured alone, which is exactly why losses are so painful.

You first learn to cope with losses in childhood. As a child with little sense of personal history you measured yourself by the situation you found yourself in. A day seemed like an eternity. Your life could be reduced to catastrophe by a cruel comment. It is easy to forget how traumatized you were by the rejection of friends or how painful it was to endure a teacher who disliked you. If your parents told you that your situation wasn't the end of the world and that someday you'd see it in a different light, this did little to make you feel better.

It is typical for a severe loss, such as rejection or abandonment, to reawaken feelings of helplessness and overwhelm you, emotionally reducing you to a child again. When this happens, other people tend to become impatient. A little sympathy and kindness can make all the difference in how you feel.

In the early stage of a terrible loss, such as the death of a close relative, it is typical for others to be there for you. While you are grateful for their help in attending to gloomy details, most of the time you are in shock. Your denial temporarily shields you from the brunt of your pain. You live in partial disbelief.

Later, when you are more likely to be alone, the impact of the loss becomes clearer to you. Other people may check in on you from time to time, but by then your denial has worn thin. You may tell friends that you're doing fine because you want to be strong and not frighten them away. As the reality of your situation descends on you, sharp pangs of emptiness tear at your heart.

Trying to rush through the stages of mourning to get the pain behind you only leaves unfinished business that will return to haunt you. Coping and accepting take a long time. No one can give you a definite timetable indicating when the pain will end. You always think your grief is taking too long, because pain slows your perception of time.

An important guideline to remember is that the more open you are, the more quickly and completely you heal. However, being open to a terrible loss is not easy. Bonding to others makes you human. Accepting when those bonds are severed initiates healing and makes you stronger. The steps between these two points can be rugged going indeed. If you do not cope with a loss, it runs your emotional life, overriding your joy and aggravating your sorrow. When you do not mourn completely, you end up feeling cheated in everything you do.

Like everyone else, you are susceptible to all three kinds of losses. However, each character type is especially susceptible to a particular type of loss, almost like an allergic reaction. In addition, each kind of loss produces a typical response in everyone.

While a dependent person is especially sensitive to the loss of a loved one and may feel helpless, such a loss also awakens an independent person's dependent longings. For an independent person, the loss of a loved one raises questions of his lovability and makes him doubt he can survive on his own, but it doesn't keep him from feeling like himself or loving again. A dependent person can seem to mourn forever. He needs another person to be complete, and so sees such a loss as a loss of self.

By the same token, the loss of power or money is taken hardest by a controlling person, who may become paralyzed, feel powerless and out of control. A severe financial setback can hurt anyone by limiting his capacity to be free to forge his own destiny, but it does not leave a permanent scar on self-esteem the way it does to a controlling person, who bitterly blames others for his loss and obsesses over getting his power back. The controlling person measures his worth by his power and feels vulnerable to rejection without it.

Finally, while almost everyone is intimidated by failure and may wish to run and hide, competitive people are terrified of failure and tend to be crushed when their dream of success proves to be a nightmare of embarrassment. The competitive person becomes driven to find some success at any cost to prove he is a winner. Life loses its meaning for him when he fails.

The three kinds of losses have a way of reducing perspective to that stage of development where the particular issue was most important. Thus, a loss of love makes you feel like a helpless baby in the dependent period. The loss of power makes you feel like a child in the controlling stage, trying to assert himself. A failure of power makes you doubt your worth, like a crestfallen student who has failed his qualifying exam and believes he has no future.

LOSSES OF LOVE

TERRIBLE LOSSES

No matter how catastrophic your loss is, you still have to feel your hurt and anger to release them.

The mourning process cleanses the soul.

When you deeply mourn a present loss, it is typical that older, unmourned losses seem to reopen and you grieve anew. The most common losses to come forward are the severe injuries of childhood that occurred when you were too young to cope with them fully. These stored losses predispose you to mourn too severely in later years. This explains why, following the loss of a loved one, you may be pushed to the edge of depression as the earlier loss is awakened and compounds your grief.

This also explains why present losses seem not only painful but disappointing. You get the feeling that something bad has happened *again,* the feeling of the old loss intruding. You not only feel hurt, but hopeless.

Although it may sound self-contradictory, it sometimes takes a large loss to plunge you into mourning so you can set your life straight. While a loss can be a terrible event, life changing and disruptive, it is never the end. Sometimes it heralds a new beginning by helping to resolve the past.

SELF-LOSS

To lose yourself does not mean that you die, but that you find yourself transformed by disease, accident, addiction, or circumstance into a person you cannot relate to. The kinds of losses included here are the onset of deafness, blindness, or other disability, and the loss of freedom by imprisonment or by falling under the control of another person or cult. A loss that symbolizes the central issue of your character type can also make you feel as if you have lost yourself; for example, the dependent person abandoned, the controlling person bankrupt, and the competitive person in disgrace.

Suddenly you no longer feel like yourself. What seemed normal just a few weeks ago now seems impossibly out of reach. Whether you are suffering from paralysis, chronic fatigue syndrome, or another disability, you no longer seem to be the self you once were.

Mourning the loss of your former self and coming to accept the self that survives can be the most important event in your life. Like coping with all losses, the loss of self ultimately involves embarking on an inner journey and finding an identity based on spiritual reality, not on external trappings. In a very real sense you finally become what you are, what you have always been.

If you can make this transition to your higher self, you can learn to accept your limitations and turn your eye to explore a rich inner landscape. When you do, you discover everything that had been missing in your life before. It was not more love, money, or fame that you really needed, but the acceptance of yourself as you are.

There is more meaning in a moment of simply being yourself than in a lifetime searching outside for answers only your heart can provide. It is sad that it so often takes a tragedy or great misfortune to learn this lesson.

Your first task is to accept yourself just as you are in this very moment.

WHEN A CHILD DIES

You never really get over the loss of a child. The child's birthday each year is always a source of diminishment. You wonder what the child would have been like at this age, what he would have become. Although he remains a child forever, in your mind's eye you somehow age him and place him in the present, imagining how splendidly he would have flourished, only to find another reason to grieve. So many hopes, so many loving expectations return. When another child acts difficult, you ask why did this one die and that one live and feel guilty for thinking so. You chastise yourself with might-have-beens.

In time the sharp edge of pain gets softer, but it never totally goes away. You can always find ways to blame yourself for the death of a child. Being a parent places you in a unique position to do so. It is hard enough for some parents not to feel responsible for every cold their child contracts. The death of a child can completely twist your logic and make you feel responsible for everything.

Because there is nothing you wouldn't do to make it better for your child, it's hard not to view a child's death as a personal failing. When a father standing in front of the hospital bed of his son who was stricken with meningitis cried, "I'm praying to exchange places with him," he spoke for all parents.

You have to learn to live with the loss of a child. Bear in mind that living a life of sorrow is not a fitting memory to a child's life, or for that matter anyone else's. The purpose of mourning is to be able to remember the good and be grateful for it.

Still, it is hard to let go. Those who have not been in your place can never really understand.

WHEN A CHILD REJECTS YOU

When a child rejects you, it is also a kind of death. Except since the separation is intentional, the anger at your child and the hurt you suffer over his ingratitude vacillate with your anxiety. You wonder whether your child had a good case for pushing you away. The uncertainty creates inner turmoil. You want to make amends, but you're inhibited because you don't want to make things worse.

When their self-esteem is weak, children are most vulnerable to being captured by powerful forces and led away. Sometimes they become involved with bad company, peers bent on indolence and negativity. Sometimes they get lost in drugs. Sometimes they become dependent on a controlling person who forbids contact with the family and helps engineer the rebellion the child wanted to stage years ago but could not find the courage to mount.

The child who becomes trapped in such a controlling relationship and uses it to push you away probably felt controlled and powerless when he was living at home. He has gone from one childish relationship to another. When the child finally wishes to make peace he may find that rejecting you has become a symbol of loyalty to his mate and now, fearing abandonment, he lacks the courage to break the pattern.

The emotional damage you suffer from the rejection of an adult child can be unbearable. This is especially true when there are grandchildren involved. At some point your child either decides to make peace or becomes caught in his own twisted logic. In order to continue banishing you he is obligated to misinterpret your attempts to reconcile as malicious and his desires to make peace as weakness.

In some ways living with such a situation is almost worse than losing a child. To live in hope when an angry child is rejecting you or taunting you with unrealistic demands, insisting you prove you really care or admit to crimes you did not commit, is a kind of hell. You are trying to mourn a loss that will not stop wounding you. Each time you think of your child you begin mourning anew.

LOSS OF A PARTNER

The loss of a beloved spouse either by death or rejection can be devastating. The people who survive this loss best were happy, open, and emotionally up-to-date with each other. Even so, close relationships are not replaceable.

The bond created by two people who love each other, who know each other's ways, can seem to shape the world. Indeed, although the couple who share everything may not live for each other, when that joy of sharing is taken away, they come to find the world flatter, less colorful. The dimension that their love gave deepened the meaning of simple things, making just being together special.

In the other's absence such love provided an air of expectation where everything the one perceived was held in excited anticipation of being shared with the other. Now the world that was once a place of surprises to reveal to the other seems to mock the survivor. The very love that provided the reason for living, when taken away, seems to challenge the meaning of life itself.

On the other hand there is little sense of closure when death ends an unhappy relationship. The more unhappy a relationship, the more persistent and pernicious the grief when a partner is lost. All the problems that previously made the relationship unhappy resurface to make the end more troublesome. Even when the end can be predicted there seems to be too much animosity to overcome in the limited time left. Reaching an understanding that would make a difference seems a distant hope indeed. There are exceptions of course, when in the face of the inevitable a couple is able to relinquish old quarrels and find an understanding at last.

More typically the survivor's quenchless anger makes him feel bitter and cheated at his unhappy union, deeming it a sham, never worth the struggle. The surviving partners often become preoccupied and sullen, dismayed by their own negativity. While not often spoken out loud, the complaint, "I should've left him long ago," is the sort of guilt-producing obsession that torments them. It alternates with self-reproach over remembered negative acts and comments. It is no wonder such people wallow in remorse.

WHEN YOUR LOVER FORSAKES YOU

Death, though cruel, is understandable. Its logic is perfect. To be abandoned by a lover is to have your heart broken. The person you trusted most, most betrayed you. The love you counted upon has proven false. The strength you drew from being together—was it false, too, a figment of your imagination?

Were you crazy to have believed the way you did? Were you so blind, so weak, so stupid, so willing to be taken for all you were worth? What was the matter with you, to give so much away so unflinchingly? Why couldn't you see it coming? Were you that needy, that desperate, that lonely?

How do you repair a broken heart when it was you that offered it up without so much as a "Please be careful"? How do you apologize for not being more loving to yourself? How do you forgive when you still feel you would take him or her back? How do you stop thinking about the other person?

You know what was wrong. You told yourself it was wrong. If it was so wrong, what was it about you that made it feel so right? How do you keep from going mad?

Dealing with rejection of a love gone sour requires confronting the unreality you embraced and the deep purchase on your being you overgenerously granted it.

Another person may have betrayed and used you, but only to the extent you permitted. This is the hardest lesson of love to learn. Blind hope and trust are the dogma of scorned lovers. If you must blame something, blame your unwillingness to see or hear.

Although it seems like a contradiction when you are betrayed, it is yourself you must ultimately forgive.

THE LOSS OF A PARENT

A parent taken in the natural course of events is a sad event, but not impossible to grieve. What causes the most pain is when a parent dies before you have had a chance to know each other or to resolve differences between you. It is hard to come to terms with the death of a parent when there are important questions still burning within you.

It is the most natural of all feelings to want your parents to accept and love you, to believe in you and to see what you have accomplished. You want them to know that you possess an identity in your own right besides merely being their child.

If you achieve these simple goals, you are a lucky person indeed. Most people spend years trying to find their direction. Often when you finally do, your parent doesn't understand. Parents can be old-fashioned, shamed by their children's divorce, unwilling to admit their abusiveness or addiction or their mistakes. It can become complicated when you try to do what is best for you and please your parents at the same time. You can never please an unhappy parent. You can become lost if you try.

When you are a child your emotional comfort depends on getting another person to see your view and accept your hurt as real. You need to both express your pain and have others accept it in order to let go. When you are growing up there is no one more important to your self-esteem than your parents. You want them to believe in you, to hear and accept your feelings.

Naturally your goal is to be responsible for your own self-esteem and to outgrow your need to please others, but many people become adults with one emotional foot still rooted in the unresolved yearnings of childhood. As adults they hunger for a parent to mellow and rescind their emotional banishment, to understand them and take them in. For your parent to die before having a chance to see you for what you are leaves an empty space in your being.

Children smarting under their parents' emotional control are tantalized by the hollow promise of conditional love. Although your parent may have explained that he only wanted to encourage you to do your best when he chided, "Four A's and a B; why the B?" the real message you got was that you weren't acceptable as you were.

The frustration you feel from conditional loves eats at your spirit. Anger replaces your love for your parent. Doubt rings deep in your soul. Why wasn't your best good enough? The question begs for an answer, a day of accounting.

When a parent dies before that time or withdraws or grows dim with the weight of years, the loss in some way feels retroactive. All those years you had projected your hope of being accepted into the future, expecting that one day, if you could somehow be perfect, you would finally be loved. Now when you realize that day will never come, you look back and feel as if your parent never really loved or cared about you.

While mourning a parent is probably the only grief you are always preparing for, it is rarely free of mixed feelings when it happens. Children always worry about their parents "going away." Should you lose a parent in childhood it is typical to find that your schoolmates tease or deride you rather than give you sympathy, because the thought of losing their parents is so threatening that your misfortune brings the possibility of their own loss to mind and they react with anger.

Parents can also bridle children by tapping into their fear of their parents' dying. This insecurity is compounded by the guilt children suffer when they are not allowed to express their feelings. Thwarted anger makes a child feel responsible for others' misfortune and leads him to blame himself for any death or separation. With all the feelings that become pent up in childhood, it's a wonder anyone can deal with the loss of a parent at all.

When your parents grow older, disquieting thoughts intrude: Could this be the last birthday? Is this the last phone call? The last Christmas? You wonder, Should I speak my mind? Should I let it go? Was it really all that important? Are they too old to talk to? All these considerations cause you to hold back in silence. Sadly, opportune moments often pass and no true reconciliation takes place. Because the surface is placid everyone thinks peace has been made, but unfinished business still abides within you. You are a rare person if you have made your peace with your parents. Be grateful if you have.

It is common to wish your parents could be here to witness your success, take pride in your accomplishments, see a grandchild, visit your new house, admire your rise to power or your triumph over adversity. The wish to "show them" lives deep within all of us. There is some part of your victory you want them to share. In the end nothing seems to matter as much as the simple words, "Good job," or "You were a good son," or "You were a good daughter."

Unfortunately for many people the death of a parent only confirms how difficult the parent was to please and what a mistake it was to allow their happiness to depend on hearing words of praise that were never destined to be spoken.

As far as you and your parents are concerned, the simple truth, spoken in quiet tones and heard, is exquisite balm to the soul. If you have not been the recipient of such generosity, at least learn the lesson. The most generous gift you can give to those you love is to allow them to be emotionally open with you.

You mourn your parent until you forgive both your parent and yourself.

THE LOSS OF A FRIEND

Friends share the same vulnerability. Therefore, the loss of a friend feels like a loss of yourself, as well as the loss of the person whose understanding supported your point of view. When you lose a friend you sometimes lose the belief that anyone understands you. No wonder you feel lost.

A friendship is an island of acceptance, a place to be validated, to get perspective on your courage, check your perceptions and motives. A friendship allows you to unburden without burdening the other. You try out rash ideas just to get them off your chest. You think out loud without penalty.

Because friendship provides such a unique way of understanding yourself, its loss feels like a loss of familiarity with yourself. Friendships make introspection easier, deeper, safer.

Special friends often take the place of parents who never had the time or interest to get to know you. Special friends bring out your specialness in their presence. You are your best with such friends because you are able to be your worst with them without prejudicing them against you. They already know you for your best. The death of a special friend feels like the loss of the world.

When a friend rejects you, it causes you to reevaluate the way you see yourself. You struggle to rationalize the loss. You go through the motions of trying to make up, and should these attempts fail, you rationalize and make excuses for your friend's rejection. You pretend not to care, but the damage hurts deeply.

LOSSES OF CONTROL

No one likes to lose money, a home, a business, a job, or their nest egg, but we live in unpredictable and risky times. Money is not as stable as it once was. Companies are bought and sold like commodities. Workers, from the secretarial pool to the managers, the mail room clerks to the designers, are all on someone's list of items to be trimmed to save costs. It is hard to know if the industry you work in will be shifted to another country where labor is cheaper or if the balance of payments will erode the value of the currency and ruin the market that merchandises your company's product.

Most people feel powerless in this economic picture but still try to achieve financial freedom. In an unstable world, it is easy to go into debt, and while only a few years ago it was unthinkable, it is possible for the value of your home to drop and to find yourself owing more on your property than it is worth, trapped in the very dream you hoped would give you independence.

We live in an economy where space-age engineers are serving hamburgers, where top managers are selling detergents door-to-door, where small businessmen who prided themselves on offering personal service and excellence are driven out of business in midlife and don't know where to turn.

While the loss of employment or fortune is important to everyone, it can be totally paralyzing to the person who relies on his power to control others. Some people have little personal strength and few resources for giving or being emotionally supportive. They dread financial diminishment because they know that others would ignore them if they lost that power.

The insecure, controlling person who accumulates money to shore up his limited emotional wealth is terrified by business reversals. Without financial strength he knows he is at risk of losing the loyalty of the people he needs.

It is the threat of such rejection that leads these people to make bad deals, to sacrifice long-range thinking just to hold on to their power base, regardless of how artificial, flimsy, or illegal it all becomes.

When a controlling person suffers a devastating business loss, he often becomes compulsive and rigid. Instead of seeking new ways to solve his problems, he tries to show that he was taken advantage of or cheated. Trying to prove he was right, he compulsively stays the course and throws good money after bad. One thing is clear: he believes that whatever went wrong is someone else's fault. He can prove it.

This rigid attitude has always been part of the controlling person's personality. When he has financial success, others tolerate him. He surrounds himself with dependent people who need him and is able to get away with his excuses and blaming. Those dependent people don't dare raise their voices. But then again they have no reason to because he is caring for their needs.

However, when the controlling person's fortunes change, those same silent people begin to protest. Dependent people need to be provided for. If the person who is charged with that duty is unable to do so, dependent people become anxious and begin to look for new suppliers. Once a dependent person doubts he's being taken care of, he becomes frightened and his loyalty cannot be counted upon.

Now the controlling person feels attacked from both sides, by the business world and by the very people around him. He accuses them of being ungrateful, both criticizing them and begging them to remain loyal. His energy and attention are diverted from coping with his terrible financial loss. He is under unimaginable stress.

It is at such a point that the controlling person becomes overwhelmed, suspicious, critical, self-righteous, vindictive, and frankly paranoid. He finds it difficult to take responsibility for anything. When he does begin to see his role in his failure, he often becomes depressed. He feels isolated. His loneliness is unbearable. He can't stand to lose, to be without power, to be vulnerable.

When you suffer a severe business loss, the correct course is to take an honest inventory of your assets and liabilities, to evaluate the current source of damage and limit further exposure. You control your expenses while you examine your options and make a plan based on a worst-case outcome. If your plan makes sense you make a gallant effort to salvage the enterprise. If it does not you consider selling your assets and you save what can be saved. There is no room for anything else. To expect a best-case scenario to replace a worst-case reality is wishful thinking.

When you are preoccupied with proving you were right or blaming opponents or maintaining control over others you squander your energy. Obsession replaces logical thinking and even worse failure results.

LOSSES OF ESTEEM

The most common response to a loss of reputation is embarrassment. Your failure has revealed you to be less than what you pretended to be, or hoped you were, or convinced others you were. Competitive people are looking to please the crowd, and therefore they fear failure the most.

There is nothing wrong with seeking success. Healthy people put their reputations on the line all the time trying to prove themselves by their accomplishments. To some extent everyone sees their worth reflected in their performance. While much of the description that follows pertains to the competitive person, it also applies to people who are highly focused on success.

The competitive person tends to live a life with too many risks. When he wins it is a triumph and he is king, an absolute tyrant of self-aggrandizement. When the outcome is in doubt, his life is filled with arresting and diversionary dramas. Should he fail, all is chaos.

To cope with these uncertain extremes, the competitive person tries to brush aside his performance failures, claiming that he really didn't try his best and therefore should not be measured by his current results. For this reason the competitive person often abandons a risk at the first sign something is not going the way he wants. He wants to cut his losses as quickly as he can and preserve his fragile image.

While his dream is to prove that he is better than others, his doubts motivate him to avoid humiliation and conceal his limitations. His fickle attitude interferes with his ability to deal with loss. If nothing really matters, then there is nothing to mourn when it is gone. Worse, if his failure is not real, it has no lesson to teach him.

The competitive person's success goes right to his head. Lofty, vindicating success takes him away from reality. He believes his press clippings, forgetting entirely that he planted them. Believing he is perfect and unassailable, he grabs all the credit and walks all over the little people. He calls his weaknesses eccentricities that do not need to be taken seriously. He continually sets the scene for his downfall.

In his enraptured self-adoration he fails to pay attention to the day-to-day problems of maintaining his success, and it begins to slip away from him. The flatterers and entourage leave the sinking ship. He feels betrayed and cannot understand why, after all he gave, he has been so forsaken. He carries on, reading yesterday's reviews to anyone who will listen.

Should his success continue, he loses humility. His need to be seen as the best, the driving force, the creative spark understandably alienates others. He doesn't feel supported so even trivial setbacks throw him into a state of childish insecurity. Because he is a user he finds himself surrounded by users. Where talent and brilliance once ruled, cynicism and sarcasm now reign. He feels out of touch with himself and the very talent that brought him to this place.

The competitive person needs to develop a sense of self, independent of what he does or accomplishes. The problem is that his need to be different and better keeps him from simply being himself. He secretly yearns to get lost in the crowd, but he can't stand the anonymity.

The competitive person often gets caught up in what seems like a repetition of losses, torrid love affairs that burn out and crash, promising but shaky careers and performances that attract a lot of attention in the buildup but are grossly flawed. He continually appears to be trying to snatch victory from the grasp of failure. He lives in the hope that the next success, the big sale, the big hit will redeem him, set him above others, define his worth once and for all.

Of course if the next success can make you, it can also break you: the competitive person's dilemma. When your self-esteem depends on externals you are easily thrown off-balance.

Whether or not you are competitive, when you suffer a failure of self-esteem, your first instinct is to try to make good rather than to mourn the loss properly and learn the lesson it is trying to teach.

Learning to accept the loss as real and allow it to point out your weaknesses, no matter how embarrassing they might seem, is the best way to deal with a loss of esteem. It's a time for reflection.

Perhaps your goals were unrealistic.

Perhaps you did not prepare enough.

Perhaps you overestimated your ability or underestimated the struggle.

Perhaps you were afraid of being measured. You wanted to be great. Being good wasn't enough. When you started to struggle and victory seemed unclear, you lost faith and with it energy, will, and passion. You quit to protect your fragile self-worth.

Accept the loss for what it is—just a loss. It is not proof that you are a failure, just that under certain circumstances you failed. Know those circumstances. Accept your role in them and take responsibility for what you contributed to the situation. Did you believe too much in yourself and prepare too little? Were you so enamored of success that you didn't pay attention to the details?

Learn your lesson and try again. No one succeeds the first time except by luck. If the thing you want is really worthwhile, it is not easy to reach. If it is too easy, it may not be worthy of you.

Accept the struggle. Enjoy it. Be grateful for the opportunity to pursue your dream. Don't be afraid of work.

Whatever loss you suffer, no matter how complicated the issues involved, understanding what has bound you to the object you have lost is the first step in loosening your emotional ties to it. Letting go and becoming free to live in the present is the next step and the work of the mourning process.

THE MOURNING PROCESS

$\mathcal{T}$HE MOURNING PROCESS AND the natural healing process are essentially the same. The losses that initiate the mourning process are almost always real and powerful, such as the loss of a loved one. Since the mourning process is usually deep and prolonged, the steps you pass through are distinct and often pronounced.

While the natural healing process is the mechanism at work at the heart of the mourning process, it also deals with lesser, sometimes imperceptible injuries such as symbolic losses, the pain of failed expectations, false hopes, and wishful thinking, and personal disappointments that lead to a drop in self-esteem.

Both processes employ the emotional dynamics of the Feeling Cycle in which healing requires releasing your defenses and facing and resolving your hurt and anger through acceptance and forgiveness.

The mourning process is really the natural healing process, slowed down, writ large, its steps prominently displayed.

DEFENSES AND MOURNING

The defenses that protect you from pain also keep pain from being resolved and cause you to suffer more. If defenses remain in place, they create an emotional detour that directs you away from healing.

It is the nature of defenses to protect you by blurring reality. This explains why it is difficult to be sure what really happened when you look back at your losses and why your best recollection of pain will always be a distortion.

Trying to remember distant painful events is like trying to recall an old dream. As you retrieve fragments of your experience, you create a story line to hold the facts together.

Imagine the severe traumas you have suffered. Sometimes you faced the abuse, sometimes you looked away or put your hands over your ears or eyes, trying to shut out the pain. You only allowed yourself to experience or remember part of the hurtful event. Sometimes what you imagined when you were looking away was worse than what was actually going on.

Thus when you try to make sense of a past event and resolve your hurt, what you are able to recall may have little to do with what actually happened. To make up for these lapses some people create villains both to explain their hurt and to provide a target for their anger. While the fact that people suffer unspeakable violations in childhood is indisputable, recollecting actual trauma is difficult and unreliable since the very act of organizing the memory tends to distort the memory itself.

While your defensive pattern can never be changed and the past may be forever distorted, you can learn to deal with the present more truthfully so that your ability to mourn isn't limited by your defenses. Even if you were totally honest, your particular defensive style would still distort hurt and complicate mourning.

The mourning process continually makes you face your hurt directly, and gives you new chances to heal.

Try to be aware of your hurts, even the small ones. If you can mourn completely, your passion for life is undiminished. Understanding the stages of mourning will show you the way to do this.

SIMILARITIES IN MOURNING

You measure the depth of a loss by how long it takes you to get over it. Whether you are mourning the loss of a beloved or the failure of your home team to win the championship, you go through the same mourning process.

You are in shock when you hear your loved one died.

You can't believe your team lost.

You blame the surgeon.

You blame the referee or the person who committed the error.

You console yourself that the other person is no longer suffering.

You accept defeat and proclaim, "Wait till next year."

You mourn your loved one for months or years. The longer you mourn, the more distinct the stages of grief seem. A sports fan passes through all these stages in an afternoon, and if he expected his team to lose to superior forces, his resignation may take him directly to acceptance without going through any other stages.

What may be a minor loss to one person can be experienced as devastation by another. A severe financial setback can have as much impact on a controlling person as the loss of a spouse on a dependent person. A competitive person may suffer for years in shame over a failure that another person might easily shrug off.

Dependent people tend to see all losses in terms of abandonment and rejection, and as proving they are unlovable.

Controlling people tend to take all losses as proof they are powerless.

Competitive people tend to see all losses as proving they are failures.

THE STAGES OF MOURNING

There are three general stages of mourning: injury, coping, and acceptance. Although the three basic defenses can be seen throughout the mourning process, one defense usually predominates in each stage. In fact the stage of mourning is defined by what defense you use to overcome your pain.

The stage of injury is dominated by denial.

The coping phase utilizes the rationalizing defenses of excuses and blaming.

The acceptance phase involves pretense.

The mourning process recapitulates emotional development. It starts with a regression to the earliest defense patterns and gradually, as healing takes place, it employs more mature defensive adaptations.

DENIAL

THE MOMENT OF INJURY

This is the stage of mourning you most dread, the moment of horror when you learn that someone you care about has died or is dying. This moment has the greatest impact of all. The death of hope animates your fantasy with terror. The prospect of such a loss arrests the attention of the entire human race. The mother who sits up late waiting for her child to come home, the child with a hospitalized parent, the friend awaiting a late traveler are all filled with the same dread. Milton's words, "They also serve who only stand and wait," reflect the anxiety of all loved ones whose lives are held in abeyance by anticipating loss and who are hoping against hope. In your mind's eye you have suffered such a loss a hundred times as you imagined the worst.

Sensing how concerned the general public is with loss, displaying tragedies, injury, and devastation has become a media obsession. Unflinchingly the reporter prods the husband to tell how he felt when he found his wife shot by an intruder, how the child felt when the tornado carried her home away, how the farmer feels about his flooded fields. Reporters ask, "How does it feel to be a survivor and lose everything that mattered to you?" This reflects the question you continually asks yourself: "How would I survive if this happened to me?" Like everyone else, you live but a telephone call from total disaster.

When life is kind to you, the injury phase of mourning begins before the loss actually takes place, allowing you to anticipate the loss of a loved one and make your peace with him. Friends and relatives are invited to say their good-byes. Attaining understanding and forgiveness reduces those excessive displays of mourning that are fostered by unresolved guilt. Business and legal affairs can be placed in order so that clarity can replace guesswork.

Unfortunately, tragedy often takes you by surprise, draining you, numbing you. When someone you love is taken away unexpectedly, you simply can't believe it. There were so many things you wanted to say. There was so much remaining to be done. There was such unmet potential, such truncation, such loss. It all feels so unfair, so cruel.

THE ROLE OF DENIAL

The injury stage begins with complete denial.

On hearing of a terrible loss or fatal illness you cry out the universal response: "No!" A hollow forms inside your chest. You feel life draining from you.

"Tell me you're kidding," you beg and then ask, "What happened?" desperately hoping to find a mistake in the report that will allow you to disprove it.

Your denial immediately begins to weaken. You gather the terrible information; how the driver of the car didn't see your friend crossing, how your dad felt tired and lay down and didn't get up, how the paramedics got there too late, how hopelessly advanced the cancer was.

How sad. How inexpressibly sad.

Whether the loss is a spouse telling you that he is filing for divorce, a lover confessing he no longer loves you, the boss informing you that after twenty years he's letting you go, or the news that you failed the entrance examination, you are so devastated you can't believe this is actually happening.

You find yourself numb, in shock. This is the state when denial is operating at full force. Nothing can come in. Nothing can go out. You can't believe. You can only plead that what you heard is not so. At this moment you are in a place of great emotional instability. The pain of the truth begins to intrude. It is too harsh to accept. You try to make sense of what you've heard, to see if there is another way around the horrible logic that leads to loss.

Your mind takes you to the far reaches of reason. You engage in wishful thinking. Maybe there was a mistake in identity. Maybe he really isn't dead. Maybe the exam papers were switched. Maybe your lover was just testing you. Maybe your boss will see his mistake and call and apologize, even give you a raise.

Farfetched and pathetic as these mental images are, they are spawned by desperation and denial. Your mind goes to any extreme to write a different ending to the tragedy in which you feel trapped. The unacceptable heartbreak of loss bestows a kind of irrationality on you. Capricious denial's fleeting balm makes you take leave of your senses. You never really understand the phrase "crazy with grief" until you find yourself in the same position.

When you are rejected you think of doing something drastic, hurling yourself at the other person, offering to reform, even to stop being yourself. To be alone and unloved, rejected by the person you most need, is to be a self you cannot accept. The persistence of former lovers, checking and stalking, leaving endless communications, is also borne out of the refusal to accept their loss.

Even if you are a well-adjusted person who has been fortunate enough to be able to make peace with the other person before he died, there are moments during the initial phase of grief when denial weighs heavily upon you, when life doesn't feel real, when it all seems like a dream. You still hope someone will wake you or change the channel.

Your reasoning tells you it is hopeless.

Your heart bids you not to give up.

RELINQUISHING DENIAL

After a while the evidence starts to mount. Your denial begins to lift. You realize that what is lost is gone, and there is nothing you can do about it.

The hurt descends on you, cutting a wide swath to your very soul, depleting you of energy and will. You are running on automatic just to keep moving. If you stop what you're doing for just a moment, you fear you may never get started again. Suddenly nothing seems secure.

At this stage dependent people become paralyzed with their abandonment, worrying about what is going to happen to them, how they will survive without the other. They obsess about their helplessness. They can't stop hurting because they believe they've lost the part of themselves they need to be complete.

Because controlling people dread feeling vulnerable, after a loss they try to act strong to prove they have not been damaged. Taking charge of the dreary details no one else has the stomach for makes them feel better. In a sense they're accustomed to isolating their feelings from the events that caused them and operating on automatic. Although they try to appear strong, they're really just on the edge of displaying their pain, which explains why they can become unnerved by other's tears or furious when even a tiny detail of their plans goes wrong. Because their grief is bound up in doing something, they sense that when there is nothing left for them to do they'll have to face their hurt. Understandably, because they make themselves too busy to cry, they can get stuck in this phase of doing for others and postpone mourning for years.

Competitive people tend to be a little too quick to see the bright side of a loss, immediately offering the interpretation, "Well, at least he isn't suffering anymore." It's common to say something positive at such times in order to take away the sting of a loss. However, if you focus on the positive exclusively, you're just pretending that there is nothing to be sad about.

In other words, saying, "He's gone through his transition and is in God's hands now," may be comforting, but as an early response to a loss it's just another defense to console yourself. Your pretense has to fade for your grief to begin. Typical of the natural healing process and mourning, you have to accept the truth of the hurt to heal.

If you don't cry, you don't mourn.

RITUALS

All religions and cultures have funeral rituals, the purpose of which is to initiate giving up denial. You have to live in the here and now to be productive and happy. When you are caught in denial, you are partially blinded and vulnerable to being manipulated.

While theologians may argue with this point, as far as the general public is concerned, the power of religion is derived not so much from the belief in God, but from the fear of death. The belief in God is used to reduce the fear of death, allowing people to give up their denial and begin to let go of their loved ones. Religion's blessed unction is to offer the promise of sure deliverance, but this relief is short-lived. While the newly widowed farmer may accept the kind words of comfort from the smiling minister at the grave site, the next month in the middle of his barren field, alone at the wheel of his tractor, he breaks down and cries inconsolably. It matters not one bit that he has been reassured of his wife's redemption. He just misses her.

The role of such rituals is to give you a bridge of hope while you're trying to deal with the unthinkable, to provide an antidote to counter the bitter finality of your loss. It is hard to admit that something is hopeless. It is hard to admit you are powerless. It is hard to admit that you will never see the person you love again or ever have the conversation you hoped would reconcile your differences.

Death cares not a bit for your hopes. Death is final. Absolute. As Hamlet acknowledged, "This fell sergeant death is strict in his arrest."

Few things in life provide such sharp edges, such unnegotiable terms, such clear-cut limits as the force you must face when you mourn the loss of someone you love.

Your spirits may be raised by the kind words offered at the funeral service, but at the same time just being at the funeral reinforces the reality of the loss and causes denial to weaken. In the middle of the service the hurt gnaws at you. What am I doing here? you ask yourself, still denying the obvious. Something finally connects within you and the meaning of "gone" takes your breath away. You realize you are not your normal self. You're numb. You'd rather be doing anything but this.

At the cemetery, there is the walk to the grave. Someone points out the grave of a relative who died years ago. You hadn't realized it had been that many years. You think about time, perhaps your time. The graveside ceremony. The casket. The reality of a grave. Prayers. Speeches. Shaking hands, hugging, farewells. The reality of a grave.

Back to the house. Sitting and talking. Too much food. A bottle of whiskey. Stories. Thanks and good-byes. The house is yours again, but it feels so empty.

The reality of the grave returns. You sit down and sigh.

AS DENIAL FADES

Giving up denial may take years to complete. That denial has started to weaken is all that matters. Mourning hinges on letting go of hope.

Linda and Ben had been each other's constant companions throughout their thirty-year marriage and planned to travel when he retired. Shortly before that, Ben, who had emphysema and still smoked, developed difficulty breathing and was hospitalized with pneumonia. Within a few days his condition suddenly became critical, and without warning he died. When the doctor told Linda the news, it seemed as if he were talking about someone else. Nothing seemed real. Linda refused to believe what had happened.

Linda kept the house exactly as she always did. Everything was in its place except for her husband. She'd lived her whole life as his partner and never saw herself in any other role. She could not get accustomed to her new situation. Each morning she waited at the breakfast table, expecting Ben to come downstairs. She even thought she heard him getting dressed in the bedroom. In the afternoon she sat at the window, waiting for him to return home.

Linda's denial fluctuated, but she was never really convinced he was gone. As the weeks passed Linda began to get confused and disoriented. Her emotional ties to her husband were in place, but there was no husband to attach to. Her mind played tricks on her. Once she even thought she saw him in the living room, but when she looked again he was gone. Shaken, Linda found herself groping for stability and balance.

One day while cleaning out a drawer Linda found a carton of cigarettes and the thought crossed her mind, Why doesn't he stop smoking? It'll kill him. A swell of hurt and anger flushed through her body as she sighed, "It *did* kill him." Six months after the funeral, Linda finally began to mourn. Her anger at Ben for not taking better care of himself flooded to the surface, and she knew for the first time that Ben would never come home.

Human tragedies occur when a person refuses to give up denial over a loss. This next case is admittedly extreme, but it reflects exactly what happens in such a situation.

Barry had been a math whiz during high school, and while he was a bright and good person, he didn't have the social graces that made boys popular with girls. In college he met Lucy, a math major, who was not only intelligent and beautiful but also found him lovable. Caught totally off guard, Barry fell in love with Lucy and they became engaged. One evening at a restaurant celebrating their upcoming marriage, Lucy choked on a piece of meat. Barry went to the hospital with the ambulance, but it was too late. By the time they arrived at the emergency room, he was screaming his protest to the walls and had to be hospitalized.

Even though Barry had been with Lucy when she died, he could not let the truth in. He refused to admit that Lucy was dead and would start screaming, "No, no, no!" whenever someone tried to reason with him. Heavily sedated, he attended the funeral, but became so disruptive, pounding on the casket trying to wake her, that he could not go to the cemetery. He was transferred to a mental hospital, and even now, some thirty years later, he is still frozen in grief, still refusing to admit Lucy is gone.

You need to give up denial in order to survive.

COPING

There is considerable overlap between the stages of grief.

The coping phase begins as soon as your denial weakens enough to permit you to ask for details about what happened. In a sense you begin to cope when you first think the loss may be true. The coping phase continues until denial is gone.

Coping is facing the unresolved feelings of hurt and anger that continually break through your remaining denial.

The practice of wearing black during the first thirty days of mourning alerted others to the vulnerability of mourners in this phase, a time of great emotional instability where a trivial comment could suddenly break through weakening denial and permit painful feelings to escape.

The coping stage is punctuated by many episodes of Toxic Nostalgia, in which the residual unmourned grief is continually being symbolically tapped. Think of the painful tasks typical of this stage and the emotions that accompany them: cleaning out closets, sorting out belongings, giving away items that will never be used again. Each task is full of memories and downloads hopelessness at the same time.

During the first phases of coping, when denial begins to retreat, the intellect takes over to form a bypass over the pain. Because you're really starting to hurt, you try to find something to do. You use your intellect at this stage to gain distance so you can function. In order to mourn you have to set your reasoning aside and just feel your hurt, a vulnerable position indeed.

You can never escape your hurt and mourn successfully. The best plan is to deal with as much hurt as you can.

BLAMING AND EXCUSES

This is an attempt to control events over which you are powerless.

During this phase of mourning it is typical to accuse others for their contributory negligence while alternately blaming yourself and making excuses for your own shortcomings. This is the time when you direct your self-condemnation outward. Even if you don't express your accusations you still secretly blame anyone you can and resent them. During this stage it is typical to define an endless list of targets, initiate malpractice suits, seek custody, and challenge wills.

Such blaming is a futile and alienating exercise, doing more harm than good. Open antagonism at this time interferes with the mourning process, further injuring everyone involved.

RATIONALIZATIONS

While bargaining, trying to undo a loss by bribing the gods, is typical of the coping phase of mourning, it is just another type of rationalization you engage in when you feel powerless.

Bargaining is usually seen as part of anticipatory grief. You are inspired to bargain when you are afraid and want to prevent a tragedy. You're inclined to promise to do anything if it will help. It is typical for people to "get religion" in the face of a terrible loss. While prayer may not be intended as a form of bargaining, it certainly is used that way.

The sentiment of this coping mechanism is, If I am spared this loss, I will do the following. The promises that keep the petitioner's side of the bargain range from the erection of Santa Maria della Salute, celebrating the rescue of the city of Venice from the plague in 1630, to pledging to give up your bad habits.

Since concern with power is the hallmark of the controlling personality, it is not surprising to find that controlling people get stuck in this stage. As they bargain to keep their loved one alive or bring him back, they obsess, perform endless rituals, make a mockery of religion by reducing it to a kind of voodoo. Should the person die, they feel responsible because they weren't strong enough to prevent it.

Bargaining only postpones mourning by leading you to believe that there is something you can do to prevent the inevitable. Bargaining is, in a sense, the intellectual version of denial. You deny that you are helpless. You try to do something that will turn the present tragedy around. You try to prove it was a mistake. Bargaining generally lapses when denial fades and you accept that the situation is hopeless.

REGRETS

Regrets make up one of the critical parts of the coping phase. What do you regret?

You regret:

That you didn't make up or forgive.

That you didn't visit or call.

That you didn't check one more time.

That you didn't say what you wanted to say.

That you didn't say "I love you" enough.

That you stayed away, broke off contact, held a grudge.

That you didn't use your good china more often.

That you weren't nicer to each other.

That you didn't take more time off together.

That you didn't celebrate each day.

You regret what you should have done, could have done, would have done, might have done, but didn't do.

You regret your inaction, your overreaction, your rashness, and your procrastination, your excesses and your holding back.

Your regrets stay with you for years, returning at anniversaries and birthdays, in settings where you spent time together, favorite haunts, restaurants. Such regrets form the bulk of the toxic nostalgic intrusions that ruin the day.

When you have unfinished business with a departed parent, some part of you continues to prove yourself to them. It is only natural to want him to know that you made it, that you were a success, that you were a good parent, that you found happiness or made a bundle of money, overcame your problems and redeemed yourself.

Understandably, when you have such an unfulfilled need to win your parents' acceptance, the coping phase of mourning can be greatly elongated. Years later, when success is finally yours, you lift the award at the ceremony and blubber, even though it's been years since you lost your parent. Your Toxic Nostalgia contains your yearning, your unmourned regrets.

RESENTMENT

The more unhappy you are to begin with, the more resentful you are likely to be following a loss. Since unhappy people are already storing old emotions, their typical reaction to a new loss is, "After all I've suffered, this too?" The type of resentment each character type feels during the mourning process reflects his life problems in general.

The dependent person in the throes of a loss feels abandoned and resents others for forcing him to take responsibility for himself. He tends to hold on to his denial and mourns slowly, wallowing in self-pity. He cannot shed his disbelief and holds on to hope long after all is gone. He deeply resents any suggestion that he try to move on. He accuses others of not understanding how much his loss meant, how painful it is just to go on. Any suggestion to try to be braver, to get a job, to let go of the past is taken as an insult and may precipitate a deepening of mourning as he feels abandoned once more. Not surprisingly, he is slow in forgiving and therefore in healing.

As the controlling person tries to conceal his vulnerability over a loss, he often loses touch with his feelings. He resents others when they point out his sadness, thinking they are exposing him. He blames everyone he can. He speaks of his hurt in intellectual terms and feels justified in punishing others for their failure to do their share. His mourning is tainted with resentment because he feels more comfortable expressing anger than admitting he's been hurt.

The competitive person pretends that whatever losses he suffered really didn't affect him that much. He would like you to believe that everything is wonderful again as soon as possible. Almost overnight he has a new lover, a new job, or a new project to involve him.

The competitive person tries to stay emotionally unattached, seeking safety through pretending. He pretends not to care about what really matters, while appearing to care too much about what doesn't. Seeking safe losses to mourn, he overreacts to minor hurts rather than admit the real loss he's suffered. It almost seems as if he is purposefully creating Toxic Nostalgia. When he chooses lesser concerns to express his hurts, he deeply resents others for not sympathizing with him, but his histrionics and exaggeration make him seem phony. The competitive person adapts too quickly to the loss of others because feeling hurt makes him feel exposed. He hurts so much that he can't stand to be himself and so pretends to be someone else, a person who is not in pain.

Any incompletely mourned loss becomes a source of hurt and anger that predisposes you to Toxic Nostalgia that will exaggerate the losses you experience in later years. This may occur as a sudden overwhelming sense of depression, but it can also occur as an unexplained resentful attitude that continually seeks out targets.

Overcoming resentment is an important part of the work of grief. Containing your resentment is the most common way mourning is blocked. Unresolved resentment can persist for years, make you appear bitter, and ruin your life. You need to release your resentment. If you don't, you cannot forgive.

Although Don managed to get close to many women, as soon as a woman asked him to commit, he would find fault with her, accuse her of hurting him, and then back away. He knew his response was illogical and felt he must be crazy. His career had also been a series of ups and downs, spoiled by other examples of such rashness.

Don related how when he was fifteen his life became a total shambles. His alcoholic mother hated his father, who worked late to avoid her drinking. Each day Don rushed home after school afraid he might find the house on fire if his mother had left something burning on the stove. On a good day his mother would be upstairs drunk. On a bad day she'd be at the window waiting to pounce on him. Don endured his suffering in silence and tried to keep his brothers from making noise and disturbing her. He made dinner, cleaned up his mother's messes, and helped his brothers with their homework while neglecting his own. When his father came home, Don would lie and say everything was fine.

One morning before school Don stopped at his mother's bedroom and found her lying in bed, very still. Both frustrated by her unresponsiveness and accustomed to it at the same time, Don shrugged and left. On arriving at school he was told to come home, his father had discovered his mother dead in bed. Now Don was burdened with caring for his father who, overwhelmed by his repressed anger and guilt, became deeply depressed. Don could not handle the responsibility, and his grades fell. He was unable to get into college. He was trapped. He'd sacrificed everything for others.

When asked if he felt resentment toward his mother for what happened, Don was quick to say no, adding that her death was "an accidental suicide." He went on to explain that she frequently took tranquilizers when she was drinking and must simply have miscalculated. When Don revealed that his mother had attempted suicide on several occasions, two of them requiring hospitalization, it was suggested that his mother knew full well what she was doing and that her death was very much intended.

Don tensed and shouted, "That's a lie!" Then he hesitated, and with amazing bitterness clenched his fists and fumed, "She did mean it!" and started to cry. It was the first time in the thirty years following his mother's death that he admitted she had hurt him on purpose. Suddenly his long-standing resentment toward women made perfect sense.

Don's refusal to admit his mother had committed suicide put him in a terrible position. Because he had no explanation for his resentment, his mourning could not resolve. Whenever a woman wanted him to commit, it reawakened his secret resentment over his mother wanting to commit suicide, and he furiously pushed the woman away, the way he wished he could have pushed his mother away and escaped from his situation.

BITTERNESS

To mourn successfully you must admit your hurt and release your anger.

It isn't easy to release your anger over unfulfilled expectations when someone has died. While some may claim that death settles all debts, it doesn't work that way in real life. You, the emotionally encumbered survivor, have no forum where you can plead your argument or present your mistreatment and abuse. There is no court in which to appeal the lack of love you suffered or your disappointment in never being told you did a good job or were loved.

The extent to which you depended on the other person's approval now becomes your torture. You still want to prove yourself to that person. You feel cheated. Your anger tastes bitter, and unspoken cries constrict your chest. It hurts to breathe.

The heart of the mourning process is to release your claim on the "if onlys" and the "could have beens" and accept the finality of your loss. You need to give up hope of reunion, approval, or success. Arguments and protests will not be heard. The case is closed.

On the day you are better:

You will give up your denial.

You will stop blaming others for your injury.

You will stop making excuses for your shortcomings.

You will stop pretending that the past was something it wasn't and admit that what you lost mattered to you.

You will accept that your life is precisely the way it has turned out to be.

You will accept that your relationship with the person you lost is over and that it was exactly what it seemed to be, no more and no less. You will prune the relationship of its false hopes and expectations.

You will stop apologizing for the other person and for yourself. Faults, weaknesses, warts and all; you were the way you were.

You will release your hurt and forgive.

You will forgive the other person for being the way he was.

You will forgive yourself for not being better, wiser, more generous or understanding, for not caring, even for being negligent.

You will accept that you deserve to be forgiven just as you are right now, in this place and as yourself.

You will accept all of this and you will move on.

Then, only then, will the bitterness fade.

THE END OF COPING

The coping phase of mourning never really ends. It returns with every recollection of what has been lost. From the time you first hear about the possibility of the loss until after you think you've let go, some hidden part of your loss seems always ready to lead you to mourn anew.

These toxic nostalgic recapitulations are a reflection of the persistence of the natural therapeutic process as it continually works to free you from past attachments, allowing you to evolve into a better self.

Don't be discouraged when, long after you've been hurt, some trivial reminder propels you into a sudden sadness. In the first year following the loss of someone you love, each event has the potential to be a symbolic anniversary. The first Christmas or Thanksgiving without the other person, their birthday, your anniversary, for that matter any event without them for the first time becomes a kind of anniversary of their absence. These reminders capture you and wring sorrow from your heart. They emphasize the finality of the loss once more and remind you there is still much to grieve.

In the first year of mourning everything you see seems to conspire to download the still-unmourned part of your grief. As this recent loss is being mourned, older losses that are still being coped with also break through to your awareness and accompany the present loss with sad remembrances. Again, all these recollections are just one more opportunity to work through the pain of the past and should be seen in the context of healing and freeing you.

ACCEPTANCE

You begin to accept a loss the very first time you set your denial aside. Acceptance accompanies coping and defines a painful and irregular journey. You have good days and bad days.

You cannot have a good day when you are full of denial, because you are fighting against the truth. However, you can seem to have a good day when you are pretending. In fact at the beginning of the grieving process, most so-called good days are merely pretense. Even though you may be admired for being a rock, holding back tears, managing a supportive smile for everyone who has come to the memorial service, this is a false front and is not to be confused with real acceptance.

THE PERSPECTIVE OF HEALING

The early use of pretense is a foreshadowing of acceptance, of the time when you will be able to say that you feel better and mean it.

Acceptance begins when you are able to speak of your loss with a bearable sadness, without having to shut it off because it reminds you of the hurt you still can't face.

When you are emotionally healed, your recollections will still be able to sadden you, but they will not trigger you into mourning again.

The perspective that healing creates allows you to develop a new attitude toward old losses. This is not pretending. When you pretend, you assert that your hurt no longer matters in order not to feel the pain. The true healing perspective, attained after the pain of a loss has been felt and released, allows you to affirm that the loss did matter but hurts much less.

That difference makes all the difference in the world. When you mourn a loss you release the pain. When you pretend to feel better, you merely store the pain in Emotional Debt and are therefore highly susceptible to Toxic Nostalgia.

For this precise reason people who employ pretense as their main defense often find themselves becoming depressed years after a loss. They have dedicated themselves to surviving happily without bothering to go through the trouble of mourning. They are forced to push more and more pain away until, finally, some loss presses their old pain forward.

The healing perspective is the exact opposite of Emotional Debt.

Acceptance is usually conferred gradually. Bit by bit the current loss is released from denial, confronted, mourned, and relinquished. At the time of grief, older, unresolved feelings are reawakened as Toxic Nostalgia and are also worked through by means of the natural healing process until they are accepted. These companion feelings may appear only as intensifiers of the loss, or as bad moods that seem to appear from nowhere, in dreams, as fragments of fantasies that seem to elude being identified, or as haunting recollections that resist full retrieval. Everyone has a collection of these fleeting threads of memory that come in and out of awareness. Their home is Emotional Debt, their meaning obscured by time.

The healing perspective can also be acquired suddenly and with great power. When it is, it is a magical confirmation. Learning to see a loss in a higher perspective can suddenly transform your world. The healing perspective is a function of the higher mind, the home of insight and awareness.

People often use religion to attain this perspective of healing, which is like a state of grace. To paraphrase the theologian Paul Tillich, once a person believes he is acceptable to God, he can begin to accept himself.

It helps to believe in a higher self to access the healing perspective. The truest healing comes through acceptance of your pain and suffering as it is happening.

Acceptance is letting go, without denying the hurt.

Acceptance is embracing what has happened, even if you do not like it.

Acceptance is being on friendly terms with your pain.

Acceptance is welcoming the truth even if it hurts.

Acceptance is being willing to admit failure, hurting others, being abandoned, your loneliness, and your powerlessness, all without giving up.

Acceptance is not easy, but it is your only hope for happiness in the face of impossible odds and unthinkable losses.

If you do not accept the loss, you are forced to harbor the pain.

If you do not accept the loss, you are required to repeat it.

If you do not accept the loss, you are bound to the past and have mortgaged your future to suffering.

Only through acceptance is it possible to find peace of mind.

Only through acceptance can you know yourself.

OTHER LOSSES

While this discussion of the mourning process has focused mostly on the loss of love, that is, the loss of a beloved other, or the loss of self, the stages are the same for losses of power and losses of self-esteem. Once again, what is different is the speed with which you move through the stages of grief and also the quality of the mourning.

REJECTION

Separation from a loved one is like a kind of death, although when another person has rejected you, false hope is continually reborn within you. This makes it more difficult to give up denial. After all, you reason, while there is life, there is hope. When you are rejected, it is hope that hurts the worst.

Some of the saddest people are those who have had their hearts broken. Not only have they suffered the wound of losing another person, but because the rejection or abandonment was intentional, the blow to their self-esteem is both concrete and lasting. While you struggle not to take the death of a loved one personally, rejection is about as personal as anything gets. You bury your anger in the hope of reuniting. You want to forgive everything and take the person back, but it is not to be. As a result your suppressed anger builds into guilt, reinforcing your belief that you aren't lovable, good, or desirable. This can result in protracted mourning, especially when self-esteem was low to begin with. For this reason some teenagers suffer for decades when they have been rejected.

FINANCIAL REVERSALS

It is common to become depressed after losing a job, a business, or a personal fortune, especially when your self-worth depends on your power to influence others. If a loss of power is of paramount importance to you, it's probably because you need such power to feel good about yourself. Your ease with others depends on being able to buy your way out of difficulties rather than trusting in your own worth.

Blaming often dominates the atmosphere at times of financial crisis and it is tempting to become trapped in legal maneuvers, such as trying to sue your boss or the competitors who put you out of business. Even if such actions hold out the promise of remuneration, they totally eclipse the lesson you need to learn. To be a success you need to accept your role in your losses, not refute it. You need to accept your imperfections.

The mourning process following a financial loss is characterized by obsessional preoccupation. When you suffer a financial loss, your energy usually turns to making another fortune as quickly as possible. As you become consumed by this materialistic quest, you make vows that this situation will never happen to you again. You may finally regain your lost fortune, but unless you learn to find value in simply being yourself, you become rigid and suspicious and risk losing yourself in the bargain.

SELF-ESTEEM

The loss of reputation following a career failure causes deep embarrassment and is also mourned like a little death. Now you must deal with the loss of your nerve, your special touch, your passion or inspiration. Following such a failure the truth is harder to ignore. Maybe you realize that you succeeded because you were lucky. Perhaps you discover that your belief in yourself was exaggerated. You wonder if the talent you once so fervently believed in was just another figment of your fertile imagination. You question the very belief in yourself that once gave you the courage to risk. Without this belief you feel like a shadow. Something is missing and you can't put your finger on it. A certain feeling is gone. You want more than anything to believe in yourself again.

It is typical to have doubts after a defeat, to question whether you were really prepared, to wonder if you were in over your head or if you should have been running the race at all. The moment of failure is especially frightening because you have no place to hide. If you continually put others down on your way up, you've also made enemies who are probably gloating. If you have grandstanded and played for the crowd's adulation, you may find your loss compounded by losing your audience.

The first stage in coping with a loss of self-esteem is to give up your pretense, the very defense that was designed to protect you from a loss of self-esteem. Beneath your pretense there are still self-doubts you concealed in order to give yourself courage. Instead of admitting that you were weak, not smart enough, or lacked talent, you pretended to be the opposite. Now you have to look at yourself as you are, facing your concern about your flaws and weaknesses.

Still, even a crushing loss of self-esteem can be a powerful stimulus for growth if you deal with it honestly. After you survive the initial shock, a serious failure can become the rallying point for success. Forced to examine your failings, you make the corrections you've been postponing, take a stand, find your true worth, and blossom.

At its heart mourning is an exercise in facing the truth, a test of your honesty. When you mourn successfully and let go of what you have lost, you are always ahead of where you started. Even if you are sadder, you are wiser, stronger, and because you better understand yourself, richer for your loss.

How a Therapist Assists Mourning

When you suffer a loss, a good therapist tries to support the natural healing process by helping you understand:

> *What hurts and why.*
> *Why what you lost was important to you.*
> *What gave the loss such power over you.*
> *What the loss reminds you of.*
> *How you try to avoid facing the present loss.*
> *How you avoided losses in the past.*
> *And what the loss teaches you about yourself.*

A good therapist helps you to accept the truth so you can know yourself, understand your vulnerability, trust your feelings, believe in yourself again, and act in your best interests.

In doing this, a good therapist helps you find the healing perspective and maintain your clarity. Honesty always heals.

EMOTIONAL DEBT

*I*F EMOTIONAL PROBLEMS WERE CLASSIFIED the same way as physical illnesses, they would be considered storage diseases. The heart of all emotional problems is that instead of pain being dealt with at the time it happens, its expression is postponed. The emotion is stored rather than expressed or coped with. Stored anxiety feeds on itself and expands. You block hurt because you cannot face the injury or its consequences. As a result hurt converts to anger and anger to guilt.

Both these feelings are stored in Emotional Debt. Denial causes you to be unaware of your hurt, creating a state of shock that ranges from a momentary confusion before you realize someone has hurt your feelings to totally forgetting a traumatic incident. You employ the defenses of blaming or making excuses to justify your anger and make others seem at fault for your problems. You pretend not to care to save face. All three of these defenses create and maintain Emotional Debt.

Feelings and memories are stored and distorted alike. There are three general levels of Emotional Debt: current, recent, and remote.

CURRENT EMOTIONAL DEBT

THE MENTAL SCRATCH PAD

Current Emotional Debt describes the unexpressed feelings of the present moment or past few days or weeks. Typically these unexpressed feelings are the reaction to an event that has just happened or is still evolving. You haven't gotten your bearings yet to be sure of what you're feeling and so you're waiting to express yourself. Generally you're keenly aware that you're hurting and why.

You spend a large portion of your life in current Emotional Debt, waiting for the opportunity to speak your mind.

Someone hurts your feelings and for one reason or another you cannot immediately express yourself. Or you are faced with a threat and stop what you're doing as you try to figure out the best way to respond.

In both cases your emotion is immediate, but your expressive response is momentarily delayed. You feel a little out of balance and unsettled. You want to release your hurt feelings or resolve the threat, but you can't right now.

Your access to the emotions stored in this current Emotional Debt corresponds to your mind's scratch pad memory, the place you store your parking space in the public garage. It's momentary storage. When you return to your car, you release the information.

Thus, to become more permanent, a current memory must either have importance to you or be associated with an emotional impression. You can intentionally make any detail memorable.

Unless you consider an item important, most scratch pad memory rapidly fades. This memory represents the brain's operating desk space. You really don't want it to be cluttered with nonsense. You need space to think and work.

It is therefore important to forget. Without forgetting, your life would be so full of mental debris you could not think your way to work and back.

Remember what is important and let go of what is not.

WHY YOU HOLD BACK

You store feelings either because it is awkward to express them when they occur or because you are afraid to be open.

The present situation may not offer an opportunity to express feelings appropriately. It may be a work situation where expressing feelings is considered unbusinesslike.

The circumstances may be uncertain, so expressing your emotional reaction might be jumping to a questionable conclusion. For example, you may feel hurt but can't determine if the insult was intentional or if you are just overreacting.

The person you need to express your feelings to may be unapproachable or seem menacing, and so sharing feelings may risk creating a crisis.

If you have unresolved emotional business with a person who just hurt you, you may shy away from expressing yourself because you don't want to start something bigger.

The insult may be a minor irritation not worth dealing with, beneath you, the words of a fool or emotionally troubled person, or a vicious taunt designed to throw you off guard.

The injury may be entirely impersonal but still frustrating. Include here a flat tire, a repeated dunning letter after the bill has been paid, today's paper delivered wet, getting a parking ticket while looking for change for the meter, cutting into an expensive melon and finding it flavorless and hard as a rock.

MANAGING

Life continually bombards you with little disappointments that add to your stress. You have to develop an attitude that permits you to adapt to frustration without responding automatically and creating an angry scene. Your objective is to be aware, but disenthralled; present, but distant; caring, but free; responsive, but not drawn into the drama.

You manage common everyday insults best by assuming a viewpoint of detachment. Decide that you won't let unimportant things upset you. Be an observer, a survivor, and still keep your humanness. Do the best you can with what you have and accept what you cannot affect without taking it personally.

When you are in Emotional Debt you find it difficult to be dispassionate because your stored feelings are always looking for release and tend to attach themselves to everyday disappointments and make too much out of them. Emotional Debt interferes with the way feelings naturally extinguish and fade. Just as when the surface of a still pond is broken by an insect, injuries create a momentary disturbance on the surface of your consciousness. If you accept and feel the injury, it will resolve and disappear by itself. When there are other currents of submerged emotions, the calm surface becomes agitated. Then, because you cannot tell where the disturbance is coming from, every injury seems offensive.

The object of processing feelings effectively is to reduce the residue of submerged feelings so that a present hurt doesn't call forth the past and cause further agitation.

When it comes to feelings, remembering what is important and needs to be expressed while letting go of what is not is the lesson you are always learning.

STORING HURT AND ANGER

Current Emotional Debt is the time between an injury and its expression. You are deciding how to react, waiting for the courage or the opportunity to tell someone how you feel. In a sense everyone is working on getting out of current Emotional Debt. You're trying to make sense of your feelings, figuring out if you were really hurt or why the other person treated you so badly and what you're going to do about it. Like everyone else you are a prisoner of your insecurity. You fear rejection, revealing your vulnerability and losing face.

STORING ANXIETY

Anxiety is stored as hurt that has not yet occurred. By allowing you to imagine what could happen it motivates you to peak performance. You work through your anxiety by figuring out how real the danger you face is, how close you are to it, and what you should do to avoid it. When the danger has passed, you measure how close you came to disaster and let go of your fear.

The purpose of holding anxiety in current Emotional Debt is to establish a state of caution and maintain your alertness until the present danger is over. The anxiety stored in current Emotional Debt is an excellent motivator, but if it is not released when the threat passes, it turns into obsessive thinking, worrying over what could go wrong. Obsessive thinking is circuitous and leads you to perceive potential threats everywhere. Anxiety grows when stored too long, just like anger. Instead of focusing on the specific problem, stored anxiety leads you to see danger everywhere.

PERFORMANCE ANXIETY. It is typical to become anxious when you prepare for an important presentation, test, or performance. Anxiety's purpose is to make you question your readiness. It leads you to estimate what will be asked of you. In terms of risking, anxiety points out your greatest exposure to failure. It shows you your weaknesses and what you must work on. Fear is a shortcut and an excellent guide, but only when it is current. Older fear is less reliable because it is distorted and blunted.

Consider the role anxiety plays in taking an examination. First you plan. If you think, "I hope he doesn't ask about the Crusades," you should review your notes on that subject. The very thing your fear points to is what you should study.

You deal with intrusive older fears: You question if you are smart enough. You remember your old failures and doubts. Will you choke and become confused or be unable to recall what you studied? Will you have enough time to present yourself in a way that shows what you know? You use these doubts to motivate yourself.

If you become obsessed, you can create a paralyzing domino theory of failure. You reason: If I fail, my record will be terrible. My grade average will be too low. I won't get good recommendations. I won't get into graduate school. My parents will disown me. I won't get a good job. No one will want to marry me. I'll never have children or a family.

As amusing as this can be from the distance of having been there, when you are experiencing the anxiety of preparation, these nagging self-doubts are nevertheless the ones that you must put aside and overcome.

The mind's capacity for symbolic reasoning can subvert the effectiveness of anxiety and allow you to become a victim of fear rather than using anxiety to prepare yourself.

In confronting physical danger you want to be strong and fast. You set your anxiety aside so you can concentrate on surviving without thinking about it. However, you cannot solve a difficult problem without using your mind. You can't use your mind if you can't concentrate.

When facing a complicated mental challenge, obsessing about a threat or trying not to think about it both limit your ability to think. The same defenses that allow you to store anxiety also limit your ability to think clearly.

Storing anxiety rather than using it to manage a threat encumbers your ability to reason. The anxiety held in Emotional Debt activates your self-doubts, which slow you down and get in your mind's way. Instead of focusing on the problem that needs your attention you become preoccupied with questions regarding your own worth, intelligence, or goodness. Every challenge becomes a test of your self-worth when anxiety is allowed free reign.

If you have pushed your fears aside rather than allowing them to guide you to study what you do not know, when it comes time to take the exam and you see a question you avoided, your suppressed fears will resurface in a flood. You panic. You can't think or remember answers that you were sure of.

After the exam your defenses lift and you remember the answers you should have given. You see your mistakes. You resign yourself to the inevitable. You may pretend not to care and adopt an air of indifference, but waves of concern still break through, giving you pause until you know for sure how you did.

Ideally the lessons learned from your performance are as important as the subject you study. Unfortunately most people do not place the focus of their education on the right place, which is themselves. Everything you study, every presentation you make, is really all about you.

Therefore, use your current fear to lead you to identify and conquer your self-doubts. When you do, everything else will fit in its proper place.

NARROWLY AVERTING DISASTER. When you have a close call, you are instantly placed in a state of anxiety. You are stunned by the realization that you narrowly avoided being seriously damaged. You also realize that the reason you were spared had nothing to do with you. It was fate or luck. The fragility of life and your powerlessness astonish and alarm you. You ponder: How close did I come to getting killed? What did I do wrong? Whose fault was this? Why wasn't I more careful? As far as anxiety is concerned, a close call counts just as much as an actual loss.

You feel like you've been living life on the edge. You feel responsible and powerless at the same time. The world does not feel as secure as it did just a short while before, when you thought you were safe, when you thought you knew what you were doing, when you thought you were in control.

The lesson of such a close call is to take your fears to heart and increase your margin of safety without overdoing it. You want to be safe and yet still live life to the fullest.

A COMMON CLOSE CALL. You are on the freeway doing sixty miles an hour, urgent to make time. You decide to pass the car in front of you and accelerate. As soon as you pull out of your lane, you discover that you are less than an inch away from cutting off a car you somehow didn't see. You pull back into the lane, frantically applying the brakes to keep from crashing into the car you originally intended to pass.

Your heart is racing. You wonder why you didn't see the other car. You try to get your bearings again. You feel shaken. You realize you could have been killed. You wonder how close you might have come to causing other accidents.

After a minute you calm down and gingerly bring your vehicle back up to cruising speed. Still a bit edgy, you overanticipate the actions of another driver and brake for nothing. You are feeling better, but you're still overly cautious.

After a while you see the car you cut off just ahead of you. You wonder if the driver will remember you or if he's still angry. You keep your distance, feeling sheepish. Your line of traffic moves past him. You try not to look but see him looking over at you and shaking his head. You decide to wave an apology, but he's not convinced. Maybe you appeared insincere.

You drive on with a feeling of tightness in your stomach that you recognize as rejection. It combines with your loss of confidence. You console yourself that at least no one was injured. You're trying to put these frightening events into perspective and get them behind you.

During this episode you stored anxiety. It kept you in a continual state of awareness that led you to search for signs of danger everywhere, causing you to overreact and brake unnecessarily. Just getting home in one piece feels like an accomplishment today.

Imagine how much worse your distress would have been if you had experienced that close call while you were preoccupied over losing your job. Your anxiety over your work could easily have contributed to an accident.

Another possibility: you could internalize your fear of the close call and combine it in Emotional Debt with your job fear. This would damage your self-confidence and lead you to doubt your judgment, make you question if you were a good driver, or perhaps wonder if you shouldn't drive at all. Feeling shaken, you might even get off the freeway before your exit to avoid additional stress. It's at moments like this that people develop a fear of driving on freeways.

You need to release your anxiety once the danger is past so you can discriminate between real danger and remembered anxiety. Anxious people always feel as if they are in danger. Even when they are safe, their anxiety drains them and places them at risk. Expecting injury everywhere, they have difficulty concentrating and act skittish. Anxiety begets anxiety when it is stored. You fear being afraid and thus take something innocent as dangerous. Avoiding it in a panic, you act out of control and create real danger.

Fortunately much of the hurt, anger, and anxiety that is stored in scratch pad Emotional Debt is relieved by the natural therapeutic process, releasing the feeling in symbolic ways, such as dreams.

As ANXIETY AGES. Stored anxiety is manifested as an attitude of heightened awareness and exaggerated uncertainty.

When the threat persists, stored anxiety grows, creating a pervasive disquiet that torments you and corrupts your logic. Sometimes when a state of anxiety is unrelieved, you do something irrational or get into trouble just to end the uncertainty.

Anxiety is stored in any situation where there is prolonged exposure to uncertainty or risk, such as working for an unstable boss who continually threatens to fire you, waiting for an aftershock after an earthquake, living with an alcoholic or in a crime-ridden neighborhood, or being sent to a war zone.

Unrelieved anxiety defeats your defenses' ability to contain it so it intrudes and interferes with your life. You become increasingly restless and are easily startled and agitated. Unlike the anxiety in current Emotional Debt, where you know what you are afraid of (such as waiting to see if your loved one is one of the survivors), when anxiety is stored it pools with other fears and often loses its connection to the potential loss it is warning you about. As a result you feel something is wrong but aren't sure exactly what. Now your mind is on an intelligence-gathering mission and urgently needs to know everything. In this state, obsession and suspicion rule and sponsor the agitated logic of distrust, which has a life of its own.

As the volume of stored anxiety grows, life feels ominous and foreboding. You misinterpret facts and take innocent comments the wrong way. As your confidence falls you become even more vigilant. You're on edge, making a case for defending yourself. In this state even a little fright can trigger your stored anxiety, causing you to act mistakenly and create the very damage you most fear. Anxiety serves you best when it is the result of a situation changing from safe to unsafe, not when it exists as a constant state of fear. If everything seems like a threat, how can your anxiety protect you?

The most compromising experiences are those where anxiety is unrelenting, real, and oppressive and the means to deal with it limited. In such situations your Emotional Debt is overwhelmed and completely distorts your perception. This situation occurs in brainwashing, where you'll cling to anything just for safety; in the indoctrination to cults, where the leader is seen as having the power to save you; and in the Stockholm Syndrome, in which hostages fall in love with their abductors, seeing them as lovable rather than killers.

RECENT EMOTIONAL DEBT
WHEN HURT AND ANGER GET TRAPPED

As feelings age current Emotional Debt becomes recent Emotional Debt. Though the transition is imperceptible, the difference is real.

Recent Emotional Debt is a more rigid, closed, and resigned position. You are determined to hold your feelings in place, and the aftereffects are significant. As your defenses become fortified to contain your hurt and anxiety, distortion begins to work its transformational ways. You become less flexible, more set in your withholding. This defensiveness consumes energy and begins to deplete you. As a result your spontaneity and freedom are diminished. You're not your best.

The feelings in recent Emotional Debt make up the bulk of your unfinished business. You are generally conversant with the details that range from coping with a recent death, rejection, or betrayal to your concern about an ailing parent or a struggling child, your failing business, or your problematic career. Some of these injuries can be as recent as a week ago or have been troubling you for years. However, you know what is causing your suffering, you just haven't solved the problem or been willing to let go of it yet.

Since hurt rapidly evolves into anger and anger makes you doubt your worth, unexpressed emotions soon make your original problem seem worse than it was. The injury that was once so clear and simple now seems complicated. You may be wallowing in self-pity, suffering from panic, entertaining dark fantasies of revenge, or feeling guilty or depressed. Your reasoning is continually being fueled by resentment. You become preoccupied with betrayal, being cheated, used, or treated unfairly.

After a while you get lost in the short-circuited courts of emotional justification and blame, gathering evidence, planning retaliation. Your negative energy is continually leaking, causing you to appear emotionally brittle. As your stored feelings begin to commandeer your mind's storage space, your memory suffers, you are easily distracted, and you find it difficult to concentrate.

As this state progresses your logic becomes the slave of your defenses, circuitous and repetitive. You tend to obsess and keep bumping into the same rigid mental detours. You find yourself at the place you started. Because you've made up your mind, no one wants to argue with you.

Because you are highly defensive, your creativity suffers. You find it easier to complete mechanical tasks rather than solve problems inventively. It is difficult to be open to new thoughts when you are afraid to face what is hurting you.

THE LOSS OF SPECIFICITY

When feelings stored in recent Emotional Debt become distorted they also lose their specificity. The older anger is, the more difficult it is to relate to a specific injury.

In time the anger from a distinct hurt merges with the anger from barely remembered injustices. While recent anger builds through obsession, older anger gradually tends to become covered with denial. Still, it is the imperative of all stored anger to seek expression. The older, amorphous anger typically appends itself to more recent anger, intensifying it, blowing it out of proportion as they try to escape together. This is why when you finally do seek to release a painful feeling or memory it can seem like an unexpectedly daunting task. No one likes to be blindsided by a wave of angry Toxic Nostalgia.

Because when such excessive anger is expressed it can't be readily justified by remembered events, people are led to exaggerate their injury. This distortion creates conflicts because it is seen as guilt producing or malicious. Clearing old feelings from the distortions of time to divine the truth has always been a problem for therapists, patients, and families.

While some creative people have the ability to isolate their feelings and remain productive in spite of huge emotional turmoil, it is nonetheless highly destructive to be embroiled in unresolved old feelings. You cannot live your best life with a backlog of unexpressed anger as your constant companion.

STORAGE CAPACITY

The emotional storage capacity of the brain seems to be elastic when adapting to modest levels of Emotional Debt. The main purpose of the natural therapeutic process is to keep storage to a minimum so you are less encumbered.

When your defenses become rigid they prevent you from resolving your feelings. When this happens you approach the storage limits of Emotional Debt. As you do, you become inflexible and preoccupied. You find it difficult to adapt to change and are easily irritated and moved to tears. When you call someone emotionally unstable you really mean that his emotional storage is at the point of overflowing.

Your life is drained by the defensive energy you expend to keep your emotional gates shut down and prevent unwanted emotions from intruding. This defensive roadblock inhibits positive as well as negative emotions. Your vitality, which reflects your freedom to access all parts of your thoughts and experience, now seems flattened. The fire that energized your personality and gave you life seems faded and with it your specialness.

Although this is an extreme example, one glance around the grounds of any mental hospital will show the crippling effects of severe Emotional Debt. Patients in deep denial become strangely inexpressive as they struggle to contain their anger. They move slowly. They hardly speak. Their emotional storage capacities are full and their lives are empty.

When your defenses limit access to your experiences, whether painful or pleasurable, you become like a drone, frozen in time and response. This is a powerful reminder to cherish all of your life, the good and the bad. The whole you is the result of acceptance, not of blocking out the bad.

Even if you are flexible, you can be shocked by a great loss and find your Emotional Debt suddenly pressed to its limits and your ability to cope with daily life temporarily overwhelmed. Precipitous losses can compromise you even if you have little Emotional Debt and make you seem fragile.

Storing anxiety in Emotional Debt often results after a trauma that is so overwhelming you try not to think about it. However, the very act of pushing a fearful thought away seems to encourage it to return.

Tim was a twelve-year-old boy who had been suffering from nightmares and sudden bouts of anxiety for the year following a brutal attack by a large German shepherd. While the nightmares and the anxiety were gradually becoming less frequent, Tim was growing impatient and wanted them to go away completely.

Tim had been walking a neighbor's dog when the shepherd broke through a gate and attacked him. At first Tim did not know what was happening. The dog had his leg in its mouth and was tearing at him. Tim lay still until the dog stopped and then got up and started to run away. The dog immediately ran after Tim and brought him to the ground, biting him and growling ferociously. Tim was too terrified to cry out and just lay there. The dog stopped, and Tim ran away. Again the animal chased him and brought him down. Tim felt caught in an unending nightmare as the dog attacked him six times. Finally two men pulled the dog off. By the time Tim reached the hospital he was in a state of shock.

Tim's recovery was complicated by infections that would not go away. He was also ridiculed by his classmates. Tim became ashamed of being bitten by the dog and just wanted the incident to disappear. The more Tim pushed the memory away, the stronger his nightmares became, and the more intense his tormenting flashes of anxiety. Finally Tim's anxiety was triggered every time he saw a dog. Repressing the memory had made his symptoms worse.

Tim was reassured that he wasn't crazy for feeling the way he did and was told that anyone who had gone through such an attack would have painful memories. Then it was explained that the painful memory was only seeking to be released and that he should not try to shut it off.

He was told that the memory would probably repeat for a while and when it returned he should just observe it and accept it. Each time it recurred, he needed to permit it to surface, admit he was afraid at the time, but tell himself that he survived the danger and that it could have been a lot worse. In a few weeks, as the backlog of stored feelings was released, Tim's symptoms began to fade. In two months the symptoms disappeared entirely.

FEAR AND RESENTMENT STORED TOGETHER

When fear and hurt are stored together it is often the result of your being deeply hurt and unable to speak up because you have low self-esteem and fear rejection. In this situation it is common for an external object to become the focus of your fear. By having something concrete to avoid you feel as if your feelings are manageable and your life is under control. Of course the thing you are trying to control eventually starts to control you as, like all stored feelings do, your fear starts to expand.

Norman complained he was afraid of heights. He admitted that he had always been a little uncomfortable with heights as a kid but that it didn't really bother him until recently. Now when he traveled he insisted on a room on the second or third floor. The idea of going up in an elevator beyond seven or eight stories filled him with terror.

The fear had been a problem for almost ten years and was beginning to limit his effectiveness at work and disturb his peace of mind. He began to worry about the possibility of having to be in a high place. It became clear that his biggest fear was taking an elevator. After close questioning he remembered that ten years earlier he and his girlfriend Wendy were at an amusement park. The conversation was about moving in together. Wendy was persistent, persuasive, and highly insistent that Norman make a commitment to a serious relationship. The thing Norman objected to the most about Wendy, and never revealed to her, was her pushiness and her ability to get him to agree to things he did not want to do.

As they went from ride to ride, Wendy became more aggressive, talking about how wonderful it would be to bring their kids to the amusement park someday. Norman could feel himself weakening. Wendy kept pressing. At the free fall ride they were strapped in. As they were slowly lifted up the eight stories to the release point, Norman could feel himself becoming entrapped by Wendy's manipulative pressure. He wanted to tell her that he didn't want to commit. He wanted to tell her that he really didn't trust her. Every time he began to speak, Wendy spoke over him. Now they were at the top of the ride. Norman was about to open his mouth when the cage was released and they fell eight stories in a few seconds. The physical sensation of the ride combined with Norman's frustration with Wendy was stored in his memory as a single traumatic event and evolved into his fear of heights.

Norman's first step in resolving his problem was to separate his feelings into individual components; his reluctance to commit, his lack of trust of Wendy, and his fear of expressing his resentment over being manipulated. He never really was that afraid of heights; the free fall ride merely provided a convenient cover for his other concerns by producing a physical sensation of fear. Had Norman taken the ride by himself, unattached from any other fearful thought, the free fall ride would have just been a physical thrill. However, combined with fears that he wished to repress, it formed a kind of hybrid memory, a synthesis of more than one event. It was easier to feel afraid of heights than admit his frustration and anger at Wendy.

Norman was encouraged to ride the glass elevator of a local hotel up and down sixty-five stories, repeating to himself that he wasn't afraid of heights but just didn't trust Wendy and felt trapped by her. Attaching his fear to the correct threats immediately lowered his Emotional Debt. After several such trips, riding in an elevator was much less frightening, and he actually became able to enjoy the thrill of looking out over the city.

Thrill becomes terror when it is invested with anxiety from Emotional Debt.

THE LOGIC OF FEAR: HOW FEAR BUILDS UPON ITSELF

Recent Emotional Debt can involve feelings as close as a few weeks ago all the way back to adolescence. When a feeling is stored from an event only a few months old, it can join forces with much older fears and seem overwhelming. Even if it is nearly forgotten, old unresolved anxiety can be reawakened and lead you to misinterpret a present danger and create a state of fear out of flimsy evidence. Anxiety has its own logic. It leads you to distort the way you see the world, creating its own justification as it does so. The following case illustrates how this can happen.

Tom was a seventy-two-year-old man who had been suffering from anxiety attacks for just over a year. Although he saw four psychiatrists and was placed on several medications, which only made him drowsy, his anxiety became increasingly debilitating, waking him in the middle of the night and lasting all day. After a while his anxiety seemed to have a life of its own, easily triggered and tenacious.

Tom's problems began shortly following a visit to his sister in England. She'd written him to say that she'd been suffering from anxiety and had had little success with treatment. The letter made Tom worry. When Tom saw his sister, she was much worse than he'd anticipated. She was reclusive, pathetic, and childlike. The question suddenly hit him: Will I become like her? It shook him to the marrow of his being. He instantly brushed it away.

While visiting England, Tom began to be troubled by memories of his childhood in London's East End, growing up in poverty and fear. His family had worried constantly about getting from one day to the next. When he was twelve Tom's father died, making the family's situation worse. Tom was broken by the loss and worried that his family might not survive, but he did his duty, left school, and went to work. He kept his doubts and hurt to himself, but his fears and resentment over giving up school ate at him in silence. His younger sister had taken it especially hard and openly expressed the very fears Tom, pretending to be strong, tried to hide. At the time he thought of her as weak and tried to encourage her to be brave. He was really reassuring himself but did not know it. He seemed to put it all behind him and went through life with a stiff upper lip but a restricted capacity to respond emotionally.

Tom's visit reminded him of his frightened youth. He also began to worry openly that since he once had the same fears that his sister did, her fate might also become his. As was Tom's style when he returned to the United States, he did not talk about his concerns. Instead he became preoccupied with his fears, and each time he became afraid, he feared he would turn into his sister.

Tom's fearfulness made him lose his concentration. He stopped doing the odd jobs he had done since his retirement to keep himself occupied and supplement his income. As a result money became a little scarcer, causing him to worry even more and also reminding him of his childhood experience of poverty and his long-buried fears.

Experiencing his old fears again felt to Tom as if his prophecy were starting to come true. Tom now worried about getting so sick that he'd have to be put away. As he imagined the separation from his family, it brought back his sadness and desperation over losing his father. The more afraid he became, the more he feared his anxiety would cause him to lose those he loved.

Instead of being happy when his children visited at Christmas, Tom could only think of what would happen if he got sick. He could picture the worst coming to pass. In the greenhouse atmosphere of his Emotional Debt, Tom's fears began to grow out of control. He began to suffer anxiety attacks triggered by minor stressors that didn't seem to have a symbolic meaning. They were just feelings that exceeded the storage capacity of his Emotional Debt, causing it to overflow and startling him when it did.

When Tom finally began to talk about his fears and admit his concerns, his fear began to lose its grip, especially when he realized that he believed turning out like his sister was his punishment for resenting his father for dying.

It is characteristic that long-repressed anxiety is easily triggered by trivial detonators. The precipitation of an anxiety reaction in a person who has already worked himself up into an expectation of dread is a foregone conclusion. One does not need to analyze the psychodynamic meaning of shouting "Boo!" to such a person. The person's imagination fills in all the details.

It is easy to put yourself in an anxiety state. Indeed, it can be said that everyone who suffers from anxiety contributes in some way to making matters worse.

OBSESSIONS AND COMPULSIONS

Anxiety is often stored with suppressed anger.

When, like Norman, you have more anxiety stored than anger, you fixate on an external object and develop a phobia. This is typical of dependent people.

When you have more anger stored than fear, you become concerned about losing control of an angry impulse. This often becomes an obsession in which you doubt yourself. This is a typical reaction of controlling people. There are many common obsessions: you may doubt that you shut off the gas, locked the door, secured what needed to be secured. Such obsessions usually have two distinct components: the forbidden wish to express the anger and hurt someone, and the fear of losing control of your anger, of putting it into action and proving you are bad. These obsessions lead to compulsions, like checking to make sure you didn't take the angry action.

Sarah had great difficulty baking her husband's favorite date nut bread. Just as it came out of the oven she would worry that she had left shells in it. Lest he choke and die, she felt a compulsion to inspect the cake by taking it apart until it was a pile of crumbs. Sarah sometimes baked four or five loaves in succession. This would infuriate her husband.

Sarah was angry at her husband and held it in. She had long been angry at her father and also unable to express it. The father was severely abusive to her mother, and Sarah had often had the thought, "I wish he'd die." Just thinking such a terrible thought alarmed her, and she developed the habit of touching everything twice to undo it. When Sarah moved away from home, the touching compulsion seemed to improve, but the hidden resentment that was behind it still lived within her. After she married, Sarah found herself in another abusive relationship. Her anger at her husband reawakened her suppressed anger at her father. The new compulsion was a symbolic attempt to manage all the anger and correct her angry inner dialogue.

When you withhold hurt and anger, it's typical to have angry fantasies. Although you would never act on them, just thinking such things disturbs you and makes you question yourself. Your concealed anger reactivates old guilt messages such as, Am I good?, which in turn lead you to wonder if you are actually capable of committing such an angry act. It is in this state of uncertainty about your goodness and your ability to control your anger that you return to check the gas. You want to make sure you haven't lost your grip and that others are safe from your hidden angry wishes.

TO AVOID STORING ANXIETY

Silence is the partner of anxiety.

Express your fears. Don't be afraid of being afraid or of what others will think. If you're afraid, they probably have some concerns as well.

Test reality. How real is the danger you see?

Resist giving in to the fear. Use it. Don't become part of it.

Assume that you are strong enough to manage.

Don't overstate your weakness, looking to be saved.

Test your strength against the fear. Fight it.

Get out of the habit of expecting the worst to happen. This leads you to over-react to negative indicators.

Pay attention to positive signs.

Remember, you are the author of your life. How do you want it all to turn out? Do everything you can to make that possible and stop doing things that go against your plan.

DEALING WITH A FEARFUL RECOLLECTION

When a terrifying memory returns, see it as an opportunity to lower the pressure in Emotional Debt. The following will help you do this.

If the threat was mostly imagined, admit that you were merely afraid of being afraid. Think of how you were then, how you've grown since.

If the threat was real, accept that the danger existed.

Realize that the danger is now past and you survived.

Allow the full memory of the danger to return without pushing it away. Look at it the way you would watch a movie.

When the memory recurs don't react to the anxiety that comes with it. Merely state, "I really was afraid then."

Remind yourself that this fear has presented itself in order to be relieved and that its reappearance is just part of the natural healing process, fine-tuning, a good thing.

Expect the memory to continue to return. This keeps you from becoming disappointed or questioning your wellness or emotional integrity when it does. Remember, healing is a process, not a one-time, snap-your-fingers-and-you-are-better event.

Learning to welcome these returning memories as opportunities to resolve the problem takes away their sting. As you let go of the recollection, remind yourself once more that the danger is past, that you were safe while you remembered the danger, and that you are stronger for allowing it to surface and facing it.

STORING HURT

This case illustrates many of the consequences of storing hurt.

Cindy was a thirty-five-year-old housewife who had a bizarre response following an automobile accident. While driving into a parking lot she suddenly found another car directly in front of her. She could not understand why she had not seen it earlier and was unable to do anything but watch herself collide with it. The accident seemed to be taking place in slow motion, almost as if in a dream. As her car hit the other vehicle, the curious thought, Me too? crossed her mind, and instantly she became dizzy.

Although the damage was light and no one was hurt, Cindy felt disoriented. She exchanged information with the other driver and went into a shopping mall, attempting to put the episode aside. However, in the very first store she became confused and clumsy, dropping a pair of shoes and tripping over a display. An employee offered her a chair and suggested that she go to the hospital. Cindy gained her composure and left. After what seemed like a very long time trying to find her way through streets that suddenly seemed unfamiliar, she finally arrived home exhausted.

In the days that followed Cindy began to feel enclosed by a distantly familiar sadness she could not place. She also had a strange sense of disconnection, almost as if she were not herself, but merely floating through her life as an observer. She began to have intensely sexual dreams in which she saw herself reunited with her ex-husband, an alcoholic whom she had struggled hard to divorce. The dreams seemed to hold an undefinable but dark presentiment, causing her to wake in a sweat. She also began to have other bizarre dreams but could not remember their content, only that they were frightening and sad and yet she felt reluctant to let them go each morning and wake up. In spite of her present husband's support and understanding, Cindy's sadness increased to the point of depression.

Cindy portrayed her present marriage as perfect and was hesitant to talk about her past and only reluctantly revealed that she'd suffered severe losses when growing up. When Cindy was sixteen her beloved older brother was killed in an automobile accident. The circumstances of his death were never clear. Cindy explained he'd been up all night arguing with his girlfriend and the next morning he fell asleep at the wheel while delivering newspapers.

Cindy really wasn't sure how the accident took place and had only a shadowy recollection of him driving into another car that he had not even seen. "Hmm," she remarked with naive insight, "just like my accident." Cindy admitted that she originally wondered how her brother's accident had happened but couldn't think about it or ask questions. In fact her memory was focused not on the facts but mostly on her fantasies about the event. She simply did not want to admit that her brother had died.

Cindy had no recollection of the funeral or of ever mourning but did recall that she actively tried to block out any mention of her brother's death. When friends offered their condolences, she told them they were mistaken, that her brother had not been in an accident and was in fact still alive. She recalls that she was full of conviction when she pushed evidence of her brother's death away, even though she was vaguely aware he had died.

Within a few weeks of the funeral Cindy began to have intense, pleasurable dreams in which she saw herself and her brother carrying on their happy relationship. These pleasurable dreams increased in intensity, creating a peculiar kind of pressure that made it difficult for Cindy to release them and return to the waking world. She felt attached to her dreams but totally disconnected from her life.

The dreams stayed with Cindy until she was nineteen, when her mother suddenly died from a stroke. Cindy struggled with her mother's death and also tried to block it, but she was much less successful than she had been in shutting out her brother's death. Curiously, as she tried to push the pain away, the pleasurable dreams of her brother that had kept her company all these years also began to fade. Thus facing the loss of her mother made her more aware of the loss of her brother. Her old defenses did not hold.

When Cindy was twenty-one she realized she could no longer deny that her brother had died. Agitated by the return of the grief she had so long avoided, she ran to a relationship for solace. She found herself powerfully attracted to a man and became lost in the intensity of their sexual relationship. They created a world together that excluded everything else. Their highly dependent relationship felt unreal. It was another fantasy of safety Cindy was acting out. She became lost in the marriage until her husband revealed his true abusive character.

Even though she had not dealt with her past losses following her divorce, Cindy matured and grew in self-esteem. With her new confidence she was more at ease and less guarded. While her old losses were still held in Emotional Debt, bound by her repressive defenses, their natural inclination still remained to surface again and be relieved. Cindy's maturity and increased openness created more favorable conditions for these old feelings to intrude. They just needed a trigger to set them free.

Cindy's dreamlike accident felt like reliving a memory. Her comment, "Me too?" touched an awareness that pierced her denial and connected her to her old pain. At that point, her brother's death suddenly seemed real, and the repressed pain both from her brother's accident and her mother's death began to flood through Cindy's breached defenses.

Almost like a study in emotional archeology, when Cindy's old pain burst to the surface it brought some of her old defensive maneuvers with it. The first old defense to reappear was the sudden disorganization and confusion that immediately followed her accident. That confusion also characterized her first response to her brother's death. Likewise when her sadness emerged Cindy felt discon-nected, again the way she felt years ago. As more old pain emerged, Cindy be-gan to have highly sexual dreams, mirroring the way she used her sexual obsession to hide from the loss of her mother. The reluctance she felt in waking from her recent dreams, even though they were frightening, reflected how years ago she had hesitated to leave her consoling dreams and face life without her brother. Finally these dreams subsided, and Cindy found herself in a depression that represented all her unmourned losses coming home to roost.

Cindy's recovery was surprisingly rapid. Once her sadness was identified with the losses that caused it, she began to make sense out of her life. The relief that she experienced in letting go also motivated her and gave her courage to talk about what she had so ardently refused to admit years ago.

REMOTE EMOTIONAL DEBT
GLIMPSES OF OLD FEELINGS

The older your feelings, the more mysterious they seem. Sometimes a shad-owy remnant of a distant memory drifts into your awareness. A present event evokes something vaguely familiar, but you cannot make out its reflection in time's cloudy mirror. The trails of the memory fade, and you are left trying to place the intrusive disquiet.

You angle your mind to pursue the fragments of the memory and press along tangential side passages of recollection. You arrive at a cul-de-sac of memory that you know well but does not contain the one you sought. You sigh, feeling di-minishment. The path to the memory seems to have evaporated. To describe what you have almost remembered, you'd have to make a conjuring leap of imagination, creating the recollection as much as remembering it.

It is likely that many of the experiences commonly referred to as déjà vu are merely incomplete recollections of feeling fragments from the storehouse of re-mote Emotional Debt.

When you have a large backlog of remote Emotional Debt you are likely to be visited by vague feelings—some pleasant, some not—that you cannot read-ily identify. The awareness of these feelings usually occurs by unexpected trig-gering rather than intentional recall. When you do recall these feelings, you cannot be sure of the accuracy of the recollection or if it is a single or combined memory. It is fair to say that you experience remote Emotional Debt almost ex-clusively as Toxic Nostalgia.

The feelings in remote Emotional Debt also fuel attitudes and ungrounded fears. These effects are often subtle and appear as a vague mistrust or foreboding. They may not seem to make sense or have any clear relationship to the present, but the intrusions still have a certain power over you. They make you pause. They cause you to doubt yourself.

Sometimes the feelings of remote Emotional Debt surface when they coincide with similar feelings in the present, adding to them silently like a shadow, making them more prominent. The feelings in remote Emotional Debt often manifest in dreams as persistent and ambiguous moods. They are the building blocks of the recurrent dream.

Charles experienced such a reaction at his high school reunion banquet. After returning to his seat, which had been marked with his name tag, he found that someone else had taken his seat and the people around the table had closed ranks, essentially eliminating his place. It was unintentional of course, but he found himself becoming deeply hurt and then accusatory, offending his old classmates. His out-of-control behavior made Charles flush with petulance and reduced him to tears, causing him great embarrassment.

Charles had a manipulative father who thought he was a crybaby, and from as early as Charles could remember, the father set his two older brothers against him to toughen him up. Charles always got the worst of these conflicts and grew up feeling both defeated and unfairly treated. Charles could only express his hurt at the risk of being belittled by his brothers. He grew up at a distance from others, a kind of emotional fugitive, always looking out for the next possible injustice. Revisiting his high school, Charles found that his memories of childhood and feeling cheated began to resurface. These feelings merged with the oversight at the table and led him to overreact and create an unpleasant scene.

This quality of vague familiarity characterizes all feelings in remote Emotional Debt. Generally, as in Charles's case, that old feeling is not recognized as itself when it appears; instead you focus on the present situation on which it is superimposed. The situation may feel familiar enough to make you acknowledge, "See, it's happening again," without even being aware of the specific context of the older feeling. This is a good example of an emotional blind spot.

OLD ATTITUDES

When you get caught in a swell of old feelings, it is common to reexperience a childlike attitude of helplessness. This frightening attitude reflects your mental state at the time the feelings originally occurred. The painful feeling and your old attitude were stored together. The reappearance of these old attitudes undermines your self-confidence. When these attitudes reappear as Toxic Nostalgia, they seem to undermine the ability of your accomplishments to reassure you.

For this reason, when you have a life-shattering experience that cuts to the core of your self-esteem and allows the release of these feelings, you are momentarily struck with childlike powerlessness and terror, transformed into an earlier self.

EARLY FEELINGS

The feelings stored in remote Emotional Debt generally represent your earliest emotions. They are, therefore, also the most difficult to remember or define. When they do manifest as Toxic Nostalgia years later, they are likely to bear little resemblance to their original form but instead appear as cloudy distortions. Sometimes all that remains of these feelings may be the appearance of irrational attitudes, baffling feeling states, or physical symptoms, the timeworn remains of a nearly forgotten reality, a vague collection of miscellaneous events and injuries, highly contorted and incompletely remembered.

Even when what is remembered appears as a discrete event, it is just as likely to be a kind of mosaic, an assemblage of various bits of old emotions. Some of these emotions are real, some are the product of distortion, while other feelings and facts are appended later to provide logic and continuity to your memory as you fill in the blank places and try to make sense of it all.

It is typical for distant events to blend together, especially when they contain a common feeling. For example, when a young child is taken to a ball game, the zoo, or the circus with his family, he does not have a complete recollection of the event but recalls only fragments. He is carried, he is hungry, he eats, he sleeps, he watches the performers, he looks at the lights, the crowd. He is frightened and delighted. It smells. It's crowded. He has to go to the bathroom. Parents are irritated. There's a quarrel in the car. Everyone is exhausted when they get home. He's hungry, tired, and irritable.

However, years later when he "recalls" such an outing as an adult, he combines several circuses or ball games and also adds other recollections of childhood to the memory, both earlier and later. He also adds his general impressions of childhood and attaches them to the memory he is constructing, such as feeling loved by his family and the feeling of being together. He makes the memory more special than it was. Thus one memory of a happy day at the beach in early childhood undoubtedly stands as the symbolic memory for many other such days in childhood, days that otherwise would be lost forever.

A child from a troubled family does precisely the same thing but also uses denial to edit out the bad times as he experiences them. He tries to convince himself that he is safe and happy, that everything is fine. When he grows up and mysterious dark feelings plague him, it is these same "happy" memories that have to be penetrated to resolve the pain beneath.

This investment of many events in a single memory explains the emotional power of early recollections and also why they seem more intense, more loving and caring, or more neglectful and abusive. You weren't jaded then; everything seemed new, wonderful, and full. The good was also the best because you had nothing to compare it to. You were taken care of. You were free. You were not happy; you were in heaven. You were also powerless then, and minor threats seemed terrifying; small losses, catastrophes. You had no one to share this with and thought your life was the worst. You were trapped. You were not unhappy; you were in hell. For this reason when you compare the present to the past, the distorted recollections you use to make your point feel so convincing to you.

The fusion of many events into one memory fragment is especially typical of negative feelings. During traumatic periods when a child is confused and needs to make sense of his frightening surroundings, a single distinct negative memory can stand for many other hurtful events. This explains why recalled painful childhood events seem exaggerated or surreal and are so difficult to resolve.

If you were able to recall and resolve a particular early trauma, the other emotions that were attached to it might be settled, but then again they might not and instead would persist as amorphous feelings. Where before they had existed as hurts in care of a more distinct memory, there would now be no emotional address to reach them. They might linger unattached or recombine with other old memories as they continued to work themselves out. This explains why when you do resolve a painful old event in therapy, it sometimes does not seem to make you feel better.

Fortunately, the healing power of the mind seems to allow it to resolve many similar emotions at the same time. The momentum of healing carries along as much pain to resolution as possible. This explains why when a person understands how a particular emotional event had the power to trigger his old negative feelings, he is often able to apply that understanding to other situations and heal them as well, sometimes without even being aware he is doing so.

You are wounded particularly, but you heal symbolically and generally.

Until they fade completely all of your negative feelings in remote Emotional Debt continue to seek expression and resolution. Understandably, a particular old memory may not be real. It may even be a false bottom, protecting you from an even older memory. Perhaps you were too young to make sense of the earlier hurt when it took place, and it was stored as a pure sense memory that later attached itself to another event. The question of early memory is complicated.

What is remembered may not have happened.

What may have happened may not be remembered.

Sometimes you invent explanations for the feelings you remotely remember. It is natural to assume abuse to explain injury just as it is to assume danger to explain fear. If you remember being afraid as a child, you tend to exaggerate the danger you recall in order to make sense of your fearful reaction.

A young child fears abandonment, rejection, or the loss of a parent above all other hurts. From the child's point of view, a little separation feels like the end of the world, like being lost forever. His fears are exaggerated by his sense of helplessness.

For these reasons, when years later you cite a negative incident to support your belief that your parents were negligent or didn't care, your explanation will sound embellished. A single highlighted memory may serve as proof of many offenses, explaining why you may find it difficult to forgive a specific old hurt. What would you do with all the feelings you cannot explain if you let go?

Although there is considerable distortion present in all remote Emotional Debt, there is no doubt that many children actually suffer considerable trauma, deprivation, and abuse. Sorting out the truth remains an ongoing challenge. Identifying these early traumas, putting a name to sorrow, and determining what actually happened to you are the driving forces that lead you to analyze your life. And yet not all these mysteries are answerable. Often the best understanding you can reach is both approximate and unsatisfying.

It is typical to become highly suggestible in your search for answers to these ancient riddles of pain. In an attempt to settle the frustration of not knowing, you can fixate on something that feels right but is not really true. It is easy to be led into false beliefs in the name of healing. Much scapegoating takes place in the therapeutic process. If this results in forgiveness and progress, it can be argued that it is acceptable. Transference itself is a kind of scapegoating of the therapist that occurs during the therapeutic release of old unattached feelings as they search for a target to explain themselves. Even in the relatively controlled setting of a therapy situation, these transferred feelings can become a problem, transforming therapy into a mockery of healing and freezing the patient in unrelenting displacement of old feelings.

Forgiveness must be the principle guiding the release of such old feelings.

The feelings stored in early childhood are older and therefore perceived as being buried deeper. The hurt or anxiety of early childhood takes place before the complete range of emotional defenses is fully developed. Denial, whose purpose is to shield the helpless child, is present in early childhood and tends to be very powerful.

Denial binds the feelings stored in remote Emotional Debt and makes them much less accessible. They are not managed by intellectual defenses, for excuses and blaming require language skills, as does pretense, which develops even later. Therefore, when these old feelings intrude later in life, they do so almost purely as feelings, with scant details or explanations accompanying them.

Additionally, the quality of the Toxic Nostalgia that results when these older feelings encroach on the present feels not only mysterious but also debilitating and regressive. You reexperience the helplessness and powerlessness you felt years ago and feel dismayed for seeming so childish.

REMOTE EMOTIONAL DEBT AND STORED ANXIETY

Lily was a thirty-year-old woman who had an incapacitating fear of being in closed spaces. Over the years this caused her to avoid anything that could shut her in, including elevators, airplanes, any conveyance that had a door that locked, small rooms, any room without windows, and enclosed spaces such as theaters. As she got older her fear became more generalized and her mobility greatly restricted.

She had been in psychotherapy and on medication with little benefit, but the focus had been to try to control her symptoms rather than understand them. When Lily tried to understand her fear, she imagined herself trapped, and this precipitated more anxiety.

Remarkably, when asked the direct question, "Were you ever locked up as a child?" Lily gave a deep sigh and reported that when she was three years old her older brother once shut her up in a closet. She recalled her fear of the dark and the helplessness and futility she felt as she cried out to be delivered. No one heard her, and for what seemed an eternity she was her brother's captive.

Lily was let out of the closet by her brother just as her mother was coming into the room but was so upset she could not make her case. She remembered only rushing into her mother's arms for safety, hurt and enraged. She could not explain herself. Her mother criticized her and sent her to her room.

Lily recalled that her brother continually tormented her and that her mother was more interested in quickly making peace than in justice. The quiet child was rewarded. The noisy or crying child, usually Lily, was reprimanded. It was unfair, and there were no appeals allowed. Therefore Lily's pain of being locked in a closet was also connected to her disappointment over her mother's unfairness.

At the age of three Lily was just developing the verbal skills to arm the intellectual defenses of blaming and excuses. Considering her brother's attitude toward her and her mother's way of dealing with it, it was likely that Lily had been storing anger long before she was locked in the closet. Thus, feeling rage at being treated unfairly and not being able to express it lowered Lily's self-esteem to the point where in some way being locked in felt like deserved punishment and confirmed to Lily that she was bad. Certainly her mother reinforced that belief.

A child from a healthier environment would have protested more and stood up for her rights, but Lily's rebellion was suppressed before it got started. Had her mother been more sensitive and aware, she would have reassured Lily and set matters straight by demonstrating a sense of familial justice. She would have made expressing hurt acceptable rather than a crime punishable by disapproval.

This support was missing in Lily's case, and her well-justified anger, the result of being maliciously terrorized, was internalized lest she risk appearing bad. Thus revealing the anger at her brother, even though she could barely remember it, frightened her with the even greater loss of her self-esteem and her mother's love. Being trapped in an enclosed space therefore stood for becoming angry and risking rejection.

REMOTE EMOTIONAL DEBT AND STORED ANGER

Monica was a thirty-five-year-old engineer who suffered from an inexplicable sadness that seemed to live deep within her. From time to time it broke through, dampening her pleasure and robbing her of energy and optimism. The sadness presented itself as waves of hopelessness, a lack of joy, or a feeling of futility. At these times life seemed like a faded old movie. Curiously, these feelings seemed to intrude most when Monica's life felt positive.

Monica's friendships suffered because she brought an air of emotional caution into them that others mistakenly interpreted as her not caring. Monica was always holding back, limiting the expression of her feelings, both the good and the painful. At the movies she would sometimes watch others laugh and wonder why she couldn't. Her sexual life also suffered from a lack of a certain intensity, which her boyfriend took as her indifference. She protested that she really loved him but somehow felt she had a governor on her feelings that kept her from reaching her potential for pleasure.

At work the story was similar. Although talented and well liked by her coworkers, who thought of her as fair and kind, she did not have the close relationships that others in the office did. Her supervisor explained to her when she was passed over for a promotion that she lacked "interpersonal energy."

A review of Monica's life revealed that everything had gone well for her. She was loved, supported, and encouraged. Teachers admired her businesslike attitude toward school. She was easily taught and took pride in her work. Somehow each accomplishment she made, and there were many, did not seem to bring with it a sense of fulfillment or pride, but rather a feeling of "Is that all?"

There was no sense of passion in Monica's life. She lived emotionally shrouded but could not understand why.

The key to understanding Monica came through applying the principles of Natural Therapy and using them to build a map into her feelings. It was assumed that the sadness was a form of Toxic Nostalgia. As such it had to be the result of some inhibited hurt. Judging from the pervasive way in which the hurt manifested as Toxic Nostalgia, the hurt not only had to have been equally pervasive, but expressing it had to have been forbidden.

This was explained to Monica to help her review her early childhood once again. What were her parents like? "Wonderful, loving and caring," she replied. "There was nothing they wouldn't do for me," Monica expanded, and then became intensely sad.

"Why are you so sad, just now?"

"I don't know."

"Talking about your parents makes you sad?"

"I guess."

"Why?"

"They were . . . well, they were Holocaust survivors."

"Were they sad?"

"They were the only family each had. I was the only child." Monica looked out the window, totally lost in her sadness.

Living with her sad parents was Monica's lifelong pain. One of the reasons that early childhood hurts are so difficult to define and resolve is not just that the child is too immature to perceive the injury correctly or not strong enough to process it, but that the injury is subtle, constant, and in the truest sense of the word, familiar, part of the family. Monica's hurt was built into everything she experienced, accepted as normal and therefore not dealt with.

Such undefinable hurts still do their damage. Often their effect is more pervasive and in a sense more malignant than the injury that is a discrete event, because a specific loss is easier to mourn. Great damage can be done to a child by living in continual fear, such as in wartime, severe poverty, abandonment, or in a family where there is great emotional turmoil. Uncertainty pervades the home, and children grow up worrying, a difficult stress to define.

Monica's pain came in part from living with her parents' oppressive sadness. It tainted and diminished every experience.

As pointed out earlier, it is not what happens to you that is so important but how you deal with it. Some children endure terrible abuse and seem to survive quite well, while others are damaged by seemingly trivial injuries. It is the opportunity to resolve the hurts of childhood that determines what negative impact they will have on later life.

Monica was so sympathetic to her parents' sadness that she would do anything to make them happy. Unfortunately nothing she did made any difference. Children develop an important sense of their own power to be positive by the reinforcement they get from their parents. It is not so much subtle as it is nonverbal. From the earliest moments in a baby's life he is continually being prodded by parents to smile or react to them. When the child makes a positive move his parents reinforce it. To prove this point one need only think of how a parent responds when a child says Mama or Dada the first time. This feedback is everything in childhood. It empowers a child to believe he has the ability to make his parents happy. It bonds a child to the possibility and expectation of joy.

It is fair to assume that even if they put up a happy front, when Monica's parents turned their interest away from her, their sadness soon returned. Children look at their parents' faces to study the expressions they see. Children often read their parents' true emotions without the parents even being aware they are revealing them. The child reacts to a fearful look by crying even when his parent is trying to reassure him he is safe. The child knows just by looking what the truth is. In the same way, Monica knew there was something to be sad about but did not know what. Like all children, she probably suspected something was wrong with her.

More importantly, because her parents were "sweet and wonderful and had suffered so much," even if Monica knew what was hurting her, she couldn't speak up. It was impossible for Monica even to think about doing or saying something to them that might hurt their feelings. Saying, "I'm angry at you for being so damaged from the concentration camp," was totally out of the question even if it revealed the dark truth. There were no other relatives to balance her parents' sadness or show another way of feeling.

Monica went through school playing the role of the perfect student. No matter how well she did, she was somehow unable to get from her parents the approval or sense of pleasure she hoped for. They said the right words, but something indefinable was missing.

Monica remained the obedient child. She never rebelled in adolescence. The idea of causing her parents any more grief was unthinkable. And yet her secret wish was to be loved and cared for by happy parents. That hurt became the resentment she stored and gradually turned against herself.

Monica sought to become independent and move out on her own as soon as possible, telling her parents she didn't want to be a burden. Her real motivation was that she couldn't stand living in their dreary house anymore, but her rationalization for leaving made it more acceptable to her.

After moving out Monica felt comfortable only expressing sadness. She felt she had to deny her happiness because being happy would contradict the reasons she gave for leaving home. After a while Monica could only find peace by making herself sadder than her parents. If she admitted she left for selfish reasons, she would have to deal with the guilt of abandoning her parents and her suppressed anger at them. By not allowing herself to be happy, she could avoid this. She was worse off than ever. Her parents may have been sad, but she made herself miserable.

Monica was stunned when these hidden dynamics were pointed out. When it was shown how she had been victimized by her parents' sadness, she saw that her anger was justified. She realized they had passed their hurt on to her and made her part of their suffering. This realization allowed Monica to forgive her parents for not being stronger and herself for being angry at them. When she did, her sadness gradually faded, and she became free.

The negative atmosphere in your family, whether from addiction, poverty, prejudice, persecution, chronic physical or mental illness, or cultist religiosity, provides the air you breathe as you grow up. Whatever their cause, negative family settings all have secrecy, dishonesty, and emotional guardedness in common.

In such families it is hard to tell what is real because parents' limitations keep them from being open. In addition, it is hard to adjust to such families, because secrecy and dishonesty create inconsistency. The children never know what to expect and worry constantly and about everything. As a result they also become guarded and, in trying to adjust to inconsistency, they may become controlling.

Unhealthy families value appearances more than feelings. They constantly worry about what other people think. If you shame or expose the family by simply being honest, you're likely to be ostracized and not forgiven. Such families have unrealistic standards of behavior and manipulative definitions. Good means to be silent or acquiescent and withhold your feelings, inclining you to develop Emotional Debt. Bad means to be open. The greatest damage done by an unhealthy family is to thwart the child's expression of feelings and undermine his courage to stand up for himself.

A healthy family has simple honesty and loving acceptance in its corner. It needs nothing else. Its greatest strength is that it is a place where it is easy to express feelings and where everyday life is simple. You know what is wrong, because painful events are not concealed. You know how others feel, because they tell you. Because your feelings matter to others, you come to believe that you matter. The mystery of hurt is removed because it is openly accepted. You learn that even the worst disappointments can be managed just by being open.

The greatest help in overcoming a negative family atmosphere is more likely to be provided by teachers, mentors, friends, and heroes than by other family members. It's hard to find someone who isn't infected when they live in such an environment. You need someone to believe in you. When you have emotionally disturbed parents, a kind word of support from someone you respect can become the pillar of your self-esteem. Having someone else agree that your parents are controlling, unreliable, unreasonably fearful, or negative makes you feel better. Just learning that your parents can't be expected to be what you need allows you to let go of the expectation that they can be different.

FINDING YOUR PEACE

When you have suffered because of your family's negativity, it is difficult to approach them about it and practically impossible to get them to see your point of view. You'll be disappointed if you insist they take responsibility for the way they were. They'll protest how hard it was in those times, how much suffering they endured, and that they did the best they could with what they had and what they knew. They will be right, of course. And of course they will also be wrong.

Even though they are your parents, try not to take your hurt personally.

Realize that, like other people, your parents sometimes became trapped, helpless, and afraid to change.

People in such a state can become wrapped up in themselves and lose perspective.

Your job is to understand as much as you can about their limitations and blind spots.

If you can see how your parents were bound, you also have a clue how to set yourself free.

Overcoming the encumbrances of your family and accepting its limitations remains a lifelong task and is probably never fully completed.

Typically, when you accomplish something important later in life, your old hopes are reborn. Even though you realize it is unlikely, you find yourself wanting your family's unconditional approval or recognition.

Understanding the influence your family atmosphere had on you and accepting it without blame allows you to let go and enjoy your life without unrealistic expectation.

No matter what you have suffered, no one can hurt you the way you have hurt yourself by holding on to the past. For that matter, no one else can save you.

Only you can let go.

ADOLESCENCE AND REMOTE EMOTIONAL DEBT

One of the reasons adolescence can be so turbulent and disorienting is that it becomes the symbolic battlefield on which the unresolved struggles of early childhood seek expression and resolution. Sometimes it feels as if all these old problems surface at the same time. Adolescence, in a sense, is just a prolonged period of Toxic Nostalgia. Old pain, partially remembered and distorted, is symbolically displayed and acted out with fury.

Adolescents disturb their parents deeply because the parents sense that, even if the war is undeclared or the prime targets are located outside the family, the rebellion taking place is clearly directed against them. Children from the best families associate with society's outcasts. The prejudiced parent finds his child in love with someone from the most hated group. The professor's child flunks out of school. It is easy to take such transparent acting out personally, as meant to hurt you, because that is its intention. The child hurts the parent by being self-destructive, the only way he feels he can do so without feeling guilty. The parent is often stirred into upscaling his controlling activity. The adolescent now points to this as proof of the parent's unreasonableness.

Nevertheless, adolescence offers a unique opportunity to resolve old conflicts. Bear in mind that as a young child the adolescent probably had only a vague feeling about his family's destructive habits and felt too weak to protest them. His expression of hurt, which has now evolved into anger, is long delayed, and while it is uncomfortable and confusing to everyone involved, it is necessary for establishing his self-esteem and confidence.

The stored feelings in Emotional Debt start to come loose. Energized by sex hormones and reinforced by peer support and his own firsthand experience and impressions of the world, the adolescent is propelled into acting out. What no one wanted to admit before is now pushed into everyone's face.

Although some adolescents go too far, adolescent rebellion is generally a sign of health. Unfortunately some adolescents are too timid or their parents too powerful, and their rebellion can be quashed. In its place self-destructive patterns blossom, and the child immolates himself trying to wrest sympathy for being a good child rather than learning to please himself.

It is at this time that eating disorders begin in an otherwise "perfect" child. It is also when obsessive-compulsive disorders show, as the mind is sent on the fruitless errand of trying to rationalize symbolically, or by means of ritual, the child's repressed anger. When there is no place left to store denied feelings, symptoms often appear. Symptoms are manifestations of Toxic Nostalgia.

Psychological illnesses in which denial plays a significant role such as manic-depressive illness and schizophrenia can become activated at this turbulent time. The fear of rebelling increases ambivalence. Unresolved feelings flood the defenses, producing bizarre thoughts and behavior. At the very same time there is a sudden flux of sexual hormones filling the adolescent's mind with unfamiliar thoughts and urges. He tries to gain control. The adolescent attempts to store more feelings in his burgeoning Emotional Debt. This creates more pressure than some adolescents can manage. It is at this point that defenses become entrenched and recognizable disease patterns become evident.

No matter how precarious or trying, a successful adolescent rebellion is a wonderful antidote to the toxins of early Emotional Debt. Some adults who did not experience an adolescent rebellion themselves can become so stirred up when their child rebels that they become as repressive as their own parents on the one hand or act out in a childish way themselves on the other.

SHAME

Instead of internalizing his anger as guilt, a young child is more likely to feel shame. The child easily comes to the conclusion that he is bad for feeling angry and feels ashamed of himself.

This shame is stored as a negative self-image and inclines the child to punish himself for being bad whenever he is hurt. A shameful child's hurt seems to evolve directly into self-castigation. The only anger he feels comfortable expressing is at himself.

In the so-called terrible twos the child struggles to express his anger through his newly acquired mastery over his body and his acquisition of verbal skills. As he tests the limits of what is acceptable he often breaks the rules and is reprimanded for being bad. Since he already feels bad, he gets into additional trouble to get punished and ease his mind. He has a flawed conscience combined with a limited capacity to store negativity. Punishing a child too severely at this age only produces more anger, which fuels his need to seek external punishment and leads him to disobey again. This explains why such children are studies in exasperation.

If you didn't learn to express hurt as a child, you become an adult plagued with shame. When you feel guilty you're likely to suffer self-criticism, sometimes justified, sometimes unreasonable. When you feel shame you often act self-destructively, with a tendency to gravitate toward hurtful situations. This explains why so many people embrace hopeless scenarios.

People who harbor inaccessible anger usually doubt their goodness and expect rejection. Because their character was formed at a time when they were likely not to be verbally expressive, dependent people particularly experience shame. They often become trapped in abusive relationships to balance their long-internalized anger. Their shame makes sense out of a relationship they know intellectually is bad for them. Probably because such relationships are often abusive, they permit the dependent person to express his old hurt in a passive way, like a child.

BORDERLINE STATES

The Emotional Debt model explains borderline states. A borderline personality is one whose feelings are mainly derived from past events but are continually being triggered into present awareness. Since others are unaware of the source of these old feelings and react to them as if they were real, the borderline person can often point to the present situation, with some justification, as the cause of his injuries. This makes borderline people extremely difficult.

When Emotional Debt becomes full, your focus becomes inwardly directed, leading you to take everything personally. Since your denial is very strong, you can't tell where your feelings come from or what they mean. Your belief that others are responsible for hurting you makes you see the world as against you.

The large volume of stored emotions in the borderline person poses severe problems as they continually mount escapes from their defenses, attaching themselves to innocent events as soon as they emerge.

In a sense a borderline person suffers from chronic and debilitating Toxic Nostalgia. His level of Emotional Debt is so high that he is continually being triggered. At any moment he can suddenly take an innocent remark the wrong way and brimming with self-righteous anger from many remembered affronts, attack his perceived assailant without mercy. To the targets of this symbolic display, the person appears crazy.

Borderline people are very difficult to treat or live with. Their high level of Emotional Debt can lead them so far away from reality that from time to time they seem psychotic, but by and large they live in a real world furnished with feelings derived from the past.

PSYCHOSIS AND EMOTIONAL DEBT

Psychosis is a relinquishment of the reality sense to the point where you accept your inner perceptions of the world as true, without questioning if they are real. In the absence of reality testing, thoughts are amplified to voices, while dreams, memories, and fantasies are taken as actually perceived external images. Logic is subverted and not to be trusted. Ideas become fixed in belief, whether or not reality can substantiate their validity. Isolation and withdrawal add to your inclination to distort. Because you have lost your bearings, fear fills in the empty spaces of your life. Confusion and terror feed on each other.

When you are psychotic, you completely believe something that is entirely untrue. A delusion is a false belief, unsupported by reality. A delusion is often a compensation, much as fantasy is, for a loss or diminishment. Cindy's insistence that her brother was still alive was not really a delusion, rather a pretense, because she really knew he was dead. A wish, no matter how unrealistic, is just a wish unless you don't know it is. A delusion is a pretense where reality testing has been at least momentarily suspended.

When one's Emotional Debt capacity is suddenly and massively overwhelmed, a psychotic reaction can result. In a sense you deny the world, turn inward, and become submerged in Emotional Debt. Since contact with the real world is tenuous during a psychotic reaction, it is important for others to get through to you and draw you out, helping you adjust to the painful loss or overpowering fear that has driven you inward. Left to yourself, you may not return. Such transitory flights into psychosis are not as rare as once thought.

When Emotional Debt and denial are great and the tendency to run from the world and turn inward becomes established as a defensive pattern, the precarious course for a more tenacious psychotic reaction is set. While many factors play into the development of different kinds of psychoses, including the anatomical disarray of cells in the associative part of the brain, heredity, substance abuse, the involution of aging, alterations of brain chemistry and the like, the psychological dynamics of Emotional Debt still remain powerful mediators of disorganizing stress. The unexpressed flood of feelings from Emotional Debt, remote, recent, and current, lead you to shut down, block your sensory apertures, and close out reality.

Left in this inner world of self-justifying logic without the correction of reality testing, you can drift far from the shores of reason. In this nether landscape of uncontested logic, a hope is as good as reality, symbols become real, and words magical. Wishing makes it so. Because the greatest casualty is the truth, no healing takes place here, merely projections of your broken heart lost in time, trying to stop the world, without being obliged to recognize its existence.

Psychotic reactions are best addressed as quickly as possible, for when defenses become too rigidly established they can become impermeable and their costly maintenance can drain your entire being. When defenses become rigid, interest in the outside world diminishes. The gaiety of life becomes a distant memory. There is little to capture your interest. It becomes increasingly difficult to reach or treat you.

Regardless of the method of treating a psychotic, the results are made more permanent by teaching him coping mechanisms to deal with his feelings in the moment. The goal is to deal honestly with the present, allowing the natural therapeutic process to work so that the level of Emotional Debt is kept to a minimum.

No matter how sophisticated the psychopharmacology of treating psychosis becomes, managing feelings more directly will always be an important line of defense and adaptation.

EMOTIONAL DEBT AND AGING

As you age, the presence of distant memories often seems more intense while recent memory seems ephemeral. Oddly, some nearly forgotten memories seem to break loose, intruding as ancient flashbacks both in the waking state and in dreams. Other memories seem to become irretrievably lost in now-inaccessible parts of the brain. Perhaps this is a function of decreasing brain cells so that some memories are cut off from access routes to consciousness while others simply fade. Maddeningly, new memories cannot find storage space and drift away before their information can be more permanently recorded. It is as if the scratch pad memory has been encroached upon and forgetfulness ensues.

Even though a specific memory may fade, the feelings associated with it may still occupy storage space and diminish the person's Emotional Debt capacity. When you age, you seem to reach the overflow stage of Emotional Debt, where now a current experience that would normally be felt as sentimental takes on tragic proportions as it couples with these older losses. This explains why the elderly are prone to emotional displays.

Unlike the borderline and the psychotic, the reality sense is well preserved in ordinary aging. However, easy irritability and self-centeredness, and a tendency to focus on your personal discomfort, are the hallmarks of aging. In addition, because you are approaching the storage capacity of Emotional Debt, your defenses are less flexible and your adaptability diminishes. You seem crabby and set in your ways as you obsess over the irritations of growing older. There are many assaults on your personal integrity: failing memory, decreased mobility, declining health, physical strength and stamina, increased dependence on people who prove short-tempered or unreliable, not being taken seriously or listened to, being patronized or treated like a child.

Chronic, unrelenting stress also ages you prematurely by filling your Emotional Debt to capacity.

THE LEGACY OF EMOTIONAL DEBT

Even though you may try to be open, face your hurts honestly, and express your emotions as they occur, there is always some residual hurt that goes unmourned. Much of this residue is processed by the natural therapeutic process without your even being aware of it. This is what is meant when we say time heals. Even so, some emotional remnant remains unexpressed and seems to get lost in the brain's storage network. Imperceptibly, this agglomeration grows and continues to combine with other stored feelings.

WHEN YOU ARE IN EMOTIONAL DEBT

Digging into remote Emotional Debt as a psychotherapeutic tactic is fraught with danger. Understanding the dynamics of the earlier times can be extremely helpful, but to insist on having someone relive these old feelings and relinquish the perspective of adulthood to reexperience them can produce such an overflow of bad feeling that the cure creates more problems than the disease.

Knowing what took place in early childhood can only be approximated, but it can still have therapeutic benefit. You do not need to know all the details. It should be clear by now that you can't know all the details. Merely being able to say, "I wasn't cared for," or "I was mistreated," or "I was rejected," will provide enough of an emotional platform to understand the prejudicial slant of feelings that intrude. You simply want to be able to identify the feeling as old business. Being able to say, "There's that feeling of being cheated from my past, making me feel suspicious again," is about as good a resolution as you can hope for.

Again, the goal is not to go onto the old battlefield again, but to admit the old hurt and forgive your oppressors.

MANAGING EMOTIONAL DEBT

The feelings in remote Emotional Debt are not easy to resolve. Not only are they blocked by denial, they are further distorted by being perceived through a child's perspective and reported with a child's limited language skills.

If you were in intensive long-term psychotherapy and succeeded in reconstructing and examining your early emotions, you might be able to place what happened to you in an adult perspective. At best you might diminish the intensity of your concern when these feelings later intruded in the future. However, since these early feelings cannot be completely resolved and the way in which Emotional Debt is stored eventually becomes your personality type, the potential for Toxic Nostalgia intruding from this early time would still remain. When it did, you'd be able to say, "There's that feeling of being cheated from my past, making me feel suspicious again."

While it is a reasonable goal to reduce the negative feelings in current and recent Emotional Debt, it isn't always possible to do this for the feelings in remote Emotional Debt. Everyone has some residual feelings from this time that exist as negative attitudes, as inner disquiet, or as character traits. However, by becoming more open and honest, you can reduce the intensity of all these old feelings and decrease your likelihood of acting on them.

A GUIDE

The following guide will help you express your feelings in current, recent, and remote Emotional Debt.

The next time you feel overwhelmed by an event that seems to release a greater emotional response than you expected, try to get a little distance. Don't permit yourself to get lost in rage or tears, exasperation or fear. Instead pay close attention to the unexplainable part of your response.

Accept that your old feelings have just been activated. See this intrusion as a privilege and be grateful for the opportunity to heal that it provides. Consider what just happened and how you reacted. Setting your self-justification aside, ask yourself: Is there any excessive volume in the feelings I am expressing?

This is a very difficult thing to admit since, like everyone else, you want to think of yourself as well-balanced and appropriate. Remember, this is an exercise in deciphering the forces that lead you to distort. Be patient and open to the possibility that you are not perfect. This may help you discover a new strength.

Ask yourself: Are my present feelings at all inappropriate, childish, prefabricated, or familiar? Try to define how. Focus again on the present event that triggered your excessive response and ask yourself: What older feeling gave this trigger its power to disturb me so? Give yourself time to hear the answer. If the feeling is vaguely familiar, ask what it reminds you of.

If this feeling brings another situation to mind, consider that other situation but don't relive it. You are a time traveler. Just observe yourself in the previous situation if you can. Your goal is to understand what happened, not to allow yourself to get lost in the old pain again.

Don't put the feeling aside because it is uncomfortable. Just acknowledge how powerful the emotion feels.

Now, still holding this older feeling at a little distance, realize that it has been triggered into awareness because it wants to be expressed.

Try to place its source as exactly as you can.

Now just feel the feeling again.

Give the feeling a name.

If it is guilt or anger seek to identify the hurt you suffered.

If it is sadness or disappointment, describe the loss you suffered.

If it is anxiety, try to define what you thought might happen to you.

Now let yourself feel the feeling again.

This time define the details of the situation.

What happened?

How old were you?

Who else was involved?

What did they do or say?

How did you react?

How did you want to react?

Why couldn't you do what you wanted?

Is that really the truth?

Now ask yourself how you contributed to this situation.

Did you have similar old feelings intruding then?

What were they, and where did they come from?

Apply these same questions to that even older situation.

Correct your responses so they are as truthful as possible.

Remember, your truthful acceptance of all you feel activates the natural therapeutic process to resolve it. If you are successful in this exercise you will create a brief moment of mourning in which you grieve the past anew. Again feel the feeling and allow yourself to let it go.

Letting go is an exercise in believing in yourself.

BEING FREE

You are here to give your gift. Your Emotional Debt prevents you from giving your best effort. You deserve to be as free of Emotional Debt as possible. The interest you pay on Emotional Debt is your lack of participation in the present. As a result your energy is diverted from pursuing your life purpose to maintaining the futile vigil of keeping the past from reemerging. When you try to shut out the pain of the past, you also rob yourself of the richness of your history. The forces that contain your pain also confine your positive emotions.

You bury the past at the risk of losing wisdom.

When you hide from your weakness you lose the ability to reaffirm your strength and the meaning of life.

When you conceal your sorrow, you also hide your love.

You need to be truthful about the past and allow the Natural Therapy process to help you come to acceptance.

You are a prisoner of all you cannot accept.

9

DEFENSES: THE INSTRUMENTS OF DISTORTION

THE NATURE AND ORIGIN OF DEFENSES

The purpose of your defenses is to cushion you from the full impact of a fear or hurt so that you can function. Your defenses are designed to provide a temporary adaptation to danger or loss. When their usage becomes more firmly established, they predispose you to create Emotional Debt.

The way your defenses screen your pain defines your style of coping. You tend to admit the friendly feelings and exclude those that hurt. Your defenses skew your view of the world. As they become more established, your defensive pattern becomes your reality.

Healing begins when you admit the truth of your pain.

You cannot get better if you refuse to feel.

You cannot grow if you are defended.

DEFENSES ARE TEMPORARY

Defenses are not designed to be used as a permanent shield against pain. If you used them that way you would never adapt to the real world but instead would retreat into a realm of fantasy. Here everything would be as you wanted it, but it would not be real. The price you would pay for such imagined happiness would be to lose the ability to risk, to love, or to find lasting fulfillment. Instead your life would become constricted and you would become a figment of your defenses. Anything that could reveal the truth you wished to avoid would create anxiety and have to be excluded. In time you would become a prisoner of the very defenses that were supposed to protect you. Furthermore, maintaining a defensive vigil is a costly enterprise, obliging you to be forever on the alert.

Your defenses are designed to help you survive, not escape from pain. Properly employed, your defenses provide you with a little extra time, a kind of emotional breathing space, in which you set aside your terror or loss, get your resources together, and act to save yourself.

Any soldier who has seen combat will testify how a certain numbness takes over in the heat of battle, shutting off feelings. In this state the soldier disregards the pain of physical injury and, though afraid, acts as if he were immune to fear. When a comrade close by is killed, he sets his grief aside and moves onward to save himself. Later, when the danger has diminished, his denial releases its grip. Then he feels the pain of his injury and the sadness of losing his companion and realizes what a close call he had. He relives his postponed feelings anew. His defenses have held his feelings in current Emotional Debt so he could concentrate on surviving. He may have guilt for not saving his friend, but in time, if his defenses are kept low, he will cope with the truth of his experience, accept that he did what he had to do.

THE NATURE OF DEFENSES

A defense is really a lie that is built into your character.

While it is true that everyone uses the same defenses, people tend to rely on one particular kind of defense more than others. Since a defense is a distortion that is built into the way you perceive, it is likely that your defenses intrude without your consent. Defenses are the guardians of your blind spot.

Defenses lead you to make decisions almost without thinking. You may believe these decisions are in your best interest, but more than likely they really work against you. These automatic responses are initiated when you are threatened. Defensive reactions tend to be generalized, like a habit, and therefore do not address the specific problem at hand. Your defenses also guard your unrealistic beliefs from being tested. Even if you know that you're just fooling yourself, you'd still like to believe you're always lovable, smart, good, strong, right, successful, and attractive. As soon as one of your cherished beliefs is challenged, you tend to act defensively.

For example, if you're insecure and fear being wrong or appearing stupid and someone offers you constructive criticism, your defensiveness intercepts to protect your self-esteem.

You may deny the problem exists. You may repeat, "I've got it," before you have even heard the other person's point.

You could attribute insincere motivation to his criticism to soften any truth it may contain by rationalizing, "He's just picking on me."

You may try to intimidate the critique by diverting him: "Don't come back here. It's dangerous." You may make excuses and insist you were just following directions. Then again you may pretend to listen and then carry on as if you couldn't care less.

All these defensive ploys infuriate the person who is trying to help you, knows exactly what you're doing, and thinks of you as difficult. Sheltered from the truth that you need to know, you do not correct your mistakes, you do not grow, and you only set yourself up to make bigger mistakes in the future.

CRUISIN' FOR A BRUISIN'

Because you don't want to look at your faults, take responsibility for your actions, or admit you're in trouble, your defenses comply and hide your shortcomings from your awareness. When something goes wrong you have to raise the height of your defensive barrier to protect yourself from reality's detracting evidence to avoid self-criticism. Each time a problem occurs, it needs to be bigger to get your attention.

When finally it all goes badly and is happening right there in your face, you are stunned. First, because you can see that you were wrong and the problem you denied is actually happening. You're also shaken because the problem has caught you unaware. You thought this could never happen. You never took it seriously, and so you aren't prepared to deal with it. Now you have to admit you were mistaken in your perceptions and reasoning. Your self-esteem slips. All the criticism you pushed away comes back to haunt you. You doubt yourself and question if you were ever right. Still, the collapse of a defensive wall provides the view you need to find the right way.

Some people just keep on raising their defensive walls and continue to hide. This explains why so many people repeat their problems again and again, marry the same losers, work for the same miserable bosses, get cheated the same way without seeming to learn their lessons. They come to believe that the world is against them. The world is just fine. It is their defensive patterns that view and sort the world in predetermined ways and come up with the same narrow questions and answers, obliging them to repeat their mistakes or hide.

GUARDING

When you are defended you seem on guard, a little distant and removed. You read hidden meanings into others' words. You find ulterior motives. You react to the world as if it is unfriendly. You don't like or trust yourself for thinking this way.

Guarding is understandable. When you're defended, you're trying to conceal your negative feelings and the opinion of you they seem to support. You'd hate people to know what you're really thinking.

When you're defended you become inflexible. You lose your ability to be subtle. You want to know too quickly what something means or what someone is trying to say. Your impatience comes from your belief that you are in danger. You just want to know where safety lies. You speak too soon without knowing the facts. Your prejudice reveals the very hand you are trying to conceal.

Guarding is a posture of fearful expectancy. Because you really don't know what you're afraid of, everything is seen as a potential threat. You cannot be openly accepting or give others the benefit of the doubt. You need to categorize people so you know how to react to them. As a result you're continually misjudging. You do not trust others, and you feel urgently pessimistic. You can't allow a situation to develop on its own, because you have a need to control the outcome. This leads you to act prematurely or in set ways that do not entirely fit the circumstances and to create the very situation you hoped to avoid.

HOW DEFENSES LIMIT YOU

YOU CAN'T SEE CLEARLY

Your eye is directed inward. You are preoccupied. You edit what you view, hear, or feel. To be comfortable you exclude disagreeable facts. This makes you even more uncomfortable, because you need to know what you're shutting out. Instead, you imagine the worst and are inclined to act on your misperceptions.

YOU DON'T SPEAK UP IN TIME

Defenses are an emotional straitjacket—sometimes looser, sometimes tighter, but when you are defended even small amounts of stress can make you feel restricted.

You become shy, afraid of what other people will think. Since your defenses hold in hurt and anger, you always feel as if you're running the risk of disclosing how you feel. When these stored feelings become exaggerated, your fear is based on a misperception of yourself as being angrier and therefore nastier than you really are. You want to release your negative feelings, but you are afraid of admitting the pain that caused them. You want to complain, but because you are defended your clarity suffers and you aren't really sure you have something to complain about.

This ambivalence robs you of your spontaneity. Instead of being open, you watch everything you do or say. You are afraid of giving yourself away. You wait for the right moment.

You bite your tongue and suffer.

You Can't Seem to Express Yourself

Even though you may have a pretty good idea of what you feel, when you are defended the words don't come. Your defensive delay, which was supposed to protect you, has allowed your feelings to incubate. The minor hurt that has built into a preoccupying anger now doesn't feel appropriate anymore. At the very moment of making your feelings known, they seem exaggerated. Doubt takes over. You wonder if you are making all this up, if you're crazy.

You puff up your case to justify all this anger and make too much of your hurt. You accuse the other person of evil intentions. Before you know it, you're in a fight. At the very moment you want to be heard, get a little sympathy, and maybe an apology, you find yourself making war, hurting the other person instead of coming to peace and feeling better. Everything seems confused. You wish you had kept your mouth shut.

Even with the best of intentions, the expression of a specific old hurt often goes badly because of the general downloading of other stored anger that occurs at the same time. Since your natural inclination is to release your stored feelings, even when you aren't entirely sure of what you're expressing, you feel good and right in letting go. You're at a crossroads; although you're feeling some relief, you don't like yourself for expressing these feelings, and you feel uncomfortable holding them in. You felt justified when you started to tell the other person how you felt, but now you're overdoing it and getting a little confused and panicky. You seem a little out of control.

Lowering your defenses to express feelings makes you vulnerable. The longer you've been holding feelings inside, the more vulnerable you feel when you begin to open up. You are revealing that you have been feeling hurt for a while. You're showing your weakness.

This show of vulnerability can be very frightening and cause you to shut down at the very moment you need to be expressive.

YOU CAN'T REMEMBER

When you are defended, your memory suffers. Defenses, especially denial, act as the gates of memory and perception. Their purpose is to monitor and intercept painful messages. Your defenses were designed to interfere with the perception of an injury. To be sure you are protected, whatever can remind you of the injury also tends to be at least partially defended against.

Since defenses are not usually highly specific, the dampening effect of your defenses will inhibit your ability to remember in general, especially details. While you may wish certain ideas and facts to cross the border into awareness, your defenses are conducting thorough inspections and slowing down the traffic of the mind.

YOU BECOME LESS SPONTANEOUS

Defenses diminish your capacity to think freely, extemporize, elaborate, and dream. Your creativity suffers. You are not playful. The poet in you withers. Lighthearted flights of imagination and humor become strangers to you.

Although your defenses are supposed to guard you from negativity, they merely cause you to carry old hurt around with you. This close association to unreleased pain sets you in an inhospitable mood. You operate more out of habit and tend to become rigid and cling to the rules. Your work seems more and more measured and mechanical as you try to hold everything in place.

YOUR EXPERIENCE IS DIMINISHED

Your ability to find life's goodness is diminished by defensively shutting out your pain. As a result your experiences tend to seem shallow and repetitive. It's easy to become cynical and ask, "So what?" You take less from the good and see the bad as a confirmation. It is as if your defenses screen what you experience.

When you go to the market in an angry defensive state, you seem to notice disagreeable customers, surly cashiers. You are unable to find what you were looking for and are irritated by high prices and poor quality. If you had been undefended and open on the very same errand, you might have had a pleasant conversation with a clerk, helped a senior citizen find an item she was looking for, come up with a creative idea for dinner, and tried a free sample of a new salad dressing.

Your defenses shape both what you recall of your experience and how you perceive the present. In fact the reason you see the present the way you do has more to do with how you have resolved your past hurt than almost anything else. If you have let go of the past you are free to live fully in the present. When you hold on to the past you are bound to repeat it.

You Defeat Yourself

Defenses limit you the most by putting you in your own way.

If you think about it, you are the person who is most likely to damage yourself. If you are in your own way, you don't need any other enemies to defeat you. In fact the people who try to beat you need only get you to beat yourself. They just find your weakness and play to it. You do the rest.

If you are unaware of your weakness, you're flying blind in a hostile world. You come from need not from strength. Because you make unrealistic demands and have little patience with others, you create enemies. Finally, since your weaknesses are obvious to everyone but yourself, it is tempting for others to retaliate by controlling and frustrating you. Without even being aware of it, you've already shown them how.

Other people can control you only if you are afraid of being open. They need only lead you into fearful terrain. Thus if you are afraid of expressing anger, someone can easily bottle you up by making you a little angry. Internally you do all the heavy work. You doubt yourself, hold back, bite your lip, all the while fearing you will blow. You become easy to manipulate.

Similarly you can never be fooled, unless you want to avoid the truth. If there is something you do not want to know, it can be right in front of you and you will not see or hear it.

Desperation leads you to compromise yourself. People rarely test a lifeboat for leaks when the ship is sinking. Your desperate needs do you in the most by making you take what you can get, not wait for what you want or what is right for you. Hungry to be loved after being jilted, you suddenly find true love in the most unexpected places. You're sure it's real this time. You've made your mind up. No one can tell you anything. You have to find out for yourself that it is you who has done yourself in . . . again.

When you avoid your pain, you are motivated into action to replace rather than mourn what you have lost. The same denial that blocks your hurt also causes you to be less discriminating. Impulsivity and rashness rule. To replace what you have lost, you accept the first substitute you find. Your poor choice causes you more anxiety. You want it to be right this time, but it isn't. Your uncertainty propagates the very climate that breeds more desperation.

You are always the accomplice in your own betrayal. Accept this for the simple truth it offers. Think back on your life, at all the mistakes and bad choices you made. Consider what motivated you to interpret the lesser path as the greater. In all these cases you were trying to avoid looking at your weaknesses, admitting your responsibility, or telling the truth.

Don't look to discover who led you astray.

You can blame your parents, siblings, friends, lovers, teachers, bosses, the system, and the times. Even though people lead you astray all the time, they are not at fault. They may have led but it was your responsibility to look and ask if the way felt right. It was your job to express your feelings and to search for a more honest way of living and being. Others may have pointed the way, but it was you who decided to follow.

Your denial allowed you to stay too long in a situation that was painful or not in your best interest. Perhaps you doubted yourself or were afraid of change. Even so, staying there eroded your courage to risk.

When you blamed others, you failed to learn your lesson. You tried to conceal your vulnerability by being powerful, and you alienated the people you most wanted to get close to or who could teach you.

When you pretended you didn't care, life began to lose its meaning. After a while others tired of your indifference and you stopped believing in yourself.

Look no further; you are the one who did all this to yourself.

You Repeat Your Mistakes

Unable to see the truth clearly, you suffer.

Unable to take responsibility for your errors, you do not learn.

Unable to be open, you do not gather new information, and your opinion becomes rigid.

Unable to admit you were wrong, you apply the same logic, come to the same conclusions, and take the same actions.

Defenses and Character Formation

Your defenses are the single most defining part of your character. Your defenses shape the way you react to the positive as well as the negative parts of your life.

Your defenses determine how honest, open, loving, trusting, giving, expressive, responsive, caring, compassionate, sharing, accepting, patient, and forgiving you are.

They also define your capacity for deceit, suspicion, resentment, dishonesty, isolation, withholding, indifference, restlessness, irritability, and cowardice.

When your defenses are rigid they lower your self-esteem and lead you to be self-destructive. They diminish your ability to see and hear clearly. They undermine your ability to act spontaneously in the moment and lead you to procrastinate. They make you fearful, mistrustful, and protective. They limit your ability to grow.

When your defenses are lowered and you are willing to be vulnerable, you learn easily from your experiences. You feel optimistic in spite of heavy odds against you because, aware of your limitations and failures, you still believe in yourself. When you are vulnerable you are not without defenses, but rather you are flexible and have a choice in using them. You don't waste energy hiding from yourself. You don't have to be perfect. You can be brave without denying the danger you face. You can accept criticism without blaming others. You can take failure without being crushed and can admit how you contributed to it.

DEFENSES SHAPE YOUR WORLD

Your defensive pattern also determines how others react to you. People tend to be more open with open people and closed with people who are guarded. Defended people are difficult to be around, harder to talk to, less rewarding to share with. Open people are fun to be with because they do not expect you to be a certain way. They allow you to be yourself, so there is less stress when you are in their presence. You don't have to work at being, you simply are.

Your defensive pattern frames your world by setting up others to respond to you in a specific way. Their response can either reinforce your defensive pattern or cause you to take stock of yourself and encourage you to change. You can insist you are right and the world is wrong, or you can decide there is something in the way you treat others that is making them act the way they do. It depends on you. It always does.

The old saying, "You get what you give," is particularly true when it comes to understanding your defenses. If you are suspicious or demanding, you get a surly response from others. The people who get the best service are not the biggest tippers, but the friendliest, most outgoing people. Ask any waiter. People respond quickly to negative people only because they are trying to get rid of them.

No two people experience the world the same way. Your defenses explain both how you interpret what you see and why the world treats you as it does.

Nature vs. Nurture

In light of this discussion of defenses, the long-debated question, Is it heredity or environment that shapes us the most? seems incomplete. After all, children from the same family with the same heredity and upbringing adapt very differently and develop entirely different personalities. The way each child develops his defensive pattern in response to life's stress is a unique inner adaptation. Each child contributes his own part to his evolution.

For example, the unresponsive child is treated less lovingly because it is less rewarding to give to such a child. While most parents would instinctively deny this and claim they loved all of their children equally, in their hearts what parent does not have a favorite?

Being a parent's favorite doesn't depend on being good, getting the best grades, or doing anything tangible. The favored child displays an emotional responsiveness or sensibility that naturally validates his mother or father. Perhaps he reveals a part of himself that resembles what the parent especially loves about himself. The child instinctively knows how the parent feels. There is a continual system of emotional feedback involving these loving issues.

Of course it can work the exact opposite way when the parent rejects the child for a trait he cannot accept in himself, especially when the parents are concerned that their child may show some undesirable behavior, perhaps revealing a family secret. Parents' self-doubts play at least as strong a role in rejection as any failure on the part of the child.

When a child is talented, a child of light, touched with the divine, receiving praise and attention, this can lead one parent to claim the child's specialness as a reflection of his own. However, an insecure, unfulfilled parent can view the same child with envy and feel compelled to put the child down, especially if the child, as talented children are wont to do, takes great joy in his accomplishments, feels good about himself, and reminds the parent of his ordinariness.

The Child's Contribution

All parental influences pale in comparison to what is going on inside the child. As he sorts out his own inner world, the child proves to be the most powerful force shaping his defenses and character.

Who can say what takes place inside the child during his sessions of internal debate? Only he knows the old injuries he recounts or the promises and resolutions to reform or overcome adversity that he makes to himself.

These oaths, made in innocent earnestness and fierce determination, reflect the secret inner workings of your will. Declarations made in the forge of your youthful discontent such as "I must never tell . . ." "Someday I will . . ." "I'll never let anyone ever . . ." and "When it's my turn . . ." continue to live in you, defining your needs and shaping your expectations right up to this very moment.

It comes as no surprise that in the same loving home a misfortune that is passed off as inconsequential by one child can register deeply within the very soul of another and shape his destiny.

For example, a financial challenge can have a deep impact on a child who, for reasons entirely of his own, feels responsible for the well-being of the family. So motivated is he by his fear of being poor that he fills himself with a dire resolve to become powerful. In his mind, far away from the awareness of his family, he acts as the dread inner cheerleader, pressing himself toward materialistic goals, silently shaping his will and his life. He must succeed. He becomes driven, always striving for more.

Or he can simply be overwhelmed and expect to be poor all his life. This also comes to pass. Similarly no one can say when a poor student will react to a failure by suddenly deciding to study harder, while another child who has always done well will take a particular failure as proof of his inferiority and just give up. Perhaps the failure echoes some long-forgotten angry criticism. Perhaps he has too much invested in the risk, such as the talented thirteen-year-old poet who never wrote again after her poem was rejected by the *New Yorker*.

Unrealistic expectations create failures that a young person finds difficult to place in perspective. When the child needs a success to distinguish himself, prove his worth, or differentiate him from his parents, his failure is exaggerated all out of proportion and difficult to explain. No one can tell for sure why a sensitive child decides to risk being open again after being injured or why the open child sudden withdraws.

How Defenses Formed

Your particular defensive shield formed as you grew. The periods in which each of the three defenses developed correspond to the three phases of childhood development.

You retain some defensive legacy from each of these three periods. However, your particular pattern of defenses is a unique mixture of all three and reflects your childhood experience, especially how easy it was to be open and express feelings in your home, how safe you felt doing so, and the support and encouragement you got to be honest. A child's defensive pattern tends to become fixed in response to stress, injury, abuse, and mostly to losses and fear. When you seek to understand what shaped you, you are really asking how your defensive style evolved.

No matter how mature and emotionally resolved you are, you still have your original defensive style. It never changes. It always exists as your characteristic potential for dishonesty. When you get into trouble and are dishonest you do so in your characteristic defensive way.

Being free and open means that you are aware of your defensive style, not that you are free of defenses. However, you are fully conversant with what makes you afraid and what hurts you. You can easily recognize your defensive reaction when it occurs. Always mindful of your weakness, you are rarely caught by surprise. When you are, you admit your humanness and accept it.

Your goal is always to face your pain honestly.

THE DEPENDENT PERIOD

THE ROOTS OF DENIAL

Denial is the predominant defense of the dependent period. In a sense every child is born with a powerful capacity to deny. The child is utterly helpless and has nothing but denial to protect him. He can only shut out the pain he cannot deal with.

A child is totally dependent on his parents for his survival. However, emotional survival involves not merely making it into adulthood but how that task is accomplished. Exposed to too much pain, some children are unable to protect themselves adequately from the onslaught of injuries that befall them and therefore become trapped in a rigid defensive position, an emotional scar that persists throughout life.

The characteristic stamp of a childhood injury and its significance is determined more by when the injury takes place than by what actually happens to the child. Thus a child who is severely hurt in the dependent period is likely to be impaired in his capacity to form loving and trusting relationships in later years.

Some children suffer severe losses in their first year, such as separations, the death of a parent, or a severe illness. Although they may be cared for by a loving relative who replaces what has been taken away and they seem to make excellent recoveries, these children become especially sensitive to dependent issues.

It is understandable. Other people held the key to their fate. Their focus was on their pain and their need to be rescued. In spite of how well-adjusted they may become later on, they are especially sensitive to abandonment and rejection, "people" people forever.

At one extreme they can be needy, empathetic to the point of invasiveness, have trouble defining boundaries with others, and have an unrelenting need for another person to make them complete.

At the other, especially when they were cherished and well cared for, they are likely to become warm, sensitive to the feelings of others, compassionate, instinctive, giving, supportive, sensitive of others' pain, patient, and willing to draw others out.

The healthy dependent person, someone who has had a strong sense of being loved, also develops a sensitivity to people without being rigidly trapped in a needy, dependent style. Instead he strives to be independent, mindful of his dependent needs. He still enjoys being cared for and given to but without unrealistic expectations that the world owes him anything. Unlike the person who was damaged in the dependent period, he doesn't see being by himself as a punishment. Healthy dependent people are wonderful companions, the best friends, the most loyal workers, the best parents and teachers.

The denial that is seen in early childhood is a powerful, totally occlusive defense that can entirely shut down the gates of perception. Such massive denial is most likely set in motion by pain or fear that exceeds the child's threshold of tolerance. When a pain is too great to be managed in early childhood, total denial blocks it.

When this happens the child retreats within. In this inner domain the child, in a sense, "remembers" what previously fulfilled his needs. Not being able to discriminate between reality and memory, he takes his memory to be real, and it nurtures him.

For example, mothers who have been tardy in meeting a child's tearful demands for a feeding are sometimes surprised to discover that the child is already sucking on an imaginary nipple when they finally come into the nursery. Sometimes the child is so sated by his fantasy that he will not take the real bottle when it is offered.

This capacity to rely on his inner fantasies for satisfaction when reality proves disappointing is a powerful force that shapes the child's reality sense. If the child makes too many of these inner journeys to avoid a hostile and unfulfilling external reality, his tendency to retreat may become established as a way to deal with stress. As a result his personality will become embossed with patterns of avoidance. In later life, he will tend to flee inward, become passive, find inner solace, hide within, or utterly disappear.

People who become substance abusers often have a similar tendency to deny pain and turn inward. The substance merely chemically reinforces their denial.

In order to learn to live in reality, every child needs to relinquish his absolute dependence on denial. To accomplish this delicate transition the child needs to be nurtured and develop a sense of trust that the world is a safe place. His strength comes in learning that he is lovable and will continue to receive the protection and caring he needs to survive. This trust allows him to feel strong enough to believe in himself.

It comes as no surprise that children are highly sensitive to rejection. They see their situation as follows: if they are not lovable, it means that they are at risk of being abandoned. When love is removed, the world is over as far as they are concerned. The time you are most likely to have a drastic feeling like this as an adult is when you are deeply in love with another person and suddenly have a falling-out. The feeling of panic and abandonment that overwhelms you is partly a toxic nostalgic recollection of childhood feelings of desperately needing another person, which were triggered into awareness by your lover's rejection.

Can you imagine how you must have felt as a child to have the very same feelings and no sense of history or perspective in which to place your discomfort? Your entire world seemed to be falling apart. This quality is momentarily reiterated when you suffer the threat of a loss of love, and it complicates your emotional response by causing your perspective to regress to that of a child's.

When children receive inadequate care, they may accentuate the pain they suffer and live in negative expectancy. These children seem to take every shortcoming as abandonment and every criticism as rejection. They are highly sensitive to loss and find it difficult to forgive, that is, let go of their hurts. For this reason they do not seem to make emotional progress. In later years, they seem on a desperate search for love but often look where genuine prospects are slim. They have unrealistic expectations of being cared for and so meet disappointment everywhere. Even though they insist they are not, they seem to be recreating old losses in order to work through past hurts.

Some children seem to have an inner strength. Hard to evaluate or define, its presence is nonetheless obvious to everyone in the family. The happy child is naturally outgoing and confident, likes himself, takes joy in his pleasures, amuses himself, delights in being paid attention to, and also enjoys being by himself.

Although the task of setting denial aside and facing the world as it is can seem frightening at times, almost every child manages to do it pretty well. The most important role of a parent is to provide a consistent source of love that the child can rely on as a guide as he makes his transition from dependence to independence.

Children are highly adaptable and are able to gather their experiences of being cared for by several different family members and assemble them into a mosaic of support, creating a general memory of having been loved. This ability to selectively cull the good from the child's mixed experience can compensate for terrible deprivations and allow the child to carry on as if he had a happy childhood.

On the other hand, when there are insufficient sources of love and the child is unsupported, he can compile evidence and prove he had a sad, painful childhood while other family members may be entirely oblivious to his struggle and think of the family as happy. This is especially true when the child seems different and, for example, goes against the emotional current of the family by saying what is on his mind when everyone else is pledged to silence.

Your view of life is also a gathering of selected experiences. Coping allows old hurts to fade into the background and happy memories to stand out. You learn the lessons from your pain and take courage from the good. It follows that when your unresolved pain is stored in Emotional Debt, your life seems sad, and hurtful experiences seem to overshadow the good. So in some way your view of your life as happy is a creation you reinforce by letting go of your hurt. You need the healing perspective to put all the parts in their proper place. That perspective can only come when denial is lifted.

As a child begins to develop motor and language skills, his dependence upon denial as his only line of defense changes. As soon as a child begins to assume control over his body, he also begins to venture out into reality where denial does not serve him as well as it did when he was totally protected. He begins to express himself. Sometimes he acts with annoying defiance, sometimes with blind curiosity that leads him into danger and places him at odds with those who love him. He is driven to imitate the actions of those he loves. He wants to become his own provider, to take without asking and get what he wants when he wants it.

The seeds for conflict have been sewn.

THE CONTROLLING PERIOD
THE ORIGINS OF BLAMING AND EXCUSES

The defenses of blaming and excuses evolve at the same time the child develops language skills and body control. A child's first communication skills are often physical gestures used to express displeasure, such as shaking his head or pointing a finger at an object he wishes to have retrieved. In a way these negative body expressions are a more active representation of feelings the child was forced to repress when he did not have such expressive skills. The young child may have turned away, but only as an act of avoidance, a retreat. The older child turns away with an air of defiance and intention.

This negative body language is greeted by the parent with a mixture of amusement and annoyance, depending on the parent's state of mind. A happy, well-adjusted parent will take the expression of negativity in stride, attribute it to the child becoming a person, and usually laugh about it. An insecure parent, on the other hand, will try to control the child's expression of negativity, taking it as a nursery rebellion, and may overreact and become punitive. This teaches the child that expressing himself risks losing his parent's love. When a young child is intimidated by fear at this stage, it contributes to the establishment of rigid controlling defenses and subsequent remote Emotional Debt.

The child also initiates powerful, positive nonverbal communications at this time such as smiling, laughing, cooing, making eye contact, hugging, stroking, and kissing. Generally, these positive communications meet with great enthusiasm and encouragement. They are the joy and reward of parenthood.

The miracle happens toward the end of the first year. The child speaks. After "Mama" and "Dada," the child's first word is likely to be "no." It is a powerful word, in fact the most powerful word the child learns for many years. Saying no from a position of weakness and helplessness elevates the child to the level of an obstacle others must contend with. He is unwilling. He is not pleased. He does not want to eat. He does not want to do potty. He does not want to go to bed. And he says so—"No!" Just like that, he makes his will known.

The impact of saying no, or acting it out physically, is not lost on the child. In a world of adults he is suddenly made an equal. Others try to reason with him. More words. He holds his ground against better-educated, worldly people who proclaim what is best for him. He has only his negativity in his corner and his magical vocabulary. He resists by repeating, "No."

All of a sudden he is picked up and transported against his will to a crib and imprisoned. There is no court of appeal. "No" doesn't work. It has failed him. He needs other words. In time he picks up a larger vocabulary and begins to deal with the pain of misbehaving with other phrases. "I'm sorry," "I'll be good," "I didn't do it," "Not fair." His language, like Shakespeare's whore unpacking her heart with words, is an attempt to absolve himself and blame others.

His motivation is clear. He wants to be lovable and loved. He wants to explain away his badness and divorce himself from it. It is someone else's fault. Remember, he is struggling with a burgeoning Emotional Debt as his hurts frequently become transformed into angry outbursts that cause him to be punished. This leads to more anger, and so he feels he is bad a lot of the time. The debate between Am I good? and Am I bad? is ongoing and causes him much pain. He wants so much to be good, but his anger makes him doubt himself.

Blaming is an obvious solution. A child learns to blame by being criticized. Even if the scolding is justified, it makes him feel bad. He is told he is responsible for doing something bad. He wants to shift the blame onto something else. The stool was slippery. The paper was already wet. He was pushed. The dish was too heavy to hold. The dog made the mess. It was his sister's fault.

As the child develops the intellectual defenses that allow him to excuse his behavior or blame it on external circumstances, he is in a real sense learning to use logic to divert the pain of responsibility, the pain of being "bad." He is establishing mental detours that shunt his pain outward, rather than allowing it to be felt. The hurt of being bad or wrong is immediately converted into angrily blaming others or external circumstances. The child exercises the diversion as long as it makes him feel better.

It becomes a mental habit.

MAGICAL THINKING

At this stage of development the child employs words, not entirely for communication but also for the magical power he attributes to them. The power of the word, of saying something and making it happen, is highly seductive to the child who, at this stage, is struggling with the limits of his own strength. The child also begins to use mental images to correct for deficiencies in reality. He imagines and reasons. He discovers that his thoughts also have the power to make him feel better.

The child begins to develop the capacity for magical thinking. He invests power in the words he speaks. His words are used to accomplish the deeds he feels powerless or afraid to execute. Children at play frequently show signs of this kind of thought process when they shout, "You're dead," at a playmate. This is not merely imagination at work here, but the child trying to establish boundaries between feeling an angry feeling and having it come true. He wishes to be all-powerful and is terrified of losing control of the power at the same time. He is continually testing.

One of the reasons behind your present fear of expressing feelings comes from your lingering uncertainty from this stage that if you did express your anger, it could do harm. You also struggled to conceal your anger out of fear that expressing it might prove you unlovable.

When a punitive parent inhibits your expression of feelings, you are likely to fear rejection if you speak up. Unable to risk retaliating in words, you entertain angry thoughts. You may wish your parents dead and suffer unimaginable guilt and fear for doing so. The old game, Step on a crack, break your mother's back, derives its dread power from this kind of thinking. You fear your thoughts could come true.

Since the distinction between an angry thought and act becomes blurred at this stage, your old angry fantasies are stored as if they were real actions right alongside memories of actual angry events. This explains why it is often so difficult for you to access your old feelings. You fear discovering that you really did something evil or that you killed someone merely by wishing them dead. This makes you afraid to examine your history. You'd rather not know what you actually did but suspect the worst. If you seek to know why deep down you feel you are bad, you need look no further than this example.

Healing this distorted perception is a matter of taking a leap of faith. You accept that you must have been hurt, that you couldn't express your anger, and that you thought your anger was lethal. You were mistaken. The next step is to believe that in spite of your anger and your self-doubts, you are a good person.

Remind yourself of that and believe it.

DEFENSIVE LOGIC

As the child's intellectual capacities grow, his ability to use logic in the defense of his innocence increases. He studies those who criticize him and picks up their style, their manner of presenting their argument against him. He's not nearly as adept as they are in stating his case, but he becomes a devoted student of obstinacy, tenacity, and the power of blaming.

In a word, he learns to lie and stick with it for dear life. At heart he wants to confess and be forgiven, but when circumstances are stressful and the adults in his life insist on being right and punishing him, he finds it difficult to admit his wrongdoing.

In some households children get the sense that they can never be completely forgiven. Because their parents are always holding a grudge, they feel they have to maintain their guard, and so their hurt feelings do not get aired or resolved. As a result they come to believe that they have not only done wrong, but that they are bad for doing so.

In a family where criticism and sarcasm reign, it is frightening to admit your wrongdoing and make yourself vulnerable to verbal attack. You grow up guarding against admitting your weaknesses or shortcomings. You get accustomed to hiding your humanness. You think you need to be perfect in order to be loved, and knowing you are not, you're on alert, ever ready to disprove or argue any challenge to your worth.

Blaming and excuses become the explanations for your wrongdoing. Again, most of your negativity comes from your anger over the hurt you suffered when you didn't feel accepted for being yourself.

How much easier it would have been if your parents told you you were good even though you did something naughty, that doing something bad didn't make you bad. When you are a child you suspect you are bad when you do something wrong. The reason you allow yourself to get caught is to test that belief. You want your parent to catch and both punish and forgive you.

When you felt unforgiven, it only reinforced your belief that you were bad. This hurt you even more and made you even more angry. This in turn convinced you that you weren't lovable and that others would abandon you. This remains the greatest fear of controlling people later in life and explains how the defenses of blaming and excuses become fixed.

The fear of being bad permeates the thinking of most people for a considerable period in their life.

THE COMPETITIVE PERIOD

ENTER PRETENDING

Like the start of the controlling period, the competitive period begins gradually. The earliest elements of the controlling period appear as soon as the child develops motor control. The competitive period begins when the child starts to use his imagination and pretends in order to make his losses seem less severe.

As the child in the controlling period grows, his intellectual defenses of blaming and excusing begin to incorporate pretense as he exaggerates his alibis, pretending that they are true. He may act deeply injured trying to prove his case against a mean-spirited sibling whom he claimed punched him. His performance is designed to evoke sympathy, substantiate his accusations, and justify his retaliation. He may act out so convincingly that he comes to believe his own story.

Where the controlling child yearns to be in charge, writing the rules and enforcing them, the competitive child dreams of winning and basking in the adulation of admirers as he effortlessly trounces his opponents, seeming not to have a care in the world.

The child in the competitive period uses pretense to escape from pain. While he is being beaten up he imagines his revenge and plots his enemy's downfall. He is continually scripting his future success and triumph, imagining himself stronger, more powerful. "Someday I'll show them . . ." his fantasies typically begin.

He takes courage from these fantasies. They compensate him for his disappointments. This wishful thinking can lead to unrealistic expectations of others and additional hurt when he is let down. A child can also be seduced by his fantasies and seek to live in a world of pretense, where in spite of a recent failure, he imagines himself important, still loved by everyone, still the best. By providing fantastic solutions to his problems, wishful thinking can deprive the competitive child of his will.

However, some pretense is necessary to protect and develop self-esteem. It would be damaging if after failing the child immediately concluded that he was a loser. It is important to pretend that you can still do it when you do fail. Your belief in yourself is, after all, the most important ingredient of success. It gives you the courage to face your weaknesses and correct them, to work hard and do your best. But wishful thinking alone will not bring success.

The competitive child is trying to find the balance between wishing for success and working for it.

FACING THE REAL WORLD

Coming to terms with reality is not an easy task. The real world is always more difficult than you expect. The role of your defenses is to allow you to tell lies to yourself to help you cope.

Denial tells you there is no danger.

Excuses prove that whatever went wrong wasn't your fault.

Pretenses convince you it doesn't matter because something better is coming if you just keep believing.

Again, defenses are designed to be momentary adaptations, allowing you to regroup, admit the truth, and continue. However, because a defensive life is a life of lies, it quickly becomes convoluted. The driving force behind all defensive operations is simplicity itself. It is your need to be lovable that motivates you to be defensive.

In the dependent period all a child had to do to be loved and protected was to be lovable. A loving parent did the rest. If that loving care was absent, the child denied it, retreated within, and hid from the pain of abandonment.

In the controlling period much more was expected of the child. He had to obey rules in order to be considered good. When he got into trouble he made excuses that explained why, in spite of what he did or was accused of doing, he was not really to blame and therefore was still lovable.

In the competitive period the child finds that his parents' expectations of him have expanded. Now he must perform, do something, compete with other children in order to be considered lovable. When a child fails, he pretends not to care about disappointing himself or others in order to protect his self-esteem, his lovability.

Pretending doesn't do a very good job of protecting you. It barely conceals pain; you just pretend that your hurt doesn't really matter because someday it is going to get better. In a sense pretending is the healthiest of the defenses because it allows you to stay in closer touch with reality than denial, which leaves you a helpless victim, or the projective logic of blaming and excuses, which can lead you to believe that others did it to you. However, you still can get lost if you live in your dreams and act as if your failures had nothing to teach you.

Pretending is a remarkable defense and is ideally constructed to deal with the issues of the competitive period. In a sense pretending seems like a combination of denial and excuses. You don't really admit that you're hurting or afraid while passionately explaining what you're going to do to make everything better. You pretend you can succeed without knowing for sure if you really can.

Everyone the child comes into contact with encourages him to pretend. His parents reinforce pretending by telling him he doesn't know how good he is until he tries, that he can always do better. Coaching, teaching, and parenting are really no more than exercises in helping the child pretend to believe in himself until he finally succeeds.

During the competitive period a child is measured not only by how lovable or obedient he is, but by what he accomplishes and how he measures up to others. Obviously for some children this comparison begins at home when they are measured against their siblings.

In a home with a competitive, insecure parent, the child is also measured against the exaggerated way his parent remembers himself when he was a child. The child may be compared to a standard his own parent failed to reach. The child only wants to please his parent and be loved in exchange. When he falls short, he understands only the look in his parent's eyes that tells him he is a failure, and it dismays him. With such manipulative parents, the child begins to believe that he must succeed at all costs. He becomes driven. Every failure runs the risk of rejection.

The child has yet to learn that you cannot please an unhappy parent who did not take his own risks.

Before a child reaches the competitive period, he is a creature entirely of his family. In the competitive period he ventures out into the real world for the first time. Here he has his own place, a desk, storage, associates, routine, other people to report to, responsibilities, another life in which to define himself.

A WORLD OF STRANGERS

This exposure can be a sobering experience. The child is introduced to a world of strangers. No one knows him. No one seems to give him the benefit of the doubt.

Some people take him for what he is. He may not like hearing the truth. Other people have a mistaken impression of him. He's not sure if they are right. If they are wrong he doesn't know how to correct them. He is puzzled but cannot put his confusion into words.

He discovers that other children have a much different agenda than his parents. They are not committed to making him feel good and may not be fair when they play with him. They may be entirely indifferent to his feelings. Other kids are out to win and don't care if he loses or feels bad about it.

It doesn't take the child very long to discover that his value is different in the real world than it is at home. He learns that some kids are much stronger. Others are better coordinated, while he feels hopelessly awkward. Some kids are really smart and know all the answers. He's not sure he understands the questions.

After a while the child realizes that he is not as capable, as knowledgeable, as experienced, as well liked as some of the other children he has gotten to know. Since he now knows the truth of his worth for himself, the reassurance he gets at home seems insincere, even disheartening. He begins to wonder if his parents really understand the competition he faces.

Of course other children come to realize for the first time that they are likable and smart when they go to school. Even then they are not home free because they have a family's low self-esteem to contend with and its expectation of failure.

CHALLENGES

The school years challenge the parents' expectations for their child. He not only carries his anxiety to school but bears his parents' hidden hopes and fears. They wonder how smart he really is, how sociable he'll be, how quickly he'll adjust and catch on to the routine. They wonder if the teacher will like him, if he'll make friends or get along. They wonder if the weaknesses that held them back will reemerge to thwart their child.

School poses a double-edged threat. The child risks losing his self-esteem and his parents' love. When he falls short he knows he is disappointing them, but he never suspects that one of the reasons they are hurt is that they expected to prove their worth through him. When he fails, they fail, too.

The child is continually tormented with challenges to his confidence. When he is asked how much two plus five is and answers incorrectly, the teacher merely says, "Wrong," and quickly moves to another student for the correct answer. No one consoles him for embarrassing himself. He finds himself on a stage where his performance is measured. He gets love and attention by knowing the right answer, being smart, demonstrating ability and talent.

If he can't get noticed in the classroom, he tries to distinguish himself in the school yard by being better looking, having the most friends, being the funniest, the most agile, the strongest, the bully, the one who smokes or skips school. The child who just a year ago languished in the protection of his home is now in a struggle to save his self-esteem wherever he can.

EMERGING SEXUALITY

To his great surprise the child discovers that he is a sexual creature. He is evaluated for his looks, seen in the context of a potential boyfriend or girlfriend, if not today, someday soon. He thinks about the older kids and their sexual innuendoes and teasing. Some kids proclaim their crushes on rock stars. The lyrics of songs don't always make sense but feel sexy. Other kids sing them. He sings them, too, imitating the artist's sexual inflection without understanding it. He pretends to have sexual feelings. While they may seem silly as he repeats the lines from a passionate love scene in a film, they find an unexpected resonance. It makes him uneasy and fascinates him at the same time.

He can practically feel the veil of innocence being torn from him, exposing him to the world as a sexual commodity. He may not have words for this. The matter may not be discussible at home. He may not understand the facts of life, but every commercial on television, every newscast, every soap opera he skims past while looking for his cartoon show exudes sexuality and reflects the sexual reality that he has found himself immersed in.

While his parents are totally unaware of what is going on, he becomes a different child than they knew.

EXPECTATIONS

Complicating matters further, the child discovers that his parents' expectations of him have also changed. Returning home, he finds himself cross-examined by well-meaning parents who want to know how he's doing, what friends he's making. School is moving into new areas so quickly he cannot even get used to where he is. He always feels as if he is on shaky ground. He is asked to recount his failures and successes. How can he report that he often feels intimidated, overwhelmed, and insecure when so much is expected of him? He may fall back on earlier defenses and blame the teachers for being unfair and other kids for being mean, but he'd rather not talk.

When parents ask him, "What did you do in school today?" and get "Nothing," as a response, the child is really pretending not to have failed again.

More than anything the child wants to find something at which he can excel, something he can use to prove his worth. If he cannot be better or show he's special, he does a complete reverse and wants to blend in and be exactly like everyone else, to dress alike, idolize the same heroes, be part of the pack . . . invisible.

A child pretends as a way to cope with the considerable stress he faces in and out of school. His self-esteem is continually being challenged, and much of the time he doesn't come out ahead. Pretending allows the child to claim that his efforts shouldn't be used to judge him because, since he wasn't trying his hardest, his achievements don't represent his best work. He may also pretend that he didn't care, so however he did simply doesn't matter. This pretense allows him to set aside any rejection he suffers as a result of his failures. He reasons that next time will be different, because he'll try. Just wait and see. He'll show you.

FAMILY INFLUENCES ON DEFENSIVE PATTERNS

At the beginning of *Anna Karenina*, Tolstoy remarks, "Happy families are all alike: every unhappy family is unhappy in its own way." Every family has its own style of perceiving reality.

As mentioned, your character is shaped more by how you chose to react to a situation than the situation itself. Still, certain family circumstances create typical response patterns in the children. The effect of these patterns is to inhibit the child's free expression of feelings and thus create Emotional Debt, a kind of familial defensive pattern in its own right.

The family perspective can become a powerful intimidating force when prohibition and taboo are reinforced with the threat of rejection. The child is often coerced and intimidated by circumstances that are so familiar he cannot even recognize them as hurtful. Instead when he feels differently from everyone's expectations, he wonders what's wrong with himself. He feels like a misfit, an outsider, and distrusts his own judgment. His self-doubt hinders his openness with his feelings, and so he develops Emotional Debt following his family's defensive guidelines. His rebellion is precarious, fraught with loneliness and self-doubt, and often extended. He wants to belong, but to be himself he must get away from the family he wants to love and be loved by.

TYPICAL EXAMPLES

The children in alcoholic families tend to grow up prematurely. They suffer from chronic anxiety based on not knowing what they will find when they get home. When they speak up they are often greeted with angry outbursts. Living with the addicted parent, the children develop a feeling of shame from their internalized anger, which leads to low self-esteem. They are always covering up and making excuses for themselves and their parents. They struggle against their self-doubt by trying to be perfect. They manage their Emotional Debt poorly. It manifests as criticism and projection. In later life they are often attracted to addicts as a way of working out their stored anger toward their parents. Finding other alcoholics to dominate lets them be critical, rescue, take control, and feel totally justified doing so. They often develop a defensive position as pathologic as their parents' addiction.

Children whose parents continually screamed and fought tend to become intimidated. They discover that their Emotional Debt is overloaded. Their bottled-up rage soon starts to leak, causing them to hold back even more feelings, finally leading them to become rageful adults, the very thing they hated in their parents.

Smothering parents undermine their children's natural bravery by focusing on all the dangers around them. Their children can become timid worriers and cling to home for safety. The children can stop taking such parents seriously and treat them with disdain and pity and end up being overprotective of their parent in later years. Then again, these children can rebel and become reckless, putting themselves at risk to torment their parents by really giving them something to worry about.

A critical, unhappy parent often projects his weaknesses onto his children, finding fault with everything and being pleased with little. He wants the children to suffer as he suffers. His standards are unrealistically high and he is nonsupportive of failure. Children with such a parent often have problems learning to like themselves because they are so angry. They often adopt the parent's projective style and put down others as well. When they pretend not to care about the way they were treated, they can become sarcastic and feign an attitude of superiority.

Seductive parents create anxious children who are continually trying to define their boundaries. The parent who treats his or her child like a boyfriend or girlfriend places the child in a difficult bind. The child wants to be close but is afraid of being so. The child often acts as if he or she enjoys playing the role the parent wants while desperately wanting to get away. Such children can become sexually active at an early age to bind the feelings that the unwholesomely close relationship with the parent has aroused. These children often have difficulty forming deep, lasting relationships because they find it difficult to trust others.

Children whose parents had military careers, or were frequently shifted around by a corporation or through foster homes, often suffer because they were unable to develop roots. In later life they tend to fear change and separation and may have difficulty forming lasting relationships.

Children brought up in poverty, like all children who live on the edge of desperation, often suffer from anxiety and low self-esteem. The parents are often emotionally drained by their misfortune and have little energy left over to give to their children. The children want to forgive their parents' failings and to believe that their parents did the best they could. However, the children often grow up feeling undeserving because they have internalized some secret resentment of their parents for being failures. Then again, some poor children attempt to prove their worth and are driven to succeed. However, when they attain success they continually need more to prove their worth and often live in fear of losing their gains.

To be rich is to need nothing.

Being poor leaves you with the feeling you need everything.

Growing up in a home with chronic illness leads a child to hold in feelings out of fear of making the parent worse. This leads the child to feel pessimistic, guilt-ridden over resenting and wanting to matter as much as the sick person, and to focus on his own illnesses to win secondary gain.

Living with a mentally ill parent creates a singular stress for a child, who is left to define reality without reliable assistance. Indeed the view he may decide is real may be at variance with his parent's belief and cause conflict. While all parents tend to slant the information they tell their children, the emotionally disturbed parent has a slanted view of life, which is totally self-justified and admits no discussion.

When a parent is obsessed or paranoid, the child learns to hide his true feelings. Any disagreement triggers an endless persecution and interrogation. There is no satisfying such a parent until you agree with him.

When a parent has a major psychosis, or continually threatens suicide, the child learns to develop a callus of indifference and to disregard the parent's utterances. He becomes a master of overlooking and not responding. He learns to be silent and evade provocation and maintain his distance. If the child permits himself to become involved with the parent's illness, trying to protect or help, he may grow up to feel pessimistic, powerless, and responsible. Should the parent actually succeed in killing himself, he may feel guilty for having secretly wished to be free. Lowering his defensive barrier is a frightening proposition to such a child. He may become insincere and patronizing in order to survive. In later life such children often feel emotionally isolated, keeping their emotional cards to their chest. While they tend to be wary of contact with another human being, they deeply yearn for it.

All these negative family defensive patterns inhibit children's honesty and spontaneity by making the child self-conscious about saying what he feels in the moment. The child's own insecurity would be enough to incur Emotional Debt. However, when the child's tendency to be defensive is combined with the family's inhibiting influence, his willingness to be open can be seriously undermined. It often takes a substantial adolescent rebellion to set these scales in balance again.

Families that impose secrecy damage children while families that are accepting of the truth make it easy for a child to find himself.

Where there are many rules, children have to fight for every breath of self-expression. They grow up questioning their judgment and point of view. They hold back even the opinions they believe in just to avoid conflict.

Every family has its own set of unwritten rules defining what is acceptable and what is not, setting forth the mythology that it uses to cover over embarrassing history, hide its secrets, and support its self-deception. What matters most is how easy it is to challenge these sacred beliefs.

In some families any questioning of the family myth is considered an act of defiance, a sign of disrespect, and a reason for expulsion. The family closes ranks around these forbidden questions, guarding its sacred honor, its cherished fantasies. If your family lived in distortion and you rebel by insisting on telling the truth at all costs, you may end up telling too much truth and also distort reality in the other direction. You have to find a balanced position.

The legacy of growing up in an unhappy family is having to search for a new grounding in reality. Some children do this too quickly and seem rigid and overly mature. Others take years to find themselves, to grow up and allow themselves to be happy.

The most important impact of your family's distorting ways is how it led you to withhold your truthful feelings and to store them in Emotional Debt. Every unhappy family is a greenhouse nurturing the bud of Toxic Nostalgia.

YOUR FAMILY'S DEFENSIVE LEGACY

Understanding how your family shaped your defensive style helps you grasp your capacity for distortion. Put briefly, the way your family encouraged you to misrepresent the truth becomes your emotional defensive legacy. Until you recognize the fears that silenced you, you continue to support the conspiracy. You may even love your family and care deeply for those who hurt you, but until you recognize the patterns of emotional concealment that corrupted your honesty, you are just like them, doing the same thing to your children without understanding why.

It is hard to say when you were first politicized by your family and how you were influenced not to notice that the emperor had no clothes on. Families create intricate systems of prohibitions. You are told to avoid hurting this person's feelings, to be solicitous of that person, not to talk about feelings, and never to mention the drinking. Everyone wonders what it would have been like to have been brought up in another family, to have grown up freely and naturally, without restriction.

A FAMILY INVENTORY

What behavior was considered inappropriate in your family?
What did you risk for being honest?
How easy was it for you to say what you felt?

How were your feelings accepted when you did express them?
Were you taken seriously or ridiculed?
Did others argue with you?
What blind allegiance was rewarded?
What individuality was punished?
What hypocrisy were you silently forced to endure?

Your defensive system is shaped by the way you experience and meet the challenges of the three major developmental periods. It is possible to have dependent, controlling, and competitive children in the same family. However, the hurts you defend against are determined by your particular family's needs and fears. Your defensive style is your own adaptation, but the issues against which you defend mirror your family's special problems.

The "Perfect" Family

Melissa was born into a wealthy mainline Philadelphia family. Every part of her life reflected the golden light of privilege. The family had a long tradition of philanthropy and a social position so esteemed that no society function would be considered complete without their attendance. Melissa was beautiful, an outstanding student, and an excellent swimmer and tennis player. She was respected by her friends and refined in her manners and taste.

There was a serious problem in Melissa's family, but it was so entrapping that every member of her family was blind to it. The family never let down their guard and behaved as if they were always in public. In that house it was forbidden to raise one's voice. The breach of the slightest rule of etiquette was elevated to a serious offense. Once when her seven-year-old brother came to the dinner table with a sloppily made tie, he was asked to excuse himself and tie it properly before returning to the table. The house was not real, but a showcase for mannequins. In addition, the father drank excessively, never showing his liquor of course, and never drawing attention to the fact that he drank.

One summer when Melissa was twelve she was sunning herself on their private beach in Southampton while her father was taking his morning swim. Melissa heard her father make a strange sound but could not see him in the water. She immediately got to her feet just in time to see him surface and sink again. Melissa dove in, pulled him to the beach, and gave him mouth-to-mouth resuscitation. He vomited alcohol and seawater all over her. She helped him onto a beach chair and ran toward the house. She met her mother on the porch. Before Melissa could say a word, her mother sternly criticized, "What is that all over your bathing suit? And what is that horrid smell? Go upstairs and change immediately." Her mother would not let Melissa speak.

Overcome with frustration Melissa screamed, "Daddy almost drowned. And the smell is booze. He puked all over me. What's wrong with you?" The outburst was totally out of character for her, especially the critical anger that exploded in her mother's face, right in front of one of the servants who was just setting places for lunch.

Her mother recoiled in shock at Melissa's indiscretion, gathered her wits, and hurried out to the beach with Melissa running behind in tears. When they got to the beach, they found Melissa's father fully recovered, acting as if nothing serious had happened, and secretly annoyed that he had been caught drinking. Her mother decided that this was all an inexcusable exaggeration. Her entire focus was to upbraid Melissa for daring to raise her voice. Melissa's father, needing an ally, immediately concurred. It was bad form that Melissa was so disrespectful. After all, there was no incident, really. He and her mother began to speculate openly on the kind of hysterical female Melissa was turning into.

Melissa became enraged and protested again that her father was drunk and that she had just saved his life. Her mother slapped Melissa across the face for making up such vile accusations and embarrassed her in front of the servants. Her father joined in sternly chastising her and insisted that she write a formal apology to each of them.

Melissa backed down and went up to her bedroom, distraught and confused. Her family suddenly no longer made sense to her. It seemed completely false. How could this have happened? Everyone talked about how generous her family was. At the beginning of the summer they'd dedicated an entire wing of a private hospital to her grandfather. No one would believe her story. Whom could she talk to? Maybe she was mistaken?

Melissa capitulated and wrote a note of apology, saying she had been so frightened by her father nearly drowning that she had overreacted. Her mother refused to accept the letter and insisted that she admit that she'd made up the incident of the drowning and rewrite the note accordingly. Melissa wrote the note without a thread of sincerity or honesty. Her mother was delighted by it.

Melissa changed. She began to realize that everyone in her family was living a lie. Everything they did or said was superficial and based on appearances. She tolerated her existence living as a pampered prisoner. While she had never before expressed her true feelings, she was now acutely aware of what those feelings were and felt pain each time she tried to suppress them.

Melissa's youthful beauty blossomed as she grew older, but she refused all suitors, acting aloof and protective. During her freshman year of college she secretly started to work as a fashion model. When she was nineteen a successful businessman in his late twenties was enraptured by one of Melissa's ads, tracked her down, and proposed to her. He came from a working-class background, totally unacceptable to her family. She quit college and married him on the spot.

The family was horrified and moved their considerable power against the couple, but the young man was very independent and Melissa allowed his strength to be her barrier as she cut off her family. The marriage was a total disaster, and by the time Melissa was twenty-one she was divorced with a one-year-old child, supporting herself as a model. The nightmares started soon after.

Every night she dreamed she was reaching for the hand of a drowning man. She almost grasped it, but he let go. She woke filled with terror. While the meaning of this dream is obvious as a symbolic resolution of her old anger at her father, its meaning completely escaped Melissa. Even though she had become an observer since the near drowning, the family's defensive pattern had dulled her memory of the event. In fact, after all these years of keeping her feelings to herself, Melissa was no longer sure if the note of apology to her mother was true or if she had in fact rescued her father. Unsure of herself, she retreated. Her style became one of passive acquiescence. She never raised her voice or protested.

It took a second marriage to a sensitive man who helped her find her worth again for Melissa to remember her past and put it in perspective. Her family, so perfect and powerful, had been too much for her to deal with even when she knew the truth. She needed to live in a family of her own, where she could break through the cloying defensiveness that had shaped her and finally say what she felt and trust that she would still be loved.

THE BEST FAMILY

The best family:

Is unconditional in its expression of love.
Is always listening to hear feelings.
Takes the feelings of its members seriously, without exaggerating or minimizing.
Interprets feelings as not only communicated by words but by facial expressions; by social, work, and school behavior; by body language; and by changes in mood or energy.
Knows the emotional strengths and weaknesses of its members and doesn't let people hide. Thus family members are aware of the feelings that should be expressed in a certain situation but are not and try to draw out the person who suffers silently.

Cares about the truth and tries to understand.

Doesn't make rules more important than people.

Has realistic expectations.

Accepts that everyone is human, that no one is perfect, and that while everyone should be given the benefit of the doubt, no one should be granted permanent immunity.

Is slow to anger, quick to forgive.

10

DEFENSES: UNDERSTANDING THEIR MECHANICS

DENIAL

THE DEPENDENT DEFENSE—A PASSIVE POSITION

Denial is triggered into play when you lose someone you love or are threatened with abandonment or rejection. Denial is the defense that dominates the dependent period. It's no mystery that in later years, when you feel powerless or like a child, you tend to deny the threat.

Denial is a powerful defense. It prevents a hurt from intruding into your awareness. The defense of denial seems to act like a biochemical block at the perceptual gate, shutting perception off when it is dangerous and opening the gate when it is safe. Denial acts to short circuit the current of association.

However, with the exception of psychotic denial, which can truly shut out the world, denial is not usually an all-or-nothing defense. It is generally incomplete, allowing you to know some part of the truth. Like the young infant, you turn away from what hurts and force yourself to forget it's there without even defining what it is you are shutting out. Even so, you suspect that something bad exists. You just hope it will be gone when you open your eyes.

The denial you experience on losing a loved one, when you go into disbelieving shock, is also incomplete. The fright of the loss stuns you. You don't want it to be true. Much of denial follows the wish, *Please, don't let these facts be true.*

Much of denial is temporary as well as partial. The soldier blocks his fear during the attack but is still aware of what is going on. The singer ignores his fear and gives his best performance, but he's still afraid. The batter shuts out the crowd and becomes one with his bat, focusing only on the ball, but he still knows he has to get a hit to win.

Most of your use of denial is healthy and is employed in the service of concentrating or as part of the accommodation process. Walking down a dark street, you hear a noise, identify it as nonthreatening, and using your denial, allow the disturbance to slip into the background. Now you can focus on looking for a house number again while being alert to other sounds that might signify danger.

Your denial rises and falls. It is lower in safe situations and higher when you feel threatened. When your denial is lowest you are most susceptible to having old pain triggered into awareness. It is necessary to lower your denial to accept some painful truth. In a sense you pick up mourning where you long ago left off in order to initiate healing.

In a sense denial gives you a chance to think without immediately having to face the danger. You close an emotional window so you can concentrate. You retreat into your mind, trying to plan your escape and survive. You're not sure what you'll find when you release your denial and resurface in reality, but you want to have some plan to fall back on.

When you use too much denial, trying to push reality completely away, you end up not caring about what is going on outside you. You just want to be safe, hiding where you are. You are content to believe what you believe and restrict your perception so you won't be disturbed by unpleasant facts. At this point denial poses a problem, for rather than protecting you momentarily and allowing you to get your bearings, it becomes rigidly attached to an event or feeling and shields you from facing it. Instead of being managed by the natural therapeutic process, these blocked feelings are shunted into Emotional Debt.

Beneath your denial, you always suffer.

THE RANGE OF DENIAL

To understand the range of denial, keep in mind that defenses are nothing more than styles of deceiving yourself that are part of your character. The following variants of defenses are arranged roughly from weaker to stronger. However, each of these variants can grow rigid and become the manifestation of total denial.

Also, while denial is the chief defense of the dependent personality type, certain forms of denial are also employed by the controlling, competitive, and mature personality. The way denial is used by the dependent personality reflects his powerlessness and his need for someone else to take care of him and make his pain go away. In a sense the dependent person denies until help gets there. The controlling person uses denial to block his feelings of vulnerability. The competitive person uses denial to fortify his pretended indifference, while the mature person uses denial to cope until he figures out how to save himself.

Some forms of denial are common, everyday occurrences without any special pathological implication.

HOPING. Denial often starts with hoping, usually that what has happened hasn't happened, that you will be rescued, that it is all a mistake, that you will be made whole and escape harm. Some people hope long after all hope is gone. They refuse to believe that the loss has taken place.

PROCRASTINATING. You seek to avoid an unpleasant event or avoid discovering some painful reality is true. You procrastinate because you fear discovering you are not up to the challenge. Sooner or later the thing you fear approaching comes to you. You tend to put off confronting any event or test that will measure you. You procrastinate to avoid a loss of self-worth.

DIVERTING. You divert others to prevent them from looking at the very same evidence you're trying to avoid. Because others don't share your point of view, they are likely to state the unwelcome truth and validate your worst fears. Diverting is an active form of denial. It requires a lot of effort to push others away. Diverting also suggests that you are partly aware of the thing you are trying to deny. Competitive people use diversion when they act out and pretend that the hurt they suffered didn't matter.

GENERALIZING. Generalizing, broadening the scope of your concern, results from storing fear and hurt in Emotional Debt, where it grows unchecked. Generalizing is a way of increasing distance from a fear. A typical example is having been bitten by a dog, you cross the street to avoid him, then avoid the street, and finally avoid that section of town altogether. You dilute the threat in the name of safety, but your expanded avoidance quickly imprisons you.

BEING LATE. Being late is an extension of procrastination, but it largely reflects your wish to deny your disappointment over where you are in your career, in a relationship, or in any other situation. You resent where you find yourself. You don't want to be there. It is pure avoidance and is related to feeling lost in your own life.

LOSING FOCUS. This is a more typical manifestation of denial. You shut out what you are being told and cannot follow the other person's logic. You fear the comment contains a truth you don't want to hear. You become inattentive to anything that might lead to a painful truth.

LYING. You misstate reality to avoid the pain of the truth. Most lies are subtle and hardly noticed. If you tape-recorded your conversations, you would be amazed at how often you alter the truth to make it palatable.

NOT KNOWING. You repeat, "I don't know," as an expression of your wish not to know and your need to deny that you do know. It's a way of keeping information from penetrating into your awareness. People who say, "I know," to block criticism when they are being corrected are really denying they made a mistake. They don't want to know they were wrong.

MISPLACING. You avoid facing painful events or situations by misplacing items necessary to deal with them, such as your car or house keys, a critical telephone number, directions, documents, or receipts.

NOT SEEING OR HEARING. This is when your denial begins to become obvious to others. You completely miss the pointedly hurtful remark. You drive right past the exit on the freeway and then past the house where the fearful confrontation is to take place. You don't see the sign. You are afraid of moving forward.

CONFUSION. It may seem strange to think of confusion as a form of denial but it works perfectly. Although you hear them and they are obvious, the facts do not make sense. Their meaning is too painful. Include here also creating a hopeless mess so you cannot find what you're looking for, another way to keep from going forward.

FORGETTING. Forgetting is the fundamental mechanism of denial. It ranges from a momentary lapse, such as forgetting the name of a person with whom you have an unresolved painful conflict, to a total inability to recall a difficult period in your life. You just can't remember what happened.

Slips of speech, while seeming like intrusive remembering, are really the product of defensive forgetting. The hidden feeling or thought momentarily overcomes the denial protecting it and inserts itself out of place into conversation or in writing; for example, calling a pet by the name of a long-lost pet you much miss. The memory of the old hurt intrudes as a slip of speech, a partial memory of your yearning. Slips are valuable keys to understanding the unresolved pain contained in your Emotional Debt.

BLOCKING. This is an example of pathological denial in which there is broad disruption of the thought process caused by rigid emotional detours. Your logic suffers because you are denied access to broad areas of your experience. Because your denial will not permit critical facts into evidence, you have to make do with what you can remember. Your reasoning and mental associations are no longer in service of problem solving but are purely defensive. Your reasoning becomes concrete as a result. You can only see the obvious. The subtle associations elude you.

When you block, your brain is made subservient to your denial and you are less able to solve problems creatively. Because blocking is so effective, many innocent parts of reality are also excluded along with the painful. For this reason you seem emotionally flat, and reality seems a bit lifeless to you.

When you block, the meaning of words can become scrambled and the sound of the word seems to lose its meaning. To get a sense of this, repeat any word out loud fifteen times. You will notice that the word seems more like a nonsense sound and less like a familiar symbol. Because blocking disrupts your memory and your ability to associate one idea with another, it makes your language seem a little unfamiliar. This in turn makes acknowledging and resolving pain much more difficult as you begin to focus on the parts of words instead of their true meaning and get lost in the syntax of speech. Words in turn lose their ability to convey ideas and feelings. They become a linguistic barrier.

A similar effect where things and words feel like they are losing their sense of familiarity occurs during severe anxiety. However, this is the result of feeling isolated or distant from yourself. It can also happen in depersonalization. Adolescents can convince themselves they are crazy because nothing seems to mean anything, a form of blocking out meant to spook oneself.

GLOBAL DENIAL. This is denial of psychotic proportions. The threat you dread doesn't exist. The painful loss has simply not happened. Your pain, however, does leak through from time to time, causing you to increase your protestations of denial. It consumes all your energy. Like Barry angrily pacing in his hospital room after his fiancée choked to death in the restaurant, the price you pay for this total insulation is to live in an unreal world with considerably more pain than if you faced your problem.

EXCUSES

THE CONTROLLING DEFENSE—AN ACTIVE POSITION

The intellectual defenses are developed during the controlling period. They are an attempt to take control after the long period of powerlessness that characterized the dependent period. Waiting for someone to notice and take care of you when you were uncomfortable and helpless was a frustrating experience. Taking control of anything seemed extremely appealing. For that reason intellectual defenses tend to be triggered into use whenever questions of vulnerability or powerlessness arise.

Where denial was invoked to block the danger because the child felt powerless, the intellectual defenses serve to deny the powerlessness itself and explain it away. Scratch a controlling person and you'll find a dependent person just beneath the surface.

The controlling defenses—excuses and blaming—lead you to interpret reality from a rigid perspective. You admit that some disappointment has taken place, but your excuses and blaming explain why and how it happened and allow no contradiction. Once you have established the real reason for the hurt, it is perfectly clear, crystal in fact, that you had nothing to do with it. It was someone else's fault.

Excuses and blaming act as built-in bypasses in the brain's logic. You experience the damage, but your perception of what happened is immediately skewed so that it supports your preconceived viewpoint that someone else was at fault. It is almost as if you have a lawyer deciding on how the evidence you experience will be perceived, weighed, and judged. You are innocent, and your imbedded lawyer will prove it. Since you are innocent you don't have to feel the pain. You'll prove it.

Excuses and blaming also employ some denial to help filter out contradictions to your prejudicial viewpoint. This allows you to make your highly slanted explanation with great confidence, totally dismissing opposing views as immaterial.

One of the least rewarding experiences is to argue with a person who is fixed in defensive blaming and excuses. He believes he is right and you are wrong. You can't win because you can't get through to the person. It's already been decided. It helps to know this beforehand so you don't waste energy or get hurt further. What does get through to a controlling person is your statement that you are leaving because he hurt you. His dependent side is aroused and no logic can slake the panic a controlling person feels over the threat of abandonment.

THE CONTROLLING VIEWPOINT

The viewpoints that blaming and excuses defend are very simple to understand. So are the defensive postures they imply.

Viewpoint: I am good. You are bad.

Defensive position: You are wrong for not loving or supporting me. Look at all I give to you and do for you. You need me and you owe me. Your disloyalty in the face of being so vulnerable is not only unforgivable, it is stupid. What if I chose to cut you off? You needn't worry because I won't. Remember I'm good. You are the betrayer. I am justified in shaming you and pointing out your selfishness and neediness. If you go too far, I could retaliate.

Viewpoint: I am strong. You are weak.

Defensive position: It was your weakness that caused this problem. You scoffed at my offer of help. You went your own way. You thought you knew better. You were mistaken. Therefore, I am entitled to belittle you. You need to accept your limitations and be appreciative of my superior strength.

Viewpoint: I am smart. You are stupid.

Defensive position: You need me. Maybe someday you will be more experienced and know the ropes, but right now you are a novice and I am the expert. I am obligated to tell you what to do and to criticize you. How else will you learn? You should be grateful for this. Who else pays you this much attention? Where would you be without my guidance?

Viewpoint: I am right. You are wrong.

Defensive position: In your heart you know that's the truth. In the future you should just do as I suggest without being so contrary. Your argument is usually faulty anyway. You lack experience and don't think things through logically. I am justified in not taking you seriously. I'd be surprised if anyone does. Just do it my way and show some appreciation for my patience.

THE RANGE OF EXCUSES

Keep the controlling viewpoints in mind when you review the range of excuses that follow. When you feel the need to justify your behavior, you make excuses. Mostly excuses defend against the fear of being imperfect, wrong, stupid, or bad. The main purpose of rationalizing defenses is to avoid admitting any vulnerability or weaknesses.

Many of the variants of rationalization that follow are exaggerations of normal tendencies to organize and quantify. Without these defenses your life would be chaos. However, you can't control or know everything. As in everything else it is seeking a balance and taking a chance that matters.

NEATNESS. To look professional, organized, and therefore important. To be in proper uniform, to hold rank and power. To escape scrutiny and criticism by being in perfect order, faultless at least on the surface. Providing others no clue to dig further. How could you be wrong if you look and act the part?

SCHEDULING AND RULES. Rules and schedules can become an extension of your controlling defenses. They are a way of asserting control over others without having to take a stand. An insecure person may find it easier to dominate others by saying, "The schedule does not permit," or "It's not in the rules," rather than asserting himself directly.

People believe that if their schedules are intact, their life is working. A tight schedule provides a way of managing others and limiting stress, giving you an excuse to cut an unpleasant conversation short in order to make way for your three o'clock meeting. The power derived from schedules explains why it is sometimes so difficult to get people to make minor changes. It's like asking them to lower their defenses and give up control and explains why pointless rules stay in place.

CRITICISM. A way to keep others in line and maintain a position of superiority over them by continually measuring and evaluating them. Criticism also allows you to take the heat off yourself by pointing out others' imperfections. Criticism is endless because you never run out of faults to discuss. The fewer faults you admit to in yourself, the more you see in others.

The best answer to a question is to question the questioner's right to ask. Criticism is the easiest intellectual defense to see through. Everyone hates a critic even if he is right—especially if he is right.

GREEDINESS. To garner more and more possessions in order to enhance faltering self-worth.

Underlying rationale: you acquire power to prevent others from abandoning you.

INFLEXIBILITY. Insisting that others comply. The perfect plan needs perfect compliance. Others can't see the wisdom of your idea because they are inferior.

So just do it! No discussion!

EXPLANATIONS. No matter what the situation looks like, your explanation will prove you were infallible, right as usual, and will offer some interesting suggestions as to where the real blame for this dilemma might lie.

MAGICAL THINKING. To act as if you believe that if this happens, then that will follow. To assume a causality between events related only by a feeling or a wish. In its most common form, magical thinking is the belief that an angry thought can hurt others and that symbolic corrective action can prevent that injury from taking place.

Magical thinking is a way of trying to attain symbolic control over your anger, fear, and powerlessness. You can come to believe that you are responsible for another person's suffering just because you were angry at them. The very defense you used to feel empowered now makes you feel guilty. You want to believe you have the power but then doubt your goodness for using it in such an angry fashion.

EXCESSIVE ORDERLINESS OR DISORDERLINESS. At first glance this seems like an extension of neatness, but it is also a more concrete form of magical thinking. You create perfect order to avoid facing internal disarray, another way of symbolically managing hidden anger or the self-doubt it sponsors. You want to appear perfect again, that is, good and lovable.

People who cannot throw out anything—pack rats—display a variant of this thinking by assuming the opposite position. They hold on to everything as a way of symbolizing holding on to painful feelings. Their physical collections of junk mirror their Emotional Debt.

RITUAL. The need to appear perfect and deserving can come to be symbolized in a ritual. You want to complete some magical routine properly so the gods will grant your wish. The ritual cleanses you of doubt and evil, allowing you to appear deserving. If the ritual is not performed in a specific order, it will not work its magic.

Some rituals are extensions of the need to be orderly, a way to keep life organized. Some are superstitious incantations, personal prayers to no God in particular. Other rituals, like having to pass three red cars on the way to work in order to have a good day, become magical petitions. When these rituals cannot be completed satisfactorily, anxiety results and can interfere with your ability to function, and thus become a self-fulfilling prophesy.

The roots for this belief in rituals run deep in all civilizations, stemming from man's helplessness in the face of overpowering nature. He wishes to placate the gods and get them on his side. In some rain dances, the need for all the dancers to be in step is an extension of this belief. If a dancer were out of step, he could be blamed for the failure of the rains to materialize. Following the proper ritual to the tiniest detail in ancient Greek religion was important in obtaining the desired result. It was always assumed that the ritual failed, not the gods.

At its heart ritual is totally absurd. If you can get the gods to do your bidding by following a ritual that you, after all, invented, are you not in control of the gods? If you are in control of the gods, are you not a god yourself?

UNDOING. This is another extension of magical thinking, an attempt to balance and correct an unacceptable thought, which in magical terms might do damage all on its own. Therefore, leaving the thought unneutralized is anxiety provoking. You nullify thoughts of being evil, prurient, or vengeful by an undoing action.

The thought or wish is generally angry, and the undoing is often an action, such as knocking on wood, checking, or doubting, a symbolic gesture that counters the negative outcome such a thought might produce.

REACTION FORMATION. Acting one way when you feel the opposite. The assertion of bravery when you are full of fear. Climbing mountains when you are afraid of heights. Your action is a form of undoing in which you deny your fear and prove it is not true. The reasoning also involves some pretense: How could I be the way I fear if I act this way?

RENUNCIATION. The ultimate in undoing. Giving up all your wicked ways, especially under the threat of being caught and punished. Include here turning state's evidence, deathbed confessions, finding religion, and other drastic life conversions made from a position of desperation. Such abdicating power to a stronger authority is often made without accepting responsibility for what you've done, without feeling genuine remorse. You want to feel worthy without admitting wrongdoing. Such people are especially susceptible to cults.

Not to be confused with sincere life changes. The acid test is that when you have a genuine conversion and feel redeemed, you experience grace, which is the state of accepting yourself. You are altogether willing to discuss your faults because true converts have humility, self-acceptance, and flexibility. False converts use the rules and the structure of their newfound absolution as another set of excuses. They do not want to discuss the past. It is all behind them now. They just want to move on. True converts continue to grow, admitting when they slip, pointing out their own weaknesses before anyone else has to.

INTELLECTUALIZATION OF FEELINGS. In a sense, all these excuses are a form of intellectualization. When your mind manages feelings, it works very hard but generally does a self-defeating job. Reasoning away hurt causes you to isolate yourself from your feelings, making you more defensive and increasing your Emotional Debt.

This places you in an inflexible mental state. You regard your rigidity as being strong, but everyone else can see through it. You may claim you need no one and that you are an island, but you are really afraid to admit you need others. A lot of intellectualization is based on the need to assert your independence and superiority and to deny your dependence on others and your fear of abandonment. Admitting you are afraid to be vulnerable would go a long way to letting down your guard and making you appear more human.

At some level excuses begin to incorporate pretense. When you intellectualize, you playact some position of power and are in a sense pretending that your feelings don't matter. You are also pretending that you can control reality. Your orderliness, your rituals, your schedules, your ornate plans, your flawless logic are just a pretense that you don't need to feel afraid or responsible.

RATIONALIZATION OF ACTIONS. You rationalize your shortcomings to avoid feeling guilty for hurting another person or to explain your selfish actions. You explain that you simply did what had to be done under the circumstances. You were the only one who saw the danger. You were the only one willing to take a stand. Someone had to do it, and you were the only one who was prepared to accept responsibility. You were the only one . . . so you did it.

Rationalizations may not absolve you from blame, but they make it difficult for other weaker, more passive people to complain. They did nothing while you moved mountains. So there were a few mistakes. That is acceptable under the circumstances. No one helped. It was all up to you. If it were left up to them, they would have died.

When you rationalize it is hard for you to accept that other people have the right and sometimes the need to fail, to put themselves in harm's way, to experience their own life danger and learn their own lessons. You'd rather rescue someone and do a less than perfect job and take the heat for it later than let them suffer. That's what you tell yourself. That's what you believe.

For some reason other people find your rescuing them hard to take. They feel bound and trapped, and no matter how much you do for them, they feel treated badly.

Could you possibly have been doing all these noble acts just to control others?

You, of all people?

BLAMING. Whatever went wrong, it wasn't your fault.

That's the rationale of blaming others. You blame to reduce the critical guilt messages.

You want to believe you are good, so you blame a hurtful result on the fact that someone else was a bad person.

You want to believe you are smart, so you blame your mistakes on others' stupidity.

You want to believe you are strong, so you accuse the other person of cheating, using unfair tactics to win.

You want to believe you are right, so you accuse others of being unreasonable in their judgment, or claim that they are operating with only part of the facts. A little more explanation will show that you are right and why you acted the way you did. You can clear your reputation if you just get the chance.

You blame others when you are afraid to accept yourself as imperfect.

You blame others when you doubt your own goodness.

You blame others when you have questions about your integrity, sincerity, or genuineness and will not admit them to yourself.

PROJECTION. It is a very small step from blaming to projection. In fact blaming is a form of projection, except that blaming usually involves putting responsibility on others one event at a time as the need arises. Projection is a preconceived suspicion that others are always somewhere behind your mistakes.

When you project:

You automatically divert responsibility for wrongdoing away from yourself.

You accuse others of your own unacceptable feelings or motivations.

You also discover your weaknesses in others and often hate them for it. This is the basis of much prejudice and suffering.

Since projection becomes generalized, it is easy to believe that others are unfair and are trying to hurt you. This makes you distrusting.

With a little pretending and denial it is fairly easy to begin to imagine that others are up to no good. When your judgment is tainted by blaming and rationalization, it is easy to discover the evidence you need to prove your distorted case to yourself. The danger comes when you take preemptive action based on suspicion alone.

PARANOIA. When you believe others are out to get you, you are on shaky ground. You support your belief system by distancing yourself from anyone who presents an opposing view. While intellectual defenses generally tend to isolate you from your emotions, in paranoia the connection to feelings is nearly severed. As a result, your conversance with reality is markedly diminished. Your logic no longer makes sense. You begin to believe that people are in a conspiracy against you or that you have a powerful enemy who is responsible for holding you back.

However, this is a delusion. As Tom Wilson in one of his cartoons had a psychoanalyst advise Ziggy, "If everyone were out to get you, they would've gotten you by now."

Paranoia is, however, a powerful and persuasive emotional state. Not bound by the rules of reality, you can argue your illogical case with total conviction. People who are dependent on you may support your twisted beliefs, but when your ability to provide for them falters, their belief in you also dwindles, and they may try to escape your influence. This explains why so many abusive and fearful marriages seem to last right up to the point of disaster. When the husband feels powerless to control his spouse from rejecting him, his distorted sense of reality may lead him to act rashly, with tragic results.

These often sensational cases arrest our attention because the feelings that are acted upon are common to every troubled relationship. When a relationship gets into difficulty, betrayal and rejection run high, sometimes bringing you to the brink of violence. In such circumstances you try to keep a grip on the most intense feelings you have ever experienced. You wonder how close you have come to losing control and what it would take to push you over the edge.

PRETENSES

Your tendency to pretend developed when you began to compare yourself with other children and found yourself lacking or the task you were trying to accomplish harder than you bargained for. You were looking for a way to manage failure. You wanted to keep your self-esteem and reputation intact. You did not want to be embarrassed or have others laugh at you. You wanted some way to deny the loss and also some explanation to make the loss seem like a win. Pretending was the perfect alternative to admitting failure.

You deny that the pain took place.

You make excuses to explain logically why what happened is not your fault.

You pretend that the pain you suffered doesn't matter to you and therefore wasn't really pain.

Pretending assumes a posture of indifference and sometimes acting *as if* something were true. You act as if you didn't really care or as if the way things have turned out is precisely the way you intended. You move away from the battle as if nothing happened.

So what?, Who cares?, Forget it!, Yesterday's news!, and Can't be bothered are some of the feigned postures of pretending. They are infuriating, irritating, maddening to others, a way of expressing anger without admitting the hurt, although some unsophisticated people may think your blasé attitude is "cool."

Of course you can pretend to care too much when you don't care at all. You can mirror passion, get consumed in a relationship, and go through exaggerated grief when it falls apart. Is it just an act or are you trying out a role to see what it would feel like? You hurt a lot of people pretending.

Confusing?

Pretending is designed to be confusing. The disappointing circumstances that cause you to pretend are usually obvious, but pretending makes them seem complicated. Perhaps the effectiveness of pretending depends on the frustrating inconstancies it creates. No one knows where you're coming from. You're hard to pin down.

Consider the person who was rejected by someone he claimed to be in love with just a few days ago and who now insists that he was only acting. His aloof position makes sense only if you understand how much pain he is suffering, the very thing he cannot admit. To take his explanation at face value makes him seem a cad, or at least shallow and unfeeling. You can't tell whether he really cared or not. That's the whole point of pretending—to save face.

Like everyone else you'll find that you use some form of pretending when you feel insecure about your worth. Pretending is the most mature of the three defensive patterns, not only because it evolved at a time of greater maturity and emotional expressiveness, but because it allows you to be in closer touch with reality. You pretty much know how you feel even if you pretend it doesn't matter.

Nevertheless pretending is also designed to hide from the truth. Its advantage over denial and excuses is that it is more likely to be used transiently.

THE RANGE OF PRETENSE

Pretense in its mildest forms has elements of familiar, seemingly innocent, everyday behavior. Everyone engages in such pretenses, and no one makes much of it. It's just a coping mechanism for dealing with the stresses of a competitive world. The underlying motivation of such pretending is to protect your self-esteem and to gain praise as easily as possible. This is a risky maneuver because the praise that is won by pretending is often superficial, not enduring, and when withheld can produce disappointment over the wrong issue.

If you stop and think about it, there's not that much difference between being salesman of the month and not being salesman of the month. However, pretending allows you to believe that it really matters. You become salesman of the month and you're on top of the world. File under *Cheap thrills.* You miss by a few percentage points and console yourself by saying you didn't try, the other fellow had a better territory, or you were taking it easy this month. File under *Sour grapes.*

The real issue is not are you winning in someone else's race, but are you doing your best at the thing you love most? Are you testing your true worth?

In its more pronounced forms, when it is used to deal with deep doubts about self-worth, pretense can consume considerable energy and divert you from your life's work. Your focus becomes appearances rather than substance. Also, as pretense gets stronger, it employs excuses and blaming as you rationalize your pretending. Finally, when pretense becomes more rigid, it also uses denial. As a result you can be led far away from reality.

COMPARING. Comparing yourself with others is a basic principle of the pretending position and is the hallmark of the competitive personality. It is natural to measure yourself by others' accomplishments, but doing so can be misleading. You can appear like a winner by choosing an unworthy opponent. Your real goal is to challenge yourself and see how you measure up to your own ideals.

PLEASING OTHERS. This is a leftover from the early days when you weren't sure of your own judgment and pleased yourself by pleasing your parents. You still tend to seek others' approval when you aren't sure of yourself. Again, you also seek to please others when you want an easy success, rather than giving your best and measuring your worth by your own standards. Of course when others are controlling, they can withhold their approval and lead you far away from yourself.

When others' praise is easier to win than your own, you can make others the standard of your approval rather than competing with your own best. When that happens you stop following your inner dreams. Rather than be creative, you become imitative. You lose your originality and specialness. Praise is little reward if you feel you have betrayed your true gift.

ONE-UPMANSHIP. You put others' efforts down to feel better about yourself, especially when you aren't brave enough to take your own risks.

BRAGGING. Fulsomely making the most of what you have. This is an overcompensation for your concealed feelings of inadequacy or dissatisfaction with your accomplishments, usually because the accomplishment was too easy and was designed to gain attention rather than to answer the question, How good am I? or What is the best I can do?

EXAGGERATION. Making more of an accomplishment to make it seem as meaningful as the risk you should have taken.

Seeking praise without having to do the work.

Overstating the worth of an inferior goal to compensate both for your fear of not being more talented and your embarrassment at not being braver.

GAME PLAYING. Minimizing the stress of a loss by devaluing how much it means to you.

Stating that life is just a game and that you're only playing or just kidding.

Also a way to test unfamiliar waters, to see what it would be like to be in a new situation without really committing, so you can leave unattached if the going proves too rough.

A way to see what others think or feel or how tough the competition is without revealing your hand.

Acting *as if* you're involved without being involved at all.

Teasing.

Thrill seeking, again.

KEEPING A STIFF UPPER LIP. Pretending all is going well in spite of obvious setbacks, keeping up appearances so to appear *as if* you aren't suffering.

Acting invincible is a brittle position and one that does not take kindly to confrontation. When you say a person has an attitude, you're probably sensing that he is suffering while pretending to be stronger and acting more assured than he feels. Pretending not to be hurt, the person still acts irritable, haughty, or above it all, putting others off and encountering negativity that allows him to play out his rejection by proxy.

PLAYING EMOTIONALLY DUMB. Denial begins to play a part in your pretending. You act *as if* the insulting remark went over your head.

You can't understand what is going on.

This can lead to smoldering anger, which is difficult to release because the hurt has been purposely muffled or confused by you.

WISHFUL THINKING. Living emotionally *as if* things were better than they are.

This pretense involves excuses as well as denial. The more denial you employ to feel comfortable in your wishful thinking, the more transparent your defensiveness appears to others. You seem pathetic and fragile, as if you are living in your own world. You don't want to hear contradictory information.

FAKING. Going from your fantasy into reality, without any work or preparation, and acting *as if* you belonged.

This can be a useful adaptive mechanism that allows you to test an unfamiliar situation and gain courage. You pretend to be comfortable until you actually become comfortable. You act as if you own the place. You act as if the sale is a done deal. In some way faking is like giving yourself the benefit of the doubt while still continuing to doubt yourself. Some people fake as a way to cope with their lagging confidence. When people fake all the time, they don't want to be judged for themselves.

If you get caught and are confronted, faking can lead to considerable embarrassment. Others focus on your insincerity and dishonesty. They do not recognize how well you did, considering that you really didn't know anything. It's hard to build self-esteem while pretending.

ROLE-PLAYING. Acting *as if* you already were the person you would like to be. This tactic, along with faking, is a common device that sometimes actually helps people grow. In any new job, you try to act like you are comfortable and are supposed to be there. Slipups in role-playing are the source of lighthearted office jokes on the new guy who doesn't know the ropes yet but pretends he does and so gets all screwed up.

Role-playing is especially typical of adolescents, who are always trying out new identities.

As you get older role-playing gives you a slippery emotional quality because you can act out either side of a conflict without really being involved.

Typical roles are the scapegoat, the victim, the know-it-all, the fool, the spoiler, the crisis monger, the aristocrat, the prima donna, the star, the hypochondriac, Don Juan or siren, the gambler, the critic, the rival, and devil's advocate.

Role-playing is a way to express emotions without taking an emotional risk. It is an obvious compensation for something that's missing in your life, namely, being yourself. Unfortunately, when a particular role becomes established as your predominant style of reacting, it can take you off course, wasting energy and time and misleading others. People don't know who you really are.

When you act insincerely, such as playing the part of a caring person just to make yourself feel good, you can lead others to expect what you cannot deliver. Letting others down makes you feel like a bad person. This explains why people who role-play and hurt others often act self-destructively. They act out the role of a guilty person.

DEPERSONALIZATION. This is the discomforting feeling that you aren't you. It's not that you are pretending to be someone else, it's just that you don't feel like you. You feel *as if* you are in someone else's body, or in someone else's life. This defense serves to distance you from situations that are overwhelming, but it is not effective in blotting out anxiety. Something's wrong, but you don't know what.

Depersonalization is most commonplace in adolescence when your identity, body, and physical hormones are changing all at once. Your ideals may have been crushed as you began to see your parents and heroes as having feet of clay. The whole world seems phony, and what is worse, you don't know who you are.

You feel light-headed, as if you are floating through the world. You continually question if you are really you; if everything that is happening around you is real, really happening. When you are young and all your cherished beliefs seem suddenly overturned, you can feel as if you are going crazy. The more denial you use to cope, the crazier you can seem. It is for this precise reason that making a diagnosis of psychosis in an adolescent is discouraged.

SPLITTING. Splitting seems a little like role-playing, a little like depersonalization. Your painful emotions seem at a distance, as if they have been split away from you, and can seem entirely remote to you. You go through your life *as if* you are viewing it from behind a glass partition.

You feign indifference by immediately covering your painful feelings with So what? and Who cares? Still, it is apparent to others that you do care, but are just too insecure to admit what exactly is wrong. Instead you become overly upset over trivial disappointments, flying off the handle unpredictably. You seem brittle, unapproachable, volatile, and unstable.

DISSOCIATION AND AMNESIA. When you're in denial, the distance you place between yourself and your split-off feelings increases, and splitting evolves into dissociation and amnesia.

In the mildest form you can still see reality clearly but cannot relate to it emotionally. You almost sound like you are talking about another person when you talk about yourself. When dissociation becomes severe, you split off your painful memories so completely that you seem unaware of them. You can develop episodes of amnesia during which you act out your repressed feelings and have little or no recall of doing so. It is almost as if your split emotions have claimed some part of your body and soul to express themselves without your being aware of it. Frequently the source of the pain that is being split off is related to severe trauma from childhood, often sexual or physical abuse, the memory of which remains split off from awareness in remote Emotional Debt. The toxic nostalgic manifestation of split-off stored pain often takes the form of an altered state of consciousness, such as a fugue state, in which a person lives out his feelings almost as if he is another person with little or no recollection of what happened when he returns to himself.

The toxic nostalgic representation of a split-off emotion is often also split off when it is downloaded and is therefore not recallable.

MULTIPLE PERSONALITY. Multiple personality is an extreme and uncommon form of dissociation in which painful emotions have been so widely split off that they give form to a discrete but partial personality or personalities living in the same body. It is as if the pain in remote Emotional Debt is being expressed through another person when it downloads. This is not schizophrenia, as is commonly misunderstood.

These people are highly suggestible, as are all people who use pretense. Hypnosis is a powerful tool that takes advantage of this suggestibility to unify these feelings as part of the same person.

THE LEGACY OF THE DEFENSES

The benefit of the defenses is also their burden. They keep you from being overwhelmed by an injury. They also keep the truth of the injury from being accepted and thus delay the natural therapeutic process from resolving the pain. The natural therapeutic process continually struggles to shear old feelings loose from the grip of the defenses and bring them to resolution.

Holding feelings in Emotional Debt, while common, is an unnatural condition, similar to an emotional vacuum. Your feelings are always seeking expres-

sion to balance this uncomfortable condition, and it requires considerable defensive energy to keep them from doing so. Energy that is committed to withholding feelings is not available for other life-sustaining activity, such as
engaging in play and laughter and all the other natural therapeutic adjuncts that
keep you vital and young.

Still, not every feeling can be expressed. Some feelings need to be withheld
because their expression would violate trust or simply be inappropriate. Holding back some feelings is necessary in the name of socialization and allows you
to get along with other people in a civilized manner.

In a real sense, no one is entirely free to express what he feels. In fact only
primitive people express whatever they feel, and then they're likely to hurt others indiscriminately. Even so, you still want to express yourself, but everywhere
you must contend with rules and expectations, laws and customs. You want to
say what is on your mind, but you also want love and respect. You don't want to
offend people unnecessarily and you don't want to make enemies. In the business world expressing feelings is hazardous indeed and likely to be viewed as a
failing, a time-consuming and unproductive indulgence.

How open should you be?

How much truth can other people stand?

When it comes right down to it, how honest are you?

No one knows the answer to these questions. You are continually testing, trying to discover the limits of appropriateness and bravery. Your defenses help you
store your feelings while you decide what to do.

You have to choose which feelings are important to express and release your
hurt as best you can. You need to accept what you are powerless to change and
learn to tolerate some Emotional Debt from time to time without making it a
habit of avoidance.

WHEN YOU DEFEND TOO MUCH

When you avoid the truth, the natural healing process is inhibited.

When your energy is spent defensively, life loses its zest.

When you deny, you block out the good along with the bad.

When you make excuses, you avoid your life lessons and do not grow.

When you pretend, you are stymied; how do you mourn something you
claim not to care about?

When you are defensive, your world shrinks. Because you have less energy
to invest in living, your work and love life seem less gratifying. You have less to

give and so life's meaning feels diminished. Your attitude toward the present isn't fresh, but an echo of the past, making the present seem boring and repetitious. You seem so preoccupied in proving an old point that the world of the present and all its pleasures slips by you.

Your defenses define a kind of emotional dam. While its original purpose was to protect you from momentary swells of feelings that might overwhelm your stability, the dam tends to become permanently established. Even when you have resolved most of your problems, you still have some defensive structures in place.

Freedom comes from recognizing and lowering these defenses, not from trying to eliminate them. You can no more alter your defensive style than you can change your character.

However, the more truthful you are in accepting what happens to you and the more responsibility you take for it, the less your defenses will intrude. The price you pay for employing defenses is that you don't learn to trust your strength or believe in yourself. You need to accept that you can deal with anything your life presents to you. It's when you doubt this that you hide and your problems really begin.

Living in the truth is always the easiest solution.

THE PERSONALITY TYPES

Your PERSONALITY TYPE REFLECTS THE WAY you deal with the natural therapeutic process. When you are open you heal quickly. When you are closed you suffer. Each personality type protects itself in its own way for its own reasons.

Your personality represents your defensive style, mirroring both your honesty and the way you avoid pain. While no two people have the exact same mixture of defenses, it is possible to describe three distinct defensive character types: dependent, controlling, and competitive. Your particular personality is a unique blend of all three elements.

Your character type defines both your negative avoidance patterns as well as your positive qualities. Should the need arise, your defensive style still exists hidden within you, a well-established detour to bypass unpleasant feelings. Even if you were a well-adjusted person, you'd still tend to employ your familiar defensive patterns when overwhelmed. However, because you were mature, you'd confront the problem, cope with it as soon as possible, and release your defenses, preferring honesty and directness to avoidance.

When you are at your best, you are uniquely yourself. Each day you create your life anew, free of stereotype and prejudice. While your character possesses typical special sensitivities, the way you realize your gift will be original and uniquely your own because the positive aspects of your character are free and open while the defensive parts are closed. When you're at your best you transcend your character limitations to fulfill your potential.

The optimism of personal growth stems from the fact that, even though your character was shaped by painful difficulties, it was influenced by positive forces as well. When you resolve your problems and release the feelings stored in Emotional Debt, you can step beyond the confines of your defenses and become a mature person who is free to choose. You can see the world the way it is rather than be limited by preconceived expectations that are defensively predetermined.

THE EVOLUTION OF CHARACTER

The dependent personality type reflects the young child's perspective of helplessness and powerlessness. Totally vulnerable, the dependent child is exquisitely sensitive to abandonment and separation. This characteristic persists in the dependent character. The larger truth is that everyone passes through the dependent period, and because parents are only human and flawed, everyone experiences deprivations, both accidental and neglectful, as well as receiving both generous and overdetermined expressions of love. Everyone, therefore, develops some dependent character traits, without necessarily becoming a dependent personality.

The same principle holds true for acquiring traits of the controlling and competitive period.

RESPONSE TO EARLY STRESS

While your exposure to stress was a powerful force in shaping your personality, it is not a perfect example of the laws of cause and effect. Much of why you turned out the way you did involves too many variables to evaluate. Still, if you suffered significantly during the dependent period, it is likely that the defense of denial will figure prominently in your dealings with pain. As a result you will tend to be passive, deeply affected by the actions of others, likely to withhold negative feelings and to build remote Emotional Debt that tends to lower your self-esteem, making you needy for others' support and love.

However, you can also have a difficult time during the dependent period but instead of becoming dependent use your denial to block your fears and become active, take life by the horns, and refuse to be a victim or dependent on anyone but your own initiative. You are still driven by the dependent character's sensitivity to people even though you defiantly choose not to be committed.

These adaptations represent opposite extremes of the dependent style. A dependent person who desperately needs other people is in some way very close to the dependent person who insists on being independent and refuses to become emotionally involved with anyone.

On balance, if you were exposed to severe hurts during the dependent period, it is far more likely that you will become dependent rather than defiantly independent. In fact the person who extols independence at all costs is more likely to be a controlling person, who has taken his fear of being powerless to heart and never wants to be vulnerable again. This is what is meant by the comment that a controlling person is a dependent person who has learned to make a good living. Unlike the independent person, the controlling person's independence is achieved by sacrificing his sensitivity to the feelings of others.

While everyone needs to be independent to feel whole, being independent feels exactly wrong to a dependent person. All his life he has yearned to be together with another person in order to feel complete. Even so he needs to learn to take care of himself without resenting it. He needs to master his weakness, his mistaken belief that he is nothing without another person. He has to learn to feel complete as he is. Then being alone will be seen as a privilege rather than a punishment and will not provoke anxiety by stirring up toxic nostalgic recollections of abandonment.

The person you eventually become is a reflection of how well you adapted to childhood stress. Were you supported and encouraged or abused and put down? Did you cling and retreat or risk being open? At each stage of development there were new challenges to shape you. Families changed. New children arrived. Relatives moved in and out. Parents separated. Boyfriends and girlfriends arrived and departed. There were other visitations: illness, death, separation, addiction, poverty, and success. The combination of influences, both positive and negative, that shaped your character was complex and unique.

Of all these variables involved in shaping you, it was your response that mattered most.

Even if you weren't aware of it, you had a lot of choices. Although you used denial to cope, you had a wide range of denial to choose from. Your choice was influenced by the severity of the pain you faced, how long it lasted, who was there to make it better, and how strong you were. Some children show great emotional resilience and are forgiving of delays, absences, and shortcomings; others are easily and deeply wounded. Some seem undaunted in the face of deprivation while others are so sensitive that a raised voice or eyebrow feels like complete rejection and reduces them to tears.

The dependent child also passes through the controlling and competitive stages. His defensive armor is elaborated upon and polished as he takes elements of controlling and competitive defenses and combines them with his characteristic use of denial.

Even though a person's character type becomes established before the age of seven or eight, the process of personality formation is still not complete. While a person may develop a dependent personality rather early, the question of *how* dependent he will become is continually being modified.

GROWING UP

Life is full of corrective emotional experiences. Even when exposed to unpredictable caretakers and unable to count on their support, a child can still learn to develop a trusting relationship with a worthy person later on. It will just take more time and patience. When the child finally learns to be open and trusting, he is still not a completely trusting person, but rather a repaired untrusting child. Should his current relationship let him down, he will discover that he is still highly susceptible to rejection and regression to the nontrusting state he "outgrew." In fact, he may become involved in unstable or hurtful relationships that seem to evoke his earlier disappointments as a way to "remember" and try to resolve them.

ADOLESCENCE REFINES CHARACTER

Adolescence plays a critical role both in resolving earlier conflicts and adjusting the defensive posture that resulted from dealing with them. Adolescence is like a second chance to reenact and symbolically reconcile past troubles, even those hurts that occurred before the use of language was established. Adolescence can be a powerful healing experience in which a sheltered child blossoms, comes into his own, and begins to assert his independence for the first time.

It can go the other way as well. A child who seemed well-adjusted but who was merely being timidly compliant can find the stress of adolescence so disruptive that it confirms his worst fears about himself. The weakest parts of his character suddenly glare at him, crushing his self-esteem and causing him to regress emotionally.

LIFE HEALS

Even though it tends to confirm your character type, adolescence is not the end of personal growth. Life still presents crises that are really opportunities to be more honest and grow again.

You mismanage these crises when you insist on seeing them as proving that the world is against you, that life is hopeless, or that you are jinxed. Then you become set in your ways.

Your defensive posture is most pronounced when you deploy your defenses rigidly. Then your responses are mechanical and prefabricated. You are at your worst and your character weaknesses most obvious. You act in a predictable manner, a caricature of yourself. Others tend to respond to you predictably as well. They push you away, undermine and hurt you, and thus seem to justify and reinforce your defensive behavior. Negativity begets negativity.

While you may not be able to change your defensive pattern, you can lower your defensive wall by deciding to be open, to accept yourself and your short-comings, and to tell as much of the truth as you know. At its heart continuing to grow requires that you face life's hurts directly and take responsibility for being in the place that allowed you to be injured.

You learn your lessons by telling the truth.

CHANGE

The blessing of the natural therapeutic process is that a person whose life has been enmeshed in rigid defensive reactions can still arrive at a point where telling the truth is the only viable option left. When he does, healing and growth resume.

It may take desperation and the realization that his efforts have been futile for him to get to this point, but he finally seems willing to admit what others have been trying to tell him all along. He lowers his defenses, lets down his guard, and concedes that he has been wrong. He admits he was jealous, foolish, insecure, or didn't believe in himself enough to take risks. He confesses that he was obnoxious and can understand why people didn't like him.

Others are dumbfounded by this apparent sea change. They can't get over the fact that the person seems in touch with his weakness. He is easy to talk to, concedes his errors matter-of-factly, laughs at himself. He seems likable in spite of his obvious faults. People realize that what they disliked about him was not his faults, but his defensiveness in concealing them, his negative character traits. His defensiveness masked his humanness.

The person has not changed. He is still the same person with the same char-acterological type and potential for defensiveness, but because he has decided to be open about his shortcomings and truthful about his hurts, he has less need to use those defenses. He has bypassed his defenses by telling the truth, letting in the pain and taking responsibility for his role in his problems.

The world responds. While some people are distrustful, others are support-ive and welcome the change. They may even feel affectionate toward the person now that his guard is down and he's no longer trying to control or manipulate them. He allows other opinions to be spoken without interruption or criticism and to stand uncorrected. Amazing! Others believe that there is hope and that the person is changing.

In fact no one really changes. When we say that someone has changed we really mean that he has grown more honest about the lies he has told. The difference between the former condition and the more truthful one feels enormous. It is.

Such gains are real but not necessarily consistent. Everyone slips and slides when he grows. Even after a considerable time of better adjustment, during which you learned to lower your defenses and be more honest, you can come into negative contact with an old lover who has open access to your heartstrings, or with a manipulative employer who knows how to press all your buttons and does so with a snide comment. Even when you swore you would never again permit it to happen, you find yourself tripped into your old defensive behavior patterns. In just a moment, you can go from loving yourself to believing you haven't changed and are therefore hopeless. Don't lose faith. We've all been there.

Progress is staying in the growth process, admitting you are only human and forgiving yourself when you do have a setback. Consider the setback a refresher course in being human. Learn from it and let it go.

Even though your positive character traits predominate when you are open, you always retain the potential for lying. It is a humbling realization and keeps you on your toes. The process of growing is simply committing to be open in expressing whatever old emotions come to your awareness while continuing to be vulnerable about the hurts you feel in the present.

Understanding the basic character types and how they developed will give you a perspective on the defensive postures you adopted and also a greater appreciation of your strengths: your capacity to care, reason, and create. Realizing your positive potential supports your belief in yourself and makes you lovable to others. When you deal from your strengths rather than weaknesses, your ability to give your gift is freed up from your need to please or manipulate others or to succeed at any cost.

When you give your gift out of strength and love, you do so for the best reason, because it gives you pleasure. When you do, your giving leads you to discover an honest representation of yourself in the world. Others are appreciative and grateful for your contribution, and you are pleased with yourself.

When you act for negative reasons, no matter what you accomplish, you never seem to get what you want. Others seem to intuit your insincerity. Your gifts feel as if they were given to get something in return. In spite of your "generous" efforts, others do not respond the way you want. Life seems futile and disappointing.

You create the world anew when you conquer your character defects and learn to be your best.

The following descriptions of character types will allow you to recognize both their inherent weaknesses and potential for good. You need to understand that even if the description of one distinct personality type fits you perfectly, you are nevertheless still a composite of all three types and have incorporated elements from all three stages of development to form your unique personality.

THE DEPENDENT CHARACTER TYPE

SHE

The dependent character is often a woman. Women are trained to be nurturers, and this role is supported by society and family expectation. The concern with love, caring, nurturing, support, constancy is more typical of a woman's expected characterological ideal than society's view of a man. Indeed women are expected to sacrifice their lives while they have children and to make a home where they can care for their family. These considerations place women around the hearth more than men. Without debating the politics of sexuality, it is the current status of women to be more dependent than men.

While exceptions to this assumption are to be found everywhere, they do not refute it. In this discussion the dependent person is therefore designated "she." However, what follows is to be attributed to the dependent person, not to women in general.

LOVABILITY

The dependent person is concerned with being lovable. Everything she is and wants stems from this. If others love her they will protect her and provide for her needs.

If she grew up in an unloving household, she will choose someone as a mate who is also unloving, as if she is hoping to win him over and resolve her old needs by proxy. This attempt usually fails.

The person she chooses is usually a controlling person. He doesn't usually give her all she wants because that would be giving away too much. He tends to hold back something to keep the dependent person dependent on him. The controlling person also needs to be loved but is too afraid of declaring his need because that would reveal his weakness and put him at risk of being rejected. Thus, while he may be an outstanding provider, the thing he tends to withhold is his love or approval, his emotional support. To the dependent person in a relationship with an unresponsive controlling person, this deficiency feels like the world.

The dependent person tends to suffer from guilt because she needs so much to be loved she can't risk expressing her hurt in a timely fashion. After a while she builds up such resentment in Emotional Debt that she begins to doubt her lovability.

Her anger chafes at her self-esteem, making her clingy. She continually asks others for reassurance that they still love her. When her demands press others to their limits and they push her away, this only confirms the dependent person's fear that she is not lovable.

This causes a tearful cycle of pouting, testing, and more clinging.

The dependent person is so blinded by her need for love that she tends to drown in her feelings. She can become so lost in her yearning that she is unable to sort out her old from her new hurts. She lives in a sea of dependency, like a child wanting to make contact but feeling undeserving or too naughty to reach out to others. She will wait endlessly for others to reach out to her, to apologize and make it better. Often no one comes, and she feels unnecessarily rejected, when a few simple words from her openly shared could have prevented all her suffering.

The dependent person tends to see others' positive emotions as a reward for being lovable. When others do not feel good about themselves, she is likely to take it personally. When the person she needs becomes sick, she often gives too much, hovering and smothering, making the other person sicker than he is just so she can exercise her "giving." Of course the person who is sick is made so uncomfortable by this that he prefers to get up and go to work with a 104-degree temperature rather than open himself up to being entrapped by "giving" that is really "taking" in disguise.

The dependent person is not willing to discuss this matter at all and takes mentioning any insincerity in giving as a sign of disloyalty. Such a discussion can precipitate so much anxiety in her that it hardly seems worth the effort. To keep peace you end up apologizing to the dependent person for her letting you down.

By the same token she takes any negative expression personally, and rather than trying to understand why someone is irritated by her, she takes it as a removal of affection, a punishment she feels deeply. Out of annoyance the people who love her do withhold their affection from time to time. Since the dependent person is so needy for a continual show of love, she finds it difficult to hear the other person's complaints. That the other person raised his voice in exasperation becomes more of an issue than how she caused the other person to be frustrated. She can only hear her own needs speaking: Love me. Don't leave.

BOUNDARIES

The dependent person has problems maintaining realistic boundaries. This is understandable because in her heart she does not want there to be any boundaries between herself and the person she loves. She would like the two of them to merge into *onetotallyinseparablebeing.* Just like that! Her need to dissolve boundaries is a reflection of her childhood need to be one with her mother, to hold on to her for dear life.

The dependent person is always being lured by the dependent dream. She believes she needs another person to be complete. She needs another person to be her best, to assuage her hurt, to comfort and love her. When the other person is not around she not only feels lonely but unloved and unlovable.

Her wish to be close causes her to disregard her safety and best interests and try to get involved with others even when she is aware that they have hurt her. She is always hoping the other person will change. She becomes so attached to her dream of being taken care of that she holds on to relationships long after experience has revealed to her the dismal prospects of getting what she wants. After forty years of rebuke, she still approaches the withholding parent with open arms, expecting that this time she will be taken in and loved as she needs to be.

Her yearning for love at all costs is a crippling need. When it causes her to abdicate the role of protector of her own boundaries, it leads her into relationships that are destructive and seem designed for abusiveness. Abuse requires an abuser and someone who will not defend herself.

Usually her boundaries are trespassed when she appeals for affection. Starved by the lack of love while growing up, she opens her borders to be sure she doesn't shut out any possible source of affection. This often results in tragedy. It is hard for her to learn her lesson because to admit that she has to love herself by herself is to give up her dream.

As an extension of her weak boundaries, the dependent person seems far too willing to admit she is wrong when she was not, just to heal a rift with another person. She is driven to make it all better. She apologizes when she is hurt. In a sense she is making amends for her unexpressed anger. She loses other people's respect for doing this and only invites more abuse in the future.

She needs to take a stand and risk rejection.

REJECTION

The dependent person is so sensitive to rejection and abandonment that she discovers it everywhere. She is so convinced others are about to push her away that she often reacts as if she is rejected when other people are merely not paying enough attention to her. Out of her insecurity she accuses others of wanting to get rid of her. This is a touchy subject. Since the dependent person can cling annoyingly, there is always a little truth in this. Her persistent needy accusations make her unpleasant to be with and can precipitate the very rejection she fears.

Because the dependent person is hypersensitive to loss, she is continually noticing and measuring diminishment. She notices that the servings at the restaurant aren't as big as they were last year, the service is slower, the place just doesn't seem the same. "Something's missing," is the recurrent theme underlying all her logic and suspicions. What she is missing, of course, is a paternal figure who is always present to care for her every need. She yearns for life the way it used to be or the way she wanted it to be when she was in the nursery, when she didn't even have to ring for room service. Things have been going downhill ever since.

The dependent person perceives loss everywhere and always seems to be in some form of mourning. This gets in the way of the natural therapeutic process by making it more difficult for her to put a serious loss in perspective and give it its due. She doesn't see a new loss in its own right but either exaggerates it or sees it as part of a series of losses or as proof of her deprivation and confirmation of her worst fears. "I knew this would happen!" is her typical response. So is "Why does this always happen to me?" and "Not again?". The dependent person frequently disdains the value of growing up by reasoning, "What's the point of being an adult if I cannot be protected from loss or have to care for myself?"

When overwhelmed with rejection the dependent person acts paralyzed, numb, helpless. Being alone is a terrifying prospect for the dependent person who somehow equates it with being bad or being punished. Exclusion is always a terrible punishment for the dependent person. A dread of being excluded from the family during childhood persists as a fear of being cut off by her circle of friends or work group.

This fear of rejection continually causes the dependent person to test the affections and allegiances of others. Since she has a deep distrust of her own lovability, reassurances do not make her feel better. Only the continuing presence of the other person will console her. She reasons that if the other person is not with her, he must want to get away from her.

This leads the dependent person into one of her least appealing behaviors—insisting that others stay with her. Such clinging may seem like a wish come true to someone who has the same needs, but it quickly becomes cloying. The dependent person will fill up all the space in a relationship and not allow her partner to breathe. A natural request for freedom seems like an opening for betrayal.

The dependent person wants others to be with her right now. She wants to know what they are doing today and tomorrow. She wants to make plans to be together and be sure they are followed. She hates being disappointed, ignored, stood up.

She overreacts when she feels rejected and never forgets. Because any hurt tends to awaken her old rejections, she suffers easily and deeply over seemingly trivial insults. Others continually have the feeling that she is oversensitive, can't take a joke, or finds offense in innocent comments. As a result she hears others say, "Grow up," a lot.

It comes as no surprise that she never really forgives a rejection. If she could, she probably wouldn't have become dependent in the first place.

SECURITY

The dependent person has a troublesome blind spot. If someone meets her basic needs she will stay with the person and brook considerable abuse. The dependent person is so concerned about being taken care of that she neglects to take care of herself. She sees getting better as getting into a more secure relationship with a more reliable person to meet her needs. She does not see getting better as being more self-reliant. "Do it yourself" feels like a taunt to her.

The dependent person becomes trapped in relationships and jobs that hold out the offer of security. Indeed, she makes up the bulk of the workforce. Loyalty is her badge. At least that is how she presents herself. While she may hang on to the bitter end, she also has an uncanny ability to jump ship and shift allegiances when she is frightened and loses faith in the person who was supposed to take care of her.

OTHERS

The dependent person always has her eyes on others.

The dependent person is often blind to others' character faults. She measures others not for who they are but for what they have to give or what they could take away. She judges others first by their ability to protect her; morality comes second. This explains why she sometimes becomes attached to tyrants, dictators, unsavory types whose only virtue is that they are good providers.

The dependent person is a people pleaser. She cares too much what others think. Her fear of being rejected, ostracized, not liked compromises her judgment. This makes her susceptible to being manipulated.

She can also become extraordinarily manipulative and flaunt her passivity and helplessness as a way of controlling other people by playing the flaccid child who needs to be carried. She can make an extraordinary burden of herself. It is as if she will do anything but care for herself.

PASSIVITY

The dependent person avoids taking any action that may cause her to lose favor with others. The only assertive position she is comfortable taking is admitting that her feelings have been hurt. Even then the dependent person generally delays and withholds her resentment by becoming a passive doormat.

Rather than defend herself when she is treated badly, she tends to display her injury, as if doing so will cause the person who is hurting her intentionally to stop. Her mistaken logic is that she believes he really cares. Parading her suffering to make others feel sorry for her frequently backfires.

While the controlling person who was attracted to her may at first have found her compliance to his liking, he soon tires of it and comes to see her continual passivity as an expression of defiance. This angers him and leads to more abuse. The abuser also feels angry to be with such a dependent loser and punishes her for making him feel this way, an obvious projection.

VALUES

The dependent person values affection, consistency, someone who is there for her, who accepts her love and loves her in return.

She values being acknowledged and remembered.

She values loyalty and keeping confidences but can be entirely unforgiving at the slightest sign of disloyalty. Then she gossips incessantly about the person who broke the rules of her group. She goes to great ends to prove that the person who betrayed her was bad.

She values others' company for company's sake. Her life is frequently filled with people who have little real meaning or value to her, other than being bodies who fill otherwise empty rooms. She becomes so obligated by nonsense relationships and mistaken concepts of loyalty and friendship that she does not ask herself if she really likes the people with whom she surrounds herself.

TOGETHERNESS

She always wants to be with another person. She avoids being alone whenever possible. She doesn't like to eat alone, shop alone, sleep alone, exercise or walk alone. She is the original "buddy."

She continually asks questions that reflect both this desire to be together as well as her anxiety over being separated.

She always wants to know: Where are you? What are you doing? When are you going to be there? Who else will be coming? Who will we be driving with? Who will I be sitting next to? Who will be there to show us the way?

If you have a telephone in your car you will be called on the way to and from where you are going, in parking lots, garages, and tunnels. The questions start: "Where are you? . . ."

All these questions about details are not the ramblings of a control freak but her need for continual reassurance that she is going to be included, not abandoned, remembered and returned to. She wants to know all the details to corroborate your story that she will be all right. She doesn't want to be left on the sidewalk while you drive off to New Jersey. Don't laugh; she's read about it happening.

She doesn't like to travel alone. She joins tours. She needs to know what to expect. Going off the beaten path may seem exciting, but she worries about getting lost and you never know what could happen. Bandits, insane taxi drivers, kidnappers. The papers are full of such things.

The controlling person may make extensive plans and try to impose them on others, but he does so to be in control, not to avoid danger. The controlling person can include some pretty harrowing dangers in his rigid trip plans. As long as it's on schedule why not climb the Matterhorn? The dependent person would rather wait until the bus arrives and look at it through the window.

Togetherness can reach a state of suffocating closeness. The dependent person wonders where the other person is all the time. When he is late or doesn't call, she doesn't think that traffic was slow or that he was detained by business; she immediately engages in fantasies of horrible accidents imagining the car bursting into flame, just like on the evening news. A partner's routine trip to the dentist for a cleaning raises the specter of a cancerous growth somewhere in the gums. The person seems relieved when she is told that there were no cavities, but she is really preoccupied with the partner's death or anything that can symbolize it. She feels safe . . . for the moment.

GIVING

The dependent person can be giving to a fault, to the point of self-sacrifice and beyond, to the verge of martyrdom. Giving without respecting yourself, however, is not giving, but a subtle form of manipulation. Even though her generosity and kindness provide some of her family's warmest memories, the dependent person's giving is often just so slightly tainted with the expectation of getting something in return.

Although many of these expectations seem reasonable—for instance, sending a birthday card and expecting to be remembered in return—what happens when her own birthday is ignored speaks volumes about her character. She sees the failure to reciprocate not as an innocent oversight but as proof that her giving is taken for granted. The injury resonates with other oversights stored in Emotional Debt, and a familiar deep sadness breaks through as a toxic nostalgic intrusion. Trivial slights lead her to feel rejected and abandoned.

She does not express these feelings directly to others but is more likely to become sullen and irritable. When asked what's wrong, she is likely to declare unconvincingly, "Nothing. Everything's *just* fine." Her pretended stoicism provokes more questioning and gives way to reveal her dark brooding. She holds her true feelings back, and they grow overblown in Emotional Debt.

Often she expresses her hurt symbolically by complaining about physical symptoms, the emptiness of life, or some other vague expression of hopelessness. She has difficulty being open about her anger, and so she continues to suffer the omitted birthday card every time she sees the other person. When she sends a birthday card to another friend, she begins to wonder if this friend will also forget her. Again, these concerns are manifestations of Toxic Nostalgia as her Emotional Debt taints innocent events with past hurt.

The dependent person finds the motif of rejection in every disappointment and takes it to heart. If you do not immediately answer her phone message she is positive you don't care. When she was young she focused on being given to; now as an adult she worries about something happening to those she loves and depends on for love. She expects you to know she worries about you and feels you should respond to her quickly to keep her suffering to a minimum.

The sad truth is that rather than take her own risks the dependent person often sacrifices her life to help insure the success of a spouse or a child. She finds herself trapped in a rigid pattern of obligatory giving that eventually drains her energy and makes her bitter. Because she hasn't explored her own opportunities and since she invested so much in others, whether she is in her early twenties or in her fifties, she believes it is too late to do something for herself.

As she continues to give to others, a cycle of expectation and rejection develops. Since nothing can really compensate her for her self-sacrifice, others' gratitude seems a little hollow. She feels taken for granted and may manipulate others and try to make them feel guilty for not calling more often or coming by. Feeling like rejecting her at this point, others usually become guarded in her presence and choose to stay away. She senses their withdrawal, and it hurts. Neither she nor the person she offends can discuss their real feelings. Both are in Emotional Debt and wish to avoid each other and yearn to be closer at the same time.

The dependent person is reluctant to complain about others' lack of appreciation openly, because she's afraid others will tell her that they didn't ask her to sacrifice herself for them. Her family would be delighted if she finally paid attention to making herself happy.

The dependent person can do for others everything she should have done for herself but lacked the courage to do. She needs to put herself first, be a little more selfish and let others do for themselves, make their own meals and do their own laundry. She is always amazed to discover that other people can actually take care of themselves. When she does she only wishes she had let go sooner.

DEFENSIVE LIMITATIONS: HOW THE NATURAL HEALING PROCESS IS DEFEATED

The dependent person uses denial almost as a reflexive barrier to ward off pain. For this reason, more than any other character type, when the dependent person is hurt, she often does not recognize or express it, leading to a built-in delay in her emotional reaction time.

This causes her not only to lose touch with the events that hurt her but to become accustomed to withhold rather than be spontaneous in expressing feelings. Because people do not usually hurt others intentionally, many misunderstandings that could easily be cleared up were she more direct linger instead to torment her. As she waits to express herself, her hurt builds out of proportion, while the other person forgets entirely about the hurtful incident, if he was ever aware of it in the first place. This makes reconciliation difficult.

The delay also leads her to wallow in her exaggerated feelings, to doubt their validity and conclude that it isn't worth expressing herself to run the risk of being rebuffed. Internalizing her pain, she overstates her case to herself: "After all I've done, to be treated like this." Even though she keeps most of her resentment to herself, her anger is palpable and distances her from those she loves.

This pattern causes more Emotional Debt and leads her to suffer. It saps her strength and makes her increasingly sensitive to injury. The denial she uses to conceal her anger slows down her emotional reaction time even more, making withholding more likely, and thus aggravates the cycle of resentment.

She still tries to be giving, naturally expecting to receive something in return, a kind of testing, a search for proof. She overdoes it. Her actions seem guilt-producing. She is hard to please and her emotional silence makes her impossible to fathom. Others feel controlled and push her away. This leads her to be wounded again. This pattern makes her susceptible to depression. Forcing others to take care of her for hurting her is sometimes the only way she can express her anger.

When the dependent person tries to deny her fears of abandonment or separation, she begins to worry about anything that could go wrong. She becomes clingy and disguises her fears as being concerned about others. Her attitude quickly becomes like a plague in the family. She becomes overprotective and tries to infantilize others, to do too much for them and intrude in their affairs. All she wants to do is help, she insists. Any resistance is taken as a sign of ingratitude, if not cruelty.

As she gets older her helplessness in the face of anything fearful makes her a living obstruction. Her solution is to suggest, "You all go ahead without me. I'll be fine." This attitude does not sit well with others. It is guilt-producing, exasperating, and controlling from a passive position all at once. If you do go without her, you have abandoned her, and when you return, no amount of reasoning is going to convince her otherwise.

VICTIMIZATION

Because she tends to be passive in the face of injury, the dependent person is more likely to be a victim than any other personality type. She fears discovering that other people do not love her, and so precisely when she should stand up for herself, she is silent. This leads her to become trapped in situations where she can neither speak up nor leave. After a while her silence leads to the storage of considerable anger, which in turn causes her to doubt her goodness, the issue that she is always debating internally.

Doubting her lovability and needing reinforcement, she is hesitant to act on her own. She is unwilling to take a risk that might leave her alone. It comes as no surprise that rather than do what is best for herself she ends up tolerating considerable abuse. She will leave an abusive relationship only when another person helps her or promises to love her. She views abuse not as unacceptable and grounds for leaving, but not really that bad, better than it could be. As one abused woman put it, "It doesn't happen all the time."

SOME GENERAL OBSERVATIONS

The dependent person is not driven by money. If she can make ends meet and the stress of debt is minimal, making money is not a primary concern. Emotional comfort is.

The dependent person finds loss everywhere and is continually reminded of some unmourned sadness. She is emotional and cries easily, but not fully. She has trouble releasing hurt, a function of the tenacity of her denial. It is not always easy to tell what she is emotional about. Past and present losses merge. There is much Toxic Nostalgia in her life. Even happy events somehow have the power to remind her of what is missing.

Once she has been betrayed it is difficult for her both to forget or rebuild trust. She will claim, out of her fear of being alone and to justify staying with the person who hurt her, that she has forgiven when she actually has not. Her old hurts bother her for a long time.

She views children as her possessions. She sees herself as the possession of her spouse. She expects to be treated like a queen but will tolerate the worst abuse.

Her self-esteem can suddenly, almost without visible cause, hit bottom. Anniversaries of deaths, birthdays of departed friends and relatives, holidays in absence of her loved ones, are all cause for sadness. She is sensitive to all forms of diminishment. Nothing escapes her sense of loss, even if she is unaware of what she is specifically mourning.

THE EVOLVED DEPENDENT PERSON

When the dependent person is secure and confident and has made a life for herself, achieved independence and success, there is no one in the world more desirable as a friend, parent, or spouse. She is the model of giving, understanding, and caring. She relates to others openly and sympathetically. Naturally empathetic, she is eager to know how you feel and quick to pick up when you are having a problem. Easy to talk to, unprejudiced and free, she is naturally nurturing and therapeutic, seemingly driven to uncover the source of pain that is bothering you and to help you to understand. She is intuitive, accepting, kind, naturally inclined to discover the best in others and draw it out, a yes person, a positive force, optimistic and resourceful.

Unlike the undeveloped dependent person, the evolved dependent person is willing to let go when she gives advice and does not need others' love to feel good about herself. She would rather you were free and solved your own problems than control you or have any kind of obligation between you.

Such people are natural spiritual or emotional leaders, swaying others by the power of their own passion rather than by elegant persuasion. They are the people who believe in causes and follow them against slim odds, simply because it feels right to them. Others believe in them because they always remain regular folks, emotionally accessible, even though they may achieve success, fortune, or fame. They believe in their convictions. They love themselves. They have the greatest capacity to love others and are the most emotionally generous of all the personality types.

Their relationships are characterized by warmth, sincerity, friendliness, openness, childlike spontaneity, and appreciation without guile. They are not fickle or petty but constant and supportive of change in their partner. They are present for their partner without dominating, giving without controlling, and inquisitive without being suspicious.

She is the soul of the family, the person whose love holds them all together. No one is more considerate and appreciative. She is the person in whose presence you feel your best, without needing to prove yourself, without feeling competitive.

In the workplace, such people are the best team managers, perhaps not the top executives, because they see the human impact of business decisions so acutely. They inspire loyalty and trust. Others follow them when they lead because they always act like a team member and do not ask of others what they would not do themselves. Their relationships with others are always personal. Formality is not their style.

Include here the best therapists, medical personnel, social service workers, team players, teachers, coaches, and interviewers. These people are the backbone of family, party, organization, team, system, and life. Wherever people are involved, the dependent type shines and fits in, truly born to it.

DEALING WITH DEPENDENT PEOPLE

It's always tempting to employ short-term solutions to deal with dependent people; to give them what they want and get them out of your way, rather than stand on principle and argue with them or take the time to encourage them to do for themselves. Of course, if you rescue them they come to expect you to do that over and over again and you quickly find yourself typecast as a supportive figure.

Bear in mind that the dependent person's goal is to take risks for herself. She needs to learn that being alone is not a punishment, and that just because you can't be with her all the time, it doesn't mean you don't love her or that she's done something wrong.

The dependent person needs support to take action. She will probably claim that what matters most is being given to. It is useful to point out that waiting for others to help her has led to her being disappointed in the past, that no one knows her the way she knows herself and therefore that she is the best one to fulfill her needs.

The dependent person always tests your love. When she claims you aren't loving her enough, don't lie or pretend. Simply tell her that you don't have to show your love every minute to love and care about her completely. It is her expectations that are false and her needs that are extreme, not your caring that is lacking. She has to decide if your caring, just as it is, is enough.

Don't allow yourself to be trapped into proving yourself or giving insincerely. If you try to make her happy and exaggerate the way you feel, you won't be able to sustain your emotional effort. Instead you'll come to resent what you have given and will pull away, believing the relationship isn't worth maintaining. Tell her that.

Total honesty is the best policy for dealing with the dependent person.

If you feel she wants too much, say so.

If you feel she is playing the victim, point it out.

Remember, she is passive because she doesn't want her anger to show and offend you. Indicating that her passivity is already pushing you away is sometimes helpful to get her to relate honestly.

If you feel suffocated by her insistence on perpetual togetherness, take a stand.

The dependent person somehow always makes her feelings more important than yours. You sense this when you are reluctant to speak up or tell her how you feel. Let her know that you don't want to hurt her and explain that because you can't be yourself with her you tend to avoid her. Her unrealistic anxiety cannot always be permitted to be the most important emotion in the relationship.

Be honest even though it produces tears. Be straightforward and direct when you offer criticism. Reassure her that you still care for her. Make your point. Pause. Smile and move on to the next subject.

Always be appreciative, respectful, and sensitive. Treat her like an adult and expect her to be responsible for herself. Be firm and gentle. Physical contact counts; pats on the shoulder and hugs often matter more than words.

If you meet with failure or self-sabotage when you try to encourage her, don't get enmeshed in a futile argument. Simply remind her that she may one day learn to feel differently about herself and shouldn't stop trying. Remind her also that you believe in her, mean it when you say it, and encourage her to try again.

The cure for whatever ails the dependent person is to become more independent.

Tell her that as well.

THE CONTROLLING CHARACTER TYPE

The controlling character became the way he is in order to have the power to protect himself from abandonment and so avoid feeling vulnerable. He is also concerned with being smart, right, and strong and acquired his defense mechanisms of blaming and excuses to make up for the times he is not. He uses his power to dispel feelings of helplessness and to keep others from rejecting him.

HE

Although many women can be equally controlling, the controlling person is usually a man. More often than girls, young boys are brought up expecting to be in control someday. Just as from early childhood a girl is told that her role will be a nurturing one, a boy is more likely to have been told he'll be a provider, protector of his family, and should therefore aspire to be a person of substance, power, or influence. These expectations intimidate him, but he's encouraged not to show it.

Right or wrong, these expectations have undeniable effects on character development. Women are generally encouraged to be more dependent, men to be more controlling. There are countless exceptions to this, but for the purpose of this book the controlling person is referred to as a man.

Indeed, history is replete with the bloody adventures of aging controlling men, compensating for their waning powers by trying to extend their sphere of influence. In their insistence that they are right they punish enemies, quash dissent, or impose on others their religion or political doctrine as the only true one. Most wars have been fought over controlling issues such as territorial claims, rights of way, and access to markets. History's record of injustice and bigotry reflects the story of men trying to assert power over others to maintain their privileged status.

There have been women involved in such controlling endeavors, but mostly they participated as support to their men, acting equally vicious or unfeeling. Today when women achieve positions of control, they are little different from controlling men, except for the fact that their struggle to overcome sexist prejudice may make them even tougher.

BOUNDARIES

In a sense establishing and maintaining boundaries is the controlling person's business.

He draws boundaries between himself and his feelings, seeking to isolate himself from any feeling that might reveal him to be weak.

He separates himself from failures by drawing the line of responsibility to exclude himself from fault.

He uses his capacity to blame others as the major force to establish these boundaries and also as the rationale for keeping them in place. He reasons since others are to blame for his problems, he must control them.

His boundaries tend to become too rigid and eventually isolate him from others and himself. This leads the controlling person to suffer from intense loneliness. His activities become increasingly solitary enterprises.

Because he originally walled himself off to enhance his sense of autonomy, to avoid contradiction and the need to explain himself, he often finds himself out of touch with others. Finding it difficult to ask others for their opinion, his decisions are highly personal, even though he passes them off as the result of superior logic. Allowing no consensus, no sharing of decision making, he becomes committed to believing he is always right. He admits error reluctantly and usually only when he fails or is unable to prevent rejection. Then when he fails, he is totally disheartened, full of self-doubt and remorse.

HE'S RIGHT

The controlling person would rather be right than happy. He's right anyhow; just ask him.

In the silent sessions of his inner court, he builds endless evidence against people who have offended him. He proves his case from every possible angle, refuting every possible argument that could be made against him. He is prosecutor, witness, judge, jury, gallery, jailer, and executioner. In some perverse way he is also the priest hearing the final confession and granting absolution before he throws the switch.

He is amazed that his right actions, his right decisions, his right thinking, and his right planning could ever hurt another person. He may act without others' consensus, but never with the intention of actually doing anyone any harm. So he maintains.

However, this irrefutable belief in his rightness, combined with his absolutist exercise of power, does a lot of damage. He tends to injure those who are dependent on him. His controlling patterns of abuse are subtle, well thought out, and difficult for dependent people to refute because they are camouflaged by the appearance of giving.

One of the most difficult things a controlling person must face is that in spite of the fact that he can prove conclusively that he is right, he is often wrong. He hates to hear this. His thinking is logical to the point of being unrealistic. Admitting any error in his logic reveals his flaws. This frightens him because logic is the cornerstone of his inner rationalizations, the way he relieves himself from guilt and blame. If his logic is faulty, his sense of self-esteem falls.

PERFECTIONISM

Even though he suspects that it isn't possible to be right all the time, he acts as if he believes he's perfect. Secretly he dreads that he may be flawed and is always on guard lest his imperfections show. He squanders his time reviewing trivial facts and unimportant procedures to be sure he is not making mistakes. As a result of all his attention to details, he may lose sight of his goal. Needing to be perfect in every detail, he finds himself unable to act. There is always something that needs to be fixed first.

Others shy away from contradicting him even when he needs to be told he is in error. They don't want to oppose a tidal wave of self-justifying logic and prefer to remain silent. Not only does this rob him of valuable feedback, it also further isolates him, increasing his sense of loneliness. He flaunts his loneliness, affecting the pretentious attitude—I am an island of superiority without peers—as if he planned and prefers it this way. This reinforces his need for unassailable perfection.

Such perfectionism is often a result of feeling out of control as a child. Children of unhappy or addictive parents typically feel powerless and yearn for a more manageable life. To conceal their helplessness they may act as if they don't need anyone and become perfectionists in the belief it will give them control over their situation. In a sense, by trying to be perfect, these controlling children try both to whitewash their present difficulties and draw as little attention to themselves as possible. They learn to hide their feelings and invent stories to cover their disappointment. When they look back in later years and remember these stories, they can actually believe they had a happy childhood.

This quest for perfection can become an end in itself as the child begins to feel comforted just by doing insignificant things perfectly. He invests simple tasks with the magical power to protect him, creating talismans everywhere. He may begin to play magical games with himself. If he can get to the bus stop before the other kids, he concludes he'll be safe. If the column of numbers has an even sum, he is secure. If it is odd, he is in danger. He is looking for symbolic predictors in his uncertain world and shies away from anything that could symbolically place him in danger.

The need to be perfect grows out of control almost as soon as it appears. As the child's awareness grows more discriminating, his imperfections glare at him and motivate him to strive even harder. He can become so concerned with avoiding mistakes that he loses the ability to be spontaneous. Realizing that he cannot be perfect, he may put down others for not being as perfect as he is. This leads him to act smugly superior, isolating him further.

At some point there comes a crisis of nonfunction, when his pursuit of perfection causes the controlling person to lose the very things he is trying to preserve. The window of opportunity for the risk closes while he is double-checking and now the project is over cost. He has lost for being too careful. His need to appear perfect also alienates those he loves.

Only when being perfect has failed to protect him from being abandoned or from making mistakes does he become open to the possibility of change. Being perfect in an imperfect world suddenly means he is wrong. He comes to realize that his biggest mistakes and losses have come about because of his very best thinking and planning.

CRITICISM

The tendency to criticize is deeply imbedded in the controlling person's character. Basically, he projects his self-criticism onto others. The only time he is willing to criticize himself is after being rejected. Then he beats his breast, shouts his faults to the world, and makes promises to change. Sometimes these deep hurts allow him to grow, but often when the other person takes pity and returns, his resolve shifts from correcting his faults to keeping the other person under control and preventing a future abandonment. He'll change cosmetically, if that is what it takes, but down deep he will not surrender. He will be more vigilant and protective next time and thwart rejection by mounting a preemptive strike of controlling goodness and displaying the ways he has "changed."

He takes criticism badly and never forgets or forgives it, especially if it is made in public. He perceives revealing his imperfections as a weakening of his power base, setting him up as an object of ridicule.

Still, he finds it second nature to criticize others. Even though he is often pointed and blunt, he always sees his criticism as being necessary, helpful, and instructive, an act of love. After all, where would others be without him? He doesn't understand why people aren't grateful for his constant constructive criticism. He drives everyone to distraction.

A thinly disguised form of criticism is his tendency to comment on everything anyone says or does, or appears to be thinking. He is an efficiency expert, a movie, TV, and drama critic, food critic, traffic cop, expert driver, automotive encyclopedia, pharmacologist, nutritionist, and fitness instructor. He knows the right way to do everything and comments on everything that falls short of the ideal.

His criticism is just another form of projection as he tries to deal with his own imperfections. Try not to take it seriously.

DETAILS AND RULES

Because of his natural attention to details and affinity for enforcing rules and regulations, the controlling person is often placed in positions where his controlling nature can be capitalized on. He is likely to become a money manager, someone whose job it is to make others account for their expenditures. He naturally gravitates toward the law, relishing especially the fine points of contracts and taxes: contracts being a set of rules, taxes being a set of punishments. Anywhere details matter he is king. He thrives on discovering loopholes and exceptions to the rule. He is born to it.

He gets lost in details and can become consumed trying to prove an obscure point for the sake of completeness. Because of his fixation on detail, he can be amazingly frustrating to others. He can pick a plan apart, seeing all its faults and none of its advantages. He immediately discerns a dozen reasons why the new idea will not work, reciting all the ways it has been tried before. He can predict what will go wrong.

However, he lacks the vision to dream the dream, to see the whole as bigger than the sum of its parts. Instead he sees the world as mechanical and fixed. He has difficulty accepting that there is slack in the universe and that just because he can figure out an ironclad theory doesn't mean it will work.

He says he doesn't believe in luck, and yet he tends to be superstitious. His judgment is easily distracted by his preoccupation with details. Finding a spelling error on a promising proposal leads him to devalue it, while seeing a second mistake makes him conclude that it is worthless. His drive to discover what is wrong often blinds him from seeing the true worth of things. His natural tendency to put down an idea that is unconventional limits his appreciation of its originality.

For this reason he is valued to maintain the smooth organization and flow in corporations, but is more likely to be given the power to say no than to say yes. No requires control. Yes requires vision.

The words *proper, legal, correct, appropriate, suitable, fitting* have special meaning as he prods others to get in step. He knows Robert's Rules of Order. His usefulness in applying for a grant or a bank loan cannot be minimized. A person exactly like him devised the form. He knows how to fill it out. It is in his genes.

SPONTANEITY

The controlling person is not spontaneous. To him being spontaneous means being out of control, unprepared, and immature. Spontaneity in others is seen as a weakness. They reveal their hand. They show how they can be beaten. Stupid!

Showing his hurt feelings as they happen is out of the question. He has to think about this. He is spontaneous only about leaking his anger and acting abusively. When he does it fills him with remorse, but he tends to hide it. He resolves to be more measured in the future.

Spontaneity just doesn't feel right to the controlling person.

CREATIVITY

Intuition confuses him. Creativity mystifies him. Artistic people seem unruly and undisciplined to him. He regards them as children who need to be reined in to conform to regular work hours and made to show concrete results for their efforts. They move illogically, jumping from one point to another. He doesn't know how they got there. He wants to dissect the creative process. He wants the logic of intuition explained to him.

Keep him away from creative meetings. He has the capacity to undermine the team's enthusiasm and freedom by simply asking, Why? He sees the creative person's ability to ask, What if we try this . . . as a weakness. He wants a plan.

Appreciate his support and enthusiasm. Reassure him that he will have the results he wants on time, even if you have to lie about it. One thing is certain, you'll have no results if you let him look over your shoulder and question your work.

FEARS

The controlling person is always fearful of losing power. He instinctively avoids any confrontation that might prove him weak or inept. He is always interested in gaining more information and doing more research before risking. He can never know enough. This need to be sure can paralyze him.

He struggles with every aspect of risk taking. Since he wants to believe he is right, he usually hires consultants who validate his point of view. Consultants are especially sensitive to his type of personality and make sure they know what he wants them to validate *before* doing their investigation. What he wants mostly is someone to agree that he is right in making the decision he has already decided upon so he can act with confidence. He just wants to be armed with facts and explanations that reinforce his decision.

Even without such support, he can set his fear aside and act incontrovertibly sure of himself, even when he is totally mistaken.

This lethal propensity for decisiveness under fire can lead him into serious difficulties. Because he sees the correctness of his course as a reflection of his belief that he is right, he can become inflexible and unable to make changes should the situation turn out to be different from what he planned. The more insecure he is, the more rigid he is likely to be. When he is challenged, he insists he is right, puts down his critics, and presses on with renewed energy.

He becomes defensive when he is questioned, and it is at such moments that he is likely to increase his risk just to demonstrate his confidence. Sometimes he completely abandons common sense by following the rules to the letter, even when they no longer fit. This kind of bullheadedness has been responsible for ruinous bankruptcies and corporate overextension and unbearable child abuse, where he does what he does for the child's own good.

His capacity to focus only on the facts that support him can lead him to believe blindly in plans that are obviously flawed. Include here devastating wartime decisions based on powering through impossible odds; Admiral Farragut commanding, "Damn the torpedoes. Full speed ahead!" Historians look back and wonder what was going on in the minds of such leaders. Being unable to admit their fears or flaws almost certainly played a decisive part on the way to ruin and victory, the difference being if they succeed they are immortalized.

VALUES

The controlling person's strengths are also his weaknesses. What he values most, most undermines him. What he is most talented at invalidates him. This is so because he pushes his strengths to extremes, never admitting any inherent weakness or limitation or the possibility of error. His absolutist need to exaggerate his strength is once again a reflection of his fear of vulnerability.

Concerned with being right, he may pay lip service to the notion that he could be wrong, but in his heart he does not believe this.

He values power to such an extent that he cannot see his own excesses of power. He cannot imagine a situation where power is not an advantage. In matters of the heart he corrupts affection by trying to use his power to control or safeguard love. He cannot seem to grasp the notion that love is free.

He values intelligence for its own sake, especially when it is quantified.

He values numbers, statistics, graphs, schedules, reports, and analyses. He loves to identify, measure, weigh, define, categorize, name, classify, and distinguish the fine differences.

He values systems, structure, plans, and organization.

He wants results, cost-effectiveness, clarity, and timetables.

He can get lost in all these details and sometimes does little more than accumulate facts. Taking action implies risk, and the threat of taking a chance sends him back to the drawing board.

He can find a home among the cases of a museum, the books in a library, and the auto parts in a warehouse. He likes constancy and predictability, security, order, and routine.

He likes any joke that is not directed at himself.

He values respect, appreciation, recognition especially of his power and superiority.

He tolerates lapses of these values poorly and keeps score of offenders.

GIVING

The controlling person likes to think of himself as generous. In fact he seems to give people almost everything they want, except the support and encouragement to go out on their own and become independent. If you examine what, how, and when he gives to other people, you discover that under the guise of generosity, his giving actually undermines others' autonomy.

He would deny this entirely. Hinting that his giving is insincere infuriates him. Just look at what he has given, how many times he has helped others, rescued, enabled, supported, and provided for them. Count the ways. If you don't he probably will.

Still, the controlling person's giving is his most subtle form of controlling. He gives others what they could not get on their own and then threatens to take it away in order to manipulate them. Others have become accustomed to using his gifts and know they could not replace them by themselves. They resent both being controlled and having their weaknesses flaunted in their faces. It is as if the controlling person is telling them they are nothing, and by continuing to remain under his influence and protection, they seem to prove his point. When they remain with the controlling person, they are likely to bury their anger and feel trapped.

Good examples of such manipulative gifts include automobiles given to teenagers as an incentive to bring up grades that are later taken away for some other offense, or giving a friend or relative a well-paying position in the family business and then abusing him, knowing he cannot get a similar job on his own.

A more subtle example is suggested by the way a controlling person asserts his weight in the family. Rather than come right out and say that he doesn't want to do what everyone else wants to do, he says instead, "We can't afford it." This clearly implies that he is the one paying for everything and making the decisions.

Go fight city hall!

Of course the people most likely to be under his control are dependent people. This means that the controlling person tends to be too manipulative with children, providing incentives that are often lacking love, which is what children are really looking for.

The problem comes when children get older and, for all their best efforts, still feel emotionally unrewarded. They have received conditional love, but they do not really understand what that means. They only know that they tried their best and still don't feel all that good about their success. What is missing of course is the simple approval they want. They want to be loved completely just for being themselves. The withholding of this reassurance causes anxiety, which makes them believe that they have to do more to be loved.

The day comes when they see through this false giving and life changes. The following may seem like an odd comparison, but when at a greyhound racetrack the dogs overcome the fake rabbit and catch it, they can no longer run. They now know they were tricked. The same is true when a child realizes that no matter how well he does he will never be loved completely by his controlling parent.

If a parent loves you completely, he loves you right now as much as he ever will. To imply that he will love you more if you succeed is a promise that will always prove false. To such a controlling parent, loving the child completely feels like giving up control. However, this is not to say that such a parent doesn't love his child, but rather that he finds it difficult to love himself, because he sees himself as imperfect even if he doesn't admit it to anyone.

You cannot love anyone more than you love yourself. You may claim to, but this is either wishful thinking or desperation.

OBSESSION

Much of what has been said about the controlling person reflects his tendency to obsess rather than admit his vulnerability, feel his hurt, and begin the mourning process. For the controlling person to admit a hurt and begin to deal with it, he must also concede that in some way he was powerless to prevent it.

This is a frightening thing for him to admit. If he were powerless to prevent one loss, might he not be powerless in general? Keep in mind that his mental process is very much tied to the laws of cause and effect. He truly believes that kingdoms have been lost for want of a horseshoe nail. He can employ this rigid causality when assigning blame to others. He can find the error on which all the damage hinges. So if he discovers he is not invincible, not perfect, not in control, there will be no end to it.

Even though he portrays himself as all-knowing, he tends to obsess over his mistakes, especially those that impacted negatively on his power. He calculates how much he would have made if he had done what he should have done. *If only* rules his ruminations.

Again, the real source of his obsession stems from his fear of being vulnerable and dealing honestly with his hurt. He has a well-established habit of repressing hurt and immediately converting it into inner-directed anger. Thus each new injury only fuels his self-criticism. This causes him to obsess about his goodness, strength, and intelligence and then to project those doubts onto others. He wavers back and forth between blaming himself and others. If he concludes that others were at fault, he obsesses over why he trusted them.

Each new decision brings with it the possibility of making a mistake that may prove his worst self-doubts true. Thus each decision carries the weight of a life sentence. He obsesses over all the points. He is looking for a foolproof formula to guide him. If he comes up with a 90–10 split favoring a decision, he feels the need not only to overstate the favorable 90 percent, but to demean the 10 percent that argues against him. He obsesses over his decision, and doing so drains him of resolve.

This is hazardous business, for at the moment of risk when he must release and leap, that negative 10 percent he was trying to downplay now resurfaces and disheartens him. Because he diminished these arguments to give himself courage, their reappearance makes him doubt himself all over again. At the very moment of taking his leap, when he should be concentrating and putting his best energy into what he is doing, he begins to obsess again, losing his focus and imperiling himself. Wanting to be 100 percent right, any diminution, any revelation of imperfection, befuddles him.

Sometimes at this point he can leap forward without feeling or thinking and put himself in great danger. At such times he becomes filled with a fearful obsessional resolve and risks hazardously, creating cruel hardship that he later explains as an urgent necessity.

While power and risk preoccupy the controlling person, he obsesses most over rejection.

REJECTION

When people finally reject the controlling person, they often do so in a pique of rebellion and defiance. Often in order to break free they must overcome a siege of dependence during which they plan their exit and script their departing speech. Their leave-taking is bound to be overblown, overstating the abuse they tolerated and rubbing the controlling person's nose in his loss of power to prevent them from leaving. They may even do exactly what he so long prohibited them from doing, even if they really don't want to. There is something about the controlling person that makes rebellious adolescents out of everyone around him.

It is typical for a competitive woman especially to act out her newly claimed "independence" when she leaves a man who has long been her protector. By showing her scorn for his gifts, she hurts the very person who has made her so comfortable. She is free and needs nothing now. Often to mock him she chooses a younger man with no position in life or means to speak of who has only the capture of her heart to his credit. With her extravagant surrender to the new man, she shifts the scales of power and allows him to defeat his more powerful opponent without making an effort or ever meeting him face-to-face. She is the true power broker now, the prize who gives herself away.

When the woman who is rejecting the controlling man is dependent, she has been debating the decision for years and is usually swayed by the arrival of a more powerful benefactor, or she leaves because she can no longer tolerate the abuse, which has a tendency to become physical and terrifying. Because leaving alone requires more courage than she can usually muster, she needs others' assistance to break free. If she does try to get away by herself, her actions are usually weak and indecisive and allow room for the controlling person to take over again.

Of course, regardless of whoever rejects the controlling person, the act strikes him as the pinnacle of ingratitude. He feels he has put up with a lot as well. Others have not made it easy for him, punishing him by overstating their helplessness, making him do everything. He has not always wanted to take care of other people, but others were so needy he was afraid of letting go. He enabled only out of the necessity and opportunity that their powerlessness created.

A rejection can be a life-saving event for a controlling person, but only if he finally admits that he needs other people and begins to accept his own vulnerability. When he concedes that he has dependent needs, he softens. He can see that the main reason he lost everything was that he held on too tightly out of fear of losing. He learns that people want to belong to another, but not be possessed.

The controlling person can also become vengeful and swear to make the person who rejected him miserable. This launches him on a life of retaliatory fantasies, loathing, and revenge seeking.

LOVE

The controlling person finds it difficult simply to say "I love you" because it is too much of a risk. The other person may reply, "Well, I don't love you," and where would that leave him? His weakness exposed and the way to manipulate him clearly displayed, he would feel in danger. Many women complain that when they tell a man they love him, he responds, "Ditto," or "Right back at you," or "Same here." Saying "I love you" feels a little too much like unconditional surrender to a person who was brought up on conditional love.

Being able to love freely depends a lot on being able to say "You hurt me." If hurt cannot be expressed between lovers, love quickly fades behind the stored resentment. This can be especially problematic to a controlling person. He is reluctant to admit that another person hurt him unless he is trying to make the other person feel guilty or manipulate him. He reasons that if he told the other person he were hurt, he'd not only be admitting that he could be hurt, but he'd be showing the other person how to get back at him. Saying "I love you" feels too vulnerable for comfort.

The controlling person much prefers love as an extension of possession. He doesn't want to be loved freely, but on command. He wants it when he wants it. He expects the person who loves him to anticipate his needs and act accordingly. Sex becomes ritualized and mechanical, the obligatory soporific before retiring. When sex is denied it is an unforgivable affront, causing a mixture of self-pity and pouting, neither posture especially sexually attractive or conducive to intimacy. There is much mercy sex in a relationship with a controlling person. It's not worth the recriminations to refuse.

Love is a fragile notion.

It abhors control, that vacuum of feelings.

It thrives on mystery and defies logic.

Its magic is unpredictable.

And yet the controlling person wants to bottle love for his convenience.

DEALING WITH OTHER PEOPLE

The controlling person is weakest in his dealings with others. He struggles to understand how people work in order to manage them better. He would like to have people function like well-oiled machines, do their job, be on time, follow instructions, and be grateful for the clarity he brings to the disorder of life. He sees himself as just and cannot understand that, in spite of all his giving, others see him as tyrannical merely because he doesn't always allow them to do what they want.

Where the dependent person's life lesson is to become more independent, the controlling person must learn to let other people be free, to do what they want, make their own mistakes, endure their failures without him protecting them. That is the only way he can learn to be free himself.

The reason the controlling person involves himself so intricately in the lives of others is that he is afraid of being alone. His protectiveness of others is nothing more than a way of insuring that he will have company. He will rarely admit this.

Loneliness's shroud of contempt is always lurking in the wings, waiting for a solitary moment to weigh him down.

DEFENSIVE LIMITATIONS: HOW THE NATURAL HEALING PROCESS IS DEFEATED

The controlling person makes elaborate excuses for his losses, explaining why his injury was caused by something other than his weakness and by someone other than himself. This defensive stance isolates the controlling person from his real feelings. Instead of mourning, he feels self-righteously resentful and there he stays put.

The natural therapeutic process is stopped dead in its tracks. Healing is limited by his inability to be vulnerable. The only feeling he feels comfortable expressing is anger. When he is hurt he tends to become abusive and damage the person he loves most. When he becomes fixed in his self-justification, the other person stops trusting him and removes her love. This throws him into a self-righteous denunciation, even more abusive. Because he has rationalized his actions as being justified, his memory is poor for the injuries he has inflicted. He makes promises but is unrepentant.

All his best thinking and rationalizing get him into more difficulty. His need to be right subverts healing. His need to be strong blocks feeling. Insisting on his invincibility, he believes he is correct, but he is nonetheless immobilized in his grief.

In his pain he tends to see others as adversaries just waiting to take advantage of his weakness. This keeps him from lowering his guard and dealing with his shortcomings. Because he doesn't take responsibility for his errors, he doesn't heal or grow but instead persists in insisting that something or someone besides him needs to be fixed. He fervently believes if other people would only change their errant ways, if the land he invested in would return to its original value, his life would be perfect.

Maintaining this rigid posture leads to obsession and further drains his emotional resources. He suffers a self-inflicted fate that causes his worst fears to be realized. The same defenses that isolate him from his feelings also isolate him from himself and others. Because his stored anger is continually turned against him, he feels guilty much of the time and is frequently depressed.

Sadly, because he refuses to be vulnerable, the true resolution of his problems often eludes him. For the natural therapeutic process to take hold and allow him to mourn, he must admit his loss and pain. This implies that he also accept his need for others and his long-unfulfilled wish to be taken care of without becoming filled with self-pity.

If he could only accept that he was lovable even though he's not perfect.

DEALING WITH CONTROLLING PEOPLE

Avoid power struggles. You'll only lose, and the controlling person will harden his position against you.

Never criticize. Pose a suggestion instead, but expect a controlling counter that puts you in a worse position than you started. You could ask a question, but to an insecure controlling person, questioning his method is a challenge that cannot go unmet or unpunished.

Allow the controlling person room to display himself. When he does, do not be offended or act hurt. Just observe and ask yourself why you allowed yourself to be trapped in this situation, job, or relationship. If you become involved with the controlling person's outbursts, you are part of the madness.

Do not start rumors about the controlling person. He has favorites who are jockeying for power and position and they will tell on you. Everything you say about a controlling person eventually gets back to him. Even people whom you don't think can be bribed are on the controlling person's dole.

Don't patronize the controlling person.

Admit you are wrong.

Ask for instructions.

When they don't make sense, don't tell the controlling person he wasn't clear, say you didn't understand.

It should be clear that you cannot deal with a controlling person from the position of needing what he has to give. It restricts you too much. He'll just punish you by taking away your privileges.

You cannot deal with him as an adversary. He'll commit to destroying you and consume your time and resources. Should you win, it will prove an empty and costly victory. You will continue to pay for it in the future.

You deal with a controlling person best by becoming strong enough not to need him. The more you do for yourself, the better off you are. If you work for a controlling boss, find some way to express your gratefulness for all he has taught you and get out on your own as quickly as possible.

If you are married to a controlling person, you can only deal from a position of strength. He needs to know that you are a person in your own right and have the means and ability and willingness to go it on your own if need be. This means that just because you are married to a controlling person, you cannot fail to pursue your own life.

THE EVOLVED CONTROLLING TYPE

In spite of all that has been said, the world could not function without controlling people. Dependent people would be leaderless, and while work would still get done, gross inefficiencies would endanger everyone. The controlling person is the backbone of the legal system, government, defense department, police department, and correctional system. He is the scheduler who keeps all the various craftsmen working on the skyscraper in the right place at the right time. He is the facilitator allowing great projects to be finished in a cost-effective and safe manner. Modern society could not be planned, built, protected, or maintained without him.

He is the statistician who tediously figures out complicated numbers upon which predictions can be made involving electrical consumption, water usage, the rise and fall of sea level. He monitors the polar ice caps and the ozone layer. He programs the computers and monitors the space flights.

He is the military planner, trainer, and coordinator. He knows the mind of the oppressor and anticipates his moves and counters them. He may have difficulty in his personal life allowing others to be free, but it is upon his talents that the successful defense of freedom usually depends.

He is the archeologist carefully sorting thousands of shards, reassembling scrolls and tablets, answering the question of where we came from. He is not as good at figuring out who we are and where we are going.

His natural propensity to document the past leads him to become the historian, the collector, the caretaker, the curator, the overseer of national treasures and archives.

He is the organizer of charities, delivery systems that get food to the homeless and distribute disaster relief. He runs the world of banking, communication, medicine, and transportation. Everything that is bought or sold, ordered, manufactured, or delivered is his work.

Without him the brilliant idea is just an idea. He is backstage at the creative performance managing the details. With him all is possible.

When he is evolved and willing to be vulnerable and allow other people to be independent and free, he is the philosopher, the sponsor, the philanthropist, the understanding and supportive patron who believes in the creative person and allows his projects to come to fruition. Without this person, who may not be able to sing a note, read a poem convincingly, or write with style, the arts stagnate, theater dies, and symphony orchestras disband.

Presenting so many negative qualities of the controlling person may seem unbalanced by this short capsule of positive traits. However, it is because the controlling person is so valuable that it is so important for him to understand and master his weaknesses. The good that an evolved controlling person is capable of delivering is enormous. Unfortunately, it doesn't take much negativity to defeat him.

THE COMPETITIVE CHARACTER TYPE

The competitive person defines himself by his actions. In a sense he is always proving something. This is what he is trying to prove: that he is the first, the best, and that he's got whatever it takes to win.

He wants to be seen as a success. Actually he may want to be seen as a success more than he wants to work at becoming one.

He needs to be seen as sexually attractive.

All these points are much more important than they may seem on the surface.

HE OR SHE

The competitive person is just as likely to be a man as a woman. They are both very much alike and very different at the same time.

WINNING

The competitive person likes to win for winning's sake. It feels good to be number one. He loves adulation, admiration, fame, attention, being noticed, being asked for autographs, being pointed out in whispers as the one to watch. He likes being the fair-haired boy on the way to the top. He likes the promise of being a future winner as much as actually winning. He thrives on the hype.

He plays to win even if it's at a casual sport. He loves to beat his best time and best score. The underlying reason is surprising. If he can see himself as still getting better or at least staying on top, he doesn't have to worry about his decline, his loss of strength or attractiveness. He doesn't have to concern himself with growing old and dying.

Being first has a powerful attraction for the competitive person. He loves showing others up, coming from behind, trouncing the competition, getting the prize account away from the other firm, winning the guy or girl away from his rival. His success is best when it is linked to someone else's failure. It seems like he is always trying to prove he is better.

The problem is that the competitive person often wins on someone else's terms, not his own. He wins to please other people. He makes the big sale but is most proud of the fact that he sold himself to the buyer. That's what counts most—winning others over. He wants to win so badly he'll choose an unworthy opponent to insure victory or a course that really doesn't test his talents.

He needs to learn to please himself, but his love of praise leads him astray.

AGING

It sounds harsh, but lying just beneath the surface, the fear of growing old, of becoming sick and dying, dogs the competitive person's footsteps.

The competitive man is never so competitive as when he is trying to prove to younger competitors that he still has what it takes. He climbs the mountain, enters the marathon at fifty, challenges a squash player twenty years younger to a grudge match. His attitude of trying to prove he's still virile and a force to contend with causes him to overextend himself and get into trouble.

The competitive woman has a lot of trouble growing older. Often she tended to use her good looks to her advantage. Although she may have made it on her own, she knew what her assets were, and no one's fool, she used them.

Unfortunately, the world has never been a fair place, and some of the benefits the competitive woman won by her looks and sexual attractiveness would not have come to her had she been plain or retiring. Others may resent her for her forwardness. While she may insist that she succeeded on her own, she still has her private doubts. When she ages she feels strangely vulnerable to whatever younger woman comes along as a possible competitor. Without her youth, she begins to question whether her ability is enough to hold the line against the competition. It makes her restless.

She frequently has the backing of some male protector who may begin to show signs of abandoning her. This is not merely the stuff of B movie plots, where a fading movie star struggles to win important roles, but the story of countless women trying to hold on to their position in a world that once favored them for their attractiveness and is now proving indifferent.

To adapt she has to consolidate her gains and come from her greatest strengths. She needs to give up trying to win at the expense of others and instead inspire others to give their best, that is, to rely on her nurturing qualities.

SUCCESS

If the competitive person didn't need to succeed so badly he might think about the goals he is trying to achieve and ask if they made him happy. He was trained to please others. It can be his downfall.

He often grew up trying to please his frustrated or unfulfilled parents. It is a common sight to see such parents, spurred on by visions of gold medals, lucrative professional sports, television and movie contracts, dragging their unwilling children from lessons to auditions as they try to get them to fulfill their own dreams.

Some parents become involved in every aspect of their children's school-work, judging the child's performance not against his true talents but against the admission standards of the university or graduate school that the parent wanted to attend.

The child of a competitive parent is fighting a hopeless battle. Even if he is good at what he does, he will never be good enough to please his unhappy parent. That is something the parent had to do for himself. Further, even when the child achieves a significant success and pleases his parents, it feels lacking to him because it is not the success that he would have sought on his own. The child's dream for himself is often not represented at the finish line of the race in which his parents entered him.

Of course when you are a child it is difficult to make a case for following your own dream. All talent starts small. If you wanted to be an artist and your ambitious parent wanted you to become a lawyer, it wouldn't take a lot of effort for him to compare your work to that of great artists and, in the nicest way possible, totally discourage you. It's just too easy to dissuade a talented child from following his dream. The parent need only use the child's self-doubt as evidence why he should give up and try a profession that is more secure and promising.

All people with talent doubt themselves. Their special sensitivity makes them acutely aware of how far they fall short of their objectives. They never feel good enough. It takes a lifetime of trial and error to overcome this fear and produce in spite of it. Talented people feel they fail all the time; however, they use their dissatisfaction to motivate themselves to try harder, to be their best.

Finding out just how good he is at what he would like to be frightens the competitive person. A competitive person has talent and energy, is prone to showy bravado, but often has little true bravery, confidence born of self-esteem. It is no surprise that he finds it easier to take risks and succeed at something that doesn't mean as much to him. As a result many competitive people achieve great success but at the wrong goal. Their drive has carried them in the wrong direction.

The competitive person needs to risk failing at a goal that he cares about rather than succeeding just to prove that he is a success. Succeeding at someone else's goal can be failing at his own.

The competitive person often has a mistaken view of what life at the top is all about. He discovers that being at the top is mostly about working, maintaining a sustained effort. Whereas before the competitive person was just another person climbing the ladder, now he becomes the person to beat. Pressure surrounds him.

Success makes him more self-critical, more vulnerable, less secure. He sees how much luck was involved in his succeeding. He finds that at the top there are few real friends, just a bunch of hangers-on and flatterers. The praise he sought before now gets in his way. Other people tell him he is great when he knows there is room for improvement. He wonders what their praise really meant if it was won so cheaply. He often yearns for the life before his success, when the world was full of promise. Being a success is more work than he bargained for. It disillusions and drains him. He wanted more of a sense of victory than this.

When he is placed at the head of the company, he is likely to get restless or reckless out of a misplaced need for adventure. He is not so much driven by greed as by the lure of more and bigger successes. His horizons are always expanding, and the opportunities at the top may not be there. This is why when companies become stable they need a more controlling manager at the top. The competitive person is better at making the company grow by functioning more as a top salesman than as a chief executive.

This explains why a creative executive changes companies not out of disloyalty but because his present position no longer offers a challenge to his competitive nature. For this reason a highly successful business type needs to look within, pick up the misplaced threads of his talent, and find fulfillment in a hobby that he embraces with the passion he set aside years ago.

He needs to know that it is never too late for him to find himself.

TRAITS AND VALUES

Competitive people can be defiantly individualistic, spontaneous and free, but they can also be manipulated when others play to their hidden needs and their blind spots. Here are some of the issues that make them susceptible to flattery and distraction.

SEXUAL ATTRACTIVENESS. Competitive people need to feel sexually attractive. When someone shows a sexual interest in them, they feel they have won. They may not even like the person they are flirting with, but they still respond positively to sexual attention. They always need to know they have the power to arouse another's sexual interest. They have a strong sexual orientation to life, but it can be entirely playful with no intention of actually following through. Once they have gotten the response that reassures them, they can seem totally oblivious to the sexual feelings they stir in others.

It also embarrasses them to get this response, because they are often unaware that they are continually putting out sexual feelers. In adolescence such people tend to blush a lot as their hidden feelings come to the surface and betray them.

It is the nature of competitive people to be flirtatious and engaging. They have a knack of paying great attention to whomever they are speaking with and making that person feel as if he mattered more than anyone else in the world. They are easily drawn into suggestive talk, but this is usually just role-playing and passed off as kidding. Competitive people are fascinated by the possibility of a conquest, however transient or symbolic, whether it is winning an admirer at a dinner party, closing the sale by making the buyer fall in love with them for just a few minutes, or seducing a big tip out of a customer.

Their sexual attractiveness is always on display. Sometimes this pseudosexual interplay is referred to as "having a lot of personality," but down deep everything depends on them establishing a sexual polarity with others and working it. As far as competitive people are concerned, receiving acknowledgment of their sexual desirability *is* the payoff. They are always looking for such acceptance. It distracts them.

They are aware of how everyone looks at them: the driver in the car next to them, pedestrians on the sidewalk, diners at other tables, and especially others in the gym. If they merely stimulate an expression of interest, they feel a sense of victory. They can live for days in a fantasy inspired by evoking a coy smile from someone at a bus stop while they were waiting for the light to change.

They have a sexual interest in others, even though they may be perfectly happy in their present relationship and have absolutely no intention of acting on it or making any changes. Being responded to is everything. They feel if they can create some sexual arousal they believe they still have a future. However, if another person responds to them in the earnest expectation of having an encounter, they often pull away. Make that run away.

Their flirting behavior can be extremely difficult for their partner, especially if he happens to be a controlling person who is likely to take the flirting as a provocation, symbolic of rejection. Always fearing abandonment, the controlling person will become angry and accuse the competitive person of torturing him. It ruins the entire evening.

The competitive person is likely to pretend that she wasn't flirting. In a sense she is right because she was really looking for esteem, not sex. She will certainly deny that her intention was to make the controlling partner jealous. However, teasing is often the only way that the competitive person can get even with the controlling partner. The competitive person also flirts with her own partner without intending to respond, just for sexual reassurance. Should the controlling partner rise to the bait and ask for sex, an argument usually follows. The competitive person will claim all she wanted was a little attention and ask with a straight face, "Why does every hug have to involve having sex?"

The competitive person walks a dangerous line.

TALENT AND BRILLIANCE. Talent and brilliance are everything to the competitive person. Everything! He believes that his brilliant performance makes up for his erratic behavior and excuses his rudeness and self-centeredness. He reasons that because he's getting the difficult job done so brilliantly, he's entitled to be arrogant. He has high standards. He's beaten the rest, exceeded the quotas. If he displays arrogance, it is merely the arrogance of pride in a job well done—correction, *brilliantly* done. So what of it? If everyone else performed the way he does, he reasons, it would be a miracle, wouldn't it? The way the competitive person sees it, everyone should be falling all over him in gratitude for bringing a little excitement into their drab lives. Other people are frankly put off by his attitude.

While it is true that the competitive person is often a dazzling natural performer who plies his talent with a casual ease, he has an annoying way of passing off his accomplishments—"Oh, that was nothing"—without seeming to realize that this puts everyone else down and is really false modesty, begging for a compliment.

THE NEED FOR APPLAUSE. Applause! Yes! Absolute nectar! The competitive person drinks it in. He wants to please more than anyone you've ever met. When he succeeds, he wants to be sure you know that he is good and why he is good and that you demonstrate your approval.

He goes around the office reminding others of the big sale he closed yesterday. He never can hear, "Good job," enough times. If you leave a message of praise on his answering machine, be assured he will play it back several times. This is a man on a string, dancing for applause.

If you can forgive the competitive person his bragging, drawing attention to himself, and exaggerating and just appreciate him, you will set him at ease and see the driven, frightened person underneath who just wants you to like him but is so afraid you won't that he beats you to the punch and praises himself. Know that he hates himself for this display of immaturity and wishes he could change. Applause calms him down, at least for the moment.

By contrast, true talent is an enduring gift. It is tied to a dream, a vision, a passion that exists without an audience or recognition, the artist creating for the sake of art. Too often the competitive person's talent becomes attached to performing for the sake of acknowledgment. It almost seems as if he wants applause more than he wants to fulfill his dream.

The truly talented person becomes a little depleted when the performance or creation is over because he loves to be in the process more than anything else. Applause is secondary.

Applause is all-important to the competitive person, who cares much less how he got there than about the recognition he finally receives. The competitive person's success often depends not so much on a specific talent but on his charming personality, his energy and drive. Unfortunately, these character traits are often the victims of time and diminish with age. Unlike an artist, for example, whose talent matures as he grows older, the competitive person becomes threatened as he ages because the brilliance and "talent" for which he was once so lavishly rewarded seem to fade. This is the price he pays for choosing to win at all costs and not taking the time to discover his gifts.

Often when the competitive person gets older and his energy wanes, he finds himself unceremoniously replaced by someone who has only his youthful enthusiasm to recommend him. What did the praise he received all these years really mean, the competitive person wonders. It becomes clear that he was just being given an incentive, prodded, played with, humored. When his productivity fell, the praise became a gold watch, and he was sent out to pasture. What was he running so hard for all those years?

Why didn't he risk to please himself?

THE NEED FOR COMPLIMENTS. When the competitive person, flush with a recent success, asks, "Wasn't I wonderful?" without the slightest trace of embarrassment, do not be offended. The competitive person is really his own best audience, and while he does not expect you to have the sensitive appreciation of himself that he does, he is signaling to you that he is now ready to accept your compliments.

A little too regal for you? Well, that is the style of the competitive person. If you rise to the occasion without gagging or feeling in competition with him and provide valid, appreciative feedback, you can make a friend for life.

To be fair to the competitive person, could you do what he or she just accomplished, get up in front of a thousand people without notes, and hold their attention for an hour, get laughs and spontaneous applause? You'd be much nicer about your success perhaps, but could you do it? His triumph is not an excuse for his rudeness, but it helps to put his lapse of manners in perspective. The truth is that no one really knows what doubts he had to overcome to accomplish his success. He only pretends it was easy. When the struggle is over, he wants praise for his tortured hard work that he will not admit to.

The competitive person is capable of considerable self-criticism. Even though he often blows his own horn, a trait that offends many who do not understand, he seriously doubts his achievements. Try to see his bragging as his way of reassuring himself that he isn't a failure and offsetting his inner criticism. He is continually coping with inner voices telling him he isn't good enough. He was driven to win love by performing. Since he never felt enough self-love, he always feels a little empty.

Thus even though he already seems to be doing a good job in praising himself, a little positive reinforcement from a friend goes a long way with him. A kind word at a moment like this, especially if it is sincere and reflects real appreciation and sensitivity, will make him humble to the point of tears. When he responds by saying, "Do you really think so?" you will see just how insecure he was all the time. The miracle is that he was able to do what he did while doubting himself as much as he did.

FEELING MISUNDERSTOOD. Because he can be so difficult and self-centered, the competitive person frequently feels misunderstood. Although it is largely his fault that he maintains a pretentious facade and doesn't reveal his true self to others, he still laments that no one really knows him. He feels that all people seem interested in is his performance. He is just a workhorse, a creator, a performing dog for other people to admire as long as he's got the goods they want. He feels a certain resentment toward others for not understanding and even more toward himself for soliciting their praise and encouragement, especially when he knows he should be doing something else.

He feels that others regard him as a freak, a thing, not a person. Others do not appreciate how hard he works. This special talent, that he throws off so nonchalantly and makes look so easy, took him years to develop.

Did other people even bother to try to do the same for themselves?

Do other people have any idea how much he had to believe in himself, knowing his flaws as well as he did, to make it all work? He is perfectly aware that he is just like other people, not a superman or star. The difference is that to make it all work, he had to believe in his greatness when no one else saw it. He alone knows that it is the dedication and belief that he put into his work that made him the success he has become. He imagined it all and worked to make it come true.

Could other people do this, knowing that the only thing that would make them a success was their belief in themselves, the same belief he feels he has to exaggerate in order to believe in *himself,* the same belief that makes him seem inaccessible and impossible to others?

This leads to a kind of bitterness, especially when the competitive person is succeeding at the wrong goal and is not personally rewarded by his success. When he is in favor, that is fine, but people easily forget and can discard him in a minute. He knows this full well. He feels tentative about his commitment and then becomes driven to make everyone love him, convinced that everyone is getting ready to turn their back on him. No wonder his success sometimes all seems so fragile. It all hangs on the thread of his inconstant belief in himself. Others seem so fickle. No one really understands. It is all up to him.

ACTING OUT. Acting out rather than expressing his feelings openly is one of the competitive person's most exasperating traits. He tends to take action rather than discuss his feelings. He may avoid or confront, but whatever he does, he acts with surprising suddenness. He lives on that line, taking precipitous action when the tension becomes too much to bear.

If he is afraid of losing an account, without discussing his plans, he may make a grandstand play, go over the buyer's head, and try to win over the president of the company. When it works, it is a fabulous success. He is seen as a self-starter, showing winning initiative. When he loses, he is considered to have acted impulsively and shown bad judgment.

Like the controlling person, the competitive person also has dependent needs. She may pretend she doesn't have these deep needs or may overstate them for effect. She finds dealing with the everyday reality of a relationship tiresome and unromantic. If she feels unable to handle a conflict, she may move out without even giving notice. She might leave a note on the kitchen table for her partner: "I can't breathe here anymore. It's just me. Don't take it personally." She signs it, "With love," and expects him not to be hurt by it. When she doesn't want emotional complications, she doesn't want emotional complications. Is that clear enough? About that "With love" closing? Well, she does feel love for him. Should she not say so?

After a disheartening defeat, rather than deal with his feelings of failure, the competitive person suddenly quits his job, moves away, starts a new career, or reenters college. On the surface none of these moves seems irrational, but as a response to the stimulus that provoked them they all seem like running away, avoiding being measured or tested . . . and they are.

In adolescence acting out is a way teenagers express feelings they do not feel comfortable revealing to themselves or to others. Similarly, the competitive person acts out feelings that he does not want to take responsibility for, that would cut through his pretense and make him admit that he actually cared, or that would embarrass him by getting him to concede failure or rejection.

Acting out makes the competitive person difficult to pin down. Now you see him. Now you don't. He has changed identities, attitudes, his circle of friends, his hobbies, or his belief system. Now he is at the feet of the guru currently in vogue, now he is taking the cure, on a macrobiotic diet, hopelessly in love with someone new, about to close an incredible deal, or totally involved in a phenomenal new project that will carry him to the very stars. His ventures may be new and different perhaps, but they always help him avoid the same old thing—his lack of belief in his worth.

EMBARRASSMENT. For the competitive person, embarrassment is the most dreaded consequence of failure. He cringes at the thought of being spurned, snubbed, laughed at, heckled, ridiculed, disapproved of, held up to derision, being made to seem pathetic, not being taken seriously, or mocked. The punishment of the pillory, in which a hapless offender used to be displayed in the town square, his hands and head secured in a board while people pummeled him with rotten tomatoes, approximates the personal disgrace that the competitive person feels when publicly defeated.

His embarrassment is an omen to him, foretelling the loss of his magical powers and suggesting that his sway over his audience is waning. This stirs his horrible self-doubt, making him question if he ever really had talent or if he was just fooling himself.

Because the competitive person is always making believe he is better than he thinks he is and presses himself to rise to that belief, the fear of being a faker always disquiets him; in a sense there is always some truth in it.

Even when he has achieved fame, loyal followers, and the status of a hero, he still wonders if he can do it again. He's always afraid of losing the knack, his strength, or the magic. In his dark moments he thinks he is all hype. Embarrassment unsettles him because he secretly agrees with his critics.

If you publicly point out one of his pretenses or suggest that he is exaggerating his worth, you make an enemy for life. The competitive person will never forgive you because his greatest hurts occurred when he felt embarrassed. He shudders when he remembers those painful incidents, even if he was just a kid at the time. He still has the same tendency to pretend, and he dreads others will discover he is a phony. The old fear lives with him.

Although the competitive person can sometimes spontaneously reveal himself and admit his shortcomings, he prefers to do so only when he chooses. He does not like to have people look at his work before he is willing to display it or be judged before he is ready to face others, that is, to give his best performance. He feels he needs to "sell" his work and win over his audience, and to do this he first needs to believe in himself. It can take considerable preparation to get himself up for the occasion because he never feels completely satisfied with his work or himself. The amazing thing is that with all his self-doubt he is the one to go before the audience and open up his heart to the world. His transparency and fragility are what make him so adored.

In the same vein a competitive woman of great beauty getting dressed for an elegant affair can only see her blemishes. She never feels she looks good until the very last minute when, against all doubts, she finally convinces herself she is presentable. It only takes one trivial negative comment to bring her self-doubts to the surface again. She needs unflinching support, an open display of appreciation from her partner, requiring him to be an appreciative audience. If he appears inattentive, insincere, or fulsome in his praise, she will suddenly flare and may find herself unable to face her public and delay her appearance as a way of punishing him.

If you live with a competitive person, remember you are allowed the privilege of witnessing the rehearsals that precede the actual performance, of seeing the incomplete work before it is ready. You need to understand that you are never allowed to humiliate the competitive person by revealing his or her preparations.

So as far as a competitive person's life is concerned, you are always looking at a work in progress and should suspend judgment. He does not want to be embarrassed by being exposed as flawed in his performance. This makes perfect sense if you remember that the competitive person *is* his performance.

This explains why athletes take defeat so hard. When television replays an athlete's error on the eleven o'clock news as a humorous sports feature, it is a source of mortification for him. He may pretend not to care, but he still takes it to heart. He studies his error, how he misjudged the ball and why. He goes through all the motions again in his head. That damn clip of the ball going through his legs! It just kills him.

Performance, pretending, and embarrassment all go hand in hand. When you look at world-class skiers before the big race rehearsing by going through the course in their mind, you can see how pretending works to get the competitor up for the real test. On the other hand, imagining his failure and embarrassment paralyzes him and invites failure. The competitive person uses his pretended victory to spur him on and his possible failure and embarrassment to keep him focused on the potential dangers.

The correct attitude for dealing or living with the competitive person is to tell him, "You can do it. Keep it up. So far, so good. You look and sound great." If you have to offer criticism, saying "Fix what you don't like" works far better than being brutally honest. Be careful about offering unsolicited negative critiques. He needs to be respected for his bravery and forgiven his presumptions. So what if his project didn't work, if he lost, if it didn't work out? Who else even bothered to risk?

Besides, there's always next time.

SELF-DESTRUCTIVENESS. The competitive person has a peculiar capacity for self-destructiveness that can best be understood in terms of his pretending.

The competitive person pretends not to care about his defeats. He pretends to be better than he is in order to set his self-doubt aside and risk with confidence. He pretends to be something he isn't, not only when he pursues career goals, but also when he deals with others. He pretends to be in love and to care just for the experience of being in a relationship. Role-playing comes so easily to him he sometimes even convinces himself. He surely convinces others with his romantic fervor. Still, he seems all too willing to abandon his relationship for the next promising upgrade. When he walks out on a partner he finally admits that even though he sincerely wanted to be, he really wasn't in love. The next time he's convinced it's real.

It comes as no surprise that the competitive person, in his selfish search for the best, hurts a lot of people along the way. When the competitive person finally approaches success, he begins to feel more confident. Now he is able to concede how difficult his struggle was and how close he came to losing. At such times it is also typical for him to admit his doubts about the real value of his accomplishments and to use the cushion of his success to indulge in some self-criticism. As he lowers his defenses his old unkindnesses to others opportunistically resurface and haunt him. When they do, he is stricken with remorse and tends to act out his guilty conscience. Right at the point of his success, he punishes himself by doing something self-destructive in a cavalier manner, something terribly stupid, painfully embarrassing, and grotesquely public, the stuff of tabloids.

This self-defeating trait leads him to seek out punishment for his past excesses. Where once he seemed to tease others sexually, he now appears the easy sexual victim, caring too much about others' affections, utterly destroyed by love, cut to the heart, devastated. He reveals the dark side of his character by acting out the self-hatred that has been so long and skillfully hidden beneath his pretense of self-love.

SUGGESTIBILITY. It comes as no surprise that a person who is so much a creature of pretense and appearances is himself easy prey to suggestion. In a sense he has spent his life taking advantage of this trait by hypnotizing himself to believe in himself. He becomes in fact as much a victim of his suggestibility as anyone he seduces.

He is so much the salesman that he finds himself on the side of anyone who is trying to sell him something and thus becomes an easy mark.

She wants to believe in love so much she falls for the most transparently insincere seduction, pronouncing it true love when everyone else can see right through it.

It is the competitive person's need to believe in believing that carries him into places where logic and reasonable reality testing do not seem to follow.

When this trait is used to create art or the like, we are stunned by its surrealistic beauty and imagination. When this trait is not tempered by asking the simple question, Is this real? life becomes blurred with fantasy. It is this trait that gives the competitive person his charm and his deepest pain. Curiously, it also predisposes him to be an especially good subject for hypnosis.

QUITTING. Pretending can be a crippling defense. For the same reasons that he becomes self-destructive, the competitive person often seems to lose confidence at the very last minute. Instead of giving the extra effort and doing his best, the prospect of discovering his true worth turns him into a coward.

He quits the race, pretending that he could have won, insisting he really didn't try. Whereas before he seemed so committed to win at all costs, he suddenly reveals an endless supply of reasons that excuse him from failure. His efforts cannot be used to measure his worth, because he wasn't giving his best. He may claim that the goal he is seeking is not really worthy of him, that he was on a fool's errand all this time and the prize he sought never really mattered to him.

Sometimes this loss of heart is the result of his old suppressed self-hatred over not pursuing his true goals resurfacing at the moment of truth. He suddenly realizes he's been a faker, a pretender. His selfishness may overwhelm him as he feels that he was not really deserving but merely outwitted others.

Whatever his reasons for quitting, he was just avoiding testing himself.

LONELINESS. Each of the defensive types suffers from his own kind of loneliness. The dependent person feels abandoned. The controlling person feels isolated from his feelings. The competitive person feels that so much of his life was pretend, he wonders if he imagined it all. Still, he becomes lonely for the self he was when he performed. He feels that was when he was his best, and he also wonders if he was being real then.

Because often he has only pretended to care, the competitive person frequently lacks the rich emotional human investments that pay lasting dividends. He was so invested in beating others that when he looks back in his catalogue of "best friends," he finds only people he has defeated or people who have bested him, rivals and conquests.

He is so accustomed to looking to the future that when his prospects become slim, he feels lost. Looking back feels like admitting defeat. There is an enormous restlessness about his loneliness. He struggles to do something to feel better. He rifles through his telephone book, looking for friends to call. He fantasizes about what making contact will bring him. But should he actually risk calling, he feels like hanging up as soon as the other person answers because he realizes that the other person will be older, too, or may have forgotten his success, or now thinks less of him. He believes others are as superficial as he sometimes sees himself. Besides, how does he call for support from someone he only pretended to care about?

If the other person answers and is happy and successful, the competitive person may be happy for him but unhappy for himself by comparison. He is competitive, after all. However, should the other person be ailing or down on his luck, the competitive person doesn't feel glee for his friend's misfortune but rather diminished because this source of support is unable to make him feel better.

He can live in his memories and souvenirs, but that makes life altogether too sad. He not only has to admit that what was, has been, he has to admit that what he could not achieve may always elude his grasp.

Still, as he tells stories of days gone by, triumphs become exaggerated. The past takes on a special glow in recollection that it never had in actuality. Now he adds the perspective of glory. Even the ordinary becomes special. War stories become embellished with time. He can look back on a moment with greater bravery than he could summon when the risk was actually taking place.

His retelling of the past becomes another performance, and for a moment his loneliness fades.

DEFENSIVE LIMITATIONS: HOW THE HEALING PROCESS IS DEFEATED

By pretending not to care when he suffers a loss, the competitive person thwarts the mourning process. You cannot successfully mourn something that does not matter to you, for the mourning process is then a thing for show, to win sympathy, not earn relief. All the competitive person's emotional difficulties stem from this weakness.

When he pretends that a loss doesn't matter, he becomes a mystery to others who see his cool reaction to tragedy as heartless. Instead of supporting him in his grief, others tend to pull away just when he needs them most. Should he act out his loss by becoming self-destructive, his self-defeating attitude will seem unfathomable or self-indulgent, causing others to ridicule him and withdraw.

His tendency to seek a replacement for what he has lost rather than mourn it also defeats the natural mourning process. It also places too great a burden on the replacement he has created. The second wife married just four months after the first is buried must not only make him happy but also make him forget. This pressure is too much and can sabotage the new relationship and create another loss. In this way he can become involved in a sequence of symbolic losses stemming from an original hurt that he pretended not to care about. The so-called repetition compulsion is really nothing more than a manifestation of replacing rather than mourning.

In addition, because he finds it difficult to admit that his failures mattered, he is slow to learn his lessons and doesn't seem to grow. After a severe setback, rather than take inventory and work on his problems, he may lose confidence, become overly cautious, and not risk enough. Then when an important risk is suddenly upon him, he finds himself unprepared and suffers another shattering defeat, this time with no place to hide.

If he finally faces his loss honestly, a misfortune can be the beginning of real growth and a life change for him. The truth is that he lost something that really mattered to him. When he learns his lesson and forgives himself for not trying or being wiser, he is often able to find his courage, commit to a goal, and finally succeed. Many great successes follow a big failure. The competitive person needs to learn that talent isn't everything and that he must do everything it takes to succeed the way he wants to.

He must always overcome his tendency to choose easy goals just to win. He needs to take risks that help him grow rather than repeatedly go over the same familiar ground. In taking risks that really matter and exposing himself to the pain of loss, he grows as a person, becoming more giving and supportive of others. However, if he doesn't take emotional risks he can end up accomplished in his special arena, but on the interpersonal level he may remain childish and self-centered, still pretentious.

In his search for personal integrity he is continually sidetracked by his old doubts. He repeatedly questions himself: Am I admirable? Am I really a success? Do people respect my talent or ability? He may try to answer these questions too cheaply and abandon his goal.

He must also guard against being misdirected by the defensive responses that subvert the natural therapeutic process. These replay in his mind at the time of loss and failure: So what? Who cares? I never liked him. I was going to quit anyhow. She was wrong for me. I didn't fail, I never really tried.

He needs to learn that it is always his fault that he fails and that he hurts because he cares. He needs to accept this graciously, just as the rest of the world does.

FANTASY

Part of the replacement of loss that the competitive person seeks is accomplished by means of fantasy. When he suffers a serious loss, his fantasies take up the slack to compensate him for his pain. In the face of bankruptcy he imagines the opulent lifestyle he will have when he regroups. He even moves into the new estate in his mind and pushes the loss away and sometimes the lesson he needed to learn as well. He envisions his triumph over the very adversaries he claims not to care about. Sometimes he is so involved in his world of fantasy that it is difficult for him to say where reality is.

These fantasies comfort him so much that he can almost forget he still has mourning to finish.

He has fantasies about the future.

He has fantasies about the past.

He edits the past.

He amends reality as it happens by attaching to it his fantasies of how it should have been or could have been. Comments like, If only this were in another place or another time or with another person, constitute his inner dialogue on how to improve on reality. It's sometimes hard for him to tell when he is pretending and when he is being serious.

While everyone enjoys fantasy and uses it to solve problems and create success, the competitive person also uses fantasy as a major escape. His loyalty to his fantasy world and to his version of the truth becomes a major obstacle in undermining the natural healing process.

He sometimes cannot let go of his dream.

THE CURE

He needs to accept responsibility for the way his life has turned out. The good and the bad.

He needs to admit that he has been hurt and that some hurts cannot be replaced. If he can replace his hurts without consequence, what value could they have had?

To succeed he has to become his best on his own terms, rather than just defeating others.

THE EVOLVED COMPETITIVE TYPE

The competitive person who has learned to compete with his best self is the spice of life. He is the inventor, the performer, the creator, the risker, the star athlete, the trailblazer, the explorer, the adventurer, the politician, the warrior, the keynote speaker, the standout in a crowd of thousands, the handsome devil, the great beauty, the actor, and the hero.

He stands above the crowd. His success or notoriety names the times, the decade, the century. His fame claims followers, fans, admirers, and detractors.

He is bigger than life. Much is expected of him that he cannot deliver. The more power he gives back to others, the greater his worth. When he is selfish or petty, the newspapers tear him to shreds.

He lives in the public eye. Whether his world is large or small does not matter as much as that he plays to it and it responds to him.

He is the subject of other people's conversations. People gossip about his weaknesses and marvel about his strength. He is aggrandized as others begin to believe the self-image he has created and diminished as others decry his tawdry showmanship.

He can be the president of France or head of her child's elementary school PTA. When he or she speaks, the star quality shows and everyone knows it. This is the personality behind the message, the dreamer behind the dream, the believer behind the hope. So large is this person's display of his confidence that others borrow strength from his vision.

He leads and builds by inspiring. Sometimes he founds a new religion. Other times he inspires people to clean up a local despoiled river. In the name of good, there is none better. His imagination becomes a public trust.

In the name of greed, prejudice, or hatred, list here all the villains who inspire others to treachery and evil. These were monsters who had to win by crushing others.

Without the competitive person, commerce would not expand and there would be diminished drive to better our lives. Here is the soul of humankind's curiosity and the search for knowledge and a better way.

Part of this trait lives in all of us, but for the competitive person, it is his life.

THE SOUL OF THE ARTIST

The personality of the competitive person has much in common with the personality of the artist. Rodin, when asked how to sculpt an elephant, replied, "Get a large block of stone and chip away everything that doesn't look like an elephant."

This comment is not entirely in jest, for it illustrates exactly how the artist's creative process transforms his vision into reality. The artist has a creative notion, an inexact suggestion of form, color, line, or sound, and allows himself to be taken by it, following it where it will go. The creative process requires that the artist accept that he is worthy and that he commit to receiving creative notions as they come to him. He is determined to take note of these creative ideas, to write them down, embellish and develop them.

The competitive person often sees his life suddenly crystallized in a creative notion that he also sets about to transform into reality, the self he wants to become. Perhaps when he was a child he saw a movie and was attracted to an actor's style or to a character's sensibility. He wanted to be like that. Perhaps he visited a wealthy friend and was taken by the way he lived. He wanted to live like that. Perhaps he met a celebrity and was sparked by the magic of his energy. He felt something familiar about that energy, something he hoped was also inside him. So he began to dream the dream and follow his creative notion, chipping away what did not seem to fit, adding what made the vision more complete, accessorizing the fantasy.

Although we all have heroes, ego ideals, after whom we model ourselves, whose brilliance and style we try to emulate, the competitive person takes this matter of becoming someone else very seriously at a very young age.

When the competitive person pretends to be something that he isn't, he is testing to see what it would be like to be a certain way. He is acting out his fantasies, rehearsing the role of success in his mind.

Most of his initial modeling begins as an imitation of his hero. Generally, young people are attracted to something or someone who touches a respondent chord in them. It is in the nature of talent that you always have love for your gift. No one had to tell Mozart to practice. They had to pry his fingers off the keyboard to make him take meals. This same passion leads the child to take risks as he develops his talent. He can always imagine something better to become. That is also the nature of talent. He needs a sympathetic teacher, who can insist on him learning the basics without dampening his enthusiasm. Without such a teacher the child is left to suffer his defeats alone and may become discouraged and fail to pursue the matter of his heart.

This is where creative people become lost—not that they don't have enough talent, but that they don't have enough experience to give them the right perspective. They need to learn patience, self-discipline, and the art of mastery.

In the absence of these supports children are likely to drift into areas where their intelligence and education, their energy and drive can give them an advantage, without exposing their true talent. They may be competent, helpful, lead useful lives, and achieve success and happiness, but unless they find and define their true gift, they never feel truly authentic.

There is nothing like *the child who has his own.*

THE MATURE PERSONALITY

The mature personality can be dependent, controlling, or competitive, but evolved and open in each trait rather than defensive and hidden. Most people are a mixture of all three types. It is rare to find a mature person who is exclusively one type, for that suggests that he has not truly grown.

A person can be evolved in one or more personality traits and still have much growing to do in the other. There is considerable variation and degree in each trait and in its balance to others, which explains why there are so many different personalities.

Because the mature personality has discovered his niche in life, he achieves his sense of independence from understanding who he is and what his life means. He loves himself so he can love others unconditionally. He is not afraid of becoming involved or committing to another person because he is committed to himself and knows that he can always save himself.

He is not afraid of being alone, because the time spent alone is spent perfecting his gift. He can just as well be with someone he loves because he chooses to be with him.

Because he has found himself, he has no need to control others.

He is able to be organized and disciplined in the service of his life's work. His life does not revolve around artificial rules and regulations. He is able to structure his work and his play. He is flexible. His life contains balance, passion, self-absorption, generosity, empathy, and sharing when it should. And when it shouldn't, it doesn't.

He does not feel obligated to be any way but honest.

He enjoys being vulnerable and is at ease admitting his shortcomings and weaknesses. Nothing else suits him.

He is tolerant of those who do not meet the standards he holds for himself and is kind and accepting rather than critical of them.

Because he is involved in creating his true life, he has no need to pretend that what is so is not, or that what is not is so.

He is patient because he knows he is on the right road.

He grows old with grace and is eager to hear about other people's success and happiness. He is always growing, always striving to be better.

Although he can seem driven and focused in the heat of a project, he can also relax and enjoy the gifts others have created. His attachment to the gifts of other people reassures him of the meaning of life and anchors him in a world that often seems adrift with uncertainties.

Rather than feeling competitive with the great men and women of the past, he finds similarities with their struggles and their ideals. He is reassured to know that he is part of that larger process by which the race betters itself.

His evolution is, therefore, part of the evolution of the whole world.

His peace of mind is contagious.

TOXIC NOSTALGIA: THE INTRUSIVE PAST

*T*OXIC NOSTALGIA DEFINES HOW, in spite of your best efforts and resolutions, you manage to defeat yourself by getting in your own way. It would not be possible to talk in depth about the mechanism of Toxic Nostalgia without first understanding the natural therapeutic process, mourning, the Feeling Cycle, Emotional Debt, defenses, and character Type.

THE LEGACY OF EMOTIONAL DEBT

SOME TYPICAL EXAMPLES

While the examples that follow seem like portraits of ordinary people in trouble, each presents a person burdened with unresolved feelings that are trying to work themselves out via the mechanism of Toxic Nostalgia. There is a complicated interplay of Emotional Debt, character weakness, and defensive style continually operating in these cases. Even the simplest forms of Toxic Nostalgia reveal a subtle blend of needs, attitudes, and defenses that keep pain from resolution. Underlying all this is the natural therapeutic process, the dynamic motor driving all that is hidden toward disclosure, pressing for the truth to be known.

Peter wanted to ask for a raise, but in spite of the fact that he had worked hard, made contributions to the company that resulted in significant sales, and received excellent work reviews, he got a tight feeling in his stomach and broke into a sweat every time he decided to petition his boss. Peter would spend hours dredging up all the mistakes he'd made over the years, almost as if to dissuade himself. He would make the boss's argument to himself that cash was tight and that growth was slower than expected. Finally, out of weakness disguised as prudence, he would cancel the appointment, feeling both resentful and powerless.

Peter's childhood fear of not being good enough had become a generalized belief that he wasn't deserving. This intimidated him in spite of his excellent work record. Also, his need to be perfect, which was his compensation for feeling flawed, made him shy away from anyone, especially a figure in authority, who just might tell him why he didn't deserve a raise and thus prove that his worst fears were true. In addition, Peter had long felt taken for granted by his spouse. He held in his resentment of her, only to express himself explosively when he was drinking. These outbursts led him to question his goodness, diminishing his sense of deservability and bleeding his courage when he needed it most.

Peter usually told his wife that the time wasn't right to ask for a raise. She would give him a hurt look tinged with disdain. She saw through his insecurity and knew he was making excuses. Peter's passive, self-destructive failure would also serve to punish her and allow him to get even with her for not being more appreciative.

Toxic nostalgic manifestations that intrude in this example:

> *Peter's self-lack of deservability.*
> *Peter's anxiety in the face of authority.*
> *Peter's identification with the forces against him rather*
> *than focusing on his own case.*
> *His pretense of prudence to cover cowardice.*
> *His pretending to be perfect when feeling self-doubt.*
> *His alcohol dependency.*
> *His explosive behavior.*
> *His passive expression of hurt.*

Julia found herself in an abusive relationship with a man whom she once pretended was everything she dreamed of. Over time their life together became increasingly difficult. Julia learned to manage him by being compliant, to give in to him sexually on demand, and never to speak when she was hurt. When they were together there were long, uncomfortable silences.

When her son was born, Julia spoiled him and became overprotective. Her husband felt that she preferred their son to him and was jealous. Julia's friends repeatedly told her she was foolish to remain in a loveless marriage. Although she recognized the truth in this advice, she felt powerless to act. She often dreamed of being alone, but the idea frightened her, especially the belief that she would be a bad person if she abandoned her husband. She just couldn't hurt her child by breaking up the family. She remained and suffered without trying to make her life better.

Julia left home to marry when she was eighteen because she couldn't stand living with her abusive parents. Without resolving her anger toward them, she sought safety in the arms of the first man who asked to marry her. She didn't grow. She didn't finish her education. She knew she had let herself down and used her husband to escape and felt guilty for doing so.

Toxic nostalgic intrusions in this example:

> *Julia's belief she would be bad for saving herself.*
> *Her fear of being alone.*
> *Her readiness to conceal her feelings.*
> *Her tendency to seek safety at all costs.*
> *Her pervasive self-doubt.*
> *Her passive self-destructiveness.*
> *Her resentment of herself for being weak.*
> *Her overprotectiveness toward her son.*
> *Her willingness to accept the unacceptable.*
> *Her guilty suffering.*

At sixteen Steve had already developed a reputation as a liar. He was continually getting into trouble by being disruptive at school. Although no one could prove it, he was suspected of several episodes of petty theft. His academic performance was mediocre, because he never studied hard enough to fulfill his potential. His parents fretted about his lack of drive and complained about his obsession with Mitzi, his girlfriend, who had a powerful grip on him. Steve claimed he would do anything for Mitzi. His mother worried continuously about his late hours and his safety, but secretly she was jealous of Mitzi. Steve was aware that his fulsome displays of affection toward Mitzi hurt his mother.

His mother was suspicious that Steve was on drugs. Feeling powerless, she appealed to Mitzi to help manage him. Steve openly resented his mother for meddling. Fearing rejection, his mother became even more indulgent and tried to bribe Steve. In fact Steve was not on drugs, but Mitzi was, and the reason Steve stole was to pay for her habit. When Steve was arrested for breaking open a parking meter, his father took notice for the first time, blaming the mother for being too soft. The family became like a battleground.

Toxic Nostalgia in this example is largely acted out, rather than a set of attitudes or false beliefs:

Steve's lying and stealing.
His dependency on his girlfriend.
Sacrificing himself for her love.
His self-destructive behavior in school.
Punishing his mother by making her jealous and anxious.
Taking unreasonable risks to hurt his father.

When you realize that Peter was married to Julia and Steve was their son, the manifestation of these toxic nostalgic symptoms takes on a different perspective.

These three people are continually expressing feelings in symbolic ways which, if you view them in terms of the present, make only limited sense. Steve resents being coddled and yet has a powerful need to be taken care of. He bribes Mitzi to love him just as his mother indulges him. Julia's smothering overprotectiveness is a remnant of her own unfulfilled childhood needs. It is insincere and irritates Steve to be infantilized. He wants to reject his mother, but that would make him feel too guilty. Instead he seeks a destructive relationship with Mitzi, where by providing for her needs he can pretend that he is an adult and in control. Steve is also angry at his inadequate father for his self-involvement and perfectionist standards. Steve holds his feelings in just as his mother does. He expresses his resentment at his father passively by hurting himself and embarrassing him. He fears his father's criticism as much as his father feels afraid of being criticized.

Julia is still angry at her parents. She is also angry at herself for not being stronger and at Peter whose abusiveness she provokes by passively undermining his self-esteem. She creates the same environment she escaped from as an adolescent but this time blames Peter for it.

Peter still resents being undermined by his father. He is committed to trying to keep up appearances, to seem like a man in control of his life, acting confident and worthy of others' admiration. Julia will not let him carry off this facade and subtly reminds him that he is flawed. He takes his anger out on her when he is drinking and resents his son in general for ruining his marriage and parading the family's dirty linen in public.

THE DELICATE BALANCE—STEPS TOWARD HEALING

If, instead of acting out his feelings, Steve could tell his mother that she was insincere in her giving, he'd feel relieved instead of guilty over his bad behavior. If he could tell his father that he seemed more interested in appearances than in his son and get him to pay attention to him, he'd feel less destructive. Then he would be less needy and feel more deserving and more likely to let go of Mitzi.

If Julia could forgive her parents, she'd be able to appreciate what Peter has done for her instead of taking out her old anger on him. This would lower her guilt so that if she found she did not love Peter, she would be better able to save herself. She would also have less need to be overprotective of Steve to compensate for the protection she didn't receive when she was a kid.

If Peter could forgive his father, he'd be able to release the store of anger that lowers his self-esteem. Then he would be able to be more successful and less envious of his son. His anxiety over his worth would diminish and he'd be able to decrease his dependency on alcohol to manage it. More confident, he'd be able to deal with Julia without punishing her for not being supportive of his failures.

A COMPLEX FORCE

Toxic Nostalgia is a subtle mixture of feelings, attitudes, perspectives, and needs of different ages all showing themselves at once as the unresolved past attempts to define the present. Your capacity for Toxic Nostalgia limits your freedom to be who you are, to act in your own best interests, or to be open in expressing yourself. Toxic Nostalgia is both your emotional history and destiny.

The quality of a toxic nostalgic reaction involves many interacting determinants. It mirrors your expressive style. For example, Julia was passive. Peter was explosive. Steve acted out.

Toxic Nostalgia reflects your character type. Julia was dependent and had many unrealistic expectations of others that led her to be hurt repeatedly. Peter was competitive with many controlling features. He thrived on praise but needed support in the form of respect. His dread of criticism made him abusive. Steve was a mixture of dependent and competitive features. He needed to be taken care of but rebelled against this need and so made a show of taking care of Mitzi.

Toxic Nostalgia is modified by your defenses. Julia was full of denial and also tried to control others passively. Peter pretended to be perfect and projected his weaknesses onto his son. Steve denied his neediness and pretended to be self-assured.

Toxic Nostalgia reflects your capacity to manage Emotional Debt. Julia was filled with unexpressed old feelings and held so much inward-directed anger that suffering became a way of life for her. Peter's Emotional Debt led him to doubt his goodness. He was so afraid of revealing his weaknesses that he could only express himself when he was angry or drinking and then usually

overdid it. Steve could not tolerate much Emotional Debt. He harbored resentment at both parents for being consumed with themselves and felt
obliged to act out his feelings almost as soon as he felt them, creating chaos
with his behavior.

Toxic Nostalgia incorporates your view of the world, your sense of perspective. Julia feared the world and sought to overprotect her son. Peter posed as the
superhero who could conquer the world in the name of the company but was
unable to ask for a raise because he doubted himself. Steve hadn't really thought
about what the world had in store for him and instead focused on getting love.
He resented not being seen as himself and gravitated to someone who needed
him, creating a little world he could control.

Most importantly, Toxic Nostalgia incorporates the unmourned losses in
your life. Julia still held on to her childhood hurt and recreated it in her relationship with Peter. Because Peter wouldn't forgive his father for continually
finding fault with him, he projected his anger onto figures of authority and criticized his son the way his father had hurt him. Steve was in the midst of acting
out his mourning of his unhappy family and adopting Mitzi's needs to work on
them by proxy.

Toxic Nostalgia is living in the past. Peter is still trying to come to peace
with a father he has never accepted. Julia cannot forgive her mother for ignoring the abuse she suffered. Steve lies as a way of rubbing their nose in his parents' pretentiousness. He sees them both as phonies and secretly dreads he is
no better.

UNDERSTANDING THE MECHANISM

Human behavior seems so widely diverse because the variables that contribute to the development of Toxic Nostalgia are as unique as a person's finger-
prints. However, the mechanism by which these feelings from one's past intrude
into the present is straightforward. Much of what follows will be recognized as
ordinary behavior. The explanation of the mechanism behind it should provide
new depth and understanding.

THE VARIABLES

All these variables have been previously identified and discussed at length.
They are now reviewed for the role they play in determining the emotional content of the toxic nostalgic episode.

CHARACTER TYPE

Your character type determines what is important to you. Each person is a mixture of types. Although you may think of yourself as one type, certain losses and conditions will bring forth aspects of the other character traits that make up your personality.

Character is the sum of your special sensitivities, and defines your needs. You have many, but your character determines which needs dominate and rule your responses.

How your needs have been met determines how sensitive you are to certain losses and therefore how susceptible you are to a particular disappointment triggering an old response.

DEFENSES

Your defenses determine how open you are to initiating the natural therapeutic process. The more rigid your defenses, the more likely you are to store feelings rather than to face them directly. Denial causes a lag between the feeling and its acceptance, while intellectual defenses make you less vulnerable to experiencing feelings in an emotional way. Pretenses make feelings seem unimportant. Denial stores feelings without processing them. When you use excuses, blaming, or pretense you still use denial to block the underlying hurt and your responsibility for it.

Everyone uses defenses from all three developmental periods. Your particular pattern and how you respond to hurt is unique to you.

How long you hold on to a defense before letting go of the feeling defines your capacity for incurring Emotional Debt.

THE CAPACITY FOR EMOTIONAL EXPRESSION

It sounds obvious, but it cannot be overstated: your ability to express your feelings honestly in the moment, to tell the person who hurt you that he hurt you, determines more than any other factor how free of pain your life is.

This in turn is a reflection of how guarded you are.

Since persistence of old thoughts and feelings is at the heart of Toxic Nostalgia, the more open you are, the lower your potential for having feelings intrude from the past. When your ability to express emotions is impaired by your fear of rejection, vulnerability, or being embarrassed, you keep your pain alive and suffer from Toxic Nostalgia.

Your ability to express pain directly is vital to being happy.

Emotional Debt

Your Emotional Debt reflects not only your inability to process the feelings of the moment but is also the record of your unique history, the sum total of your adaptation to all the hurts and nurturing, the coping, the forgiveness, the accomplishments of your life.

Your Emotional Debt directly reflects your self-esteem. A high Emotional Debt reveals a low self-esteem. Low self-esteem predisposes you to incur additional Emotional Debt, because you so deeply fear rejection, losing control, or failure. This makes you more likely to hold on to negative emotions.

Understandably, people with low self-esteem are most likely to suffer from Toxic Nostalgia. Their Emotional Debt is high and therefore more likely to overflow. Their need to prove themselves combined with their feeling that they have been cheated or abused inclines them to view innocent comments as hurtful and makes them susceptible to being triggered.

Flooding

The confusion you feel when the past is loosed upon the present is easy to understand. These old emotions come from many sources and many different times. These old feelings come forward as if released from a time capsule, drowning you in past remembrance. You loose your chronological footing.

Toxic Nostalgia: What You Bring to the Moment

Toxic Nostalgia is the feeling, behavior, thought process that envelops you when your old emotions escape into the present. Sometimes these feelings carry your old negative attitudes with them, such as the belief that you are unworthy, unlovable, doomed to fail, stupid, incapable, or hopeless. While your present situation may suggest that these beliefs have some merit, the emotions that return as Toxic Nostalgia with your past history attached to them seem to prove it conclusively.

How free you are to react in the present depends on how much you are holding on to the past. You can be independent or attached, free or bound, full of suffering and remorse. How you are is a choice. Your past bears witness to your experience, but that testimony is merely commentary that needs to be put into perspective. The most important perspective on your history results from your acceptance of what happened to you. It reflects your willingness to forgive others and yourself.

Put simply, how you see your past is how you feel about yourself. Because toxic nostalgic intrusions overstate the negative legacy of the past, they tend to undermine your confidence. They do this because you see the return of old feelings as confirming your worst beliefs about yourself.

Just because this morning your boss told you the memo you drafted was unacceptable doesn't mean that by doing so he corroborated your critical father's negative prediction for you when you were a rebellious adolescent.

You didn't please your boss today.

You didn't please your father when you were a kid.

Today's events are similar only in that your work wasn't acceptable to another person. The past was not predictive nor was the present confirmatory. Except for your lingering self-doubts about your adequacy, these events are not linked. They are separate. The feeling process that connects them is Toxic Nostalgia.

If you think your present performance confirms your old prejudices against yourself, that is merely your opinion, not necessarily a fact. However, if you take it as a fact and act on it as true, it becomes true.

You have a history. You must come to terms with it.

THE HEALING DYNAMICS OF FORGIVENESS

If you had come to terms with your difficult father and had forgiven him and were now feeling positive about yourself, you would probably react to your boss's criticism much differently. You might be embarrassed that the memo wasn't your best effort, but you wouldn't be defeated. You might be reminded how you used to deal with your critical father and how, seeing it was impossible to please him, you often tried to get by with as little work as possible. You might also notice that your old pattern of wanting to avoid working for a critical person still lives within you. However, instead of being dismayed, you'd smile to yourself and rewrite the memo. Doing your job, you'd affirm that you live in the present, not the past.

Forgiveness creates self-acceptance. You accept that you have weaknesses. You don't need to conceal them. Instead you use your awareness of your shortcomings to be sure you do your best. You know you can fail but realize that no single failure can define your worth as a person. You realize that your success is limited more by your unwillingness to confront your weaknesses than by your lack of talent. Your false negative beliefs are your biggest enemy. When you are at peace with yourself, you simply accept your limitations without condemning yourself. You treat your past experience and the events of the present as independent events. You learn from everything instead of lamenting or feeling cheated when something goes wrong.

When you are in Emotional Debt, your self-acceptance is low. Your concealed feelings are continually trying to seek expression by establishing links to events in the present. That is their natural imperative. These connections are inexact matches, based on a similarity of feelings. Although they tend to be overly generalized, these reemerging old feelings feel true when they break through, which is why they are so hard to distinguish from current emotions and have such power to discourage you.

The difference between feeling positively or negatively about yourself is, therefore, mostly a reflection of your Emotional Debt. When it is low, you easily accept yourself. You are open to criticism because it does not stir up old self-deprecation. You have a kinder perspective on your earlier failures, because you view them in the context of seeing how far you have come.

When you are in Emotional Debt, every shortcoming has a tongue to denigrate you. Present criticism reinforces past weaknesses and validates your worst opinion of yourself. You see your past as an insurmountable legacy.

Forgiveness rules your self-esteem. If you truly forgive that difficult father, you release not only your hurt from the specific incidents you recall but many other hurts he inflicted that you probably can't even remember. That is the only way you can forgive and why forgiveness that is selective is not forgiveness at all. However, since your old hurts are commingled into an amalgam of anger from many sources, when you sincerely forgive your father, you also forgive all these other injuries collectively, as part of the same batch of hurt. Should you later recall an old hurt that you hadn't before remembered, it will immediately fall under the same global covenant of forgiveness you committed to earlier and be seen as just another piece of your history, not as more evidence to warrant a retrial and conviction of your father, which is how you react when you don't forgive.

You hold a self-destructive grudge when you don't forgive.

You need to forgive others in order to forgive yourself.

You need to forgive to be fully present in the moment.

THE INTRUSION OF THE PAST

A toxic nostalgic intrusion feels like someone is suddenly playing the feeling track of a news clip of your life and superimposing it on the present moment. This happens with little warning, so you are likely to be caught by surprise, feeling a way you thought you had long outgrown. Often you are so overwhelmed you believe these feelings are really happening in the present and allow them to misdirect you. You take your feelings as confirmation of some previous negative assessment of yourself. You suddenly lose faith in yourself. You regret the choices you've made.

How do you know that what you are feeling is real? The question reaches to the essence of all human emotions.

Obviously the meaning of any emotion is distorted by the Emotional Debt of the person experiencing the emotion. Only you can tell what something means to you, and sometimes you really aren't sure. If you haven't forgiven the hurts you've suffered, you have no way of telling how much of what you are feeling is current or merely a memory.

Without understanding how your past feelings intrude, you can't tell what you really feel. Recognizing Toxic Nostalgia is the first step to take in gaining control over your life.

The lower your self-esteem, the more difficulty you will have dealing with Toxic Nostalgia. You lose your perspective and take everything personally. You become hypersensitive to criticism and see it as punitive. You always tend to assume the worst, which leads you to panic in the face of danger, to hide or run, to close down or become defiant. This attitude creates even more Emotional Debt and sets the scene for more such intrusions.

During an episode of Toxic Nostalgia, even if you are confident, your self-esteem tends to fall. You are likely to become hypersensitive, irritable, and find it difficult to think creatively, preferring instead to blame or to evade responsibility for what has gone wrong.

When you have a truer perspective, you are better able to function and meet the demands of the moment. You see the present situation as a problem with limits, rather than as a recurring proof of your lack of worth. Gaining perspective means removing the high drama from life and just going about your business as directly as possible. You just take the next logical step. You ate lunch. Now you wash your dishes. Keep the moments simple. Don't let the past bleed through the spaces between the moments.

In an important golf tournament, Jack Nicklaus had to shoot a sixty-five to win, a daunting task. On a final hole he took a bad swing and, just like any rank beginner, topped the ball, which bounced a few feet in the air and rolled to a stop hardly a yard from its original position. Nicklaus smiled at his error along with the amused crowd. The pressure was on.

Nicklaus could have argued that his error was proof that his career was fading and have said with some justification, "I've never had a shot as bad as that since I've been on the pro tour. It's time to quit." He could have made his worst fear a reality by yielding his competitive edge to his negative beliefs and returning to the clubhouse a loser in more ways than one.

However, Nicklaus knew that he had to rise above the pressures that had built up over the course of the tournament and take each moment as it came. He had to accept that his next shot was an independent event in its own right, with neither history nor memory.

He knew that the only context the moment had was the way he felt about himself. Each moment is unencumbered, always new. It is tainted or ennobled by the perception of the performer. The performer makes the moment.

Nicklaus relaxed and hit a remarkable shot. The ball hit the flag and landed in the cup. He was one under par for the hole, made his sixty-five, and won. He had chosen to see his error as just another obstacle to overcome on the way to his goal. It was not to be taken as the reason he failed.

You could argue that Jack Nicklaus is, after all, Jack Nicklaus and has all his incredible experience to fall back on, but the larger truth is that he became Jack Nicklaus by paying attention to countless difficult moments in the exact same way and creating that greater experience. It was the sum of the moments that made Jack Nicklaus, but it was also Jack Nicklaus who made each moment work for him.

Winning over Toxic Nostalgia is exactly like this. You have to live in the moment even though your past emotions divert you. The real issue is, what point do you want to make? You have all the evidence you need to prove whatever you want about yourself. You can press the negative argument your Emotional Debt suggests, become self-destructive, and fail just by holding back that extra effort that it takes to make you perform at your peak. No one would blame you, certainly not those people who are trying to surpass you. They'll be the most understanding and forgiving of your failure.

Forgive yourself for your past mistakes. Put your errors in true perspective. An error only means that you made an error and aren't perfect. What a relief! Now take the energy you get from accepting a worthy challenge and use it to concentrate. When you see the moment as exciting rather than fearful, you conquer your doubts by becoming more alive. You may argue that you have to believe in yourself to do this, but the truth is that you have to do this to believe in yourself.

Toxic Nostalgia represents the continuing appearance of your unfinished emotional business pressing for resolution. You need to enhance your ability to recognize these symbolic intrusions so you can become aware of the work you need to do to settle your old pain, forgive others and yourself, and be free.

THE FIVE COMPONENTS OF TOXIC NOSTALGIA

When an old feeling is symbolically triggered, it does not return as a perfect replay of the original event but as a mixture of feelings and attitudes, reflecting several stages in the mourning process. Because there are many parts to these episodes, they can be confusing and difficult to understand. They can be disquieting because you probably hoped that these triggered feelings had been settled long ago.

1. THE UNMOURNED FEELING: THE PAIN THAT STILL NEEDS TO HEAL

When you are in the throes of acute mourning, there are moments when your denial seems to have blocked the full impact of your loss, giving you the illusion of peace. It is an uneasy arrangement. You know you are just catching your breath. After a while your pain breaks through again, flailing your spirit with renewed strength. Even so, that returning hurt is only part of the larger loss, the part you are ready to face. There is more behind it to be felt before your pain is resolved. You feel a loss bit by bit, depending on how much you can tolerate, how open you are, and how much what you have lost meant to you.

In the mourning process your suffering is eroded gradually by waves of the truth. Denial holds back the pain, lets you regroup, and then exposes you to it again until it is gone. Mourning is a struggle between the forces of truth and the defenses shielding you from it until, after a while, relief begins to dominate.

Therefore, each toxic nostalgic event is just another in a series of exposures to resolving pain. However, when the acute mourning period has passed and the pain has aged, it may be combined with other unresolved pain and mourned together. This makes the later reappearance of several old feelings seem illogical and confused.

It makes perfect sense that the part of the old feeling that intrudes is the unresolved grief you must still attend to. This is why it feels so painful.

The return of unmourned pain is a powerful part of the toxic nostalgic experience. It catches you by surprise. Your belief in your invincibility is challenged, and you are stunned with a renewed sense of loss and sometimes hopelessness.

2. DEFENSIVENESS: THE WAY YOU PROTECT YOURSELF

When unresolved old pain breaks through, it has just defeated the defenses that have long held it in place. For that reason not only is the pain visible, so are the defenses that have contained it. Because it takes considerable effort to contain the pain, the defenses are likely to assert themselves with renewed vigor, a logical reaction to having just been overwhelmed.

If you can get some distance at this moment, you can gain great insight into your avoidance patterns. The defenses that reveal themselves at this time may not only involve denial, blaming, excuses, pretending, or one of their variations, but also character traits and automatic behavior. In fact the defining element of the toxic nostalgic manifestation is the defensive and characterological style that is brought forth to contain recently released feelings.

Another way of seeing Toxic Nostalgia is to think of it as a sudden defensive response to a stimulus.

Roland was a psychiatrist who was having a great deal of difficulty in his own psychotherapy coming to terms with his personality flaws. Although he portrayed himself as open and honest, when it came to discussing his own feelings he was secretive and elusive, a trait that he refused to admit. When he was threatened Roland would act superior and self-righteous and find ways to put down his adversaries as he pulled away. He would usually do this with a laugh that had a peculiar, annoying edge to it.

Roland refused to accept his psychiatrist's suggestion that they discuss his character traits and insisted in talking about his troubled childhood instead. When the psychiatrist refused to listen to his endless blaming and told Roland that at the next session they would focus on his personality quirks and his avoidance, Roland laughed in the psychiatrist's face, accepting the challenge, ready to prove he was perfection itself.

When Roland knew he was going to discuss a touchy subject, he sometimes would be late to his therapy session, always with an excuse that revealed how important he was to his patients. His therapist once commented on this as a form of avoidance, so Roland on the day of the important appointment left a half hour early so he wouldn't be late.

On the way to the session Roland reviewed his situation and thought of his psychiatrist's allegations. How mistaken he is, Roland thought. How perfectly silly. Roland's concerns began to lift as he pictured himself in his mind's eye defeating the therapist, proving he was open and brave. As he traveled along the highway he became more and more convinced he was right. He felt stronger with each mile and used that as proof to reassure himself that he wasn't afraid to confront the truth about himself. In a moment of absolute giddiness, Roland began to laugh his odd laugh. It sounded so odd even to him that it woke him from his reverie.

Roland suddenly began to scream. He realized he was traveling in the wrong direction at over a hundred miles an hour. The reason he was feeling better with each passing mile was that he was a mile farther away from the confrontation he claimed he was not afraid of facing. He saw through his obvious defensiveness of pulling away for the first time.

Roland's Toxic Nostalgia was shaped by his exaggerated defensiveness. The defensive behavior that is triggered by the symbolic threat is designed to smooth things over, to prevent abandonment or limit further loss. It is a desperate attempt to ply the old defensive habit once more in the hope that this time it will work.

Every example of Toxic Nostalgia involves a display of defenses or personality style, sometimes obvious, but often so subtle that it is hard to see. When a person becomes arrogant like Roland, his behavior is easy to recognize, but people also exhibit less obvious forms of defensiveness at such times. They may act strangely indifferent, falsely modest, prideful, overly generous, or inappropriately apologetic to the very person who has hurt them.

As it did for Roland, understanding the triggered defensive style can be the greatest gift of the toxic nostalgic experience.

3. REGRESSION: THE WAY YOU WERE WHEN YOU WERE HURT

Sometimes even more debilitating than the returning feeling is the sudden displacement in time you feel as you are transported to the moment when the old hurt took place. You feel like a child again, helpless, frightened, and overwhelmed. You are remembering not only what happened to you but what you were like at the time. Since you were probably less able to defend yourself then, you feel more vulnerable and have a greater need to be defensive. This explains why when some people are triggered in this way they become rigid and frozen, as if expecting the worst.

In a toxic nostalgic episode you feel as if you have been transported back to the time when the old triggered injury originally occurred. You tend to see the world, not as your mature self, but as the person you were then, someone who lacks your present experience and wisdom. In spite of knowing better, you tend to act childishly; revealing your character flaws, becoming needy, controlling, or impulsive. You're certainly not at your best, and your performance feels obligatory, not a matter of choice. You are acting from weakness and doubt. Even though you're pretty sure you're no longer this way, you begin to wonder.

Such regressions can be deeply demoralizing and difficult to put in perspective, because it is your perspective itself that is compromised when you regress. What complicates the matter further is that the perspective that you regress to may be much more childish than the feeling that is triggered and therefore even more difficult to place. The following case illustrates this point.

When Doris's boyfriend impulsively broke off their engagement, she panicked and developed severe stomach cramps that put her to bed for days, unable to hold down food. Her roommate was unable to reassure her. Doris talked about how this always seemed to happen to her. She began to obsess about a boyfriend who had rejected her when she was in high school as if it had just happened.

Doris became infantile and helpless. The two rejections seemed to combine to torment her, but neither could fully explain her severe regression. She became negative and whined and was so unwilling to accept her roommate's helpful suggestions that the roommate finally went away for the weekend in disgust, leaving Doris to solve her problems by herself.

All alone in the apartment, Doris began to remember being abandoned by her mother after her father died in an automobile crash when she was five. Her mother had never gotten along with Doris's father and after his sudden death began to date compulsively, often leaving Doris alone without a baby-sitter. Doris was close to her father and saw her mother's actions as a betrayal both of herself and of her father. Fearing punishment if she cried, Doris held her mourning inside. Over the years it evolved into a yearning for a man to replace her father and a tendency to expect more in relationships than was realistic. This in turn led her to act needy and to possess the men she loved, causing them to push her away, thus creating the very abandonment Doris feared facing but still had to work through.

When her boyfriend rejected her, Doris "remembered" the state of abandonment she experienced after her father died. She attached this point of view to the memory of losing her high school boyfriend, the first person she ever risked depending on after her father died. The isolation Doris felt when her roommate left intensified her feeling of abandonment and allowed her to remember her old state of mind. In the middle of her pain, Doris realized that although she was sad over both her boyfriend's rejection and the memory of how her teenage relationship had gone sour, it was recalling how powerless she felt after losing her father that cut so deep. Once she realized the source of her regressed perspective, Doris was able to talk about missing her father and her anger at her mother for the first time.

Allowing yourself to feel your old feelings and follow them where they will go can have the power to integrate past and present. Spontaneous cures probably use a mechanism similar to what Doris experienced, a vivid reexperience of a forgotten hurtful episode.

4. Guilt: The Emotional Debt to Be Released

It is a rare person who cannot relate to the following.

Someone hurts you in a way that feels vaguely familiar. Before you begin to express yourself, you are caught in a confusing web of doubt that stymies you. Instead of having the courage to speak up, you feel unworthy. Even though the other person is clearly at fault and the hurt unprovoked, you question whether you did something to deserve it. Your mind considers the possibilities. Perhaps you're really a bad person and the other person senses it. In your heart you know this reasoning is not true, and yet these guilty thoughts resonate within you. Your self-doubt keeps you from defending yourself.

Part of your response can be understood as a downloading of old guilt from Emotional Debt. There is always some guilt accompanying a triggered emotional episode. These old feelings of unworthiness lead you to react incorrectly to the events of the present. Since you doubt yourself, you do not speak up for your present hurt but withdraw instead. This keeps you from resolving the present problem and insures that the original problem stays hidden. These feelings of guilt can also lead you to overreact defensively to the present by protesting too much.

For some people the emergence of this old guilt at the time they are hurt precipitates an emotional decompensation, as it did when Richard saw presents fall from his grandson's piñata, reminding him of his old anger over being deprived. Instead of being able to use the toxic nostalgic event as a second chance to resolve old guilt, Richard took the reappearance of old guilt as a confirmation that he was bad; the older couple turning off the highway proved it conclusively.

It feels unfair that you should be punished from within and without at the same time, but that is the essence of Toxic Nostalgia. The external injury you suffer may be unintentional, the result of thoughtlessness or the residual irritation from someone's bad day. However, the internal torture you put yourself through is the crueler of the two and has deeper roots. You have concluded long ago that you were bad. The person who now hurts you only reawakens that old belief.

This guilty intrusion leads you to delay your emotional response, to act self-destructively and thus reinforce your belief that you are unworthy. In this way old guilt is sanctioned to throw you off-balance and can become the determining event of so-called emotional breakdowns. It is important to realize when you are suddenly feeling guilty after being hurt that the experience is Toxic Nostalgia and a function of your internalized anger. You need to act against it and speak your hurt, not give in to it and be sullen.

Again, as uncomfortable as these intrusive feelings are, they are all part of the natural healing process. They reappear because they still need to be resolved. Their return should be seen as an opportunity to heal.

Welcome these feelings into your life and allow yourself to experience them. Some guiding thoughts:

> *Put aside your self-doubt.*
> *Resist getting lost in your emotions.*
> *Try to learn from them.*
> *Take some distance.*
> *What is the feeling you are feeling?*
> *What does the feeling mean?*
> *If it is anxiety, what loss looms?*
> *If it is hurt, seek the cause.*
> *If it is anger, seek the hurt.*
> *Accept that the feeling has some truth in it.*
> *Try to remember when you first felt this way.*
> *Ask yourself:*
>> *How was I hurt before?*
>> *What feelings did I conceal at that time?*
>> *Why? What did I fear?*
>> *With whom do I still need to make peace?*

5. THE RECOLLECTION OF HEALING: THE PATH TO RESOLUTION

When an incompletely mourned pain is triggered into awareness, it not only brings with it the original context of the hurt and the old guilt but also some of your acceptance, the healing perspective. Some part of the old pain has been processed. Reminding yourself that you have worked through much of this pain before and have found some peace can give you the strength to face the part you have not mourned.

Unfortunately when a negative feeling is triggered the part that is most prominent is the unresolved part, the part that still hurts. It generally commands all your attention and makes you lose your sense of well-being. While much of what you feel seems raw, you need to remind yourself that you have also settled some of the pain as well. You don't have to go through all of it again to find peace.

For example, when settling a loved one's residual affairs a year after his death, you experience great sadness. In some way the loss seems even more real, because after all this time, all your wishing and yearning have still proven fruitless. The loss still stands. Even so, you have surely mourned some part of the loss before and that mourning has not been wasted. While you may be unhappy going through your loved one's belongings and settling the estate, it is not as painful as it was some months earlier.

Still, there are sharp edges in your recollection, moments when your grief captures you anew. You catch yourself seeing a familiar face in a crowd, hoping against hope it is your loved one, but you really know all along the hoping is futile, because some mourning has taken place and supplanted false hope. Peace is settling in on you.

Sadness gradually replaces shock as the healed part of the loss is brought forward with it.

You need to remember the healing that has been accomplished and allow it to reassure you. Even if it makes you sad, you are getting through it, even if it is taking a long time, even if it doesn't seem to be getting better.

You need to remember that the injury was then and this is now. A lot of healing has taken place. Persist. Be brave. Look at what still must be faced. You need to reassure yourself that you have already endured the worst.

This painful episode has shown you that you are capable of resolving the past and moving on. Hold on to that resolve. Move forward.

Remember this healing perspective in the middle of a toxic nostalgic recollection, to identify and experience your feelings and then let go.

Say to yourself, "I am better now—not completely, but better nonetheless."

TRIGGERS

The natural therapeutic process is dedicated to the continual dislodging of unresolved pain and to pushing it to the surface so it can be worked on.

The power of the triggers that launch this healing mechanism is derived only from their reflection of a concealed truth. Even though it may appear otherwise, these triggers have no power of their own. Still, it's common for people to come to fear what has triggered their pain. People need to be reminded that although the triggering event is innocuous, it has touched on something real, and that while the old hurt is merely being remembered and not happening in the present, it urgently needs to be dealt with.

This explains why a therapist who tries to be too supportive can prolong your hurt. Minimizing a painful truth undermines the natural therapeutic process and in a sense encourages you to bury your pain again. Without facing all the truth, you allow residual pain to remain in Emotional Debt, which leaves you vulnerable to being triggered again.

The self-acceptance of healing only comes with the acceptance of all the triggered truth.

TRIGGERING EVENTS

While triggered feelings are usually negative, the triggering event itself may be unpleasant, neutral, or even happy, such as attending a joyous family gathering and realizing that a loved one's absence can no longer be denied. The precipitating event encapsulates the dynamics of a toxic nostalgic episode. You can't understand the event if you don't understand what precipitated it.

Understanding the precipitating event takes into account your character type, your defensive armor, and your past history. It also measures your emotional fatigue and your resilience. If you have suffered many losses, you become brittle and are easily brought down by a disappointment you could have shrugged off perhaps just a year or so ago. You are still the same person type with the same defenses and life experience. All that is different is that your emotional reserves have been depleted.

Emotional resources are consumed by the work of maintaining defenses to contain feelings. Thus when Emotional Debt is high, you have less energy available to cope and adapt and the likelihood of being triggered is greatest.

KINDS OF TRIGGERS

The events that liberate your unresolved pain are usually losses that remind you of older losses. Sometimes a memory intrudes on its own. Sometimes it returns in symbolic form.

DREAMS. A series of troubling dreams, in which a feeling from the past reappears in disguised form, can precipitate a toxic nostalgic episode. It is the disguise of the dream that allows the feeling to come to the surface. Although dreams are renowned for their ability to conceal the true identity of unresolved pain, it is common for dreams to be disturbing.

People often wonder about a dream's significance, especially when it shows them hurting someone they are supposed to love. It is the excessiveness of the feeling in the dream that makes it worrisome. However, when that disturbing feeling is placed in the context of the Feeling Cycle, the real meaning of the dream becomes apparent, and the power of the dream to initiate such episodes becomes understandable.

For example, if you dream that you kill your friend, it doesn't necessarily mean that you want to kill your friend. In the language of dreams killing is simply a symbolic expression of anger. You often use the word *kill* innocently, saying, "He killed me with his backhand," or "That just kills me." You didn't mean "kill" as literally as your dream depicted. Killing someone in your dreams needs to be seen in the context of the natural therapeutic process and means only that you have been injured and are angry.

A disturbing dream can become a triggering event when it unlocks the unadmitted truth of your feelings. A period of troublesome dreams can free up a blocked mourning process and precipitate inhibited grief.

REPETITIVE HURTS. A series of repetitive hurts can overwhelm you and act like a trigger by making it impossible for you to avoid what is bothering you. When we speak of people hitting bottom and reaching their breaking point, we really mean that a series of hurts has finally exceeded the capacity of their Emotional Debt to conceal the truth. They have to face themselves. There is no place else to go.

People go from one loveless relationship to another before they get to the point where they are getting so little out of life they finally ask, "What am I doing to myself?"

Sometimes it is only after suffering the additive effect of a series of disastrous alcoholic relationships that people who have survived an alcoholic upbringing finally realize alcohol has been a problem in their life and begin to do something about it.

This same principle applies to survivors of incest. It is almost as if they need to place themselves in abusive situations over and over again until finally their accumulated abuse exceeds their ability to deal with it and triggers their awareness of earlier episodes. When it does they realize it has been going on all the time.

In Max's case the trigger was a hurt that closed off his emotional escape valve. It came at the end of a series of losses when his resistance was low enough to allow a final hurt to pierce his defensive veil and precipitate a crisis.

Max was a businessman whose father had little belief in his business ability and had relegated him to managing a division of the family company that was of minimal importance so if Max failed he would not damage the entire company. Being treated like a failure caused Max considerable pain, which he counterbalanced by telling himself he would have been a huge success as a professional athlete.

After his father's death Max took over the company and started to act imprudently. His self-destructiveness was his way of dealing with his guilt over being so angry at his father. When his subsidiary failed, he felt obligated to support it with renewed influxes of cash from the main company, depleting resources and pushing the main business to the point of failure. At the same time, his wife had an affair with a close friend. Next, right after providing his daughter with an expensive marriage that he borrowed to finance, she informed him that she didn't want to talk to him anymore. On top of all this, for the first time in a decade he lost his club golf championship and became deeply depressed.

While it took a series of losses to soften Max up, it was the loss of the club championship that finally triggered his depression. He'd always believed that if all else failed he could someday turn professional. Now that he had lost his country club tournament, he knew this was no longer true and he had no fantasy place to hide in to console himself. Max suddenly felt trapped in his failure and forced to deal with all the feelings he had buried.

TEARS. Sometimes you can be triggered into recalling a loss by simply allowing yourself to cry. The present hurt may be entirely unrelated to the buried emotions that are stirred. What is important is that some safe situation in the present provides an opportunity for you to cry. Even nonspecific tears can suddenly open an emotional connection to some forgotten loss for which tears have not been shed. The flood of such released tears can be overwhelming and their intensity deep. These distant sobs from a forgotten source can be puzzling. "I just couldn't stop crying," you say, and then you feel vulnerable as all the elements of the toxic nostalgic episode surround you without identifying themselves. Sometimes you catch a glimpse of an old loss and have a chance to mourn it. Other times the source of the old tears remains a mystery.

PROXY. Observing others in a painful situation that you once suffered can act as a trigger. You find yourself supporting them with an unexpected yet familiar passion and become deeply involved. Because it reminds you of how you were unfairly treated as a child, you overreact to the boss's mistreatment of a new employee by becoming outraged or obsessed. Which injury are you defending—his or yours?

Discovering the context of your pain depicted in art, theater, film, or literature can provide both the cathartic experience to resolve your pain by proxy and also act as the precipitant event for pain that is defensively walled off. Art has a way of sneaking behind the defenses and making you feel.

The proxy mechanism is typical for the triggering of episodes of posttraumatic stress. Flashbacks are usually triggered by the sufferer mistakenly perceiving parts of his repressed experience in his current reality. The stirred emotions can sometimes annex themselves to the triggering event, making the past event feel as if it is actually recurring. These experiences are especially terrifying. Not only is the person unexpectedly confronted with the past he has blocked, he is also now worried about what is real and what is imagined as well as whether or not he is crazy.

For some sufferers merely reading the previous paragraph serves as a trigger of past uncertainty.

SIMILAR LOSSES. Any current loss that feels similar to an inhibited old feeling can serve as the emotional trigger that reactivates the unmourned pain.

CHARACTEROLOGICAL TRIGGERS

Any loss that represents a significant character issue can act as a triggering event for the respective character type. Often it was such a loss that was instrumental in shaping the person's defensive style to begin with.

DEPENDENT TRIGGERS: DEATH, ABANDONMENT, AND BETRAYAL. While everyone is susceptible to being triggered by the loss of a loved one, dependent people are highly sensitive to losses that suggest rejection or abandonment.

It is typical for an old inhibited grief reaction to be triggered by a current loss. The earlier loss has silently eroded the sufferer's flexibility and primed him to react catastrophically. When the old grief is awakened, it attaches itself to the present loss and creates a situation of protracted mourning that often evolves into depression. As a result the grief reaction in the present cannot be fully resolved until the earlier loss is also identified and addressed.

CONTROLLING TRIGGERS: DIMINUTION OF POWER. Any financial setback or threat of reversals has the power to trigger the controlling person because he invests so much of his self-esteem in his hopes for acquisition of power and influence. Typically the controlling person responds to financial crisis by being triggered into acting more rigid and self-willed, so his anxiety may not even be noticed. Erosion of his power base makes him fear he will lose control of others and therefore makes him highly vulnerable to abandonment, his underlying dependent concern for which his controlling behavior was originally designed to protect him.

COMPETITIVE TRIGGERS: FAILURE. Any failure, but especially one for which responsibility cannot be avoided, can create an opening in the competitive person's awareness and trigger a crisis of confidence. When self-confidence plummets, defeating his ability to pretend, the competitive person can now see his previous failures as his fault.

It is a sobering moment, shaking him deeply and triggering low self-esteem. Instead of saying, "I have failed," the competitive person says, "I am a failure," and may actually display his shortcomings in detail to prove this point. Sometimes his protestation of *mea culpa* becomes overly dramatic and gets carried to such an extreme that it seems as if the competitive person is exaggerating, merely pretending to be a failure in order to claim later on that he was not a failure at all.

Still, anything that symbolizes failure will trigger the competitive personality to be overwhelmed, or pretend to be overwhelmed, or not to care as usual.

FORMS OF TOXIC NOSTALGIA

Whenever you hide from a painful truth you become susceptible to Toxic Nostalgia. Even though a toxic nostalgic event can be deeply disturbing, it should always be seen as part of the natural dynamic by which healing operates to restore and maintain emotional balance.

The readjustment Toxic Nostalgia tenders is entirely necessary to put your accounts in balance. It is as natural as rain. Toxic Nostalgia can appear in as many forms as there are human symptoms of suffering.

First of all, mourning is not Toxic Nostalgia. However, excessive mourning that is tainted by past losses is.

Included in Toxic Nostalgia are:

Excesses beyond the expected feeling response to an event, such as paralyzing caution, prolonged suffering, persistent anger, or unremitting remorsefulness.

Oversensitivity to the success or failure of others, especially in the form of jealousy or envy.

Continual intrusions of self-doubt and low self-esteem.

Mood disturbances or unexplained extremes in feelings, whether acute, such as anxiety states, or more chronic, such as depression, guilt, and shame.

Obsessional problems such as addictions, eating disorders, and behavioral problems, and of course, brooding and obsessive dwelling.

The triggered manifestations of characterological flaws are also included, such as suddenly acting rigidly and willfully dependent, controlling, or competitive. Another example is when a person is triggered to feel unlovable, powerless, bad, stupid, a failure, or unattractive, the guilt messages again. These reemerging feelings can disguise themselves and contribute to bad relationships, poor job performance, difficulties in getting along with others, and a fear of risking or commitment, making them difficult to identify and define.

HOW TOXIC NOSTALGIA APPEARS

Typically when the emotions of the past are triggered, your reaction to the present seems inappropriate. With only your response to guide them, others have no way of knowing what lies behind your actions when you overreact, seem excessive, or act out of control.

In the middle of a toxic nostalgic episode it is common to believe that the past is repeating itself. You can easily find villains and betrayers, crooks and liars, ingrates and abusers, and you can point to evidence to support your belief. However, your inappropriate attitude has merely re-created a response in others similar to your past experience. There is great power in understanding this.

In a toxic nostalgic response:

The dependent person, by claiming others are abandoning her, makes others want to abandon her.

The controlling person, feeling cheated, tries to control others, who feel taken advantage of by him and want to get even and use him.

The competitive person acts as if he doesn't care, that nothing really matters, and so others, offended by his selfishness, feel he had his failure coming to him and offer no sympathy.

TOXIC NOSTALGIA VERSUS REMEMBERING A LOSS

Simply remembering a loss brings forth sadness as parts of it are felt again. It is easy to identify the feelings that return as being related to the particular memory. While something in the present may remind you of your loss, such as coming across an old picture, the memory is not an unwelcome or disruptive intrusion. The memory may bring sadness, even alter the feelings of the moment, but the old loss is only remembered, not relived, not presented as an urgent feeling to be resolved.

The strength of the stimulus that provokes a memory determines the depth of the recalled feeling, whereas in Toxic Nostalgia the response may be out of all proportion to the event that stirred it.

The remembered feeling tends to resolve quickly. The old loss can be discussed because it is not defended against and also does not present with a trapped, negative force that needs to be discharged. However, if tearful memories are excessive and frequent, they are a manifestation of inhibited or prolonged grief and as such are a form of Toxic Nostalgia.

By contrast, in Toxic Nostalgia feelings or behavior intrude without warning, "out of nowhere," without your being aware of their origin or meaning. The precipitating event is usually symbolic, without reminding you of what you've been secretly repressing.

The toxic nostalgic response is sudden, excessive, and produces anxiety and sometimes a feeling of going crazy as the emotional dam bursts. There is no comfort in what is recalled, merely more pain. The feelings of Toxic Nostalgia displace you. They feel familiar and alien at the same time.

The triggered emotional state does not fade in an orderly manner. More likely, it initiates an extended period of discomfort, a bad feeling that you don't understand and just cannot shake off.

In the toxic nostalgic episode you may act out your old hurts, creating a psychodrama in the midst of your present life. It is as if you need to have some event to which you can attach your old feelings. You insist, even though you don't really understand why, that a present event caused your feelings.

It is difficult to see past connections to the present Toxic Nostalgia episode because the events are clouded by defenses. Time has distorted the details, responsibility is avoided, and the coalescence of other feelings held in Emotional Debt blurs the facts.

While a remembered hurt also suffers from the distortions of time, it tends to remain a much clearer recollection. Even if it is painful, it is discrete and understandable. The emotions feel in scale with events. There is nothing surprising about it. Just consider the loss you are remembering, and your reaction makes perfect sense.

TYPICAL MANIFESTATIONS OF TOXIC NOSTALGIA

While many toxic nostalgic manifestations are precipitated feeling states, others manifest as illogical behavior or unproductive attitudes that are maintained over a long time, such as prejudices, false beliefs, self-destructive living, and work patterns. As many of the following examples will show, these confusing, painful episodes create a powerful momentum to heal.

REPETITIVE RELATIONSHIP PROBLEMS

Relationship problems that repeat are seldom about the issues that appear on the surface. Some relationships can be a toxic nostalgic experience all by themselves.

Although at the age of twenty-three Paul was the top luxury car salesman in his dealership, he needed constant adulation. He lived with Michelle, who lived in fear of abandonment. To control Paul Michelle focused all her energy on him, making him feel as if he were the center of her world. While the attention felt wonderful to Paul at first, Michelle soon became jealous and suspicious. She accused Paul of wanting sex with every woman he looked at. She even became jealous of his male friends and would drop in at the dealership unannounced and become jealous when he talked with customers.

Paul's father had divorced his mother when he was four. His mother could not bear feeling abandoned and cast Paul in the role of her "little husband." When Paul became an adolescent, his pain over being controlled was unbearable. He tried to break away but was thwarted by his mother, who made him feel guilty by demanding to know how he could be so unappreciative of all that she had sacrificed on his behalf. His buried anger caused his self-esteem to deteriorate.

Paul found himself highly susceptible to Michelle's smothering behavior because it reminded him of the way his mother controlled him. Michelle also punished him by entrapping him. This seemed to neutralize his hidden anger.

Two days after he broke up with Michelle, Paul found himself attracted to a woman just because she showered him with intense attention, which made him feel like the center of the world again. Within a week she moved in with him, except this time Paul began to feel anxious as his new girlfriend immediately started to follow him from room to room. He found himself blowing up at her for clinging to him and suddenly realized that he'd chosen two identically difficult women in a row. Although the situation felt familiar, he could not imagine what would lead him to do something like this.

Paul was stunned when it was pointed out that he wasn't really interested in either woman but was still angry at his mother and needed someone to punish him the way she used to. When he realized that it was possible to feel angry and still be a good person, Paul was finally able to forgive his mother and break his repetitive cycle.

FAMILIAR DISCOMFORT

Whenever Joanna was verbally and physically abused by her husband, instead of becoming angry she became powerless, overwhelmed with feelings of self-hatred and hopelessness. She would regress to thinking the way she did as an adolescent and conclude that she instigated the abuse and deserved to be treated this way.

In telling her story Joanna recognized that she first felt this way when she was sexually abused by her brother. She had tried to get help from her parents then, but they did not believe her and punished her instead for even suggesting such a thing.

Although she did not want to stay married, Joanna found herself mired in familiar feelings of discomfort. The abuse felt so much like something she was accustomed to that she thought it would be wrong to take her husband to court. She feared she was the one who would be declared at fault because her pent-up anger might leak out and show everyone she was not a good person, a common theme in Toxic Nostalgia perhaps, but also the source of shame for the incest survivor.

One day Joanna's husband threatened her with a knife. She became faint but found a reservoir of strength, stood her ground for the first time, picked up her child, and ran out of the house to start a life of her own.

Some months following her separation Joanna went on a camping trip with some old friends she hadn't seen since her youth. Unfortunately, they told her how to dress, when to get up, and criticized her for wanting to spend some time by herself. The second morning of the trip Joanna awoke after a night of troublesome dreams, feeling transported back to childhood. She awoke reasoning that she had no clothes to wear to school and was afraid of being laughed at. She found it impossible to get out of her sleeping bag. The abuse of Joanna's friends caused her old attitude of hopelessness and powerlessness along with her old point of view to resurface.

The more emotion that is stored, the more easily it can be spilled. Because Joanna had lived a life of secrecy and concealed her hurt, she felt somehow in collusion with her abusers. This made it difficult to defend herself and allowed her to tolerate abusiveness. Since Joanna suffered years of abuse from many sources and kept it from expression, she was susceptible to experiencing multiple episodes of Toxic Nostalgia. Joanna was brimming with so much hurt that her suppressed rage could be triggered by any abusive event. At the same time her old defenses would be activated and redirect her anger inside, causing her to believe she deserved to be hurt, and the cycle would continue.

Fortunately, learning to fight one battle gave Joanna the courage to correct other wrongs. As she lay in the sleeping bag with her friends barking orders, Joanna remembered how brave she had been when her husband threatened her with the knife. It gave her courage. To her friends' surprise she got up, packed her camping gear, and walked out of the forest. Little by little Joanna began to substitute a pattern of assertion in place of her automatic victim response.

The healing process gathers momentum from each success.

IRRATIONAL OBLIGATION

An irrational obligation is almost always a cover for concealed guilt.

Jim wanted to be less connected to Emily, his twenty-two-year-old daughter, now that she had left home and was married. However, he felt compelled to send her money and acted overprotective whenever he was with her. He knew something was wrong but couldn't place the feeling.

Jim took custody of Emily, his only daughter, when she was fourteen. His wife had lost custody because her new husband had molested Emily. At the time Emily moved in, Jim was living alone with few social contacts. Because Emily had not grown up in his house, Jim did not expect her to be so grown-up. Unsure of what a father should do, he regarded Emily as his companion. They went to the movies, out to dinner, and hiked in the woods together. Emily was Jim's only female companion since he divorced.

Jim felt a powerful obligation to be protective of Emily that was only in part a response to the fact that she'd been molested. Although he could not identify them clearly, Jim also had some sexual feelings toward Emily, which he had never experienced before. He set the frightening feelings aside and concentrated on protecting Emily from ardent suitors without ever realizing that he was really a little worried about his own interest in her. As Emily grew into a woman and left his house, these unrecognized feelings remained in place and with them feelings of shame and discomfort, which prompted him to feel over-protective.

It was pointed out that Jim's feelings were not uncommon. It was suggested that had he friends to confide in he would have realized he was not abnormal to have such feelings and would have quickly dismissed his fear that he might be a molester like his ex-wife's husband. When this was explained, Jim's anxiety faded and with it his need to be overly protective.

Always ask what you are making up for by fulfilling the irrational obligation. What is the hidden fear?

REPEATING THE ABUSE

Sometimes a pattern of abusive behavior becomes established as a toxic nostalgic response.

Felice was afraid that her unsuccessful attempts to manage her sixteen-year-old daughter would cause the daughter to leave home, something Felice greatly feared. Felice restricted her daughter severely, refusing to allow her to leave the house after school or visit friends even at reasonable times. The daughter was an excellent student, had never been any kind of a problem until, wanting to be like the other girls, she began to resist her mother's unreasonable demands.

Felice was in a panic, knowing that her demands were unreasonable and that it was her daughter's task to grow independent and eventually leave. She could not understand what drove her to be so controlling.

Felice revealed without the slightest hesitation that she was the youngest of six children and, as was customary in her culture, her mother had insisted that she not marry but stay home and take care of her. When asked how she had felt about that arrangement, Felice admitted she didn't like it but had played the role of the obedient daughter and had to struggle to leave home. Then, to her complete surprise, Felice blurted out that she hated her mother for abusing, beating, and controlling her.

When it was pointed out that Felice was treating her daughter the same way her mother treated her, she gave an audible gasp of disbelief. As obvious as her motivations were for controlling her daughter, Felice had never made the connection. Felice realized that her daughter was expressing the very feelings she had wished to share with her mother and was making the rebellion Felice wished she'd started. The daughter's protest became doubly fearful for Felice because she was still trying to suppress her old rebellion.

Felice had always wanted her mother's power, and when she finally became a mother she claimed it. When Felice's own inhibited adolescent rebellion was brought to the surface by her daughter's defiance, she felt she not only had to control her daughter but herself as well.

The event that triggered Felice into acting like her mother was very subtle. Her daughter reached the age when Felice was first abused, and Felice identified with her.

The victim of abuse, by victimizing someone in the way he was abused, becomes an abuser as a way of symbolically ridding himself of his old hurt and anger. Unfortunately the plan is flawed and serves to create more guilt and another generation of abusers.

EMOTIONAL BLOCKS

Sometimes a toxic nostalgic event is characterized by the sudden intrusion of defenses that leads to an absence of emotions where one would expect to have intense feelings. The blocking of an emotion is not as dramatic as the abrupt appearance of a triggered emotional state and yet it can be every bit as painful. When a veil of indifference descends between you and those you love, you feel separated and adrift. The blocking of your feelings impoverishes your entire world.

Sharon was a sixty-year-old fashion designer who complained that she was no longer able to show affection. Although she loved her two grandchildren and got along well with her daughter, not to feel love for them made her so uncomfortable that she made excuses not to visit. She knew she loved them, but her belief did not feel attached to any inner feelings of love. The disconnection made her feel "spacey" and intensely anxious.

When asked if there was anyone she didn't have difficulty expressing feelings of love to, Sharon immediately responded, "My husband." He had died a few years before. Sharon continued, "When he got sick I suddenly felt I had to be strong for the whole family. It was my duty. I felt I had to set aside my negative feelings and act as if everything was going to be okay." This was a brave face, having been told that her husband had terminal cancer and would not survive the year. In spite of knowing the truth, Sharon assumed her posture of pretending and maintained it with total conviction. She was so successful in blocking her feelings that she was unable to cry at the funeral. Ironically, everyone felt she was magnificent.

Sharon gradually felt herself becoming more distant from people. She felt she was a stranger locked inside her own body as she observed her affection for others fade. The birth of her first grandchild just six weeks after the funeral posed a threat to her. Sharon was aware that she loved her granddaughter and wished to express it, but the risk of opening herself up made her anxious and so she backed away. Her daughter assumed that this was a delayed reaction to the death of her father but did not mention it to Sharon.

When her grandson was born a year later, Sharon's daughter began to ask why she didn't want to spend time with him. However, as soon as Sharon allowed herself to feel her positive feelings, the hurt she'd blocked began to return. These raw, unprocessed negative feelings frightened Sharon. She immediately closed down again and distanced the world. Her discomfort over feeling nothing finally became the force that motivated her to seek help.

Sharon didn't give her relationship with her husband the dignity of her tears, and so his death had no closure. Any expression of feelings frightened her because it symbolized becoming open, challenging her pretense of "being strong," and dealing with her unexpressed grief.

THE EXPRESSIVE PATHWAY

Positive and negative feelings use the same expressive pathway. For that reason when you lower your guard to feel a positive emotion, you also increase the likelihood of feeling unresolved negative feelings. The vulnerability works both ways. This explains why people cry at weddings. They become so open in order to feel all the joy of the event that they also become vulnerable to feeling the related sadness, such as realizing that their child has grown up and is leaving home or that a grandparent didn't live to see the happy day. In fact the positive emotions serve as an emotional shoehorn, allowing the hidden pain of the past to surface. Again, the return of such old negative feelings is a function of the natural healing process that, although it is always getting you to work on unfinished business, often manages to catch you by surprise.

The guiding rule is to let all your feelings flow and experience them as they are.

CHARACTEROLOGICAL RESPONSE PATTERNS

It could be argued that any person with a predominant character type is already displaying Toxic Nostalgia. In fact the sudden intensification of a character flaw is probably the most common form of Toxic Nostalgia. Everyone has a potential for such negative displays of weakness. It is the purpose of the natural therapeutic process to bring you to the point where you can admit the buried hurts that trouble you. Only then can you lower the negative energy that predisposes you to act your worst.

When you suffer a disappointment, especially when you are overloaded with fatigue and stress, it's common to revert to an old defensive attitude, behavior pattern, or rigid style of responding. Your reaction may feel childish and a bit prefabricated, as if a button has been pressed. You don't feel that your true self is responding. The main reason behind this reaction is usually your wish to avoid taking responsibility for your feelings and situation.

What follows are some typical characterological toxic nostalgic responses.

DEPENDENT RESPONSE

You suddenly feel like a helpless child, betrayed and abused by everyone and everything. You parade your injury, displaying how you've been wronged. You give a full recital of the abuses done to you and tell the story of how insult was added to injury, how heartless and cruel others acted. You parade your innocence, how defenseless, pure, trusting, giving, believing, and kind you were. You appeal to the world, crying, "Look at the damage that was done to me." All this is done to get others to join you in blaming your abusers and to make allowances for why you haven't grown up, are still needy, haven't succeeded, overcome adversity, or done better. Poor thing!

The lesson you need to learn is that it's still your fault that your life has turned out the way it has, your complaints about others notwithstanding.

When someone takes advantage of you it's your job to defend yourself. The day you get better you will decide to do that. Until that day you will suffer and feel sorry for yourself and lament that no one cares as you drown in self-pity.

Even if no one cares it's still your responsibility to make yourself happy on your own terms.

CONTROLLING RESPONSE

You are instantly transformed into a self-righteous, arrogant know-it-all.

You have caught the other party red-handed. You declare that you will never forgive or forget what has happened. You make a detailed list of the charges against the other person. You rehearse your argument. You feel totally justified in assuming a punitive, withholding attitude. You alienate even more people when you do, and you blame them for withdrawing from you.

The lesson you need to learn is that regardless of your ability to disprove this, it was your fault that the situation turned out the way it did. If subordinates failed you, you should have known better than to hire them in the first place or to delegate responsibility to them. The question you should ask is not why did they fail, but why didn't you know they weren't capable. It's your responsibility.

Focus on what you did wrong, not how others reacted. You need to risk showing your humanness and your flaws. Your rigid defensive edge isolates you from others.

Your disappointment resulted from concealing your weaknesses. Instead of being open about your shortcomings, you insisted on making others appear wrong or bad. Now they want to break away and be free of your controlling.

What difference does it make if you are always right if no one wants to be with you?

COMPETITIVE RESPONSE

I'll show them. It didn't matter. I wasn't really hurt. You're confusing me with someone who gives a damn!

You declare your indifference a little too arrogantly. You protest your immunity with too much force. It's obvious to everyone that you really care and have been crushed by your failure or rejection and are just trying to save face. However, instead of acting in a way that is honest and vulnerable, you act as if you don't care. This causes others to mistrust you. If you act as if you don't care when you lose something that once seemed important to you, others wonder how much you could care about them. By acting full of pretense you have demonstrated that it is possible for you to appear as self-important a loser as a winner.

The lesson you need to learn is that the people who love you love you because you're human, not because you're perfect. They love you most because you're vulnerable. They respect your successes more when they know how frightened you were when you risked and how brave you were to overcome such deep self-doubt, for that is what a hero is made of. Trying to pass off your accomplishments as if they were easy and your failures as if they were trivial may have been the way you tried to impress people when you were young, but people respect you now for your real talents, for your effort, for your persistence and reliability. The show is over in a flash. What remains is real.

Your most important lessons come when you are honest about your failures.

HELPFUL POINTS

No matter what your character type, when you respond to a stress by suddenly reverting to an old pattern or fixed attitude, you need to pull back a moment and try to stop the automatic replay.

These transformations are often so sudden that you're completely caught up in them. Before you realize it you are pouting like an abused child, ranting like a prosecutor, or acting above it all. In other words you immediately feel phony. You hate yourself for acting this way again. You probably feel obliged to persist in your triggered attitude just to prove your point and cover your psychological trail.

Remember, even though it feels natural and practiced to act this way, you don't have to continue. You can stop.

Become silent. Take a little distance and reevaluate your response. Do you really believe the things you just said? If you don't, tell the other person that you misspoke and correct the false impression that your response conveyed. Granted, this is not easy, but it is a crucial step.

The most important point to understand is that when your characterological pattern is activated, you are almost certainly distorting the truth. Again, correct whatever lie you just told. What is the real source of your hurt? Be brutally honest and admit it to yourself. You may share it if you want, but don't misrepresent it to yourself if you choose to be silent.

If other people have hurt you, why have you not defended yourself or taken steps to free yourself from them? If other people have hurt you, why are you still holding on to your injury as an excuse for your life not being any better? You are always the main obstacle in your way, not other people. You have to risk to be free, not wait for permission.

Instead of trying to be in control, consider what you are afraid of. Hint: you're probably more afraid of being weak than anything else.

If you have failed, ask how you disappointed yourself and what you can learn from the event that just made you act so indifferent.

BASIC RULES

If you are afraid, identify the threat and share it.
If you hurt, say so.
If you are angry, mention your hurt again.

RETURN OF AN OLD DEFENSIVE STYLE

When an old defense pattern is reactivated it sometimes feels as if you have been placed in a trance.

Rick was a forty-year-old writer who sought help for his self-destructive isolating behavior. He had separated from his wife, a crack cocaine addict, after she had severely bitten his ear in a terrible fight during which he felt completely unable to protect himself. So abruptly did he distance himself in the fight that he became totally passive until the flow of blood woke him from his defensive fog. "When I was a kid and had to protect myself," Rick remembered, "I used to pull back and act invisible." Following the fight, he moved into his studio and hid until his loneliness became too much to bear.

As a child Rick had been massively obese, weighing over two hundred pounds by the age of ten. His obesity made him the target of abusive ridicule and also served as the place into which he retreated when he was threatened. At such times he became a passive, silent mass. When he lost weight, he seemed more outgoing, but his pattern of triggered passivity persisted, and whenever he felt threatened he retreated within and waited for the danger to pass. Which is what he did when his wife attacked.

DEFENSIVE PRIDEFULNESS

Pridefulness is a much more subtle form of Toxic Nostalgia to discern since it is often a well-established part of a person's character. However, following a loss or even a series of minor losses that have not been dealt with directly, the hurt that is concealed in Emotional Debt can cause pridefulness to expand to such proportions that it seems to take over a person's life.

Lawrence was a highly successful attorney, an honor student and college football star who married Sally, the homecoming queen. Originally they were a passionate couple, but over the years their relationship gradually lost all intimacy, communication, and physical closeness. Neither partner could recall ever arguing or any conflict. According to them their relationship just faded.

On the surface they appeared like the model family. They were attentive, if not overly affectionate, to their child and maintained a beautiful home. Unfortunately, after they put their child to bed, they were totally isolated and hardly talked.

Lawrence came from a family of "positive thinking, goal-directed over-achievers," to use his words. His overblown sense of pride was an early adaptation to his parents' lack of affection. He got incentives instead. When his father demanded A's, Lawrence became valedictorian *cum arrogance* to show him. At graduation when his father bragged about "*my* son's accomplishment," without bothering to praise Lawrence, Lawrence disdainfully proclaimed, "I could have done better," belittling his father for accepting less than perfection, his pretentious way of covering his hurt.

Lawrence's defensive pride continued to grow more arrogant and separated him from his feelings to the point where he could not admit any need or reveal any weakness. He reacted to stress by portraying the picture of absolute confidence. One weekend Lawrence was robbed at gunpoint. When the police arrived they found him so calm and detached they were convinced he had staged the robbery for the purpose of defrauding the insurance company. During the big Los Angeles earthquake while the family was running for safety, he calmly walked into the bathroom and put on his contact lenses and then with total indifference stepped over the glass and rubble and asked Sally why everyone was so frightened.

Lawrence took on huge amounts of work, trying to demonstrate to his partners that he was Superman. When he and Sally finally took their first vacation in years, he was continually beleaguered by the work he brought along and the frequent phone conferences that he invited. Sally's demands that he relax, have a good time, and be romantic so overwhelmed him that for the first time he was unable to get an erection. While sex between them had been decreasing in frequency for years, at least he had always been able to perform before. Following his sexual failure, Lawrence was shaken, but so bound by pride that he was unable to discuss the problem with Sally.

Sally had confided to a friend that they hadn't had sex in over a year. The friend told her husband, and the word eventually got back to Lawrence. So great was Lawrence's pridefulness that the public embarrassment shocked him more than his own personal discomfort.

Feeling exposed, he experienced a virtual meltdown of self-confidence. He doubted his ability and suspected everyone knew he was a phony, his underlying self-dread in spite of all his accomplishments. He sought help, scheduling his session in midday between an important appointment and a court appearance, in order to carry on the pretense of business as usual. However, he was at his limit and immediately confessed his need for love, his fear of rejection, and when he admitted his prideful arrogance, he broke down in tears.

Lawrence's Toxic Nostalgia was obvious but subtle in design. Whenever Lawrence faced rejection or injury, a compensatory wave of pridefulness captured him, making him seem arrogant and unapproachable. Since pride was part of his character makeup to begin with, the way he handled his family's coldness, it did not seem unusual but merely a continuation of his customary behavior. His toxic nostalgic episode lasted for decades, more apparent at some times than others.

DEFENSIVE CRITICISM

When you live or work with a controlling person, you're well aware of how critical he becomes whenever he is threatened, challenged, or when something does not go his way. This reflex critical response is one of the most common forms of characterological Toxic Nostalgia. When the critical trait flares, it can appear in many forms, all of them irritating.

A typical example is the businessman who comes home after a day's work and when asked about a problem, instead of just being one of the family, barks instructions, treating his family much worse than he would ever dare treat his employees. He just wants to fix the problem with as little discussion as possible. He thinks if he solves the problem he doesn't need to be nice and so comes across as rude and disrespectful of others' feelings. He has done his best to help and can't understand why everyone is angry with him.

The most common manifestation of this critical trait is seen in relationships in which one partner is dependent, weaker, or addicted. The controlling person blames his partner for his unhappiness and feels justified in taking over, which only makes the other partner worse.

In this situation the critical response is usually triggered by the controlling person feeling powerless when the partner's helplessness or addiction is out of control. This is a time of great ugliness on both sides of the addiction. The controlling partner points out the affected partner's faults and broken promises. Everything is blown out of proportion and perspective is lost.

MANAGING THE CRITIC

Dealing with this irrational critical attitude is a touchy subject, because the critical person believes he is right and will recite a list of rationalizations to put you down. Wait for a calm moment and begin with something like the following:

"There is something that is causing me to love you less than I want to love you and it is disturbing me."

This gets the controlling person's attention because he dreads rejection. Continue hesitatingly:

"I know you only mean the best when you do it, . . . but it hurts my feelings . . . and causes me to feel a resentment I don't want to feel."

Wait a moment for a response. Ignore any critical resistance. If you are cut off, begin the conversation again at another calm moment. Then continue.

"If you and I aren't equally important to each other our love will fade."

The controlling person now will insist you come to the point. Pause and with great restraint indicate your hurt. Some samples:

"When you don't listen to my ideas, even if they are wrong, I feel devalued. . . . I just need you to hear them and allow me to be wrong without demeaning me. . . . Respect my right to be wrong."

Or:

"When you order me around I feel hurt."

"I need to be able to disagree with you without going to war."

"Is it all right if my opinion and yours differ?"

Finish your comment in one or two sentences. Immediately thank the other person for listening and say, "See, all I needed was to be heard and to feel I mattered."

Smile and mean it.

This may sound like barely scratching the surface. These questions are designed to be general and unthreatening. You only want to get your overall point across. Try to stay away from specific details. They will provoke an argument. If you can get the controlling person to hear that you are hurt by his style, you have won. Now when he is critical again, and expect him to be, you can remind him of this conversation.

SOMATIC COMPLAINTS

Whenever a physical organ becomes the expressive pathway for an unresolved emotional problem, Toxic Nostalgia is at work. The examples are familiar and include cardiovascular disease, gastrointestinal problems, hormonal dysfunction, and skin diseases, to mention only a few. It is common knowledge that stress creates muscle tension and anger causes headaches. One of the most important parts of any treatment for high blood pressure or angina is learning how to relax.

Often the illnesses that are precipitated by unexpressed emotions become chronic, and when the emotional origins of the symptoms are clouded by time, these illnesses seem especially mysterious and puzzling. The problem is further complicated because the physical symptoms create more stress, which in turn creates more symptoms. Unfortunately, even in enlightened times like today, treatment is often directed at relieving the physical symptoms and not at trying to understand the underlying emotional dynamics.

Any inhibited emotion can find its expression as a somatic symptom.

HIDDEN ANXIETY

Annie was a sixteen-year-old girl who developed severe sinusitis that was unresponsive to treatment. The only findings were some redness and swelling of her nasal passages. Antibiotics and sprays had no effect. After seeing a team of experts, Annie still complained she couldn't breathe.

A sweet girl who had never been a problem before, Annie began to become disruptive in school by suddenly getting up and running out of the classroom. When questioned about her behavior, she would become hostile and sullen. To her parents' dismay Annie also started to hang around with some tough girls.

The problem was obvious, but no one asked Annie what she was afraid of. It turned out that "I can't breathe," meant "I am afraid of suffocating." During the 1994 Los Angeles earthquake, all the contents of her bookshelves fell down onto her bed along with a large section of plaster that crumbled in a choking cloud of dust. In the thirty seconds of violent movement Annie had the feeling that she was going to be buried alive.

In the months following the earthquake, a period of time punctuated by many disturbing aftershocks, Annie adopted a child's perspective and refused to sleep in her room. Instead she slept in the hall outside her parents' bedroom, believing that being closer to her parents was safer. There was some logic to her choice because the hall was also closer to the front door, a possible escape.

Annie was afraid to talk about her feelings because she feared that people would think she was a sissy. This increased the anxiety she stored in Emotional Debt, which made her increasingly vigilant. Each new tremor reinforced her fears that she would be buried in debris and would suffocate.

It was Annie's refusal to admit she was afraid that caused her problems. She didn't think it was "cool" to be afraid and hid her fear from her parents and from her schoolmates. She made friends with the tougher girls to help give the impression she was tough, but the fears that she tried to repress kept intruding. When they did she would find herself in the middle of a replay of the feelings she repressed during the earthquake, causing her to jump out of her seat. To conceal her sudden burst of agitation she pretended she was being rebellious and ran from her reawakened memories and out of the classroom, just as she had wanted to run from her bedroom that night.

Although Annie's behavior was obvious, it wasn't noticed because other family members were also denying their anxiety, being brave as they tried to get their lives back in order. Since Annie's room actually suffered minimal damage compared to the rest of the house, she was told she was lucky and that she should feel thankful instead of afraid. The only acceptable way she could talk about her feelings without losing face was to complain about her inability to breathe. When she admitted she was afraid of being smothered, her sinusitis cleared, virtually overnight.

HIDDEN ANGER

Sometimes you have a suspicion there are emotional causes to your physical symptoms without even being sure how it all fits together.

Laura was a fifty-five-year-old woman, just starting menopause and embarrassed by her moodiness. She developed painful skin eruptions of shingles on her back and chest and wondered if these were psychological in origin because the symptoms developed shortly after a stressful meeting.

Laura was a strong and loyal worker in a company in which byzantine power struggles constantly roiled and threatened stability. During a meeting with her supervisor, who was jealous of Laura and wished to install her own younger friend in Laura's position, the supervisor noticed that Laura was having a hot flash and pointedly asked Laura if she were hot. Then pushing bad taste to the extreme, she went around the table polling the other people in the meeting one by one to see if they felt warm.

Laura was understandably humiliated, but because of the supposedly professional nature of the situation she was unable to defend herself. Instead she internalized her anger, and as a result, her self-esteem fell. Laura felt her rage burning inside and felt powerless and worthless. Shortly after this she developed her skin problem.

Factors that contributed to Laura's Emotional Debt:

Laura's father died before she was four. He was a powerful, controlling person who convinced her mother never to remarry. Laura's mother was cold and repressive and unable to tell Laura she loved her. Laura was raised in an atmosphere that forbade her from expressing her pain of rejection. She grew up angry but didn't know why and struggled to conceal it. She developed a deep hunger for love and affection from an older woman, believing that if she could find that love she would be happy.

When her supervisor humiliated her, Laura's forbidden anger at her mother was reawakened and joined forces with her anger at her supervisor. Stunned by the volume of her response, Laura became convinced she was and had always been bad and therefore had never been deserving, justifying her mother's withholding. Laura's need to suffer to atone and make herself lovable again coincided with her outbreak of shingles.

Laura had to learn that being angry didn't make her bad or make her deserve to suffer.

OTHER FORMS OF TOXIC NOSTALGIA
SUDDEN OUTPOURING OF BLOCKED FEELINGS

Blocked feelings keep coming to the surface until they finally break through.

Edna was a thirty-year-old woman who had been sexually abused by her father and had spent her entire childhood defending herself from his advances. Edna always suspected that her mother knew about her father's activity. His pawing and chasing her were obvious, but her mother remained silent and so Edna was forced to conceal her turmoil. Unable to tolerate living in the house, Edna finally ran away at seventeen, right into another abusive relationship.

When Edna's first baby was found dead in the crib, her husband blamed her and called her a "bad mother." Like all mothers who lose an infant, Edna was already suffering pangs of guilt, and so her husband's accusations fell on fertile emotional grounds. Edna became profoundly depressed. Her old anger at her own mother for being negligent was also stirred up. As was her custom, she tried to bury all these feelings, putting on 150 pounds in less than a year.

Edna's brother, whom she hadn't seen in ten years, came to visit. No sooner had he walked through the door than she realized he looked exactly like her father. She started to spin around in a frenzy, looking for someplace to hide from her reemerging old anger, which had long ago turned into guilt. The guilt over her child's death also surfaced, and when the two combined, Edna suddenly believed she should be punished.

In a delirium of old feelings mixed with new, not knowing whether she was the victim or the villain, Edna found her husband's pistol and tried to shoot her brother. Fortunately, the gun was wrested from her. Unable to tolerate being in her brother's presence and still taking him to be her father, Edna ran out of the house and jumped in front of a truck, trying to kill herself. The truck narrowly missed her. Her brother left, having seen enough. She hid in her room for days until she calmed down.

The next year, just before the Fourth of July, her mother died. When she saw her father at the funeral she became thunderstruck by a powerful urge to kill him and knock over the casket. All she could think of during the service was staying in control and keeping calm. Shocked by the urge, she could not contain herself. Right in the middle of the eulogy, she stood up and ran up in front of the open casket. She was about to start screaming at her mother when she somehow gathered all her strength and once more repressed her anger.

She stood there for a moment, her hands clenched in a fist. Her father approached to calm her. Just as she had run out of her parents' home as a young girl, Edna ran out of the funeral home in a panic, lost in time. She started down the sidewalk, totally immersed in all these feelings and about to lose control. At that very moment a boy threw a firecracker that exploded inches from her face. The effect was to mimic her inner struggle. Edna was not sure if she had exploded.

She collapsed on the sidewalk, unable to continue running from her feelings. At that moment all her repressed memories of abuse returned. All her hurt and anger seemed to be connected to the sources that originally caused them. Edna became severely depressed with the weight of the reality she'd been avoiding, but the acceptance of the truth and the origin of her pain finally initiated healing.

THE HEALING MECHANISM REACTIVATED

It is possible to analyze an old toxic nostalgic episode and initiate the healing process many years later, even after a prolonged period of unexplained symptoms. Indeed, for the natural therapeutic process to be reactivated, it is entirely necessary to return to the former moment of triggered symptoms and dissect the various elements of the episode. For this reason, in relieving anxiety attacks, understanding the very first attack is crucial to healing.

In all such situations some healing has taken place, but the natural process remains arrested by the defenses that have blocked the whole truth from being experienced.

INHIBITED GRIEF

It is common for a grief reaction to be precipitated when a forgotten loss is triggered into recollection. However, if that therapeutic opportunity is ignored and healing is not embraced, the toxic nostalgic event can persist as a lifetime of unexplained symptoms.

Vincent was an eighty-year-old man who suffered from recurrent bouts of anxiety. These began when he was in an army hospital being evaluated for fever in the last days of World War II. On the day of his discharge he discovered a soldier hanging from the pipes in the lavatory. Vincent got beneath the soldier, lifted him on his shoulders, and called for help.

It was a horrifying moment while Vincent stood there waiting, holding up the dead soldier. The weight of the soldier's body and the growing realization that he was dead had a strange and terrifying effect on him. Just as he was about to burst into deep sobs, a chastising thought crossed his mind: Don't you dare cry. Be strong. Then, with the soldier still on his shoulders, Vincent forced back his tears and, for some inexplicable reason, began to worry how he would be able to survive all alone in the world after leaving the army.

After a few minutes two nurses arrived. They removed the dead soldier from Vincent's shoulders, but his anxiety never left him.

From that moment Vincent spent his life in fear of death and dying. He visited doctors regularly and complained bitterly of physical discomfort. He was always in pain, but no treatment improved his situation, and his anxiety was a mystery that could not be solved.

Vincent related that when he was eight his widowed mother had died, and in an attempt to manage their own grief, his brothers and sister forbade him to cry. They insisted that he simply had to be a man now. Vincent did the best he could to minimize his mother's death, but not expressing his hurt weighed heavily on him. He recalled that his childhood was a time when he felt disadvantaged. Nothing felt certain. In his teens Vincent developed an unexplained fever, which he described as a hot feeling building up inside him.

It was suggested to Vincent that the weight of the dead soldier reminded him of his mother's death, the heavy burden he'd been carrying around with him. The fear that began at that moment and persisted for years was his triggered memory of how afraid and helpless he'd been when she died. When it was pointed out that he didn't have to feel guilty over crying in the lavatory for being weak, because he had just been reminded of how much he missed his mother, Vincent broke down and began to mourn his mother for the first time.

For over fifty years all the elements of Toxic Nostalgia lay dormant in Vincent, waiting to be released again: the unmourned loss, the defensive suppression of grief, the regression to a childlike perspective, and the guilt. What was most striking about this case was that the tears of mourning were so close to the surface all that time. The mourning process that was finally permitted to continue lasted just a few days, after which Vincent's anxiety totally subsided.

ANACHRONISTIC REACTIONS

Barbara was a sixty-five-year-old woman who was driving with her friend when she was hit by another car. The driver was a young man who immediately became terrified about what would happen to him if his mother ever found out, saying that she would "kill" him. When he begged to give her a check to cover the damages, Barbara was deeply touched and asked him to follow her home where the next-door neighbor, a police officer, ran a check on the car and verified his license. The young man continued to share how frightened he was of his unreasonable parents. Barbara listened with great interest and agreed to take the check.

After the young man left, Barbara's girlfriend noticed that she was trembling. Assuming that this was a result of the accident, the friend offered, "Would you like me to give you a hug?"

"Oh my God no!" Barbara screamed, recoiling in terror from the friend as if she were a little child under attack. "Get away from me." She became inconsolable and ran away, trying to hide in the house.

It was not the accident that precipitated Barbara's inappropriate response, but two other events. The young man's terror, fearing his mother's reprisal, stirred deep feelings in Barbara, which led her to go out of her way to make it easy for him. When her friend offered to console her, Barbara also recalled the way her own mother used to trick her into hugging and then, without warning or reason, beat her with belts and wooden clothes hangers.

When questioned about this Barbara repeated, sobbing like a child, "Why is this happening to me again?" However, when it was suggested to Barbara that she was probably still hurting over the abuse she suffered as a child, she vehemently denied it.

Barbara insisted that she had already forgiven her mother, "Because it was her 'sugar diabetes' that caused her actions." It was pointed out that diabetes was just an excuse and that, in spite of her protests, Barbara had not forgiven her mother. Barbara immediately became testy as her old anger was ignited by the comment. A wave of guilt surged over her. She mentioned her mother's illness and again excused her. This guilt acted like a dam holding her hurt in place. Any expression of her old hurt ran the risk of liberating some anger, which would make her appear like the person her mother accused her of being, that is, deserving of being beaten.

All the components of Toxic Nostalgia were present in this case. Barbara remembered her unmourned hurt when she saw the young man with a fear similar to her own. This was triggered anachronistically when her friend asked to hug her. She regressed to the perspective she had at the time of her injury, displaying her childlike terror over being beaten. A flood of guilt came forward, restating her original defensive logic, which excused her mother's behavior and assumed Barbara herself must be bad for being angry.

There was also the remembrance of a partial forgiveness. In Barbara's case that forgiveness was premature and granted to her mother insincerely without really letting go of the hurt, merely because Barbara felt too guilty to be unforgiving. After all, her mother had diabetes.

The trigger is also interesting in this case not merely because it echoes the words of her mother, but because prior to those words having been spoken, she was primed by identifying with a young man who was being terrorized by *his* mother the same way she had been.

OTHER TYPICAL MANIFESTATIONS

The following brief descriptions of toxic nostalgic reactions are given to arouse your index of suspicion in looking for old feelings revealing themselves in current illogical or unexpected behavior.

RECURRENT THOUGHTS——PREOCCUPATIONS

Recurrent thoughts and preoccupations are integrally related to Toxic Nostalgia. Any incompletely resolved feeling is in an unstable condition and is easily stirred to an awareness, which becomes obsessive when you try not to think of it or refuse to act on it. The unresolved conflict continues to disrupt your consciousness.

The imperative of an unresolved hurt is to get your attention, preoccupying you until you settle the matter. When the issue is not brought to resolution, the pain incubates, gaining strength and fueling even more rumination.

This condition can commandeer years of your life. You become preoccupied about danger, your appearance, betrayal, or any issue related to the original event. You dwell on your guilt and ruminate on your revenge.

You hold on to the hurtful moment and relive it in a mixture of hurt and anger, regressing to the way you were rather than releasing and growing.

You toy with the idea of letting go, but in the meanwhile in fantasy you conduct courts-martial and sentence your oppressors to medieval torture. Torquemada, the Grand Inquisitor, had nothing on you. Understandably these ruminations only make you feel more guilty.

Until you finally let go of your hurt, your preoccupation predisposes you to minor episodes of Toxic Nostalgia. People think you are difficult, irritable, critical, as your exaggerated character defects reveal themselves.

INAPPROPRIATE RESPONSES

This list is incomplete, but includes:

Too loud a volume of emotional response, especially to an innocent comment.

Too soft a v]olume of emotional response, especially to a serious loss.

A phony response or one that seems predetermined, as if it were just
*   waiting for an opportunity to display itself.*

A response that is only tangentially related to the stimulus that provoked
*   it. You feel that just because you've been given the opportunity to download one*
*   emotion or opinion, you must unload every complaint you've been carrying,*
*   getting more angry and more convinced of your rightness as you do.*

Accusing another of sinister intentions with minimal evidence.

Taking a setback or rejection as incontestable proof you are bad.

Triggering of a flight response.

Sudden and meaningless arguments that you find difficult to set aside.

PREJUDICE

A prejudice is a preset emotional response based on withheld hurt that instead of being directed at yourself is projected outward. Instead of saying, "I am bad," you insist, "You are bad and so is everyone in your group." Prejudices tend to be generalized, reflecting the loss of specificity that occurs when a feeling loses touch with the event that causes it.

CONFUSION

Technically confusion is another form of denial and on the surface does not seem like a manifestation of Toxic Nostalgia. Being confused is another way of saying you do not want to know what is happening to you.

However, when a state of confusion is triggered, it is usually to shut off unacceptable feelings. Such confusion represents the tip of the iceberg, concealing a toxic nostalgic event just below.

For example, you become confused rather than angry when you find evidence that your lover is cheating on you. Instead of drawing the obvious conclusion that everyone else can plainly see, you ask: What is going on? What does this motel receipt mean? Who keeps hanging up on me? Your state of confusion is your way of separating from all the evidence, current and older, in order to postpone the hurt you are avoiding.

Instead of feeling outraged, you feel more comfortable being confused. After a while, in spite of not knowing what is going on, you begin to display hurt, anger, and anxiety, just as if these feelings had been triggered. Thus the confusion plays the role of a weak form of denial that slowly allows the Toxic Nostalgia to penetrate its facade.

Of course you need to remember what started all this confusion in order to make sense of the leaking hurt and anger.

AMBIVALENCE

The same mechanism that explains confusion describes what happens when a sudden feeling of ambivalence is triggered. Beneath the ambivalence is a feeling you don't know how to handle. You know what happened, you just don't know what you want to do about it.

It is likely that you have been trying to make a decision regarding the same question for a while. You have reasoned it out both ways. You can make the negative case, the reason you want to act, but as soon as you do the positive argument that you made to rationalize staying in the situation rises to the surface and grips you in paralysis.

The failure to take action only causes negative feelings to be turned against you and keep you from taking positive action. The solution for all problems of ambivalence involves taking a risk.

PREDETERMINED ATTITUDES

An innocent situation triggers an unreasonable attitude.

These attitudes reflect both characterological flaws and the remote Emotional Debt of early childhood. This makes them pervasive and repetitive. Although it is not always easy to tell that they are a form of Toxic Nostalgia, any unreasonable attitude should prompt you to ask, What made this person see the world the way he does?

FEELING ABANDONED

Finding abandonment as the common theme in every disappointment is usually a reflection of deprivation in childhood and lifelong disappointment with nurturing figures.

FEELING TREATED UNFAIRLY

This is the universal response to having been controlled.

When you grow up in a controlling environment you feel that you have been manipulated by your weaknesses to do what stronger people want. You feel others have misused their unfair advantage over you.

If you feel treated unfairly, part of your reaction is probably Toxic Nostalgia.

Grow stronger and do everything for yourself. Forgive the person who controlled you. They would not have had the opportunity to do so unless you were weak.

FEELING CHEATED OR USED

Controlling people often have this attitude, feeling unappreciated and taken for granted after they did or gave so much to others.

The controlling person feels cheated because what he wanted was the undying loyalty, or obedience, and respect of others. When he discovers that others obey him only as long as he maintains power and have no real respect for him, he is deeply hurt. He is especially susceptible to this feeling being triggered when he loses his power and others withdraw.

BEHAVIOR AS TOXIC NOSTALGIA

REPETITIVE DESTRUCTIVE RELATIONSHIPS

People who end up in abusive or alcoholic relationships are often acting out some earlier unresolved life situation. The relationship is, therefore, a toxic nostalgic form of behavior. The relationship is difficult to correct because it is not a relationship in its own right but a projective opportunity in which to replay the dynamics of the past.

Many such relationships are, therefore, not amenable to treatment. Unfortunately, they not infrequently come to the attention of marriage counselors, many of whom have limited experience in understanding the powerful binding effects of these earlier dynamics and the way they contribute to the forming of an outwardly stable but deeply troubled union.

To heal such relationships each partner must deal with his troubled past. This is a formidable task involving forgotten issues in remote Emotional Debt that shaped character type, not easy to do for one person, let alone a couple. Sometimes the only way to resolve these relationships, which are often thinly concealed attempts to reexperience an inaccessible painful past, is to end them. A great majority of them do end by themselves. However, the partners often seek out another partner exactly like the one they have left. They now continue to live out the unresolved dynamics of their early years without ever facing what is truly motivating them.

It is only when a person accepts responsibility for himself that such a repetitive pattern can be broken. It usually takes a monumental loss in which denial is rendered useless for this awakening to take place.

CHILD ABUSE

The person most likely to be abusive to his or her child is a person who was himself abused. The pattern of abuse imprints as a restriction of the expression of feelings in oneself and one's child.

As has been pointed out, the greatest damage done to the abused child is done by inhibiting the expression of his feelings.

When such a person grows up and has a child of his own, he tends to inhibit the child from expressing feelings the same way he was inhibited. This can be disguised by the parent glossing over problems and punishing the child for bringing up painful issues. Because the parent's Emotional Debt is high, anything his child does or says that can reveal his deficiencies is a threat and triggers a swift attempt to limit the criticism.

The parent's obligatory attitude is his Toxic Nostalgia.

The parent suspects but does not want to believe that he is like his own parent. Further, because the abusing parent often denies that he was abused, he often feels obliged to maintain the myth that his parent wasn't abusive. This makes it doubly necessary for the parent to maintain the appearance that he is not abusive either.

COMPULSIVE BEHAVIOR PATTERNS

This includes compulsive eating, drinking, gambling, and sexual activity.

Whereas obsessional thinking is a reflection of internalized anger that has been directed at the self and is manifested as guilt, compulsive behavior is the self-destructive acting out of these guilty feelings. The damage done by the compulsive behavior is a form of self-punishment designed to alleviate the guilt. However, it only creates more problems.

Recovery from these compulsive behavior patterns requires that you take responsibility for the feelings of the moment, accept yourself just as you are, focus on what you can do about your life in this place with what you have, and manage your life moment to moment without looking back on the past to justify failing or self-destructiveness.

TOXIC NOSTALGIA AND ALCOHOL ADDICTION

Alcohol interferes with the healing mechanism in the most sardonic way. While it makes the alcoholic exquisitely susceptible to toxic nostalgic recall, it also disables him. Although his emotions are easily triggered, he cannot integrate them or put them to therapeutic benefit. It all sounds vaguely similar to Shakespeare's night watchman in *Macbeth* expounding upon the effects of drink on sexual ability.

> It provokes the desire,
> But it takes away the performance.

Alcohol awakens memory but blocks healing.

In a sense the alcoholic lives in a toxic nostalgic world. He is full of regretful recall, self-pity, unresolved hurt and anger. The slightest negative stimulus provokes gales of overstated affect and scenes of high drama. An innocent criticism unlocks his mind's filing cabinet of evidence, proving he is bad. The best intentions of caring others are defeated by his shame and repressed anger. All the richness of emotions that are brought forth by the bottle might just as well be bottled themselves for all the good they are allowed to do.

Mourning under the influence of alcohol is merely suffering.

Suffering is not mourning at all.

The following case presents a special window on the mechanism of Toxic Nostalgia and helps to explain the prolongation of suffering that alcoholics and other addicts endure.

One night Lisa heard a strange noise beneath her window. She made sure her six-year-old son was safe, shut off the lights, and then went outside to check. Finding nothing, she went to look in the neighbor's yard. When she returned to the house a half hour later, she found her son lying dead at the foot of the stairs. Apparently he had gotten up, tripped, and fell, breaking his neck. She tried to resuscitate the child, but it was too late. She ran to the next-door neighbor, carrying her child and screaming in anguish.

So sympathetic was her family physician to the intensity of her pain that in a misguided attempt to help her through her sorrow he overmedicated her with barbiturates. Lisa went through the funeral and the following weeks in such a daze she wasn't sure if she had actually lost her son or was just dreaming. Whenever she tried to omit the medication, painful memories immediately rose to the surface, and she pictured her son lying lifeless at the bottom of the stairs. Unable to bear the pain, she took more medication and in doing so shut off the healing each time.

After a while Lisa found herself becoming confused. Did it happen? Was her son really dead? She wasn't really sure, because she had not been allowed to feel. She had only dreamlike images to measure her life. Because her important feelings had been sealed off, the mourning process could not progress.

Lisa's concealed hurt evolved into guilt. Although her son's death was an accident, Lisa felt responsible and obsessed over how she contributed to it. She chastised herself for not leaving on the light in the hall and for having a small hooked rug at the top of the stairs and wondered if her son had slipped on it. She assumed he was looking for her and must have panicked when he couldn't find her and ran down the stairs and tripped. The only emotion Lisa could feel was her regret.

Over the next year Lisa's obsession improved, but she became depressed. She was barely able to concentrate at work and lost her enthusiasm for life. The memory of the events surrounding her son's death seemed enveloped in a haze. She knew she had lost her son, but thanks to the barbiturates, the specifics were as remote to her and as difficult to recall as memories of what had happened to her when she was six months old.

Lisa began to have troublesome dreams as the natural therapeutic process continued to push her pain forward. Although she could not remember any details, the dreams disturbed her sleep. She became preoccupied but did not know what it was she was preoccupied with. She only knew the dreams awakened some obscure terrible feelings from which she wanted to escape. Lisa could not identify those feelings or link them to the loss of her child, but they made her anxious. The memories of these vague, dark dreams felt like demons trapped in her head.

Lisa started to drink in an attempt to bridle the disturbing feelings that were waking within her. Although she could not place it, she dreaded accepting in her heart what she already knew in her mind. She feared making the connection that would prove her son really was dead.

Lisa's drinking progressed over the years. At first she drank when a bad feeling returned, but eventually she drank whenever she feared that a bad feeling *might* return. Lisa began to experience uncontrollable rages as her repressed anger, which had totally lost its relationship to her hurt, was easily triggered by trivial disappointments. This caused her to misinterpret reality and find cause for a show of rightful disputation wherever she looked.

Whenever Lisa drank she immediately became sentimental and tearful and acted as if she were transported back in time to the moment where she left off mourning. Then she would protest vehemently that her son was not dead. However, the quantity of alcohol it took to allow her to experience these feelings also made it impossible to remember them when she was sober. Since that pain could not be recalled, it did no work in the grief process. It was wasted suffering.

Until Lisa could accept her loss, she remained disconnected from it. The knowledge of her son's death was only an intellectual awareness, because she was afraid to feel the feelings that would make it real. She could not permit herself to have any memories of her son because they symbolized his absence. Because Lisa did not mourn, she had no compensating pleasant memories of her lost child. She could not enjoy looking at his picture. She could only cry. She could find nothing to feel grateful for, no promise of happiness.

As with all addictions, alcoholism became Lisa's main problem. During recovery her sobriety was repeatedly tested. Whenever a sad feeling intruded, Lisa had to mourn anew. It was in the toxic nostalgic intrusions that followed her getting sober that her mourning was allowed to progress. Gradually she built up a history of resolution of her son's death and came to believe she could get through it.

Lisa needed to face her unmourned pain.

She needed to overcome her guilt and forgive herself.

She needed to understand her continual regression to the perspective of shock when she discovered her son and how pushing it away kept her from moving forward.

She needed to accept the horror of that moment and feel it instead of running away.

Most importantly Lisa needed to remember the healing she was able to accomplish, take strength from it, and build on it. Before she became sober this was impossible. Alcohol prevented Lisa from gaining a therapeutic perspective. Instead it caused her to focus on the loss, which always seemed fresh, as if it had just happened. This is why it was easy for Lisa to feel hopeless and to believe that her life was never going to get better.

Alcohol has powerful antianxiety properties. It defeats the part of the brain that censors unacceptable thoughts and feelings, permitting them to surface in the intoxicated state. However, at the same time alcohol seems to block feelings

by generally depressing all brain functions. The emotions that are blocked ran-
kle and build. When the drinking subsides, these feelings press forward again
with renewed strength. It requires increasing amounts of alcohol to inhibit the
constant runoff of unwanted emotions, thus the predisposition for dependency
and addiction and for repeating toxic nostalgic episodes.

ANOTHER OPPORTUNITY TO HEAL

The light of the truth continually exposes unresolved feelings to resolution.

It is the mixing of past and present that dismays you. The chagrin over realizing that ghosts of old feelings still haunt your consciousness and have the
power to intrude at will is a disquieting thought. No one likes to believe that
something is amiss and not be able to identify it and fix it.

Repairing the old damage done to you is not merely a matter of resolving to
be better but the result of a willingness to be vulnerable, to accept that you are
not perfect, to admit that what you have lost mattered to you, and to take responsibility for the way your life has turned out.

Lowering your defenses is a key factor in the resolution of the complex ar-
ray of emotional factors that predispose you to Toxic Nostalgia.

Letting go of the hurt you have stored in Emotional Debt is the necessary
healing step. Releasing hurt is the central act of forgiving. You release others to
be released yourself.

This is not possible unless you are willing to change and grow, to admit your
weaknesses and accept them as part of yourself.

Your ease in accepting yourself determines how easily you deal with the pain
of your life and the hurt of the moment. You cannot be free in the moment if you
are guarding against realizations that wish to speak to you from your past.

What are those old realizations? They are many:

You were hurt, abandoned, injured, cheated, abused, and betrayed.

You were not loved the way you wanted to be loved or the way you needed
to be loved.

You were not cherished for the person you are.

You compromised, you gave in to the belief that you were less.

You took the easy path, betraying yourself and your gift.

You held grudges, acted in anger, sought revenge, and in denying your hurt,
you allowed your anger to grow out of control and sometimes hurt others in
the very way you were hurt, the very thing you promised yourself you would
never do.

You became the enemy you hated most.

Your sudden recollections of unresolved pain are another opportunity to correct these imbalances.

You can never go back and relive the past.

Accept that.

You can never make someone who does not already love you, love you.

Accept that as well.

You have no power over others; you barely have control over the events in your own life.

You need to let go of others and release them to their own destiny and you to yours.

You cannot win the esteem of the world, please everyone, or win every time.

You need to reach for your own stars and find victory on your own terms.

The purpose in dealing with so many painful issues and negative feelings is not to get you depressed, but by guiding you through the depths of human suffering to allow you to become familiar with sadness so that dealing with grief is not strange to you.

Embracing the good of life is not possible unless you have found a way to come to terms with the truth.

Toxic Nostalgia, though unpleasant and unpredictable, is an optimistic reminder that healing is still possible and a better and happier you is still evolving.

Be patient and trust in the natural therapeutic process. It is the heart of your being and the key to your happiness and self-acceptance.

Toxic Nostalgia is the wake-up call of the soul.

13

POSITIVE FEELINGS: HOW THEY ARE DEFEATED

WHILE MUCH OF THE PREVIOUS DISCUSSION has centered on painful feelings, it is just as important to look at life's pleasure and consider how it fits into the natural healing process. When you think about it, life is about pleasure. Pleasure encourages you, helps you form healthy bonds, inspires love, teaches you to develop trust and to give and share.

Pleasure is the great motivator and the reward, the relief and the fulfillment. The promise of pleasure keeps you going when the obstacles you face seem insurmountable. The experience of pleasure helps you find comfort in accepting yourself even though you are flawed. Finally, the memory of pleasure shared together fortifies you when loved ones are not their best and allows you to give them the benefit of the doubt.

Of course all this can work against you. You can live in unrealistic expectations of pleasure. This sets you up to be disappointed when life doesn't turn out the way you want it to. Having too much hope keeps you from recognizing and solving little problems as they come up. Neglecting to deal with what you know needs your attention only diminishes the good that life has to offer.

Expecting to be rescued, find the perfect mate, win the lottery, or achieve a big success that will redeem you are simply ways of staying unhappy. This life is the only one you have. The way it is going to turn out is largely a reflection of the way it is currently evolving. When you get to the next point in your life it will not be because you were reborn or transfigured, but because you moved to the next step. Your path will be logical and understandable even if it did not seem predictable at the time.

There are no mysteries of the soul looking back.

The greatest pleasures come only when you are aware of yourself and know your strengths and limitations. Your capacity to enjoy pleasure is limited by your self-acceptance. More than anything else, it is your openness with yourself that allows you to enjoy life fully.

AVOIDING PLEASURE

It seems understandable, even natural, that people would avoid pain, but denying oneself pleasure seems almost perverse. It may seem pigheaded and contrary perhaps, but it is not at all uncommon.

Everyone who has had a child in the terrible twos is aware of how difficult it can sometimes be to entice a moody child to play with a friend, go to a pleasurable event, or just enjoy himself. Rather than let go of his pain when he is hurt, the child allows it to turn into anger and feels obliged to punish himself. In some self-defeating way, denying himself pleasure allows him to continue to feel angry.

When people withhold their hurt and anger and become willful and negative, it is often impossible to get them to enjoy themselves. For all their years, they seem trapped in their own terrible twos and believe they deserve to suffer rather than be happy. If you have ever tried to encourage someone determined to grieve, you probably lost patience and began saying things like, "What's wrong with you?" or "Come on, grow up."

Happiness is letting go of the past.

THE BLOCKING OF PLEASURE

Just as it is impossible to feel love when you are trapped in hurt and anger, so too is your ability to feel or desire pleasure diminished when you are in pain.

All pleasurable feelings involve expressing love and can be defeated by the same forces that block love. Fear interferes with your ability to anticipate pleasure. You expect pain instead. Hurt focuses your attention inward and limits your ability to make contact with the good in life. Anger cuts you off from your affections, making you less willing to see positive traits in others. If you recognized the good in another, you wouldn't be as comfortable staying angry at him. Guilt lowers your self-love and undermines your belief in your attractiveness and deservability.

When your feelings of love are blocked, you find it difficult to attach yourself to your work, to the things you love, to the person you love, and to the force that drives life itself. You are isolated from the sources of affirmation within yourself and around you.

DENYING PAST DEPRIVATION

Because the contrast reminds them how bad life has been for them, people who have suffered deprivation sometimes find it difficult to enjoy themselves. They minimize pleasure so they can continue to maintain that what they had was at least tolerable. Instead of admitting they went without, they say, "It could've been worse." They may even claim that they prefer the way it was.

This sour grapes reaction is typically seen in parents from impoverished backgrounds when visiting their successful child. They feel uncomfortable enjoying the material comforts they once insisted they didn't need, saying, "I don't need so many towels." They may even make fun of the comforts offered to them. "Who needs a fancy boat? Why can't you fish off the dock like everyone else?" Of course this is maddening to their child, who just wants them to enjoy themselves. In former years these same people probably said things like, "Who needs an indoor toilet?" or "Running water is unnecessary," when they visited their kinfolk in the city.

Some people will act excessively frugal and self-denying long after they have become successful, pretending that since they now choose to maintain their old ways, it wasn't that bad before. They often get trapped in this kind of thinking and feel uncomfortable giving to themselves or treating themselves well.

THE POSITIVE FEELING CYCLE

Just like the name given to pain, the name given to pleasure depends on when it occurs.

Pleasure in the future is excitement. Pleasure in the present is joy. Pleasure in the past is contentment.

If you spend too much time anticipating pleasure, you neglect the moment. If you live in past pleasure, the present seems empty. It is the balance between positive feelings that gives life a sense of eventfulness.

EXCITEMENT: FUTURE PLEASURE

Anticipating pleasure inspires you. Like all emotions, positive feelings have a purpose. Excitement prepares you to heighten your sensory awareness so that you are as open as possible to the joy of life.

The model for excitement is the state of sexual arousal and its logical outcome. A man is attracted to a woman, and during courtship they plan and dream together of the happiness they will share. Their dream inspires the man to work hard and the woman to make sure the new baby has a good home and the best opportunities. Their shared hope becomes a commitment. They go on to dream about building a family dynasty, a business, something that can be passed on and expand. This is the driving force of civilization.

Your life is built on the motivation provided by future pleasure. You dream about how much better your situation could be. Your attraction to your dream motivates you to build a happy reality.

Be flexible. People become troubled when they become too set on a dream and don't allow room to make adjustments. Growing is mostly about editing out the things that don't work.

Much of what goes wrong in your life is supposed to go wrong. There are no mistakes. If you have been trying to please others or win love from the wrong people, then the fact that you have failed is a good sign. You were probably fighting gravity. If you succeeded you'd most likely be trapped in an unstable relationship and suffer continual anxiety over its imminent collapse.

Keep an open mind. Look at the good around you. Follow your love to the place it leads you. Continually becoming your best creates a life of genuine excitement that will not disappoint you.

Although excitement often creates a sense of urgency, learn patience in dealing with future pleasure. Enjoy the excitement. Use it to prepare yourself to risk. When making choices, be mindful of yourself, of what you really want. You want to be sure you are on the right path so you can surrender to your passion and your work without reservation and yet without becoming totally lost.

LIVING IN THE HAPPY FUTURE. Sometimes life seems completely taken with future pleasure. Although you plan, the future you desire never works out the way you thought. Little disappointments alternate with pleasant surprises. If you allow the disappointments to dishearten you, you don't enjoy the surprises. The surprises can be the best part.

A new relationship fills you with the hope that this time you have found true love. You extol the virtues of the person you love, and one day you discover that like you, the other person is only human. The exaggerated view you had was just your attempt to make yourself feel better. You have to correct your perception for the relationship to survive. Holding the other person up to an unrealistic standard will inhibit him from showing his best and will destroy love.

When you have a baby you make plans and dream about your child's future.

Your anticipation makes you want better things for your child. When you discover that your child is his own person and may be growing differently than you expected, you have to adjust your dreams. You can destroy a child by insisting he be something he is not. A parent's greatest love is in setting aside his own unfulfilled hopes and loving his child unconditionally for what he is.

When you get a new job, you are filled with excitement. You feel endorsed. You have a clean slate. You feel everything is possible. You dream about rising to the top. Your excitement inspires and allows you to believe you can make a difference, that your work will be appreciated, that you can be your best and be rewarded for it.

Follow your opportunity with care. Your real reward is always how you feel about yourself. Try not to get lost in a flush of excitement where you believe your potential is unlimited. You'll only disappoint yourself. While some of the excitement you feel comes from the new situation validating your worth, it does not eradicate the past. The lessons you have to learn are always the same and repeat until you accept them.

You need to allow yourself room to make mistakes. That is how you grow.

MATERIAL ACQUISITION. It is quite stunning how caught up everyone becomes with the prospects of acquiring a new material possession. There is some truth to the belief that compulsive collectors live for the next big discovery, almost addicted to the thrill of excitement.

New acquisitions produce a mixture of pain and pleasure. You are about to purchase a new house. You imagine yourself entertaining, impressing your friends, living the good life. It is so intoxicating you practically tremble thinking about it. You drive by the house, show it to friends. You want it so badly. Then terror strikes. You ask: Am I paying too much? Is the house really what I want?

Buying a new car makes you swell with pride. Owning it proves that you are someone. When young people yearn for a luxury car, they do not realize that what they want most is not the vehicle but to be the person who can afford it.

All materialist pleasures are great in the anticipation, giddy in the acquisition, but become ordinary after a while, a form of accommodation. This explains why people who are materialistic always need more in order to hold on to that special feeling of excitement.

THE EXCITEMENT OF RISKING. The greater truth is that winning and always wanting more has nothing to do with being happy. In one episode of Rod Serling's classic *Twilight Zone,* a gambler dies and finds himself in a casino where he discovers he cannot lose. After a while he becomes bored and then desperate as the excitement, the feeling he lived for, begins to die. He complains to the proprietor that he is sick of the place and would rather be in hell instead of heaven. The proprietor replies, "Where did you get the idea that this was heaven?"

True excitement is based on the fact that the desired result may not turn out the way you want. There is risk involved, and it is the risk of losing, of being disappointed, that gives the race its psychological worth. It also explains why, since the pursuit of a positive goal involves failure, so many people do not seem able to follow their dreams. They are afraid that they will prove themselves a failure or unworthy and would rather live in hope.

It is the risking involved in the doing that defines your life and gives it its fullness. No easily won goal ever gave lasting pleasure. The worth of the things you have is the worth you attached to them and the energy you invested in getting them.

Like anxiety, future pleasure has not yet happened and in some sense is not real. The pleasure you hope for is subject to more disappointment than any other emotion. Think of all your optimistic plans that went wrong and the relationships and opportunities that didn't work out. Your expectations were false. What happened to you was real. If you had no false expectations, you wouldn't have been disappointed. The mourning process helps you reconcile your false expectations with reality. Healing is accepting the world as it is.

When you insist that the future unfold in a certain way, you only create problems. Because you want things to go perfectly, you become controlling and get lost making too many adjustments. Future pleasure always involves the risk of disappointment. If you accept yourself as you are and pay attention to the road, you will get where you want to go.

A BALANCED ASSESSMENT OF EXCITEMENT. You are naturally inclined toward growth. The possibility of further expansion and self-realization excites you and keeps you alert and youthful. Each new possibility also presents a risk and initiates the taking of a personal inventory. The questions you need to ask as you risk are:

How am I doing?
Whose standards did I use to answer that question?
Do I really need or want this? Why?
What am I trying to prove? And to whom?
Are the reasons I want this the right ones?
   How do I know?
Are the answers I just gave true?
How may I be deceiving myself?

Why would I do that?

Am I being honest? If not, why not?

Why am I attracted to this person?

Am I able to be myself when we're together?

Am I being manipulated? By what?

Will this risk lead me to a better self?

Are other people telling me the truth? How do I know?

How much growth am I sacrificing for security?

Is someone offering me something I should more properly
*   provide for myself?*

What can I lose if I risk?

What may I lose if I do not?

Living in the future is not possible. You cannot go there. You are always here. The only way you can get to the future is by embracing the present with joy and passion.

JOY: PRESENT PLEASURE

Joy is your reward for doing the right thing.

The purpose of joy is to motivate you to do more of what makes you happy, to enjoy what is good for you. Sometimes this involves nothing more than being present to observe the good, without editing, correcting, or adding to it.

Joy is acceptance of the present just as it is. To see a walkway in spring covered with pink cherry petals and think that the walk needs to be swept is to mar your appreciation of a special moment in nature. Nature and people are simply the way they are, and if you can be witness to the ongoing miracle of the creation without commentary you can be part of it.

Joy is living in the moment.

Joy is the simplicity of life.

Joy is openness, the willingness to be seen without disguise and to be heard without censoring your true feelings.

Joy is self-acceptance, without making allowances for the way others may not approve of you.

Joy is the dissolving of self-consciousness that allows you to be yourself.

Joy is natural without guile and spontaneous without defense.

Joy is being fully present for someone you love and realizing that he is also present for you.

Joy requires sharing in innocence, listening without correcting, seeing without editing, and hearing without rejection.

Joy is being generous of spirit without the expectation of being given to in return.

It is your ability to be free in the moment that teaches you joy.

The paradox of joy is that as you become absorbed in personal fulfillment, you surrender fully to the moment and begin to merge with the greater world.

LOSING YOURSELF IN THE MOMENT. Losing self-consciousness allows you to touch the infinite and dissolve loneliness. Surrendering to the feelings of the moment is the path.

The artist becomes lost in his work and makes contact with future generations. In giving himself away he finds himself at last. At one with his work, he blends into the moment and makes contact with the tradition that has come before and everything that will follow. Surrendering to the moment places him in his own history.

The novice worries as he tries to create: How will this turn out? What will the critics say? Will my work survive? Will I be a success? Am I great? and so he loses his confidence. His concentration breaks. He doesn't support his originality but instead imitates out of fear and so produces little.

Self-consciousness blocks joy. You question yourself: Is this the way I am supposed to feel? Is it all right to be doing this? Do I have a right to feel the way I do?

Be willing to be imperfect. Be willing to fail.

It is through the creative arts that humankind has defined how to enjoy life. What is beautiful is noted. Animals are painted on the walls of caves, the idyllic life depicted on the tombs of Egypt, and the loveliness of seaside afternoons caught on impressionistic canvas. Temples, cities, theater, fountains, dance, music all define the joy of life.

Joy is for celebration. Celebration comes from the Latin word *celeber,* meaning famous, known by many. The purpose of joy is to share the joy. In the act of sharing joy, life is affirmed. When others celebrate the same feelings at the same time, those feelings become most real and the world becomes one.

Great news events are powerful because many people relate to them in a personal way all at once. Each person measures time by these events and knows what he was doing when man first landed on the moon, when Kennedy was shot, or the earthquake hit.

Shakespeare said, "One touch of nature makes the whole world kin," but one touching event can reaffirm your place in the world as well and make you feel you belong.

All great performances unite the crowd into a single feeling being. We continually yearn to have some sense of unification with others, a communion with nature, and a sense of connection to the cosmos. When we permit ourselves to get lost in the audience we also discover that we have gotten closer to ourselves and in so doing we find we are no longer lonely.

This phenomenon of being in the moment together is also the hidden power of sports events. Watching the magic moment in the World Series when in the top of the ninth with two men out and a full count against the batter, he hits a home run and our team wins, we find we are part of the crowd. We have lost our identity. We could not be happier. Everyone around us feels the same way. We do not wonder if this person is expressing as much joy as we are. It doesn't matter if people feel exactly the way we do, but that they contribute their joy to the moment. Some people are clapping in quiet amazement. Some are just shaking their heads. Others are crying. Others are hooting and jumping and screaming. We are at that moment just another cell in the organism of joy. The moment is replayed on television and recounted in the newspapers. Everyone wants to be there, to be part of the joy.

There is joy in sexual bonding. It is spurred by desire but fueled by loneliness. In fact, the ecstasy of simultaneous orgasm is derived as much from its ability to dissolve loneliness as from its purely sensual power. We all want to be one with another.

There is joy in accomplishing, discovering, awakening, and disclosing.

There is joy in forgiving and understanding, growing and teaching.

There is joy in gratitude, heroism in survival, passion in involvement, kindness in giving, and peace in identifying with others.

Joy has to be taken in balance. Surrender to it with an eye to reality. A life that is lost in pleasure seeking is lost indeed, because it is focused on seeing what the world has to give rather than what you have to give to the world.

The meaning of life has to do with what you contribute to it. You are the gift and giving yourself away the greatest joy.

Artists struggling to be understood by a rejecting public yearn in their hearts for some future generation to pick up their book, cherish their painting, and love their music.

You are that future generation. As such you are the rightful heir to all the creativity and artistic striving that has preceded your existence here. You are both the beneficiary and the inspiration. Your willingness to be present for the moment defines your life and the compass of your joy.

CONTENTMENT: PAST PLEASURE

Contentment is being at peace with the sum total of the past, liking what has become of you, being pleased with your work, satisfied with your effort and how you persisted in your struggle. There's pride and satisfaction in fighting the good fight and giving it your best.

Contentment comes from remembering the good that remained after all the negativity settled. The argument that sealed a friendship. The confrontation that made your parents take you seriously. The way you stood on your own two feet and took a stand that ended the bullying. Contentment is coming into your own.

No life is a seamless procession of joyous occasions. Every life is filled with tribulation and discontent. It is the perspective of viewing the past from the forgiving present that softens the rough edges of life and makes the trials understandable. You learn that other people really did not mean to hurt you, that parents did the best they could. They had struggles and fears, felt bewildered and wanted to give up or run. Sometimes they did.

There were lessons everywhere for you to learn:

To trust yourself.

To believe in yourself.

To know that you are good.

To realize that you can do anything you really set your mind to.

You've heard these over and over again, but it took some event to bring the lesson home to you. No matter how painful that event was, if you learned the lesson, the event was a gift and you can look back on it with pride. Seeing the difficult events in your life in a positive way requires adopting the healing perspective that comes with acceptance. You find your strength in failures honestly faced and lessons painfully learned.

In recollecting your life you think of the happy times like pearls strung on a necklace. Between each happy event are struggles, times of trial and adversity, periods of loneliness and alienation, confusion and bewilderment. Each of these periods of sadness is designed to teach you something. If you have not been willing to accept the teaching of your pain, you cannot look back in kindness or travel the corridors of time with ease. You dread touching the unsettled past again and stirring up the dust of mummified emotions that have not been granted rest.

Being happy comes from accepting the past and taking responsibility for your part. That acceptance allows you to view yourself as a work in progress, so your imperfections do not argue against your worth.

It is only when you accept your humanness and vulnerability that you can see the past clearly and gain strength, not only from the good that happened to you, but from the way you dealt with the challenges.

Acceptance of yourself allows you finally to put the world in loving perspective, to know what matters to you and to remind yourself to take the time to enjoy what you enjoy. Simple advice, but hard won.

If only you knew then what you know now. Why did you force it, try too hard? What were you running so hard and so long to capture? If only you could have stood still and loved yourself where you stood, as you were.

Your history becomes the loving past when you accept yourself. Freed to be what it was, rather than what you needed it to be, the past is a beacon illuminating the fleeting moment of the present and fixing it in the context of the truth, allowing you to tell what is real, what makes sense, what feels right, and what is illusion.

Perhaps it is all illusion, this life. All you have of the life you have lived are the memories you carry. You edit these memories and make them fit some scheme. If you are in pain, your memories are bent into shapes that support your justifications and prejudices. If you accept yourself, your memories are edited in the light of forgiveness. Grudges are settled. Unanswered love is seen as a blessing in disguise that kept you from sure disappointment and absences are remembered as times when you finally discovered yourself.

Peace of mind comes from knowing that you did what you had to do. It is a singularity of accomplishment that is hard to share, impossible to explain, simply your own moment. You had to live it to comprehend it. Others can only tell that you feel content. You experience it and know that whatever comes, you are prepared to do what you need to do.

The pleasure of the past ennobles and protects the present, giving it worth and lending meaning to life, and in so doing, it safeguards the future.

TOXIC NOSTALGIA AND THE DEFEAT OF PLEASURE

The pleasure of life often falls victim to the unresolved pain of the past. This is especially true when old characterological attitudes intrude, diminishing joy, spoiling the good, and finding injury where none is intended.

The Dependent View of Pleasure

EXCITEMENT. Excitement is enough to throw the dependent person into terror. Excitement involves change. Excitement is destabilizing. This is all she can see.

The excitement of expecting something good is overshadowed by what she fears she will have to give up. She sets her pleasure aside and first needs to know how she will be rescued and protected. She wants guarantees. The dependent person is afraid of losing the security she has. This makes exploring new sources of pleasure seem risky and fearful to her. Her neediness makes her cling to what she knows rather than take a chance. The unknown perplexes her, and she invests her worst fantasies in it.

As a result when she should move ahead she holds back and the opportune moment to take the risks that will make her happy passes. When it does, she is relieved even though she is left in an unhappy position. Clinging to what she knows, even if it is abusive or painful, feels better to her than risking.

She sees danger everywhere, expecting rejection, the way she suffered in the past. She does not trust her ability to protect herself, and she finds it difficult to trust anyone else. Her fear puts a damper on everyone's enthusiasm. Her world shrinks as a result.

In the middle of all this doubt she often acts precipitously to form a bond with someone who is not right for her but who seems to be offering the security she needs. She seems calm in the new situation but soon becomes trapped in an unhappiness she cannot easily admit. It is now even more difficult for her to risk changing.

JOY. In the present moment the dependent person is haunted by fears of the future and memories of the past.

In the moment of love's offerings, she is tormented with her fear of abandonment. She misreads others' motives, cross-examining them, testing their loyalty, questioning when they will leave her. In so doing she pushes others away and creates the very rejection she fears.

In the middle of joy she is distracted by her knowledge that the moment will be short-lived. She anticipates the tearful parting, and when she should be enjoying herself, she is already living in the expected absence.

On the other hand she can just as easily overstate the joy of the moment and make it seem forced and artificial. She can also try to hold on to the moment too tightly and thereby diminish it. She so much wants everyone to participate in her happiness that she removes herself from the moment to make sure others are having a good time. They would be if they could get her to sit down and join them.

Her expectation of abandonment turns innocent events into betrayals, spoiling the moment.

Andrea's husband was a half hour late at the restaurant. Although she knew he'd had a busy day she greeted him coldly, commenting, "You're late." Instead of showing appreciation for his difficult schedule, she acted injured by circumstances that were clearly beyond his control. When Andrea's husband snapped back at her, it confirmed her belief she had been intentionally hurt. Andrea began to act unreasonable and demanding. The evening was ruined.

Joy is quickly debased by the dependent person's old fears of abandonment. At the height of passion she fantasizes about being alone and the moment mysteriously decays into a laconic sadness, where the question, "What's wrong?" brings forth the pitiful answer, "Nothing." The present has been swallowed up by the past.

The dependent person is always anticipating truncation and diminishment. She hates herself for feeling this way. Should she attempt to repair the damaged moment, it feels false, overworked, and the passion has passed.

Dependent people's joy is often bittersweet.

The nostalgia of the past holds the dependent person in a grip of remembrance that makes the present seem hollow. The unresolved losses of the past continually visit her and cause the joy of the moment to escape in sentimentality. Her wish that others could be here and share her joy spoils the good for her. She is so plagued considering how much better it would have been if only . . . that she does not surrender to the moment, and true joy eludes her.

CONTENTMENT. The dependent person views past joy with sadness simply because it has ended. She is the keeper of nostalgia. When you return home you find your bedroom the way you left it twenty years ago. She cannot throw anything out.

Her life is furnished with events so rich in meaning that they seem to leak nostalgia into the environment. She ponders the fading pages of scrapbooks and family albums for hours. She goes through trunks in the attic and smells locks of hair and fingers flowers pressed between the pages of dance programs.

Every picture brings an old loss to mind. Finding a hair ribbon, she mourns anew. Her life is so imbued with the past that the past almost seems to be alive. She seems a creature of another time, a living anachronism unable to shake her attachment to what has been.

She always seems to be getting over the past. Rather than using a past love to sustain her, she looks forward to joining her beloved someday. Others find her morbid preoccupation depressing and tend to leave her to her involvement with what has been.

THE CONTROLLING VIEW OF PLEASURE

ANTICIPATION. While he may be guarded about showing it, the controlling person is anxious in any situation in which his needs and vulnerability may show. As a result he seeks to control any possibility that he may be hurt.

His anticipation is so fraught with obsession that he turns the prospect of pleasure into a worrisome concern for what could go wrong. He becomes so lost in the details, trying to make sure everything will be perfect, that he leaves little slack for exploring or adjusting should reality happen to differ from what he projected. His plans for enjoying pleasure become more important than the pleasure itself.

If you go on a trip he has organized and depart from his schedule, he becomes unnerved. All he cares about is getting back on his timetable. Because his rigidity leaves no room for discovery or invention, he cannot enjoy the discoveries your curiosity has uncovered. Since joy is often improvised, he limits it because his plans are likely to exclude fortuitous opportunities. He is afraid to leave anything to chance and will choose an inferior restaurant just because he can get reservations, passing by charming places that aren't in his guidebook.

He doesn't realize that you cannot plan every moment in life. You have to live it openly, embracing the future as it becomes the present.

Some of his greatest pleasure comes from planning the future, the only place in his life he feels totally in control. He will spend hours at his computer, manipulating an electronic spreadsheet as he plays with financial variables, increasing sales, cutting costs, and making himself a billionaire on paper. He loves statistical models and games, probability theory, and curiously enough even gambling, a situation where he is totally out of control but believes he can beat the odds with his system. He thinks he can figure out anything, even the future.

In anticipating emotional involvement, the controlling person feels especially frightened. Since down deep he is a dependent person, he dreads exposing his feelings of affection and being humiliated and rejected.

The idea of allowing himself to be equal with another person makes him uncomfortable. When he anticipates romantic closeness, he tries to control the other person and keep the upper hand. Unfortunately in trying to safeguard his vulnerability he also restricts intimacy. This is why controlling people feel so isolated and alone even in intimate circumstances. They are afraid of letting go.

The controlling person likes excitement, but only where he is the one controlling it. He loses the moment by trying to secure and structure it. The thought of surrendering to another person frightens him. He cannot abandon himself unless he is in charge.

Sometimes he can go the other way and allow himself to be totally controlled in a sexual relationship involving domination. Even so he is usually the one who structures the encounter. The control he gives up is only an illusion and a temporary one at best.

He frightens off pleasure by trying to possess rather than experience it. He also scares off others who feel that their freedom to express themselves is limited by his wish to control them.

JOY. You would not think that experiencing joy would be such a problem to the controlling person, but so many things get in his way. When his need for another person's affection becomes obvious to him, he becomes confounded by his vulnerability. So frightened is he of feeling needy that he assumes a posture of strength. He wants to show he does not need what he so much desires.

Right at a tender moment he may act sarcastic and cynical as a defense against showing that he cares. He may do this by suddenly finding fault with the person he loves. He shows his criticism by making an insensitive comment, pushing the other person away and keeping himself from getting closer.

Except for when his love turns into an obsession, as it can when he becomes addicted to another person, the controlling person finds it difficult to say, "I love you." When he is addicted, he says it over and over, like a mantra, with obsessive desperation but no real passion.

This reluctance to say, "I love you," becomes a living torture to the people who need his love. His children wait for years in vain to hear these words. He is afraid of telling a child he loves him or even praising the child because he believes he will remove the child's incentive to seek affection from him. His love is therefore often conditional and is easily withdrawn at the slightest failure to comply with his unrealistic expectations.

Saying "I love you" to a lover is an especially dangerous commitment. This risk, while it may seem almost silly to people who routinely tell each other how much they care, is a continual bone in his throat. It fills him with the dread of rejection.

When he does say, "I love you," it is during a highly emotional occasion usually in the face of danger or illness far removed from passion. Other people, remembering him, apologize for his reticence, or to reassure themselves usually say, "I know he loved me even if he didn't say it." It would have been so much better if he could have risked being vulnerable and said it himself.

His critical nature and false standards of perfection also intrude on his enjoyment of the pleasure of another person's performance. He focuses on their mistakes, their fall from perfection. He demands unrealistically high standards of performance. He unfairly compares his eight-year-old daughter's drawing to Rembrandt and his son's performance in Little League to DiMaggio. While he is full of himself, he leaves everyone else feeling empty.

You cannot win unconditional praise from him, because he does not feel comfortable accepting himself. Believing he knows everything and cherishing perfection, he feels obliged to find everyone else wanting. His temperament is the stuff critics are made of. Rather than enjoy the moment, he even notices the mistakes people make when they sing "Happy Birthday" to him. His unfailing allegiance to his standard of excellence always manages to reveal some flaw that diminishes his enjoyment and allows him to withhold his enthusiastic approval.

There are exceptions. He will pay homage to the greats of history, and especially deep obeisance to those he idolized in his youth. These he speaks of in an unrealistically reverential way, lionizing them, admitting no contradiction. These were the great ones, the standards of excellence. Why should he pretend, in this age of flagging standards, that those who do not measure up were anywhere as good?

This need to find fault with the present isolates him from the main flow of life, making him a perpetual outsider and in a real sense painfully self-conscious. His jaded intellectual prejudice always manages to find something lacking, tainted, missing, incorrect, inappropriate, or not up to his standards and alienates him, limiting his ability to participate in the moment.

The ironic part is that he hates himself for being this way and wishes he could stop.

Martin arrived at his beach house after work to find his wife and five-year-old son playing in the surf. Martin bristled. All he could think of was that he had called to request they wait for him, but no, they had already gone in the water! He obsessed how his simple plea had been totally ignored. He felt unappreciated, as if he did not matter. He went up to his room in a rage and spent the entire weekend sulking, acting self-righteously indignant.

His wife tried in vain to explain that this was an entirely innocent event. It was a hot day and their son was getting impatient. They just decided to go into the water. It wasn't meant to hurt Martin, although he mentally filed it with the many rejections he'd suffered all his life.

It was pointed out that instead of taking this as a personal insult and ruining the weekend, he could have stood on the porch observing them. He could just as well have said, "There are my wife and kid. What a beautiful moment. How lucky I am to have them and this wonderful house right on the beach. I should get my camera and capture the two of them playing together."

Martin immediately teared up as he realized that he had exercised a negative option to be bitter and incriminating. He confessed that he hated being alone and sulking but somehow felt unable to forgive others for excluding him. He realized that when he was a child he continually created situations where he was the outsider just so he could feel justified in being angry over being left out.

The controlling person uncovers evidence everywhere that warns him that it is not safe to be accepting or forgiving. His rigid attitude re-creates his isolated past all around him.

The controlling person finds it difficult to be open to the joy of the moment because it makes him vulnerable. The new and the different arouse his suspicions. He is a tough audience. He is only reluctantly amused. Instead he finds comfort in order and predictability and pleasure when things go his way, the proper way, when and as he wants.

Other people learn to let him alone and let him have his own way, but by himself.

CONTENTMENT. The controlling person has difficulty looking at the past because his failures glare at him. Time makes it even more difficult to justify bad decisions, even though the pain has faded. Although he still believes he was right, he would love to return to the past with his present knowledge and set things straight.

He would really know all the answers then. He would get all A's. He would buy that thousand-acre parcel by the airport that sold for practically nothing. He would buy IBM at three, well before it went to a hundred and split three for one. He would have chosen other people to go into business with. He would have done so much so differently. Although he frequently thinks about the past in this way, he still maintains that he always did the right thing. This is a paradox. How could he insist he was right and yet yearn so badly to correct his actions?

Perhaps he wants to return to the past in order to have the advantage of knowing what the future holds and to be able to risk without taking chances. Perhaps he just wants to appear perfect? Perhaps he wants to be the richest person in the country? A quest for power? To play God? Acting omniscient, helping people avoid accidents and getting them to love him, the rescuer, the savior?

In a sadder vein, the controlling person regards the past as his failure to keep those he loved under his control. His abandonments chastise him. He obsesses over the love he has lost. Although he makes excuses and blames others for leaving him, he is mostly struck with how exposed he was to injury and how little he could do to prevent it.

His view of the past causes him to pledge that he will never let anyone hurt him again. Even when a former relationship was mostly loving, the fact that it ended plagues him. He assumes that he must have lost control over it. That is all he can see, not the joy. He blames others for his sadness and overstates how much he gave.

Although he tends to ruminate over the good that is no more, the losses he could not prevent, the people who have injured him by removing their love and affection, he is also prone to idealize the past. He has the capacity to see his past in an exaggerated way. In his self-aggrandizing moments of recollection he endows himself with brilliance he did not possess, power he did not control, wisdom that was not his to access. He replays his defeats with new words in his mouth and makes them moral victories. He rewrites the script of his life so many times that his actual memory of what happened becomes contaminated by the annotations he has added over time. Although he's no longer sure what really happened, he strongly believes his rehabilitated view of his history.

In a sense the controlling person is always re-creating and reinventing the past, making it coincide with the history he would like to use as evidence to support his beliefs and conclusions.

His peace of mind is, therefore, thin indeed and easily disturbed by any contradiction to his fantasized correction of life. He will become irritable when someone challenges his recollection and deeply hurt when his saints are portrayed as villains or his villains exonerated from blame.

He is really a creature who is always living in the past because he carries so much unforgiven resentment within him. Like Martin, it interferes with his perception of pleasure and erodes his peace of mind. He would have you view his past only through his eyes and have it explain all his eccentricities and inability to enjoy the present.

THE COMPETITIVE VIEW OF PLEASURE

EXCITEMENT. The competitive person lives in the expectation of pleasure. He imagines his next conquest, his next triumph, his future successes. He lives in these fantasies, offsetting his present disappointments with the reassurance that something bigger and better is already underway.

His dreams for future pleasure are his drug of choice. He rewards himself in fantasy. He consoles himself in fantasy. He gets even, succeeds, and proves himself in fantasy. His anticipation of how much better it will be often causes him to neglect what he already has. It interferes with his ability to concentrate and give his best effort in the moment. His dreams for the future interfere with that future actually coming to pass.

The competitive person is so fixed on the future, so eager to attain the conquest, that he often acts insincerely just to win. He becomes the seducer and charmer, working toward his desired effect. He wants to make the fantasy come true but shies away from doing the actual work. This is true in matters of love and work.

He is always running from the present to the future.

JOY. The competitive person is not satisfied with what he has and is always seeking to upgrade his life. His present joy taken at face value tends to disappoint him. Since he is always living in the future, the present cannot live up to his expectations unless he exaggerates the good. The competitive person therefore does a lot of pretending, which he is perfectly suited to do.

He exaggerates intimacy and closeness. His partners feel that they have found the real thing, someone who is capable of great passion and emotional expressiveness. He gets so caught up in his fantasy of what a relationship could be that he lives out his fantasy in pretense. Others suspect his passion may be insincere but go along with the excitement, at least for the moment.

He is a creature of the sale, not the follow-through.

As his intense feelings fade, he begins to compare his present situation with greener pastures both in the past and the future. Realizing that the present relationship falls short of his fantasy, he is momentarily saddened, and just because he can imagine something better, he feels justified in backing away. His partner feels totally deceived, led astray by his seduction and discarded. He cannot understand her disappointment and sincerely feels she should have enjoyed the good time while it lasted. They had fun. It's over now. What's the big deal?

He has no idea that he was only acting out his fantasy or that he could have hurt another person with his pretending. He is off, just like that, to his next conquest.

Whether in matters of career or love, the competitive person's ability to appreciate the joy of the moment is hindered by his continual comparison of the present with the future. The present is always falling short of his expectations, and he cannot bear to be disappointed. Instead of being satisfied with what he has, he protests being measured by his performance. As good as it is, he declares that next time it will be even better. This makes it difficult for him to stay in the moment and enjoy his success.

He finds it difficult to accept the moment on its own terms. He exaggerates, embellishes, reinforces, and blows it up with dramatic annotation. His need to hype his accomplishments makes them seem fabricated, even to him. Thus, even though the competitive person is capable of doing wonderful things, his tendency to exaggerate makes him doubt how good his work really is and robs him of fully enjoying it.

For this reason, when he finally sets aside his exaggeration and reflects on his accomplishments in a true light, they seem disappointing, less than they really were. This prevents him from taking from his efforts the full measure of support that they could have offered had he only been willing to see them more realistically in the first place.

To others the joy of the moment is simply what it is. The competitive person so much wants it to be even better that he loses touch with it. Driven by his unrealistic expectations he moves to his next triumph, rather than savoring the moment and enjoying life.

CONTENTMENT. The competitive person looks back on the past and laments, "If they could only see me now." The people who loved him who are now missing are seen as people who could offer recommendations of his specialness, missing members of his audience. This does not mean that he did not love them, but that their absence is also a loss of their testimony to his worth.

He sees people as special who saw his specialness.

He tends to see his past pleasures as a résumé of his accomplishments. He views the past like a publicity album, what he did, how he scored, whom he slept with. He keeps count. His past life is filled with trophies and mementos of himself, not of others.

When he looks back over his career, he tends to minimize his failures and overstate his successes. He diminishes the value of those who rejected him. He makes too much of those who saw his talent. It is difficult to separate the fantasy from the reality, and oddly, he really wants to do this. He wants to discover that he really did have talent, that he was good, that he gave his best, but he has so much imagined attribution to remove from what he actually did that he looks back in fear sometimes, afraid to find that it was all the stuff of dreams.

He is of course delighted when he discovers that he really did do well. When this happens the feeling is tainted with sadness as he realizes that though he wasn't everything he thought he was, he was a lot better than he feared he would be. If only he could have found peace with that.

Now the mirror is his enemy and time is against him. He looks at his past accomplishments and wonders how much good stuff he has left. Are his best years behind him? He does not want to know the answer and turns his attention to the future once more. He will not look back. He is still a going concern.

Besides, he has this idea that could just be the best thing he has ever worked on. You'll see.

ACCEPTING YOURSELF AS YOU ARE

Your response to pleasure is a mixture of all three character responses. The way the past intrudes to exaggerate or diminish your pleasure is a highly personal matter. You will gain much if you study the way nostalgia surfaces in happy moments. It will reveal yourself to you.

In happy moments your defenses are lower and you will be able to concede how much you miss those who have gone before. You will be able to see, their faults notwithstanding, how much they contributed to your life. In wishing others were here to share the good times, you gain a special perspective both of the gifts they gave as well as what you still yearn for, what they could have given.

Like everyone else you want more but have to learn to accept what you had and what you have in order for more to make any difference.

In the end it seems like such a small token of self-appreciation to accept yourself, but it makes all the difference in the world.

No one can bring you to this place but you.

No one can make you give up your pretension, excuses, or denial but yourself. It is a leap of affirmation.

You, as you are right at this moment, reading this sentence, are good.

Accept that.

You as you are now are worthy and lovable, but only if you take the risk to accept yourself, not as how you will be someday, but as you are right now.

Risk this. Be willing to accept yourself.

You, for all your faults and weaknesses, for all your mistakes and shortcomings, deserve the best.

Come to this place. Accept yourself.

All that you hope to accomplish hangs in the balance, waiting for you to take this step.

Let go of your self-doubt. It is just the excuse you keep with you to justify not trying harder, not giving your best.

Believe in yourself.

It is the difference between joy and suffering, for if you believe, you allow yourself to feel your feelings and let the natural therapeutic process heal you.

The belief that you are good becomes your happy life. Anything less undermines that natural process by causing you to store pain and mistakenly conclude you are bad.

Just believe you are good.

Everything else will follow.

14

PEACE OF MIND

PEACE OF MIND COMES with self-acceptance. It is not conferred by achievement, it is the gift you give to yourself.

You need to place your life in balance, the good with the bad, your strengths with your weaknesses, and your hurt with your pleasure.

Life is a continual process of reconciling the past with the present. The object is for you to become as openly conversant with your history as possible so you are able to enjoy the moment without fearing the intrusion of the past. Be grateful for the healing opportunities that Toxic Nostalgia presents to you to resolve your past pain.

Keep your Emotional Debt as low as possible so you have all your energy at your disposal and don't squander it by trying to keep the past a dark secret.

You need to be free to dream, to create and live in a better world.

Your life should be open and natural, simple and unpretentious.

Your life should be yours, not lost in an attempt to please others who may not even notice.

Please yourself.

Make yourself the judge of your own work.

Your purpose in the great evolutionary plan is to make your contribution by discovering your gift.

In giving your gift away you find meaning and reaffirm your belief in life itself.

You can only find peace of mind when you accept all of yourself and are willing to surrender to the truth of the moment.

You are the answer.

Spend your life defining the question.

The Do's and Don'ts of Natural Therapy

Do

Tell the truth.
Face life openly. What you avoid imprisons you.
Say what you mean, feel, and believe.
Accept yourself as you are.
Accept others as they are as well.
Know and admit your weaknesses.
Stop trying to prove yourself.
Let go of the past.
Give up your false expectations.
Take responsibility for your life and how it has turned out.
    What you are willing to take responsibility for frees you.
Have a dream for a better life and commit to it.
Be kind to yourself every day.
Find something to be grateful for and remember it.
Forgive.

Don't

Try, just be.
Lie.
Try to change or fix others.
Try to control others.
Expect the person who hurt you to apologize.
Expect people to be nicer to you than they are to themselves.
Expect others to recognize your goodness or accomplishments.
Expect people to understand you.
Test others.
Blame others.
Hold a grudge.
Expect the world to be anything but the way it is right now.
Wait for permission to do what is best for you.

INDEX